Everyday Occupation

In this rich history of everyday encounters between US soldiers and Chinese civilians, Chunmei Du explores their entangled relations from the end of World War II to the founding of the People's Republic of China. Drawing upon official, popular, and personal accounts from both countries, Du examines the sensorial, material, and symbolic exchanges that took place between GIs and ordinary Chinese people – stall vendors, pedestrians, rickshaw pullers, "Jeep girls," and suspected thieves. Through the conceptual lens of the everyday, this book reveals how interactions such as traffic accidents, sexual relations, theft, and black-market dealings impacted larger political dynamics during this pivotal era. Du shows how mundane struggles made imperialism and sovereignty tangible, fueling anti-American sentiment. Meanwhile, these encounters fostered informal diplomacy, shaping identities and forging new bonds that left a lasting imprint on both countries. This title is also available as Open Access on Cambridge Core.

Chunmei Du is a historian of modern China at Lingnan University.

Everyday Occupation
American Soldiers and Chinese Civilians after World War II

Chunmei Du
Lingnan University

CAMBRIDGE
UNIVERSITY PRESS

Shaftesbury Road, Cambridge CB2 8EA, United Kingdom

One Liberty Plaza, 20th Floor, New York, NY 10006, USA

477 Williamstown Road, Port Melbourne, VIC 3207, Australia

314–321, 3rd Floor, Plot 3, Splendor Forum, Jasola District Centre, New Delhi – 110025, India

103 Penang Road, #05–06/07, Visioncrest Commercial, Singapore 238467

Cambridge University Press is part of Cambridge University Press & Assessment, a department of the University of Cambridge.

We share the University's mission to contribute to society through the pursuit of education, learning and research at the highest international levels of excellence.

www.cambridge.org
Information on this title: www.cambridge.org/9781009600682

DOI: 10.1017/9781009600705

© Chunmei Du 2026

This publication is in copyright. Subject to statutory exception and to the provisions of relevant collective licensing agreements, with the exception of the Creative Commons version the link for which is provided below, no reproduction of any part may take place without the written permission of Cambridge University Press & Assessment.

An online version of this work is published at doi.org/10.1017/9781009600705 under a Creative Commons Open Access license CC-BY-NC-ND 4.0 which permits re-use, distribution and reproduction in any medium for non-commercial purposes providing appropriate credit to the original work is given. You may not distribute derivative works without permission. To view a copy of this license, visit https://creativecommons.org/licenses/by-nc-nd/4.0

When citing this work, please include a reference to the DOI 10.1017/9781009600705

First published 2026

Cover image: People talking on the street, Shanghai, China, May 1949.

Credit: Jack Birns/The LIFE Picture Collection/Shutterstock

A catalogue record for this publication is available from the British Library

A Cataloging-in-Publication data record for this book is available from the Library of Congress

ISBN 978-1-009-60068-2 Hardback

ISBN 978-1-009-60066-8 Paperback

Cambridge University Press & Assessment has no responsibility for the persistence or accuracy of URLs for external or third-party internet websites referred to in this publication and does not guarantee that any content on such websites is, or will remain, accurate or appropriate.

For EU product safety concerns, contact us at Calle de José Abascal, 56, 1°, 28003 Madrid, Spain, or email eugpsr@cambridge.org

For Lincoln 長天
Semper Fidelis

Contents

List of Maps	*page* viii
List of Figures	ix
Acknowledgments	xii
Transliterations and Citation Practices	xvii
Introduction: Everyday Encounter	1
1 Occupying China: Mission Impossible	21
2 Sensory Contact: Life in the Orient	59
3 Embodied Vehicles: Jeep and GIs	94
4 Intimate Relations: Jeep Girls and Gendered Nationalism	124
5 Entangled Goods: American Charms and Harms	154
Epilogue: Revisiting the Lost Era	196
Notes	213
Bibliography	265
Index	287

Maps

1	Map of China, 1945.	*page* xv
2	Map of North China, 1945.	xvi

Figures

1.1 A US Army captain holding a flag of China, greeted by cheering civilians in Chongqing upon news of the Japanese surrender, August 1945. *page* 22
1.2 Marines entering Tianjin, welcomed by local crowds giving a thumbs-up, October 1945. 29
1.3 The Japanese surrender ceremony in Tianjin, 1945. 30
1.4 The Japanese surrender ceremony in Qingdao, 1945. 31
1.5 China division parade in the Japanese surrender ceremony in Qingdao, 1945. 32
1.6 China division parade in the Japanese surrender ceremony in Qingdao, 1945. 32
1.7 General DeWitt Peck (standing, far left) and Chinese workmen flee for safety as a mine explodes on railroad tracks in North China where the general's train had been halted by previous damage, November 1945. 39
1.8 General DeWitt Peck inspects the marines in Tangshan, December 1945. 40
1.9 Navy carrier planes in a "show of force" flight over Beijing with the Forbidden City in the background, September 1945. 49
1.10 Japanese defendants in the Hankou trial, featuring Major General Masataka Kaburagi standing, February 1946, Shanghai. 50
2.1 A European-style mansion in Qingdao, serving as the residence of the US Marine Corps commanding general. 62
2.2 A team of Chinese staff, including cooks, servants, drivers, and butlers, providing services at the Marine Corps commanding general's quarters in Qingdao. 63
2.3 Marines posing for a photo while preparing a meal in North China. 65

List of Figures

2.4 A marine in a Chinese cap checks out goods from a street vendor. 70
2.5 Local bumboats cluster around a Seventh Fleet cutter in Shanghai for business, September 1945. 71
2.6 United States military leadership, including Admiral Charles M. Cooke Jr., accompanied by Chinese hosts, enjoying a Mongolian barbeque at the Summer Palace in Beijing, 1945. 77
2.7 Two American servicemen on liberty examining raw ducks for their Peking duck dish at a local restaurant. 79
2.8 Cartoon depicting a verbal exchange between a GI and a Chinese man. 84
3.1 Mao Zedong getting into a Jeep with Patrick Hurley, Zhang Zhizhong, and David Dean Barrett, en route to the Chongqing Negotiations, Yan'an, August 1945. 95
3.2 "The Jeep becomes a general-purpose vehicle," 1946. 99
3.3 "Jeep rhapsody," October 1945. 101
3.4 United States Army Air Force officer riding in a rickshaw during a race in Shanghai, December 1945. 115
3.5 American soldiers, along with local rickshaw pullers and pedicab men, gather around the scene of a traffic accident. 119
4.1 American sailors in intimate contact with hostesses at the Diamond Bar in Shanghai, 1949. 127
4.2 American soldiers socializing with Chinese women in postwar Qingdao. 129
4.3 "Shanghai characters: Jeep girls," 1946. 133
4.4 "A tribute to Jeep girls," 1946. 133
4.5 Tsinghua University students protesting "American brutalities" in Beijing, January 1947. 146
5.1 Drawing of a streetside coffee vendor in Shanghai, 1946. 160
5.2 Drawing of an outdoor coffee stand in Shanghai, 1946. 160
5.3 American canned food on window display in a Shanghai store, featuring a Coca-Cola poster on the outside wall, 1947. 164
5.4 Weekly DDT spraying by a C-47 transport over US military accommodations in Shanghai, September 1946. 165
5.5 "How many coins for a pound of American goods?" Shanghai, 1946. 173
5.6 United States soldiers guarding supplies on deck in Qingdao, December 1949. 177

5.7	Marines exit China, giving thumbs-up and "ding hao" farewells in Beijing, 1947.	194
E.1	Illustration of an American military truck rampaging down the street, killing innocent people, part of the "Brutalities of American Troops in China" series, drawn by Ding Hao, 1951.	199
E.2	Illustration of two drunk American sailors assaulting a rickshaw puller outside a nightclub, part of the "Brutalities of American Troops in China" series, drawn by Ding Hao, 1951.	200
E.3	Illustration of the rape of a Chinese woman by an American soldier, with a Nationalist official bowing to the American authority who exonerates him, part of the "Brutalities of American Troops in China" series, drawn by Ding Hao, 1951.	200
E.4	Illustration of a Chinese workman shot by an American guard outside a military compound, part of the "Brutalities of American Troops in China" series, drawn by Ding Hao, 1951.	201
E.5	"Indifference to life," *Sanmao Stands Up* by Zhang Leping, 1951.	202
E.6	"Mass denunciation meeting," *Sanmao Stands Up* by Zhang Leping, 1951.	202

Acknowledgments

On a bright June day in 2017, I sat in the Shanghai Municipal Archives on the Bund, immersed in historical documents glowing on a computer screen. The room was still, save for the hum of the air-conditioning, when the iconic melody of "The East Is Red" suddenly echoed outside. The chime, emanating from the nearby Customs House clock – the Chinese Big Ben – rang out every fifteen minutes with deliberate, resonant notes. I looked up and turned to the towering windows. Below, the Huangpu River shimmered under the summer sun, while across the water, Pudong's futuristic skyline rose, its glass towers cutting into the sky. The melody lingered, reverberating through the air, and I felt a parallel universe unfold – a merging of opposites: the extraordinary and the mundane, foreign imperialism and daily life, war and peace, remembering and forgetting. It was as if China's history, with all its triumphs and tribulations, floated on the air with every note. The spell was broken by the footsteps of patrolling staff, pulling me back to reality. I sat quietly, reflecting on humanity's enduring quest for survival and connection and the layers of historical amnesia.

This project has been made possible by the generosity and support of many individuals and institutions. My initial archival trip to China was supported by a scholar grant from the Chiang Ching-kuo Foundation for International Scholarly Exchange, Western Kentucky University's sabbatical leave program, a residential fellowship from the International Center for Studies of Chinese Civilization at Fudan University, and a visiting fellowship at the Xueheng Institute at Nanjing University. I am also deeply grateful for a one-year fellowship from the National Endowment for the Humanities (USA), grants from the Humanities and Social Sciences Prestigious Fellowship Scheme and General Research Fund provided by the Hong Kong Research Grants Council, as well as direct grants and faculty research grants from Lingnan University. My sincere thanks go to the reviewers of these grants for their support and thoughtful feedback.

Acknowledgments　　　　　　　　　　　　　　　　　　　　　　　　　xiii

I have had the privilege of presenting this research at numerous conferences and venues around the world. I am indebted to Chang Li, Janet Chen, Jian Chen, Hu Cheng, Louise Edwards, Jin Guangyao, Li Gongzhong, Ma Jianbiao, Mei Jianjun, Niu Dayong, Sun Jiang, Hans van der Ven, Jeff Wasserstrom, Wen-hsin Yeh, Yang Yuqing, Zhang Ke, Zuo Chengying, and Zuo Shuangwen for sharing materials, research, and wisdom with me. I am especially grateful to Zach Fredman and Judd Kinzley for organizing two workshops on Sino-American relations at the grassroots, as well as to other participants, including Mary Brazelton, Covell Meyskens, Jack Neubauer, Ke Ren, Linh Vu, Zhiguo Yang, and Yanqiu Zheng, whose insights enriched this project. I also learned a great deal from the Warfare in Modern China Revisited workshop at Academia Sinica, organized by Kwong Chi Man and Su Sheng-hsiung.

Several colleagues have graciously read various portions of the book or provided feedback on grant proposals, including David Cheng Chang, Ian Chong, Mark Hampton, Tony Harkins, Yunte Huang, Chin Jou, Diana Lemberg, Ji Li, Aaron Moore, Shellen Wu, Zhiyi Yang, and Ying Zhang. Thoughtful comments from two anonymous reviewers for Cambridge University Press helped me refine the book's focus. My former advisors, Ben Elman, Sue Naquin, David Howell, and Liu Houbin, continue to offer guidance and encouragement despite the passage of time and distance. I am truly grateful to all of them for their wisdom, generosity, and support.

Long-standing friendships have been a source of strength and joy throughout the years this book took shape. I am grateful to Huaiyu Chen, Liang Cai, Miao Feng, Min Ye, Enhua Zhang, and Yinghong Cheng for their unwavering support and camaraderie. In Hong Kong, I have had the privilege of learning from many remarkable colleagues, including Grace Chou, Haoming Gong, Peter Hamilton, C. P. Lau, Zhang Lei, Vincent Leung, Youjia Li, Carmen Tsui, Yuanfei Wang, Guoqi Xu, Bin Yang, and Emilie Yeh. I am also fortunate to be part of several nurturing and empowering intellectual and social communities in Hong Kong. My warm thanks go to Lang Chen, Tingting Chen, Agatha and Jonathan Fong, Janet Ho, Xiao Hu, Loretta Kim, Connie Lam, Donghui Li, Yu-Chieh Li, Pei-Yin Lin, Jianmei Liu, Jia Tan, Denise Tang, Yan Wei, Shengqing Wu, Zeying Wu, Catherine Yau, Minlei Ye, Yang Zhan, Lawrence Zhang, and Feifei Zhou. Their friendship, intellectual companionship, and emotional support have made this journey all the more meaningful.

My editors at Cambridge University Press, Lucy Rhymer and Rosa Martin, have been exceptional throughout the publication process, bringing professionalism and care that made this experience smooth. Connor

Au-Yeung, Wenkuo Ma, Tiffany Yung, Jiahui Dong, and Nianhong Qiu provided invaluable research assistance. Xu Jianing kindly shared an American Navy photo from his collection. Special thanks go to Ann, Vincy, and Alston at the Department of History office, whose warmth and kindness made my transition to Lingnan University seamless and the campus truly feel like home. I also thank Miriam for her indispensable help, which gave me the time and flexibility to work late and travel for conferences and research trips.

This project would not have been possible without the generous assistance of archivists and staff at numerous institutions. I am deeply grateful to those at the National Archives in College Park, Maryland; the Marine Corps History Division in Quantico, Virginia; California State University, Northridge; the Hoover Institution Library & Archives at Stanford University; the Radcliffe Institute at Harvard University; the Needham Research Institute at the University of Cambridge; Academia Historica and the Archives of the Institute of Modern History at Academia Sinica in Taipei; as well as the municipal archives in Beijing, Chongqing, Nanjing, Qingdao, Shanghai, and Tianjin. I also thank Cambridge University Press and Oxford University Press for permission to include revised versions of my previously published articles: "Jeep Girls and American GIs: Gendered Nationalism in Post–World War II China," *Journal of Asian Studies* 81, no. 2 (2022): 341–363, and "Occupational Hazard: American Servicemen's Sensory Encounters with China, 1945–1949," *Diplomatic History* 47, no. 1 (2023): 55–84.

Looking back, I feel fortunate to have begun this project at a serendipitous time, before the Covid-19 pandemic, the tightening of archival access in China, and the devastating federal funding cuts to American archives and institutions. Now, as the book reaches completion in 2025, the eightieth anniversary of the end of World War II, we find ourselves at another major crossroads in Sino-American relations and world geopolitics, facing an uncertain future.

Seven years have passed since I moved from Kentucky to Hong Kong, where this book came together. As I navigated new personal and intellectual terrain during this journey, the Du, Shi, and Powell families were my most steadfast support, enduring my exhaustion, frustration, and absences with patience and love. To them, I owe my deepest gratitude. Finally, I dedicate this book to Lincoln 長天, with the hope that he will embrace the motto *Semper Fidelis* and strive to make a meaningful difference in writing the next page of our shared history.

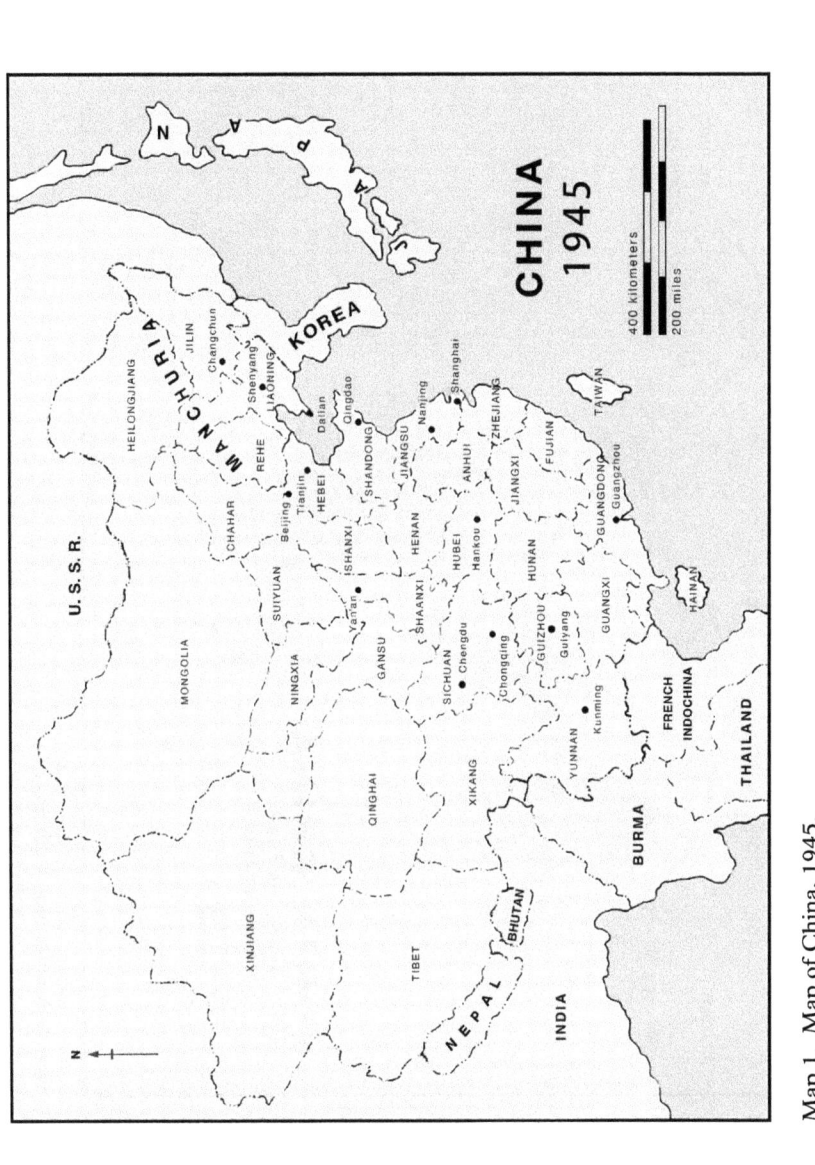

Map 1. Map of China, 1945.

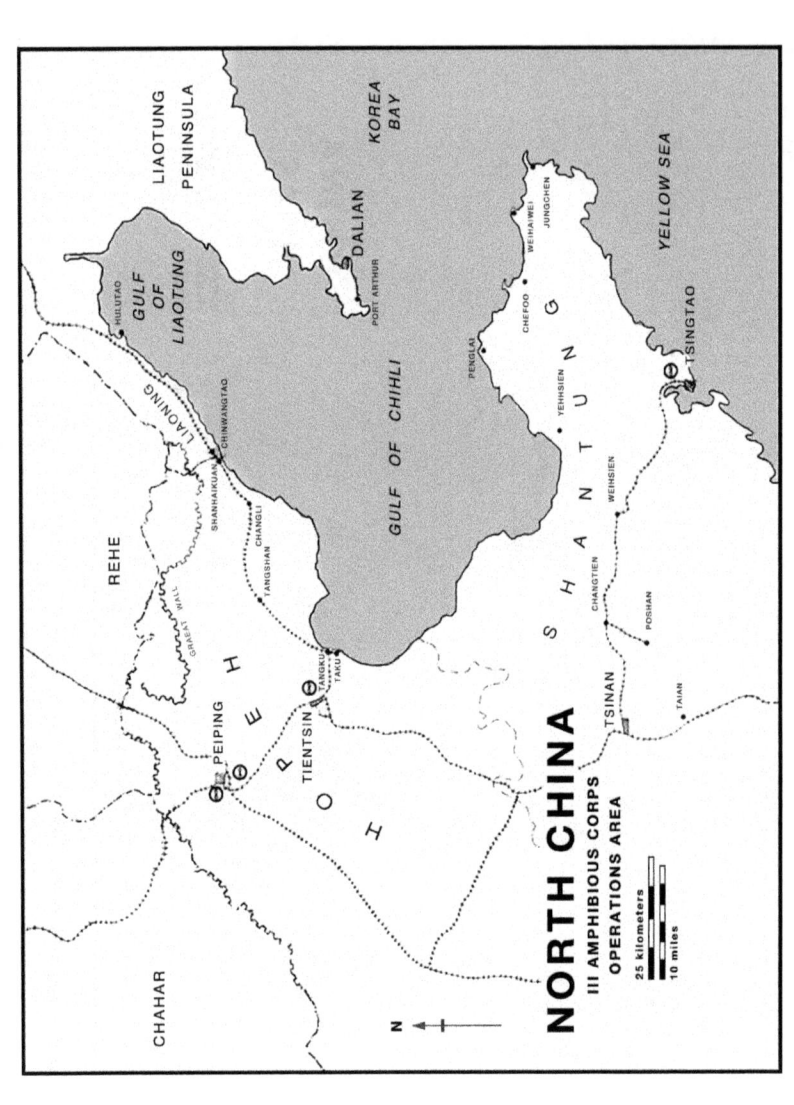

Map 2. Map of North China, 1945.

Transliterations and Citation Practices

Transliterations

For consistency, pinyin is used for all Chinese names, except in cases of direct quotations or customary usage, such as Peking University and Chiang Kai-shek. When applicable, the romanization system used at the time is included in parentheses upon first mention.

Citation Practices

In the chapter notes, the first reference to a source includes a full citation. Subsequent references to the same source use shortened citations. The bibliography provides full bibliographic details for all cited sources, except for historical newspapers, periodicals, and archival entries, which are only cited in the chapter notes.

Introduction
Everyday Encounter

Nanjing, Christmas Day, 1946. General George C. Marshall, US Special Envoy to China, was attending a concert organized by his hospitable Nationalist hosts in the capital when his Jeep with the special "USA20593633" plate went missing. As it turned out, the Jeep was stolen by a local thief who quickly turned it on the thriving black market. One Chinese critic called the Jeep incident an omen and allegory of the American failure in China.[1] However, it was not just the failure of Marshall's mediation in the Chinese civil war, or even the failure of US policy in China at large, but also America's failure to sustain the image of a good and special ally just a little more than one year after winning World War II (WWII). One day earlier, and more than six hundred miles to the north, in the ancient capital of Beijing (Peiping), nineteen-year-old college student Shen Chong had been raped by an intoxicated US marine. Nationwide protests broke out over the next few days, calling for severe punishment of the American rapist and the complete withdrawal of the US military from China. But as we zoom in to the actual scene of the protest, GI spectators inside a locked compound were spotted joining outside protesters, who were shouting "Get out of China" (*gun chu Zhongguo*), by shouting back, "I want to go home!"[2] The exchange of these messages, steeped in emotions, reveals a highly volatile and ultimately defining moment in Sino-US history that is often called the "loss of China."[3]

Everyday Occupation provides a microhistory of the quotidian encounters between American soldiers and Chinese civilians and their entangled relations from the end of WWII to the founding of the People's Republic of China. Drawing upon official, popular, and personal accounts from both countries, it focuses on the sensorial, material, and symbolic exchanges between GIs and ordinary Chinese people – pedestrians, rickshaw pullers, suspected thieves, stall vendors, and the "Jeep girls" (*jipu nülang*) who were seen as fraternizing with US soldiers. Through the microlens of the everyday, this book reveals how grassroots interactions affected larger political dynamics during a critical era in Sino-American relations. I argue that ostensibly mundane matters such as traffic accidents, sexual relations, theft, and black-market dealings provide a key to understanding the intensity and longevity of popular Chinese anti-American sentiment, as the abstract concepts of imperialism and sovereignty became legible in the common language of life and death, gain and loss, and fairness and injustice. Meanwhile, American servicemen and Chinese civilians engaged in a form of informal diplomacy, developing new tastes, languages, consumption habits, and identities, as well as individual and institutional bonds, all of which left a lasting imprint on both countries.

Shortly after the Jeep incident, General Marshall, newly appointed secretary of state, declared the end of his peace mission in China and returned to the United States in January 1947. As President Harry S. Truman's special representative, Marshall had spent a trying year in China, working tirelessly to end civil strife and bring about political unification. The Truman administration aimed to limit Soviet influence in the country by forcing the ruling Nationalists and the rival Chinese Communist Party (CCP) into a coalition government under Chiang Kai-shek's leadership. On January 10, 1946, Marshall succeeded in securing acceptance of a ceasefire agreement, and an executive headquarters was set up in Beijing to supervise the truce, led by three commissioners representing the United States, the Nationalist Government, and the CCP. However, the resulting resolutions quickly broke down as both sides violated the ceasefire and fought over the strategically important region of Manchuria. Full-scale civil war broke out in June. To pressure Chiang to become more compliant in the peace negotiations, the US imposed a ten-month arms embargo from August 1946, and a US financial loan was also put on ice. In November, Chiang Kai-shek unilaterally convened the National Assembly, but both the CCP and the Democratic League refused to participate. By the spring of 1947, the Nationalists were in a dire predicament. The tide on the battleground was shifting as the CCP went on counteroffensives. The huge gap between government expenditure and income continued to increase, and the solution of printing money led to record high inflation and devastating consequences for the urban economy. Facing increasing social unrest and widespread student protests, the government cracked down on "Communist infiltration" and banned leftist publications and organizations. The military, economic, and political crises deepened throughout 1948, and on all major fronts the Nationalist Party lost public trust and legitimacy. Despite the considerable advantages it held over the Communists at the end of WWII, the Nationalist Party was defeated in the civil war that concluded in 1949.[4]

Introduction: Everyday Encounter 3

In world history, the immediate postwar era is celebrated for the victory against fascism and the beginning of postwar occupation and reconstruction. It is also known for the emerging Cold War conflict between the two superpowers that were directly involved in China's postwar struggle. On August 8, 1945, the Soviet Union declared war on Japan and attacked Japanese forces in Manchuria, following its pledge at the Yalta Conference. The Soviet forces treated the Japanese with little mercy, plundered Manchurian "war booty" valued at well over USD 800 million, and secretly aided Chinese Communists by sending arms and supplies.[5] Moreover, they tried to maintain a physical presence in China. On August 14, the day before Japan's surrender, the Sino-Soviet Treaty of Friendship and Alliance was signed by the Soviet Union and the Nationalist Government. The pact included the agreement that for thirty years, Lüshun (Port Arthur) would be a naval base used jointly by China and the Soviet Union, and Dalian (Dairen) would be a free port granting the Soviets privileged access rights. As a result, the Soviet military occupied these two strategic ports, securing advantageous positioning in the Asia-Pacific region. The full withdrawal of its forces from Manchuria, supposed to be completed within weeks, was delayed several times and not finalized until early May 1946. Even then, the Soviets continued to maintain a presence in both ports until the mid 1950s.[6]

The US occupation of North China occurred in the intertwining of these two crucial contexts: the internal tension culminating in a civil war and the global expansion of the US empire in the emerging Cold War.[7] Fearing that the Chinese Communists and Soviets would fill the void left by Japan's surrender, America acted quickly. In September 1945, more than fifty thousand marines of the III Amphibian Corps (IIIAC) were sent from the Pacific to North China for a new mission code-named Operation BELEAGUER. Its key occupation duties included accepting Japanese surrenders, repatriating more than 3 million Japanese soldiers and civilians, transporting half a million Nationalist troops to North and Central China, and liberating and rehabilitating Allied internees and prisoners of war.[8] The IIIAC elements, including the 1st Marine Division and the 6th Marine Division, together with naval forces from the 7th Fleet and the US Military Advisory Group, formed the bulk of the US troops in China after WWII. At the peak of the US military deployment, 113,000 American soldiers were stationed in China for various duties, expanding their presence from the wartime hinterland to areas formerly occupied by the Japanese.[9] While certain marine units were assigned to remote outposts in North China and Manchuria, American military personnel were concentrated in China's major political, economic, and cultural centers: Beijing, Nanjing, Qingdao, Shanghai, and Tianjin. There they lived in city centers rather than separate camp towns and came into close contact with all types of Chinese people going about their daily lives – a major difference from their wartime predecessors who had been housed in designated hostels provided by the Nationalist Government. The nature of the mission also changed: American servicemen, including both veterans and new recruits, were no longer engaged in combat operations against Japanese forces like those who came before them. Instead, they participated in a variety of new activities, from occupation duties to humanitarian assistance and peacemaking. This shift marked a new stage for US military personnel's interactions with Chinese society, expanding their engagement with local populations in roles and capacities beyond traditional wartime functions. But ultimately, the mission's ambiguous, vague, and sometimes conflicting objectives, such as assisting the Nationalist Government while maintaining neutrality in the midst of an escalating civil war, made it a mission impossible to execute or succeed.

Despite the initial warm welcome extended in postwar China by locals who had suffered for years under Japanese rule, anti-American sentiment quickly developed in response to seemingly trivial incidents involving traffic accidents, sexual relations, and American goods. Rampant misconduct among American soldiers, coupled with systemic inequalities that pervaded individual and institutional interactions, provided fertile ground for grassroots frictions. Nationwide demonstrations broke out in the wake of the Peking rape incident, leading to the hitherto largest anti-American movement in Chinese history.[10] The CCP seized upon the growing animosity and launched a major propaganda campaign against the continued presence of US military forces in China, American aid to the Nationalists that prolonged the civil war, and US imperialism in the world. By linking American imperialists with the reactionary Nationalist regime that acted as its "running dog," the campaign contributed to the Communist victory, especially in advancing its political cause among urban populations.

In hindsight, it is tempting to see this historic encounter between US servicemen and Chinese civilians as a doomed failure. The late 1940s marked a turning point in Chinese perceptions of America: deep appreciation and gratitude turned into grievances and animosity, and public sentiment shifted from pro-America (*qin Mei*) to anti-America (*fan Mei*).[11] According to a *Time* magazine report, American imperialism had replaced both Japanese imperialism and British imperialism "in the average Chinese intellectual's dictionary of opprobrium," and street urchins in Shanghai's alleys sang the little rhyme of "*Mei kuo lao, Chen pu hao*" (American fellows are really no good)![12] While previous research has demonstrated the significant impact of US imperialism and

Communist propaganda on this transition, viewing these unprecedented grassroots exchanges only through the prism of political domination and manipulation risks overlooking individual agency and historical contingencies. We also miss the opportunity to investigate how these two large political forces worked in relation to the messy world of mundane struggles. For example, how did the US system of law and justice fail in China despite its ideals of liberalism and realpolitik in the early Cold War environment? How did the Communist anti-American campaign manage to attract such a broad spectrum of supporters, ranging from outspoken leftists and liberal intellectuals to students, businessmen, and the urban poor? Moreover, what kinds of roles did Chinese individuals and American servicemen play in the nexus of Sino-US relations and everyday frictions? Answering these questions is crucial for understanding the postwar US global empire, the rise of Chinese anti-American nationalism, and the making and unmaking of Sino-US relations during a watershed moment in history. It also provides valuable lessons for today, when the world is once again caught in polarized ideological confrontations and nationalist conflicts.

Uneven Reciprocity: Locating China in the US Empire

"The years from 1945 to 1949 will go down in Chinese history as the American period," stated Graham Peck, a seasoned traveler who served with the US Office of War Information in China throughout the 1940s. This was evident as "former U.S. Army vehicles, uniforms, and arms became most conspicuous" across the country, with military advisors active in the capital, warships patrolling the seacoast, and military planes frequently flying over the interior.[13] The United States after WWII, with its enormous soft and hard powers in both territorial and nonterritorial forms, includes a crucial military dimension – what many scholars call an "empire of bases."[14] The critical lens of empire provides a powerful framework for analyzing the US military in China, and it is essential to link its presence with that in other areas colonized, occupied, and stationed by America. In particular, power asymmetries embedded in Sino-US interactions at the national and individual levels were similar to those in occupied Japan and Korea, despite dramatic differences in political status and circumstances. Contemporary Chinese critics already compared GIs in China to the occupying forces in Japan, warning that the US was treating China as a colony. The US military's policy perpetuated systemic racism and injustice against Chinese civilians in their policing and judicial process, and American servicemen expressed Orientalist views, held racist and sexist attitudes toward Chinese elites and commoners, and enjoyed immunity from local laws. In his recent book *The Tormented Alliance*, Zach Fredman convincingly shows the prevalence of GI misconduct and the unequal relationship imposed by US imperialism on China throughout the 1940s. However, framing grassroots interactions with the Chinese, including frictions, solely through the lens of "brutal, everyday racism of imperialism" does not adequately account for the complex nature of the US military involvement and modes of domination in postwar China.[15]

Unlike its East Asian neighbors under US occupation and the Philippines – a former colony and later client state – China was an ally and a sovereign nation. Officially, GIs were "invited guests" of the Nationalist Government, a status that was not in name only. For example, despite their critical contributions to the war effort and an initial plan to send them, black troops, in deference to the Chinese government's racist requests, were not stationed in postwar Chinese cities.[16] Since WWII, the American military had tried to educate its soldiers to respect the Chinese as civilized equals, while American propaganda celebrated China and its people with flattering portrayals.[17] In the precarious environment of the civil war between the Nationalist and Communist Parties, the American government promoted a liberal image of itself as a "benevolent leader of the world," in contrast to the Soviet Union. Meanwhile, it promulgated the economic agenda of a free world economy based on the open market and free trade, secured favorable terms for American businesses and investors, and enabled further domination through various instruments of influence. In principle, the US government intended to showcase democracy and provide a blueprint for a future liberal China. This projected sense of equality and fairness was crucial to the legitimacy of the expanding empire in the early Cold War era.[18] Back home, the new American middlebrow intellectual representations highlighted mutually beneficial exchanges between Americans and Asians "within a system of reciprocity."[19] In China, US strategic objectives called for appeasement of rising anti-American sentiment among the Chinese, which the US actually attempted, and it was reluctant to directly intervene in the civil war. This peculiar power dynamic affected how US imperialism worked in China and shaped the inner workings of the Sino-American partnership.

The everyday interactions, especially conflicts, between American servicemen and Chinese civilians embodied the power struggles between the two governments. The Nationalist Government held an ambivalent and often conflicting attitude on the issue of US occupation. On the one hand, it hoped to prolong the US military's stay during the civil war and remained dependent on US assistance, and on the other hand, it was resistant to foreign encroachment on Chinese sovereignty. As the Generalissimo declared victory against Japan and embarked on postwar reconstruction after eight years of devastating war, China claimed unprecedented national pride and a leading role in the region and even the world.[20] The country embraced its new international status as one of the "Big Four" nations, along with Britain, the United States, and the Soviet Union, and became one of the five permanent members of the newly established United Nations Security Council. Known for his sensitivity regarding national equality, Chiang flagged unequal treaties as a "national humiliation" that hampered Nationalist efforts to "build a nation" and acclaimed their removal as the start of a "new epoch" in history and "the most important page" in Chinese history.[21] The Nationalist Government took sovereignty seriously and referred to US military activities in China as "presence" (*zhuHua*), rather than "occupation," the term used by the US military for its mission in North China. The government was also careful in not setting legal precedents for other foreign countries. For example, although the US Navy saw Qingdao as a potential permanent naval base and used the port as a major fleet anchorage in the Far East until 1949, "no formal written agreement on stationing U.S. Naval vessels at China ports is known to exist," as the Chinese government desired to "avoid written agreements of this nature."[22] Such a lack of formal agreements with clearly defined terms regarding the US military presence in China often led to unrealistic expectations, inconsistent assumptions, and disappointing outcomes on both sides.

By its nature, the presence of an invited foreign military in a sovereign nation is a significant military matter as well as a complex legal and political concern testing key issues of jurisdiction and sovereignty. The continuing system of extraterritoriality, dating back to the First Opium War, remained the most sensitive issue of the day.[23] As an Ally, the United States relinquished its century-old rights of extraterritoriality on January 11, 1943, when the Sino-American Treaty for the Relinquishment of Extraterritorial Rights in China and the Regulation of Related Matters was signed. The historic treaty positioned China as an equal sovereign in the system of international law as opposed to the colonial system of unequal treaties.[24] But it also necessitated the articulation of a fresh legal basis for the rights and privileges of American individuals and entities. Jurisdiction over American military personnel in China was the first issue to be settled according to these new terms. On the basis of reciprocity, a Sino-American agreement in 1943 recognized the US military's exclusive jurisdiction over criminal offenses committed by its members in the country until six months after the war. The agreement was renewed in June 1946, extending the wartime legal privileges of US troops for another year, and was extended again in July 1947 until the complete withdrawal of US troops. Due to its sensitivity, the issue was raised well before 1943, but both sides waited to sign the agreement until after the monumental Relinquishment of Extraterritorial Rights treaty in order to prevent a potential negative influence on the latter.[25]

The GIs' extraterritorial rights in China, both on and off duty, affected the dynamics of everyday interactions on the ground. They provided legal shields to servicemen whose misconduct toward Chinese civilians was often tolerated or prosecuted lightly. Today, the agreement is still widely criticized as a continuation of American extraterritoriality in China and an instance of the Nationalist Government's trading of sovereignty for US support. But a close look at the negotiation process shows a more nuanced picture of the Nationalist Government's role. Before the Agreement between the United States and China regarding Jurisdiction over Criminal Offenses Committed by American Armed Forces in China, Exchange of Notes (處理在華美軍人員刑事案件換文) was signed on May 21, 1943, the Chinese side had requested that a reciprocity clause be added. Whether it was done purely as "a matter of face," the Exchange of Notes stipulated that "insofar as may be compatible with military security," the US military trials would be conducted "in open court in China and within a reasonable distance from the place where the offense is alleged to have been committed" to facilitate witness attendance.[26] Further, US authorities "will be prepared to cooperate with the authorities of China in setting up a satisfactory procedure for affording such mutual assistance as may be required in making investigations and collecting evidence," and "it would probably be desirable that preliminary action should be taken by the Chinese authorities on behalf of the United States authorities" when witnesses were not members of the US forces.[27] On October 1, the Regulations Governing the Handling of Criminal Offenses Committed by Members of the Armed Forces of the United States in China (處理在華美軍人員刑事案件條例) agreement was promulgated. Except for Article 1, which extended the jurisdiction of the US military over its members in China, all the other six articles placed restrictions upon such jurisdiction. For example, Article 4 provided that the US jurisdiction did not "under the Chinese law, affect the right of questioning, arresting, detaining, searching, attaching or investigating members of the United States armed forces who have committed criminal offenses or who are suspected of having committed criminal offenses." Article 5 stated that Chinese authorities may request copies of American judgments "prior to the rendering of a judgment" and "make inquires as to the status of a case."[28]

As we will explore later in this book, the Chinese government tried to set some limits on the "exclusive jurisdiction" of the US military and introduced terms that would restrict US privileges and enable Chinese participation or intervention in the process. But these provisions were difficult or impossible to implement without the collaboration of American military authorities in China. Even as late as June 1948, the Executive Yuan continued efforts to improve the judicial procedures for handling such criminal cases. It issued instructions to local governments, reaffirming the principles laid out in Articles 4 and 5.[29] In practice, American authorities often simply disregarded and bypassed Chinese officials, distrusting local police or the government in general. Hampered by legal restrictions and, more importantly, the political necessity of depending on US military and economic aid while pursuing nationalist endeavors, Chiang Kai-shek's government ignored, denied, or trivialized the GIs' misconduct, insisting it was merely an isolated individual event, a strategy that eventually backfired. To many of its critics and supporters alike, the government failed in its mission to protect its citizens and defend the nation. It lost credibility and legitimacy when it failed to secure compensation, settle disputes, provide relief, and deliver justice to victims. Consequently, the Communists seized the opportunity to attack the Nationalist regime, accusing it of serving as America's agent and signing new unequal treaties that made China its colony.

In recent decades, Chinese scholars have formulated various frameworks for understanding the new Sino-US treaties signed in the period leading up to and following WWII, ranging from viewing them as neocolonial treaties, completely and unapologetically unequal, to seeing them as equal in form but unequal in content. Revisionist histories have argued that these agreements, based on international law, should not be simply called a mere revival of extraterritoriality. Instead, they demonstrate progress in creating new bilateral treaties after the termination of extraterritoriality, thus signifying milestones in China's journey toward integration into the new international legal order.[30] In this case, American demands, usage, and abuse of legal privileges in China were intended to achieve American rights, privileges, and justice on their own terms. But they should not be equated with colonial treaties or simply dismissed as empty talk, fake trials, or sham pacts. These demands and treaties stipulating American rights and privileges in China show what I call a relation of "uneven reciprocity." On the principle of equality and reciprocity, the two countries signed major agreements such as the provisions granting extraterritorial rights for US military personnel; the controversial 1946 Treaty of Friendship, Commerce, and Navigation; and various treaties on tariff relations, arbitration, educational exchange, and economic aid.[31]

Nevertheless, these agreements were unfavorable to China because it did not have the capacity to take advantage of the reciprocity rights or implement their terms, thus only ensuring American rights and privileges in reality. Such uneven reciprocity in Sino-US legal and political negotiation and practice mirrors the power asymmetry in the bilateral relations at large. It also showcases the new system of law and order that the US empire was developing after WWII, in which China, alongside other postcolonial and postwar states, struggled to negotiate equitable terms with the United States while striving to forge a "special" allied relationship through both collaboration and resistance.[32] During a period of significant political and social fluidity in China and around the world, the Nationalist Government hoped to lay a foundation for postwar reconstruction and development. It sought to leverage the emerging global order while addressing American demands and balancing various – often conflicting – political agendas. Ultimately, it failed to overcome these challenges, particularly in dealing with the US military presence.

Overall, China in the late 1940s was subject to US political and economic domination. American servicemen, while conducting their "peaceful" missions, engaged with local populations in the context of national and systemic inequality. However, adopting a stark imperialist perspective reduces the intricate grassroots encounter to a dichotomous story of aggressors versus victims. This perspective also overlooks a crucial opportunity to deepen our understanding of the CCP, which launched the most successful anti-American campaign to date, targeting the very issue of American military presence.

Brutal Imperialists: Locating America in Communist Propaganda

In January 1947, *Time* magazine described the presence of "many thousands of ambassadors abroad – all of them in official uniform" as a historic first, which stoked animosities toward America globally, but especially among the Chinese.[33] When widespread anti-American movements broke out in the late 1940s, it was baffling to the American elites and public. John Leighton Stuart, the US ambassador to China and a dedicated missionary educator, lamented that even with billions in financial aid, decades of philanthropy, no annexation of territory, "Why is there never anything but anger with America?"[34] A *Wall Street Journal* piece called the protests "a peculiar form of 'reverse lend-lease,'" a puzzling way of expressing "gratitude" for the crucial aid that the United States had provided in defeating the Japanese.[35] To many Americans, Chinese animosities against the United States were a complete shock, as they vividly remembered the close wartime friendship embodied in such representatives as the "Flying Tigers" and Madame Chiang, not to mention the rousing Chinese cheers for marines on their recent landing that were featured in so many media and personal accounts.

Communist propaganda seemed the only plausible explanation for the about-face, and it became the answer supplied by the Nationalist authorities, the US military, and major American media outlets alike. The Nationalist Government did not acknowledge the legitimacy of anti-American sentiment or make serious attempts to address the key issues raised by the protestors. Not so unlike the Communists, who used these incidents as ammunition to fire at the enemy, Generalissimo Chiang Kai-shek condemned student protests as products of Communist instigation through underground operatives and spies, instructing his officials to repress these elements rather than address students' demands. It might seem ironic that the two sworn enemies at war quickly settled on such an important assessment. But we know that both made persistent attempts to promote and manipulate nationalist sentiments for their own political gains, adopting such measures as planting agents on university campuses and waging propaganda wars.[36] Anti-imperialism had remained a central theme in both parties' legitimacy claims since their founding. A key difference, perhaps, was how effective their maneuvers were. While both groups claimed to be the true defender of Chinese sovereignty, the Communists succeeded in winning the propaganda battle, not only against America but also against their Nationalist rivals in the civil war.

According to the Communist Party's own narrative, the anti-American movement of the late 1940s was an integral part of Mao Zedong's broader strategy of "opening the Second Battlefield" in Nationalist-controlled areas. This strategy operated alongside the military front, featuring the struggles between "Chiang Kai-shek's reactionary government" and the patriotic, democratic movements led by students, workers, and other urban populations.[37] The Party's official history weaves a cohesive account that positions nearly all major demonstrations under its central leadership, leading toward the Communist victory in 1949.[38] In the summer of 1946, with the civil war intensifying, the CCP began to highlight American misconduct in China, educating the public about "brutalities" committed by GIs. In late September 1946, ten civil organizations in Shanghai launched "US Troops Quit China Week," a campaign featuring a series of public meetings, press conferences, and news releases.[39] Following CCP directives to expose American military misconduct, the campaign expanded to Chongqing, Beijing, Yan'an, and even Chinese communities abroad. It called on American progressive groups, the United Nations, and peace advocates worldwide to demand the immediate withdrawal of the American forces from China. Three months later, in the wake of the Peking rape incident, the Party launched an "Anti-Brutality" (*kangbao* 抗暴) movement that quickly expanded across the nation and lasted several months. The campaign positioned the US military presence in a direct lineage stretching back to the Eight-Nation Alliance in the Boxer Uprising at the turn of the twentieth century. With unwavering resolve, the Communists proclaimed the abolition of "all the treasonable treaties" made with imperialist countries, especially those brokered by the Nationalists, and demanded all US troops be withdrawn from China.[40] In May 1948, during the final phase of the civil war, another major protest movement, "Opposing the US Support of Japan" (*fanMeifuRi* 反美扶日), broke out over the new US occupation policy in Japan, especially the plan to assist in its postwar reconstruction. Fueled by resentment against Japan and fears of renewed Japanese aggression, college students and intellectual elites across the country initiated a new wave of protests. They were quickly joined by workers and urban residents, who were drawn by the pressing issues of hunger, oppression, and American intervention in the civil war.[41]

In general, the CCP campaign condemned the continuous American military involvement and exterritorial rights, US aid to the Nationalist Government, and support of the civil war, framing these issues only as a matter of foreign imperialism. Despite the relatively short duration and limited scale of the US military presence, the CCP was able to make this a central focus and headline for the nation. Upon the Allied victory in WWII, American prestige and standing within China reached unprecedented levels, and there were great hopes for US aid in the country's socioeconomic and political developments. In the early postwar years, Chinese experiences and discussions of America could be described as a mixture of fascination and uneasiness. Critiques of America came from both the left and the right: while leftists criticized capitalism and economic imperialism for endangering Chinese industries, right-wing ultra-nationalists warned against cultural and racial corruption through American influence, and both were concerned about national sovereignty and American intervention. Nationalist discourses concerning American influence encompassed a variety of conservative, leftist, and liberal groups and continuing debates over Westernization and modernization from earlier decades. Nevertheless, as Communist propaganda fired up and political and economic situations worsened in Chiang-controlled urban areas, these multivalent debates over American society, culture, and commodities became increasingly politicized and singular.

Certainly, the CCP played a key role in organizing and leading the anti-American campaign in the late 1940s, contributing to its overall success. But we should be cautious of the seemingly coherent and almost teleological narrative espoused in its official history. For instance, Party cadres in Beijing were initially surprised by the rapid development of student protests in reaction to the Peking rape incident, concerned that the issue was too local to attract support from other campuses.[42] The number of underground Party members among students remained relatively small, and they had to navigate an oppressive environment with care. Despite many students chanting anti-American slogans, some directed appeals to Chiang Kai-shek, seeking justice for the victim. American diplomats and observers also acknowledged that these anti-American movements were not all Communist-instigated but had a broader base, with some arguing that attributing them solely to the Party would be "paying the Communists too great a compliment."[43] There were even instances when Nationalist agents might have helped stir up anti-American sentiment. The American consul general in Dalian compared the Communist and Nationalist attacks on American policy, describing the latter as "if less direct, in the long run ... rather more than less insidious and destructive of popular liking for the United States."[44] In reality, not every campaign launched by the Communists in urban centers achieved success. For example, the 1947 boycott campaign against American products in Shanghai did not gain widespread support, as it jeopardized the livelihoods of certain groups of workers, vendors, businesses, and local residents.[45] In essence, the Party's calls to oppose US imperialism did not always work. Rather than orchestrating a series of cohesive and coherent movements, as is often claimed, the CCP actually seized the opportunities, capitalized on popular sentiment, and co-opted the protests into a political campaign that was taking shape.

Beyond the Communist ideological attacks, the intensity and longevity of popular anti-American sentiment should also be understood in the context of everyday struggles. Ultimately, grassroots frictions provided a decisive weapon for Communist anti-American propaganda, effectively fueling Chinese nationalism. The visceral perils of daily life affected Chinese people across the political and socioeconomic spectrum – whether college students, local officials' wives, illiterate migrants to the city, or rickshaw pullers – as they fell victim to drunk US soldiers, speeding Jeeps, and the excessive use of force. Based on these events, the Communist media set a new script for Sino-US interactions, assigning the two parties the binary and collective roles of everyday victim and bully.[46] This affective formula featured key ingredients of American racism, sexual aggression, and physical violence as a result of extraterritoriality and unequal treaties. As such, seemingly frivolous disputes over speed limits, fair bargains, physical and social boundaries, economic compensations, and moral and legal responsibilities embodied the otherwise abstract issues of national inequality and infringement of sovereignty. While the Communist propaganda of this era played the familiar notes of anti-imperialism from the early twentieth century, it was the new theme song of everyday brutality that struck an emotional and responsive chord among a wide base of urban residents, from outspoken leftist and liberal intellectuals to businessmen and even government officials. It is perhaps not surprising that the Communists, who positioned themselves as champions of the common people, emphasized the suffering of ordinary victims. Ironically, this focus, also borrowed from wartime tropes and imagery about Japanese atrocities – some of which Americans had propagated in their war against Japan as well – was now conveniently adapted to target American soldiers.[47] The stereotype of the US soldier-imperialist committing "atrocious acts" toward Chinese civilians spoke a clear, strong, and intelligible message to all.

Entangled Relations

> The everyday: what is most difficult to discover.
> – Maurice Blanchot, *The Infinite Conversation*, 1992[48]

Anchored in micropolitics, *Everyday Occupation* examines how the quotidian encounter between US serviceman and Chinese civilians was experienced, embodied, and narrated by both sides.[49] It foregrounds the experiences and agencies of ordinary individuals in Sino-US relations through the everyday actions they took to survive, cope, appropriate, resist, and prosper. While diplomatic negotiations settled issues of economic aid, political policies, and occupation terms between the two nations, the grassroots protagonists of this historical account engaged in day-to-day struggles to cope with the dangers of war, social disintegration, political chaos, and psychological stress amid some of the most devastating conflicts in modern Chinese history.

Turning toward the everyday, as this study does, is both historically necessary and theoretically critical.[50] "The personal is political," declared pioneering feminist scholar Cynthia Enloe, emphasizing the role of the private, domestic, and mundane in shaping international politics.[51] Micro-actions by local agents have a cumulative power to shape larger dynamics.[52] In postwar China, mundane matters were not only crucial in shaping the new Communist anti-American trope and collective memories, but also fundamental to how the Chinese experienced, perceived, and challenged America and Americans. On the national and international stage, massive protests against GI misconduct garnered a wide range of supporters, and the tale of Sino-US reciprocity and equality continued to be questioned. In their day-to-day interactions, local civilians negotiated prices and payments with American servicemen, capitalized on complex economic and cultural exchanges, and undermined the US pedagogy of fairness and justice using their own tactics. Methodically, an alliance between the history of everyday life and international relations also provides an antidote to the two aforementioned teleological traps in the study of Sino-US interactions, American imperialism on the one hand and Communist propaganda on the other. As Harry Harootunian has argued, history writing driven by the nation-state often conceals, disguises, and suppresses the everyday.[53] The messy mundane world, its contingency, fragmentation, and cacophony, does not easily fit into a linear narrative of the past leading to national destiny. To the majority of Chinese civilians, against the backdrop of the US occupation, daily preoccupations remained primary, especially in a time of war and disorder, and the motivation to survive and prosper overshadowed national issues in their interactions with American soldiers. In the official history and existing literature, however, the dynamic roles assumed by these parties are often reduced to a simple dichotomy between victims and perpetrators, depriving those involved of voice, identity, and even name. Dominant nationalist historiographies leave little space for the struggles, actions, and agencies of local protagonists that are deemed trivial or irrelevant.[54] Many of their stories are ignored or silenced, and those that are told are often filtered through patriarchal nationalist agendas.

The matter of occupation is both extraordinary and mundane. The theater of operation encompasses not only key defense sites and railway lines but also the loci of households, streets, bars, markets, and recreational spaces. This study prioritizes the everyday space as a microcosm of larger systemic relations between nations, races, genders, and classes, as well as a dynamic contact zone where spontaneous and calculated micro-actions take place. I foreground the materiality of the daily life, emphasizing its multiple situated contexts, and dwell on individual actors' experiences and stories. The mundane acts of eating, dancing, going to a theater, playing sports, shopping, and using the toilet rarely appear in the grand national histories and might be difficult to locate in government archives that were compiled and preserved with concerns over national destiny in mind. But once we shift the focus and zoom in to the human moments and quotidian actions within micro-arenas, the ubiquitous presence of ordinary individuals and the roles they play begin to emerge.

The everyday is both a geographical and a social space consisting of concrete places and symbolic microcosms.[55] In this story of the Sino-US encounter, the actions take place in the Nanjing parking lot where General Marshall's Jeep was stolen, outside a Tianjin warehouse where suspected thieves were shot dead by GI sentries for stealing several boxes of stationery supplies, within a Beijing dance hall where American and Chinese soldiers fought over dance girls, and on the wall of a marine billet where watching US soldiers joined in with Chinese protesters' slogan shouting. The everyday space also includes the representational and imaginary space of newspaper advertisements, tabloid reports, and magazine columns, where Chinese women wrote letters asking what to do with their GI boyfriends, adoption agencies advertised mixed-race babies, satirical poetry mocked American men as "toad-like" or "over-innocent country-bumpkins," and Communist and leftist editorials condemned atrocious American acts against the Chinese people.[56] The everyday space expands further to take in the legal and political space of the American courtroom, where Chinese witnesses were invited to participate and yet not heard, and the Nationalist Government meeting rooms, where victims' families and representatives from professional associations gathered to appeal for compensation, intervention, and justice.

In this book, US servicemen and Chinese civilians are cast as the main characters and treated not as political pawns but rather as local actors with transformative potential. American soldiers were problematic agents of the empire. They were, first and foremost, foreign armed forces – occupiers, guards, humanitarian aid workers, advisors, and peacekeepers – performing assigned military duties. They were also tourists, consumers, fashion setters, sexual partners, and cultural messengers on the ground, there to cultivate alliance and represent and spread US democracy and values. In their daily lives, while American soldiers savored the taste of victory and Oriental city life, they were also confronted by the harsh realities of China's economic devastation, social unrest, and renewed civil war. The GIs were preconditioned by Orientalist views and racist behaviors, but they also stepped out of their comfort zone and engaged with novel experiences and forged new relations with the locals. Upon their return, veterans brought pieces of China home via souvenirs, photos, spouses, and children, as well as tastes, vocabularies, tales, aesthetics, and identities, which were all woven to a varying degree into America's sociocultural fabric in the mid twentieth century. Servicemen joined missionaries, journalists, scientists, teachers, students, donors, and Chinese-Americans throughout the 1940s in creating new transpacific networks, institutions, relationships, and dynamics in Sino-US exchanges that helped lay the groundwork for a postwar world order.[57]

On the Chinese side, most people, including protestors, harbored a mixture of resentment, misgivings, and fascination with respect to GIs and America at large. Dance hostesses, prostitutes, rickshaw pullers, houseboys, cooks, restaurant owners, tour guides, street vendors, black marketeers, thieves, and gangsters endured and resisted, as well as seized opportunities to capitalize on the presence of US servicemen. While some locals loathed them as violent bullies and evil imperialists, others welcomed, desired, and depended on them for the material, cultural, and political capital they brought as liberators, customers, patrons, and purveyors of Western goods and culture. As this book will show, the US military presence left overt and covert imprints on China's physical and mental geography. The GIs instituted the practice of right-side driving, affected local economies – including restaurants, brothels, and rickshaws – and participated in a booming black market for American goods. Servicemen also introduced new technological and commercial products and cultural spectacles, such as Jeep rides and Western courtship rituals. As locals emulated GIs in drinking Coca-Cola, sipping surplus coffee, using DDT to spray their houses and soil pits, and receiving penicillin shots, the United States entered the intimate and public spaces of Chinese life – bodies, households, streets, soil, and water, as well as memories, legends, and propaganda. Through these iconic and everyday products, together with US soldiers who visibly consumed, represented, and advertised them, Chinese society at large came to see, feel, and interpret America. Although American commodities and culture had been present since the old China trade, it was in the late 1940s that ordinary people on the coast and in the hinterland gained access to a more substantial American experience. This direct encounter affected their daily lives and views of a country that had previously been too remote to reach or even imagine. Through this newfound connection, the once abstract ideals of America became a tangible reality.

Both Chinese citizens and GIs crossed many boundaries in their encounters at the crossroads of micro and global spaces. Like the "anonymous hero" who, in the words of Michel de Certeau, uses context-specific "tactics" in everyday practices, they had to navigate unfamiliar worlds, speak each other's languages, develop new tactics to deal with foreign situations, protect their individual interests and the "face" of their nation, and even adopt new names and identities.[58] Such encounters were shaped by local and global knowledge and beliefs, sociocultural biases on both sides, and the larger political dynamics between the two nations. But these interactions were not simply a replay of the official guides that instructed them on how to act toward each other. Nor were they an enactment of formal treaties or agreements signed by national leaders. They were also spontaneous, messy, and inconsistent and often went beyond the official ideology and even common wisdom. It is in the micropolitics of the everyday where the macro-order of the US global empire was negotiated, contested, and potentially transformed.

To argue for a causal relation between the "micro" of everyday politics and the "macro" of international relations involves a huge interpretative leap. For instance, one may ask: Did the American military staying on end up doing more harm than good for the Nationalists? Could greater efforts by the US government to address soldiers' misconduct or a willingness to relinquish extraterritorial rights for its servicemen have prevented anti-American sentiment? These counterfactual questions, like the "lost chance" hypothesis, have no definitive answers. Yet it is reasonable to speculate that a clearer and more cohesive mission, and one attuned to local realities and grassroots tensions, could have lessened the tragic loss of life on both sides. It could also have reshaped Chinese perceptions of America and perhaps influenced how the civil war unfolded – even if not deciding its ultimate outcome.

It remains a methodological and narrative challenge to strike a balance between elements of human agency and larger, more impersonal forces that impinge upon it, to stitch together all the causative factors and weave the enmeshed fabric of micro-relations into a coherent pattern. But it is precisely such elusive specificities that lie at the core of historical and humanistic inquiries. The contradictions, ambiguities, and subtleties at the micro-level of this global encounter are not mundane distractions from the larger story but rather keys to unlocking a more authentic one. Overall, this book uncovers a forgotten history of entangled relations between GIs and Chinese civilians that was profound for both nations. It hopes to shed light on this complicated history of US-China interactions that mixed military occupation, economic expansion, imperialist aggression, nationalist assertions, Communist maneuvers, and day-to-day struggles, mundane resistance, everyday desires, and hopes for new beginnings. While the "loss of China," often attributed to state policies and ideological struggles, speaks of a failure that is evidenced by the withdrawal of the last GI from China in 1949, *Everyday Occupation*, focusing on the micro-level, sheds light on dynamic and mutually transformative quotidian encounters. Full of perils and opportunities, this process of entanglement tells a story different from the inevitable fall.

Chapter 1 examines the US military operations in China within the volatile context of the civil war and emerging Cold War. As the US forces accepted the Japanese surrender, clashed with Communist forces in sporadic skirmishes, and adjudicated trials of Japanese criminals in China independent of the Nationalist Government, they staged

American victory, might, and justice for both enemies and allies. The tactic of "show of force" was used in a "peaceful" mission to ensure submission and deference. However, its diverse, ambiguous, and at times contradictory objectives created significant military and political challenges. Ultimately, occupying China became a mission impossible.

Chapter 2 explores American servicemen's everyday lives through their sensory encounters with China. While largely maintaining a privileged lifestyle separate from Chinese society, they also forged intimate connections with local populations by exchanging goods, service, language, and culture, an encounter that both followed and contradicted official policies and popular representations. As tourists, consumers, cultural messengers, and diplomats in the field, their encounters with China were characterized by both fascination and contempt, enchantment and alienation. While their sensorial experiences and narratives were conditioned by preexisting Orientalist beliefs and racist prejudices, GIs' cultural identities were reshaped by daily interactions involving new sights, smells, tastes, sounds, and touches.

While Chapters 1 and 2 focus on American servicemen's experiences and narratives, Chapters 3, 4, and 5 examine the three largest sources of Chinese grievance or fascination – traffic accidents, intimate interactions, and American products. Chapter 3 investigates the frequent accidents caused by American military vehicles, the most common trigger of everyday tensions, as well as GIs' turbulent relationships with rickshaw pullers. Following frequent accidents caused by drunk driving, speeding, and negligence, the American Jeep turned from an object of enchantment, a symbol of Allied prestige and a cultural spectacle and popular commodity, into a military tool of intimidation, danger, and harassment, threatening the existing order of Chinese society and the nation. As the two sides fought over speed limits, economic compensation, moral responsibilities, and legal justice, the Jeep-GI duality, embroiled in local street politics with rickshaw pullers, became the ultimate symbol of prolonged American occupation trampling Chinese sovereignty. Chapter 4 examines American soldiers' actual and perceived sexual relations with Chinese women, the most sensitive subject that triggered the strongest anti-American sentiment. While Chinese conservatives, out of racial and sexual anxieties, maligned women who consorted with GIs, liberals and self-identified "Jeep girls" ingeniously invoked the language of modernity and patriotism. However, in the wake of the Peking rape incident, the once lively debate over modernity was quickly silenced as nationwide protests raged against American imperialism. Chapter 5 analyzes the everyday impact of American goods on Chinese lives and views of America. Massive quantities of industrial products, such as instant coffee,

Coca-Cola, canned food, penicillin, and DDT, poured into postwar China through American aid and war surplus sales, creating new and the only direct experiences many had of America. This growing consumption engendered Chinese fears of capitalism crushing domestic industries and US materialism corrupting Chinese morality. Meanwhile, the American military's stringent "halt or shoot" policy, implemented to protect US properties from theft and black marketing, led to frequent killings of members of the civilian population. The policy gave rise to the deadliest type of grassroots encounters, resulting in legal disputes and political crises.

The shadow of the American occupation remains long and haunting. The recurring persona of the Chinese victim facing American brutality, further popularized through propaganda during the Korean War, continues to influence Chinese anti-American nationalism. After all, the postwar US mission in China unfolded within the vital space of the everyday, where the occupying GIs encountered Chinese civilians in their preoccupations with daily life. It is in this forgotten story of the quotidian encounter, in the entangled relations, that we find connections – disjointed and faulty at times – that paved the historical paths of China and the United States.

1 Occupying China
Mission Impossible

On the afternoon of August 15, 1945, thirteen-year-old Gu Weiqing suddenly heard the deafening sounds of firecrackers, drumbeating, and victory chants from outside. The whole family rushed out and found the streets of Chongqing flooded with paraders in tears and exaltation. "It finally dawned!"[1] Paul Child, then serving in the Office of Strategic Services in Kunming, observed:

> The streets of the city are filled with windows of red exploded-fire-cracker-casings. Everywhere are national government flags and victory signs in both Chinese and English. Some of the inscriptions: "Thank you President Roosevelt and President Chiang" – "Hooray for final Glorious Victory" – "Let us now fight for Peace as we fought [fought] for War!" Crowds jam all streets, with happy faces. Dragons 60 feet long, made of flowers and paper are whirled through the alleys accompanied by gongs, flutes, drums and firecrackers. Every store front has red paper victory signs in gold on red... this afternoon, in this Chinese city, with its crowds of happy faces, its firecrackers, its wildly-twisting dragons, its drums and gongs, its flags and inscriptions has given me the feeling that perhaps the God damned war is finished.[2]

As American air units flew in a V shape overhead, overseeing the ground filled with crowds and joy, the glorious news of the end of war exploded in China and became perpetually engraved in the memories of all who had long fought and survived the most devastating war in history (see Figure 1.1). Unlike the meticulously planned D-Day landing and subsequent liberation of Paris, the abrupt end of the war in the Pacific, accelerated by the catastrophic atomic bombs, surprised both the Nationalists and Communists. Months passed before the Japanese and collaborationist forces were finally replaced by Chinese troops who rushed to reach former Japanese-occupied areas. The continuous presence of more than a million armed Japanese forces before their repatriation was not to be taken lightly.[3] The dire situation was further complicated by the direct military involvement of the Soviet Union in Manchuria. In the contentious environment of the Chinese civil war and the emerging Cold War, the Japanese surrender did not mark a clean line between war and peace, but rather the beginning of intense postwar struggles.[4]

22   1 Occupying China: Mission Impossible

Figure 1.1 A US Army captain holding a flag of China, greeted by cheering civilians in Chongqing upon news of the Japanese surrender, August 1945. NARA.

Upon Japanese surrender, the Nationalists' main concern was to prevent Chinese Communists from taking advantage of any potential power vacuum. Generalissimo Chiang Kai-shek, Supreme Commander of Allied Forces in China, ordered that Japanese forces must remain in their positions, keep good order of those areas, and only surrender their weapons and turn over their occupied territories to personnel authorized by him.[5] Because of such strategic priorities, the Nationalists generally did not treat Japanese troops in China harshly. To the initial surprise of many Japanese officers who expected much more severe punishment, Chiang announced the principle of "repaying hatred with benevolence," invoking both Confucian morals and Christian ethics. War trials were held, and Japanese soldiers occasionally were beaten in the streets by local civilians, but rarely was there any mass retribution. Unsurprisingly, the Communists ignored Chiang's instructions of standing still and took quick action. General Zhu De, commander of the Communist forces, announced that "any anti-Japanese armed forces can take the surrender of the Japanese."[6] Although they had to abort the campaign to seize large cities, opposed by both the United States and the Soviet Union, Communist troops seized more than 150 towns at the county level and above in North China and succeeded in consolidating rural areas.[7] They confiscated Japanese weapons and equipment and fought with those who refused. Like the Nationalist army that used Japanese soldiers to assist in preventing Communist takeovers in certain areas, the Communists also recruited some Japanese divisions, especially the much-needed technical and medical staff, into the 8th Route Army to fight in the civil war.[8] But unlike the lenient policy of the Nationalists, the Communist Party called for severe punishments of Japanese war criminals and Chinese collaborators and attacked the Nationalist policy on Japanese surrender as "a hoax."[9]

This was the chaotic environment into which US occupying forces entered in the wake of WWII. Before delving into the everyday encounters between American GIs and Chinese civilians, it is crucial to understand the complex and evolving nature of the US military's postwar involvement in China, the tactics that it adopted, and their impacts. At the official invitation of the Nationalist Government, American service members carried out a wide range of activities that extended beyond the scope of wartime engagements and traditional warfare. These heterogeneous operations, including occupation missions as well as noncombat duties and "peaceful" tasks, not only defined the principal tasks of GIs in the country, but also set the stage, terms, and tone for their daily interactions with the Chinese populace. Rather than solely relying on decisive battles and supreme firepower, the US employed a "show of force" tactic within the changing geopolitical landscape. This strategy included large-scale military exercises and parades, positioning of naval forces in key waterways, protection of rail lines and key installations, and regular reconnaissance patrols by air and land. It also featured dramatic ceremonial events such as the official Japanese surrender and public war crime trials. These spectacles, intended to stage American victory, might, and justice, targeted both enemies and allies, friendly and hostile groups. The use or mere threat of force aimed to ensure submission and deference by showcasing America's readiness and capacity to act. The goal was to demonstrate the United States' military strength, power, and dominance in the postwar world. However, faced with a mission of near-impossible objectives in a precarious environment, the display of American force was only partly effective, with varying degrees of success when it came to the Japanese, the Communists, and the Nationalists.

An Untenable Position

More than fifty thousand marines had arrived in North China by October 1945. Initially, Lieutenant General Albert C. Wedemeyer, Commander of US Forces, China Theater, had called for six or seven divisions to serve as a barrier force aimed at deterring Soviet expansion in the region. Two were sent: the 1st Marine Division infantry that occupied positions in Tanggu, Tianjin, Beijing, and the Qinhuangdao area, and the 6th Marine Division that moved into Qingdao. Concerned about Soviet assistance to the Communists and American strategic interests in the region, the US Navy used the port of Qingdao as a major fleet anchorage in the Far East. The number of US military personnel in China almost doubled following the end of WWII, reaching a peak of more than one hundred thousand, but it fell to below twelve thousand by the end of 1946, when a series of deactivations and reorganizations was implemented. In January 1947, when George Marshall's mission to bring peace and stability to China was declared unsuccessful, President Truman ordered military personnel home. Several thousand personnel remained on the eve of the Communist victory, and the last group withdrew from Qingdao in late May 1949.[10]

The United States Marine Corps' primary occupation duties included disarming and repatriating Japanese troops, liberating and rehabilitating Allied internees and POWs, and assisting the Nationalist Government in reoccupying key areas. On behalf of Chiang Kai-shek, the American military accepted Japanese surrenders in North China before the arrival of Nationalist forces. The subsequent repatriation mission involved disarming, subsisting, and transporting a large number of Japanese military and civilian personnel, as well as Koreans and Taiwanese. By October 1946, more than 1 million people had been deported from Manchuria, mainly through the port of Huludao. This massive undertaking continued until the summer of 1948, as many remained stranded in Communist-controlled areas, further complicated by transportation disruptions caused by the civil war.[11] Weary of Soviet aggressions together with China's civil war development, the American army and navy helped transport by air and sea Chiang's major divisions to northern and eastern China to prevent Communist takeover of these areas. In addition, marines guarded key rail lines, bridges, and mines to ensure vital coal and supply train transportation between North China and Shanghai, as well as to Manchuria. More broadly, and long after these initial goals were achieved, American military personnel continued their involvement in China. They engaged in a variety of roles that would later be known as MOOTW, short for "military operations other than war," including nation assistance, humanitarian assistance, and peacekeeping.[12] Army and marine officers provided personnel for the Executive Headquarters in Beijing, which directed truce teams to conduct field investigations and helped supervise the agreement between the Nationalists and Communists. To "assist and advise the Chinese government," nearly a thousand members of the Military Advisory Group in China, known as MAGIC, helped train and strengthen the efficiency of the Nationalist military. The last group withdrew from Nanjing by March 1949.[13] Moreover, American servicemen supported the relief efforts of the United Nations Relief and Rehabilitation Administration (UNRRA) in China, which was its largest single-country program, with a total estimated cost of US$670 million. They helped distribute massive quantities of war surplus supplies, providing food, shelter, and medical supplies to civilians across China. The final activities of the UNRRA mission were completed by March 1948.[14] Throughout their deployment, US soldiers acted as a "police force" while upholding their traditional role as protectors of American lives and property. As the Communist takeover approached, the final groups evacuated citizens, defended the naval base in Qingdao, and provided cover and support for the retreat of Nationalist forces from the area.[15]

In general, US servicemen were tasked with maintaining neutrality in the civil strife while assisting and advising the Nationalist Government, an ambivalent goal that reflected the unsettled American policy toward China. At the conclusion of WWII, the American government saw the utmost importance of a strong, united, and democratic China and pledged support for the Nationalists. But it did not want to get involved in China's civil war, a principle of Truman's foreign policy.[16] The American military and the US Department of State disagreed both on whether the CCP would pose a real threat to the United States and on the appropriate level of aid and intervention to be provided to the Nationalists. As "an instrument of American policy," the marines served in what Secretary of Defense James Forrestal described as "the balance of order" in China.[17] However, amidst a fratricidal war with ambiguous instructions to "abstain from active participation" while "cooperating" with Nationalist forces, the marines essentially "walked a tightrope to maintain the illusion of friendly neutrality."[18] This untenable position created critical challenges in the field. As Second Lieutenant John B. Simms put it, "It was probably more the political consideration of not having a major clash with the U.S. forces than our strength" that prevented Communists from "moving in and taking over." While "only marginally effective as a unit" and handicapped in movement and knowledge of the area, Simms added, "The greatest handicap was trying to maintain a neutral status."[19] Deployed across Nationalist, Communist, and contested areas, US combat troops faced stepping into a "hornet's nest" and becoming embroiled in a violent conflict, with the containment of Communism looming on the horizon. In the absence of a clear victory or timeline, the uncertainties surrounding their deployment, including how long it would last and how to determine their success, imposed serious constraints on the operations as well as on soldiers' morale.

Many of the soldiers were unprepared and untrained for the prolonged peace operations in a setting of potential conflict. According to an official Marine Corps account, "the average Marine on postwar duty in China found himself an uneasy spectator or sometimes an unwilling participant in a war which he little understood and could not prevent."[20] While the new recruits lacked adequate training and experience, the battle-hardened veterans who had fought in some of the bloodiest Pacific campaigns were plagued by homesickness, boredom, post-traumatic stress disorder, and low morale. Due to the scope and complexity of their duties, American servicemen encountered a wide spectrum of situations from surprising guerrilla attacks to widespread urban crimes and civilian hostility. In the rural environments, "a strange never-never land of allies who were not quite allies and not-quite-at-war hostiles who took pot shots and mined tracks," they were vulnerable to assaults from Communist forces, local bandits, and sometimes even Nationalist soldiers.[21] When under attack, GIs were directed to exercise restraint and avoid escalating the conflict – a frustrating and perilous experience. In the unstable urban environment plagued by poverty and social unrest, they lacked clear instructions and effective tools to handle a range of challenging situations from armed gang robbery to petty theft. As a result, guard duties turned into "accidents" and deadly incidents, and military operations became an ad hoc, improvised response by individual soldiers and officers at the front trying to manage uncertain situations and unexpected crises, sometimes resorting to unnecessary and excessive force.

Ultimately, the China operations proved untenable. Even the commanding generals felt that the occupation's goal was "ill-considered and ambiguous in meaning," making it "an intangible mission" difficult to execute or even explain to soldiers.[22] While some of its initial goals were considered successful, the results of others were more mixed and controversial. As American servicemen accepted the Japanese surrender in official ceremonies, engaged in sporadic clashes with Communist forces, and adjudicated Japanese criminals in China without authorization from the Nationalist Government, they engaged in perilous encounters with friends and enemies as well as various groups in between.

Staging Victory: Japanese Surrender Ceremonies

The first and foremost objective of the American occupation was to disarm the Japanese and accept their surrender. To most marines who landed in North China in the autumn of 1945, it was their first close encounter with individual Japanese soldiers in a noncombat setting, making it an "experience in itself." When describing their initial contact with the Japanese, Officer Simms observed: "Here was an armed U.S. Marine watching an armed enemy pass by within spitting distance. Neither they nor I really knew what measure to take," and "we ended up simply ignoring the existence of the other."[23] In an odd fashion, Japanese officers continued to reside in the genteel old Astor House Hotel in Tianjin and dined next to American officers in the same breakfast room for the first few weeks.[24] Out in the countryside in Hebei Province, Private E. B. Sledge recorded the visual shock of encountering Japanese troops on duty: "a Japanese officer in dress uniform and cap, Sam Browne belt, campaign ribbons, and white gloves standing erect in the turret – with his samurai saber slung over his shoulder."[25] Besides a few incidents of gunshots, the initial American encounter with Japanese troops in China was mostly marked by silence. The "clackety-clack of the swords clanging and the hob-nailed kind of boots" of the Japanese soldiers walking in silence, as well as the heads-down Japanese civilians dressed in disguise fearing revenge from the Chinese, were all markers of defeat.[26]

The Americans' initial attitude was to "go hard on the Japanese."[27] Commanders bore their victor identity clearly with the sentiment that "we have won the goddam war, and to the victors belong the spoils."[28] Brigadier General William A. Worton, Chief of Staff of the IIIAC, instructed his subordinates to take the "bloody houses" from enemy aliens for commanding generals' accommodations in the city. Since "there were no guidelines for this duty in the Marine Corps Manual," the general suggested giving them three days to get out, and "be dressed for it" when giving such an order, as "if you're going to kick their asses out of their own houses, make sure your boots are highly polished."[29] Major General Lemuel C. Shepherd, commander of the 6th Marine Division who took the division from Okinawa to Qingdao, commented about the Japanese in the city: "We kicked them so badly that I think we took all the sting out of them for a while, anyhow, and they are very nice to us, for they know where their bread is buttered." Rather than appear "too kind," he was further advised by his aides to be "forceful" with the regional Japanese representative for surrender.[30]

"To be forceful" with the Japanese was a result of American sentiments after the brutal Pacific warfare. Commanders and soldiers shared indignation toward Japanese troops who were seen as "bastards" and "rattlesnakes." American wartime propaganda often invoked racist images to motivate their soldiers, and dehumanization of the Japanese soldiers as animals or subhuman was a common practice to justify the killing.[31] Japanese cruelty was extensively covered in the media, creating widespread loathing. Displaying a forceful attitude was also a deliberate military strategy based on psychological manipulation, namely to prevent potential resistance and promote cooperation through intimidation, threat, and warning. When the war ended suddenly, the massive number of Japanese troops in China had little sense of defeat; many believed they "never lost any war" and didn't feel they had lost this one.[32] So the line of victory needed to be clearly drawn.

The American exhibition of force was immediate upon arrival, as thousands of marines made a dramatic entrance, riding through the major cities on trains, open trucks, and Jeeps. Their victory parades were truly a spectacle that invited gazes. As American soldiers waved, throngs of local civilians flooded the streets, holding flags, horns, banners, and streamers, while others crowded windows and rooftops along the path (see Figure 1.2). Shortly thereafter, the American military continued to impress with additional marches along these thoroughfares. On October 19, 1945, for example, the first marine parade was held in Beijing, when "tanks, artillery, and vehicles were freshly painted field green and were wiped with a thin film of oil so that they glistened in the bright sun." The troops "looked sharp," with all parts of their uniforms ordered to be "tailored to 'fit perfectly'" and "squared away and paraded with absolute precision."[33] In Tianjin, troops marched "for psychological purposes which worked both ways: it gave the Chinese a fete and a big pat on the back, it gave our Marines a thrill, and it said something to the Japanese."[34] While displaying sharp-looking GIs armed with powerful artillery and air force, US commanders also deliberately used a "rumpled appearance" and "sartorial insouciance" to accomplish "a subliminal strategic purpose of some sort." Anticipating that the leadership's landing in Tianjin would be "received very formally at the airport by a battalion of Japanese," General Worton gave orders of dressing casually in khaki – that is, to "counter-balance the icy propriety of the Japanese officers' uniforms with an American informality that would do something to their psyche."[35] Upon entering Shanghai in September 1945, Admiral Milton E. Miles, "the dare-devil Commander of U.S. Naval Guerila Forces in China," who had carried on a "Lawrence of Arabia" type of guerilla activity in the war, inspected a Japanese ship, ate some spam, and "appropriated a couple of hara-kiri knives and samurai swords." The ship was seized by Elmo R. Zumwalt Jr., then a young navy officer and a future

Figure 1.2 Marines entering Tianjin, welcomed by local crowds giving a thumbs-up, October 1945. MCHD.

admiral himself, who had led a very small crew from the Pacific to Shanghai to gather intelligence. Upon his initial days in the city before reinforcements came, Zumwalt successfully secured Japanese vessels, docks, and warehouses by teaching the "vanquished" a lesson. He answered the "truculent demands" from a Japanese captain bedecked in full regalia by taking his pistol, spinning him around, and rooster-walking him away using a grip on the seat of his pants.[36]

The most significant American spectacle was displayed in the formal Japanese surrender ceremonies held in Tianjin and Qingdao. On October 6, 1945, the United States Marine Corps accepted the surrender of more than fifty thousand Japanese troops in the Tianjin-Tanggu-Qinhuangdao area in front of the former French Municipal Building, now headquarters of the IIIAC. Beginning at 8:30 a.m., invited Allied guests entered and the marine guard of honor and band took their positions. Shortly before 9:00 a.m., Japanese representatives arrived in two vehicles escorted by American Jeeps. At 9:00 a.m. sharp, Major General Keller E. Rockey, commanding the IIIAC, and his chief of staff, General Worton, walked out of the headquarters and took

30   1 Occupying China: Mission Impossible

Figure 1.3 The Japanese surrender ceremony in Tianjin, 1945. MCHD.

their seats. The Japanese representative, Lieutenant General Uchida Ginnosuke, commander of the Japanese 118th Division, was led to the draped signing table, saluted the American leaders, and signed the surrender documents, ten copies in English and ten in Japanese (see Figure 1.3).[37] Then General Rockey signed. Afterward, the honor guards fired a gun salute, and the marine band played the US national anthem, followed by the Chinese anthem. After another round of salutes, seven Japanese delegates removed their swords and laid them down on another long table. The brief ceremony ended in twenty minutes as the Japanese delegates were led out of the site by marines.[38] Notably, General Uchida Ginnosuke wore his boots and full uniform during the ceremony with "a dozen medals tacked to his tunic," together with his sword, and he "stood rigidly in front of their command company of soldiers." In contrast, General Rockey, General Worton, and their subordinates, "by design and by order," wore their "most casual khakis; no neckties, no medals, no frills."[39] Ceremonial officers who escorted the Japanese representatives sported open-collar khaki uniforms without belts or insignia,

Staging Victory

Figure 1.4 The Japanese surrender ceremony in Qingdao, 1945. MCHD.

and crowds of marines stared and cheered in close distance, packing the headquarters stairs, windows, and roof.

By contrast, the two-hour-long surrender ceremony in Qingdao on October 25, 1945, was a more direct show of might. At 11:00 a.m., the surrender ceremony of about ten thousand Japanese in the Qingdao garrison took place at the spacious oval racecourse that had been built during German occupation in the late nineteenth century. Flags of five nations – the United States, Great Britain, the Soviet Union, France, and China – flew from the grandstands (see Figure 1.4). More than twelve thousand marines from the 6th Division paraded in battle dress, together with forty rumbling tanks; four hundred armored, military, and communication vehicles; and self-propelled artillery. During the ceremony, six squadrons of Marine Air Force aircraft swooped over the racecourse and hovered over the city and along the coast (see Figures 1.5 and 1.6).[40] As Major General Shepherd recalled, "I turned out every man in the division

32   1 Occupying China: Mission Impossible

Figure 1.5 China division parade in the Japanese surrender ceremony in Qingdao, 1945. MCHD.

Figure 1.6 China division parade in the Japanese surrender ceremony in Qingdao, 1945. MCHD.

Staging Victory 33

and every vehicle in the division" to show "the strength and fire power of the division."[41] During the ceremony, Shepherd in his formal military attire and Lieutenant General Chen Baocang (Chen Pao-tsang), Chiang Kai-shek's representative, were seated on the platform, while the Japanese representative, Major General Nagano Eiji, unbuckled his samurai sword and laid it across the table while bowing, an act followed by ten other Japanese delegates. Nagano then signed the surrender documents. Afterward, the division band played the national anthems of America and China, as all attendees including the Japanese officers saluted. After the signing, the entire marine division plus the air force members paraded.

The American-held ceremonies departed from previous Chinese ones through two major innovations. First, an open field was chosen, and the general public was invited to the collective witnessing, together with guests and journalists. An estimated two to three hundred Chinese surrounded the Tianjin ceremony, while one hundred thousand people reportedly gathered in the vicinity, shouting victory chants and clapping their hands.[42] In Qingdao, while the Japanese delegates struggled to complete their mechanized exit as their car broke down, according to a Chinese report, "Not even racket of fighter planes overhead could drown the roar of laughter that came from 10,000 Chinese throats."[43] In contrast, from September to December 1945, the Nationalist Government accepted surrenders across China in fifteen designated districts, including northern Vietnam and Taiwan, and held ceremonies that were mostly brief and unembellished. Even the carefully choreographed and meticulously planned national ceremony in Nanjing was not open to the public and only lasted fifteen minutes for signing documents.[44] Another major American innovation was to include a formal sword surrender act in the proceeding. Commanding generals saw the Japanese sword as "the symbol of his defeat" and a "token of surrender."[45] Thus, before or after signing the surrender document, the Japanese representatives formally laid down their swords on the assigned table. Chinese leaders also saw the sword as crucial to the Japanese but chose a more accommodating approach. In the national ceremony in Nanjing, the Japanese delegates' swords were submitted in a separate resting room before entering the ceremonial space and were not photographed or recorded in the formal program. In fact, this arrangement was a result of Sino-Japanese prenegotiations. The Japanese representative was given the choice of submitting the swords or not carrying them during the ceremony.[46] General Okamura Yasuji, who signed the Japanese Instrument of Surrender in Nanjing, chose the latter option.

These American shows in China might have been directly inspired by the spectacles at the Tokyo Bay on September 2, 1945. On that occasion, the Japanese delegation in their ceremonial suits and uniforms arrived beneath the guns of the battleship USS *Missouri* and were surrounded by thousands of American sailors and marines wearing daily service clothes and plain open-collar khakis. General Douglas MacArthur, Supreme Commander for the Allied Powers, had Matthew C. Perry's 1853 flag delivered from Maryland and chose the ceremonial spot because it was where Commodore Perry had come ashore for the first time and "opened Japan." These symbols were intended to convey defeat and humiliation for Japan's past deeds, as well as dismissiveness and contempt toward its future. MacArthur was determined to put on full display the superiority of American forces with an armada of 258 combat ships and a formation of B-29 Superfortresses that had brought destruction to Japan.[47] This demonstration of force was an admonition to quell any potential resistance and a show of America's new status as a nuclear superpower. Although surrender terms were all predetermined, the actual ceremony was significant as a meaning-making ritual occupying highly charged political, mental, and emotional space. Throughout Asia, American-held surrenders "relied on displays of force and potent symbols to convey the irremissibility of Allied power and impress upon the Japanese the unconditional nature of their defeat."[48]

Under close scrutiny by all parties, the Act of Surrender also became an act of power transfer. "I thought of the moment as unembellished, stark history," Walter J. P. Curley, aide-de-camp to General Worton, commented on the Japanese surrender in Tianjin, which he helped organize. "After the ceremony, we invited Chinese, British, French, Swiss, Swedish, and American officials into our III Phib Headquarters. We drank champagne, and clapped backs."[49] In Qingdao, General Shepherd recalled, he signed the articles of surrender and "had the local Chinese Commander also sign them."[50] These seemed accurate descriptions of the event except that the Chinese appeared in these American accounts as supporting characters in the background, as observing guests by invitation, and as cheering audiences of the grandiose march. The whole scene was presented or even designed as an American victory. Notably, the signing page of the surrender document in Qingdao indicated that Major General Lemuel C. Shepherd and Major General Li Yannian, Deputy Commander of the 11th Chinese War Area, were "duly authorized representatives of the Generalissimo Chiang Kai-shek." General MacArthur's General Order No. 1 provided that the Japanese forces in China excluding Manchuria, Taiwan, and northern Indochina were to surrender to Chiang, and all Japanese forces within Manchuria were to surrender to the commander in chief of the Soviet forces in the Far East.[51] However, on the cover page of this Act of Surrender, the document was said to be signed by General Shepherd "on behalf of the United States." The surrender paper ended with this statement: "In case of conflict or ambiguity between the English text of this document and any translation thereof, the English text shall govern."[52] Ten copies of English and Japanese documents were signed on that day. Surrender did not always mean an acceptance of defeat by the signers of the official documents who might be operating in very different political and discursive spaces. As Japanese army leaders in China continued to question whether they had indeed lost the war in China or lost to the Chinese, signing the surrender paper to the Americans made the Japanese surrender in China even a less clean act.

The apparently reversed roles between American guests and Chinese hosts, as well as the explicit and implicit message of American victory in the American-led ceremonies, did not escape the eyes of the Chinese. In their own reports of these two ceremonies, local news media often profiled photos of Chinese generals inspecting American forces and portrayed the two allies equally. But bitter feelings often surfaced in personal accounts. According to the memoir of Major General Lü Wenzhen, who was leading the advance commanding team of the Nationalist army to North China and in charge of handling Japanese surrender affairs in the region, he was quite surprised when an American officer informed him that the Americans would be accepting Japanese surrenders in Tianjin instead. He questioned why foreigners would be handling such matters in China. His unease extended to the actual ceremony, where the raising of the American flag and the playing of the American anthem sparked confusion among the Chinese spectators. They felt a mix of bewilderment and dismay, wondering, "Now with Japan gone, here comes America?" The mood shifted only when the Chinese anthem started and the crowd burst into roars and applause.[53] Perhaps bearing this sentiment in mind, General Lü decided to create a proper Chinese ceremony. After witnessing the Tianjin ceremony, he recommended relocating the surrender ceremony in Beijing that was to be held four days later from the modest Hall of Embracing Compassion (Huairen Tang) to the expansive open space in the Forbidden City, stating that as the "American military accepted the Japanese surrender in public, we will also hold a public one."[54] As a result, an estimated one hundred thousand to two hundred thousand locals gathered on the historic day. The ceremony was presided over by General Sun Lianzhong, the commander in chief of the 11th War Area and a war hero known for leading the Battle of Taierzhuang in 1938, China's first major victory against Japan that provided a tremendous morale boost. Also following the example of the Tianjin ceremony, a formal sword surrender act was included in the proceeding, as the Japanese delegates turned over their swords after signing three copies of the surrender document, this time in Chinese and Japanese. There were also new inventions. At 10:00 a.m. sharp on the national day of October 10, after a spectacular band show and gun salute, a moment of silence was observed for the fallen soldiers and the Japanese representatives were asked to bow low and repent to the Chinese people. While learning from the American ceremonies, especially the creation of spectacles, the Japanese surrender ceremony in Beijing also represented an upgrade, not only in scale, but also in its insistence on public contrition. It demanded explicit Japanese acknowledgment of defeat, responsibilities, and even war crimes.

Surrender ceremonies consist of a deeply visceral encounter, a physical and symbolic exchange concerning victory and defeat, dignity and shame, agonies and forgiveness. They are moments of political and cultural reordering, "a complex configuration of social and cultural forms," what sociologist Robin Wagner-Pacifici calls the "transfer of power and reconstruction of identity."[55] In Tianjin and Qingdao, marines put on a formidable show of force in the official ceremonies. The actual display of power took different forms, from masqueraded casualness to overt intimidation. However, the shared goal was to underscore a clear relationship between victory and subordination, contempt and humiliation. More than achieving straightforward military success, this effort aimed to showcase an American victory to ensure both defeat and domination. These ceremonies thus became not only the victorious conclusion of the war but also a rehearsal of incoming postwar politics.

These staged acts of surrender seemed to have worked like a charm. According to General Worton's personal aide, "the American takeover and occupation of North China from then on happened remarkably smoothly." The Japanese commander was "scrupulously cooperative, if sullen, and understood the tasks at hand," and Japanese officers and soldiers virtually disappeared from general sight.[56] Similarly, the American military in Qingdao after the ceremony supposedly "never had any trouble."[57] Diehard Japanese officers who had infamously pledged never to surrender were said to become surprisingly cooperative in following American orders. It went so well that they gained new respect from the American military leadership and became subordinates who could be entrusted with rearmament and responsibilities such as fighting Communist forces and defending marines in isolated areas. For example, General Shepherd provided Japanese troops with arms and ammunition and permitted them to keep their rifles. He explained it bluntly: "If anybody's going to be killed fighting Communists, it's not going to be Marines, it'll be Japanese."[58] Indeed, the

Japanese tried to stay on good terms with the Americans after the country's surrender and occupation. Many continued to hold the Nationalists in contempt and considered themselves defeated by the Americans rather than by the Chinese. Japanese troops of all ranks in China saluted all marines regardless of rank. For the most part, they stayed in their camps and were on their best behavior around Americans.[59]

Staging Might: Dangerous Encounters with the Communists

On October 26, 1946, just one day after the official surrender ceremony in Qingdao, Marine Aircraft Group 32 planes began regular reconnaissance patrols to check the status of railway lines and ensure "adequate warning of any Communist move" against the city. At this time, the Communists controlled most of the coastline and vast areas of the interior in Shandong.[60] These aerial demonstrations served as not only a warning to the Japanese, but also as a deterrent to the various groups of Chinese spectators, including collaborationist armies, local bandits, and especially the Communists. General Shepherd explained that the "show of force" during the Qingdao ceremony targeted "both the Japs and the Communists," adding that "it did impress the local population when the word got out that we had this tremendous military force and they'd better damn well be good or else we'd destroy them."[61] Despite such optimistic portrayals, the actual effects of this massive display were mixed. The CCP did not really buy the American claims of dominance and tried to stage its own shows of strength. Ultimately, there was a limit to the power of American spectacles within "a Nationalist island in a Communist sea."[62]

The initial attitudes of the CCP seemed cooperative in their interactions, yet these were already marked by underlying tension. In September 1945, General Worton arrived in China with an advance team, becoming the first group of Allies to arrive in North China. In Beijing, he was said to have met with Zhou Enlai, Mao's right-hand man and a skilled diplomat. In their intense hour-long exchange, Zhou made it clear that the Communists would fight fiercely to prevent the marines from taking Beijing. In reply, Worton emphasized that he was not looking for trouble, but the battle-hardened IIIAC, backed by superior air power support, could overcome any resistance if necessary. Shortly thereafter, the marines arrived in Beijing without facing major opposition.[63] The CCP also abandoned its plan to seize Qingdao because US military personnel had already landed there and refused to relinquish control. The city ultimately remained the last Nationalist city in Shandong to fall to

Communist forces. Throughout the period, the CCP waged fierce propaganda campaigns against the US forces but steered clear of direct military conflicts, recognizing their superior strength. However, the American threat of force did not always deter the Communists' actions. Their army, along with irregular forces, frequently disrupted US operations by destroying roads and rail tracks, attacking local repairmen, and orchestrating ambushes and sabotage missions. This guerrilla-style harassment, which Mao elucidated clearly in his writings, avoided open battles but posed a constant and continuous challenge and threat to the occupying forces.

Frederick W. Mote, then a young officer with the Office of Strategic Services, recorded an incident shortly after the marines' landing that, while "in itself of little import," symbolized "the overall situation then developing in North China." On October 30, 1945, during a short train ride from Tangshan back to Tianjin, he was traveling with a Japanese army major when soldiers from the 8th Route Army stopped the train by placing a barrier across the tracks and firing rifles. They boarded the train, disarmed the Nationalist officers onboard, ripped off their epaulets with official insignia, and confiscated their wallets, while leaving civilian passengers unharmed and treating the American serviceman with respect. Afterward, these Communists shouted slogans, fired shots into the air, and quickly vanished into the dense millet fields. Mote, who would later earn a bachelor's degree from Nanjing University and become a founding figure in the study of China and East Asia in America, provided a compelling interpretation of the event. He noted that although Chinese Communists at the time were "capable of no more than making an occasional, well-planned display of this kind," this "staged event was to enhance their presence and to diminish their opponents' dignity." He further explained the Communists' way of demonstrating power: These "ostentatiously ragtag soldiers were telling us that the Japanese military was no longer important, the helpless Chinese government officials could be shown utter contempt, and the Americans were a negligible anomaly."[64]

Chronic small-scale raids and intermittent conflicts were a constant presence during American routine operations. Marines "riding shotgun" on coal trains and trucks faced frequent harassment and were vulnerable to sniper fire and explosions on tracks and roads. For instance, on November 14, 1945, the train carrying Major General DeWitt Peck, commander of the 1st Marine Division, was attacked while traveling from Tangshan to Qinhuangdao. Near Guye (Kuyeh), where a break in the railroad tracks had occurred, snipers exchanged fire with the marines for more than three hours. The attack was described as "never very big," but "enough" to prevent laborers from repairing the tracks. The following

Figure 1.7 General DeWitt Peck (standing, far left) and Chinese workmen flee for safety as a mine explodes on railroad tracks in North China where the general's train had been halted by previous damage, November 1945. MCHD.

morning, fire continued, and a Chinese workman triggered a land mine that exploded, killing several others (see Figure 1.7). In response, General Peck secured permission for an airstrike on a nearby village suspected of harboring the attackers. After a warning was issued and simulated strafing runs were made, the hostile fire ceased. With the repairs expected to take days, General Peck returned to Tangshan and opted to fly to his destination instead (see Figure 1.8).[65]

Direct armed confrontations were rare but deadly. Between October 1945 and December 1947, there were thirteen fatalities and forty-three wounded among navy and marine personnel.[66] The first major clash between Communist and American forces occurred in the Anping Incident on July 29, 1946. A marine convoy was ambushed en route from Tianjin to Beijing by approximately five hundred Communist troops.[67] The convoy consisted of twenty-three vehicles carrying marines and Chinese National Relief and Rehabilitation Administration supplies. The attack resulted in three marine deaths and twelve wounded, out of forty-three American military personnel. According to the American investigation, such a heavy toll occurred because the marine personnel were "completely unaware of the premeditated danger as evidenced by the disorganized manner in which they deployed and defended themselves."[68] The Anping Incident caught the attention of the highest

40   1 Occupying China: Mission Impossible

Figure 1.8 General DeWitt Peck inspects the marines in Tangshan, December 1945. MCHD.

leaders in both nations and thereby left a rare collection of detailed archival materials unmatched by other similar incidents. As it occurred in the middle of the Marshall Mission to China, all three sides of the Peiping Executive Headquarters conducted an investigation of their own but reached opposite conclusions.

Both the Communists and the Nationalists tried to exploit the incident for their own political gains. The Communist side insisted this was an American intrusion into the "liberated area," together with the Nationalist forces, and that the Americans fired first. Although their later investigation reports revealed new information that local Communist forces initiated the attacks without the prior knowledge of the Yan'an authorities, the Communist leadership did not change its initial claim and instead continued to frame incidents like Anping as evidence of American direct assistance to the Nationalist Party in the civil war. The Nationalists, on the other hand, hoped to stir anti-Communist sentiment and ease tension from the killings of anti–civil war democratic leaders Li Gongpu and Wen Yiduo about two weeks prior to the Anping Incident.[69] Under American pressure to downplay the incident, Nationalist media did not launch a full-scale propaganda war. However, Chiang Kai-shek could not ignore this opportunity and instructed subordinates to organize a series of public memorial services and events. On August 2, several Nationalist high officials attended the American memorial in Tianjin, and Chiang himself sent condolences to General Rockey to express "deep sympathy and regret over this loss and suffering."[70] Another public memorial service was organized by the Tianjin municipal government and attended by several thousand locals. The Nationalist Government instructed various local social organizations to send condolences and demand the punishment of the criminals.[71] As Theodore H. White and Annalee Jacoby, correspondents for *Time* and *Life* in China, described in their best-selling book *Thunder Out of China*: "Communist guerrillas, who had watched American marines league with Kuomintang troops to bar them from the railway lines for so many months, grew trigger-happy. ... The Kuomintang greeted the incident with sedate good cheer as finally sealing Communist-American enmity; the Communists immediately unloosed a barrage of propaganda denouncing America."[72] In the end, with fake evidence from both sides, General Marshall observed, "Delaying tactics, vicious propaganda, et cetera, have been the order of the day."[73] Indeed, the joint Nationalist-Communist-American investigation of the Anping Incident broke down in September, soon followed by the collapse of the peace talks.

Another major attack occurred in less than a year. In the dim light of dawn on April 5, 1947, four well-organized groups of armed Communist forces, roughly three hundred troops assisted by another three hundred locals, attacked the Xinhe (Hsin Ho) ammunition dump near Tanggu in Hebei Province. The little-known attack resulted in five marines dead and sixteen injured, the vast majority being the guards. Twenty-eight marines were on patrol at the arsenal at the time while a total of six hundred marines were stationed in Tanggu. The ambushing forces led by Wu Hong (Woo Hung) from a local branch were reportedly well equipped, using a mixture of arms, including Japanese and Soviet automatic weapons. After the successful raid on ammunitions, they burned down the dump when the marine reinforcements arrived.[74] In fact, it was not the first time the 1st Marine Division at Xinhe was attacked by locals led by Wu Hong. On the night of October 3, 1946, "dissident forces" attacked the same ammunition supply point. A private on guard in the sentry tower was fired upon, followed by several hundred Chinese men armed with rifles and three automatic weapons and dressed in nondescript blue-gray coats with leggings, resulting in one marine wounded. Afterward, commanding general S. L. Howard recommended that the commander of the Seventh Fleet file an official protest to Communist leader Mao

Zedong, demanding the responsible people be punished and thirty-two cases of stolen US ammunition returned.[75] The request presumably was not met, as the second attack scaled up in just half a year.

More common than the aforementioned major incidents were the ever-present impromptu or organized attacks. For flyers conducting extensive patrols to provide intelligence, cover, and support for ground troops, their reconnaissance aircraft frequently landed with bullet holes in their fuselages. Although MAG-32 bombers flew well above the range of Communist small arms, the constant risk of being shot at, crashing, or captured remained a persistent threat.[76] For marines stationed in the middle of a "hornet's nest," danger was constantly looming. Lieutenant Simms was in charge of a remote detachment in Hebei Province, which consisted of eighty troopers tasked with protecting the bridges and railway tracks. In March 1946, they were caught between the Nationalists and the Communists in the area, literally in the heavy crossfire.[77] Sledge recounted a typical "incident at Lang Fang," an unwalled village of about five hundred people located along the railway line between Beijing and Tianjin. Forty marines under the command of a lieutenant were sent to protect the division's radio relay station and stayed inside a walled compound with barbed wire on top of the parapet. They were surrounded by a variety of troops, ranging from friendly to hostile, "all armed to the teeth and vying to fill the power vacuum resulting from Japan's surrender." On the night of October 26, 1945, his company was caught in a fierce fight between several thousand collaborationist troops and members of the Communist forces with eighty-one-millimeter mortar shells. The American commanding officer eventually had to send the Japanese troops to guard the railroad station instead in order to avoid involvement in the conflict.[78] In the words of White and Jacoby, "The United States marines, the Kuomintang, the former puppets, and the Japanese army, in one of the most curious alliances ever fashioned, jointly guarded the railways against the Chinese partisans ... Our flag flew in the cockpit of a civil war."[79]

To live in isolated areas in North China, especially extended outposts close to Communist-controlled territories, was a lonely and perilous affair. Sometimes, accidental encounters could turn hostile. On December 4, 1945, two marines hunting rabbits were shot by suspected Communists near Anshan, forty miles southwest of the marine-held city of Qinhuangdao. One private was killed and a corporal survived by feigning death, despite being shot in the leg while lying on the ground. In response, a light infantry force was dispatched to a small village just a mile southwest of Anshan to confront the gunmen, issuing an ultimatum: "to surrender the murderers within a half hour" or the village would be shelled. When the time expired, the marines fired "24 60-mm mortar shells" toward the Chinese village.[80] Afterward, *The Washington Post* published a critical editorial titled "Semper Fidelis," the motto of the United States Marine Corps, which began with a question: Is it to "the tradition of American justice" that "the United States Marines are forever faithful"?[81] A. A. Vandegrift, Commandant of the Marine Corps, responded by sending a letter to the editor and publisher, protesting this portrayal. He clarified that the gunfire was not directed into the village but into the open ground before it, breaking two windowpanes without causing any bloodshed. Vandegrift defended the actions of the marine officer in charge, explaining that his purpose was twofold: to coax the village residents into the open for questioning and searches for firearms, and "to remind the community, which appeared to him to be harboring the assailants, that force was available and would be used, if necessary, to prevent assaults upon Marines."[82] Although opposed to the continued presence of marines in China and critical of Chiang Kai-shek, the four-star general – who had served in Tianjin and Beijing in the 1920s and 1930s – felt compelled to defend his men and the Corps in the face of public criticism. The editorial, however, critiqued these actions, noting that to the Chinese, the American act of taking the village as a collective hostage and firing at it resembled the recent atrocities committed by Japanese troops – ironically, the very forces currently facing trial in American military courts. Furthermore, the editorial argued that this show of force, intended to "'civilize' these stubborn 'natives,'" failed to achieve its aim.[83] At the end of the ultimatum, not a single villager emerged. Four days later, on December 11, *The New York Times* reported another incident under the alarming headline "U.S. Marine Is Shot by Chinese Civilians." The article detailed how an unarmed marine sergeant had been shot and wounded by three Chinese people he encountered on the outskirts of Tianjin. According to the headquarters' report, the sergeant, who was on horseback, smiled and greeted the civilians. In response, they also smiled before drawing pistols and firing.[84] It was only a logical speculation that the second group of gunmen were inflamed by the earlier shelling of the North China village.

The deadly confrontations involved life-threatening situations and chilling details. But more often, marine "intruders" in Communist-controlled areas were fired upon, with some captured and later released. The length of their detention varied, depending on the success of their rescue missions, which in turn was contingent on the larger political environment, local dynamics, rescuers' maneuvers, and sheer luck. In December 1945, photo planes sent from Okinawa to Qingdao crashed en route and three crew members were captured in northern Shandong.

Thomas E. Williams, an intelligence officer, led a successful mission of five men and later received a Bronze Star for rescuing three American aviators from the Communist territory. Williams attributed his success to the rapport he established over friendly and elaborate talks, meals, group photos, and most importantly drinking a local brandy together. He painted a rosy picture of local Communist captures, and the two sides seemed to have eventually established a set of "working relations." Several Communist officials even went to Qingdao with Williams, followed by other members who brought back an injured aviator, carrying him on a litter, as well as the bodies of ten marine aviators who had been killed in the crashes. The deceased were transported in elaborate Chinese caskets, their bodies having been carefully prepared by an undertaker.[85]

Another successful operation involved seven members of a detachment guarding bridges on the Beijing–Shenyang Railway, a critical route the Nationalists used to move troops to Manchuria against the Communists. On July 13, 1946, these leathernecks from the 7th Marines were captured and held for eleven days by Communists in North China. The group had gone out to procure ice from a nearby village to celebrate a private's scheduled homecoming and upcoming twentieth birthday.[86] While one member escaped capture by hiding in the icehouse, the marine search team was unable to locate the captives, who had been quickly relocated. The seven marines were eventually released on July 24 by the Communists, who demanded the Americans apologize for their unlawful entry into the liberated area.[87] Despite the ordeal, the marines later described their detention experience as "prisoners' adventures" that involved rough rides on mule carts "touring" Communist areas no one had visited before. One marine even said, "We would have had a fine time – if we hadn't been so scared."[88] A *New York Times* article, filled with vivid details, described how local Communist leaders, with a sense of sincerity or naivety, propagated their message to the American servicemen and even tried to convert them to the Communist cause. An interpreter named Mr. Li, a graduate of Princeton University, spent most of the morning lecturing them on the accomplishments of the Communist government. After discussing the political situation of China with the American captives, the CCP commissar further reminded them how his unit had saved and smuggled the crew of a crashed B-29 through dangerous Japanese lines back to their interior base three years earlier.[89] Upon their release, the commissar invited the marines to a fourteen-course meal, which ended with a group photo. Despite these "good gestures," the American captives were said to have maintained their victor identity and appeared "ungrateful" in the eyes of the Communists. In a "friendly game," the marines played basketball with CCP soldiers who carried pistols. The American team, including two loaned men from the Chinese side, "lost the game" and "a little 'face' at the same time." But the former captives insisted that they saved some face after their dog, now also a captive, won every fight against the dogs the Communists brought in for a match.[90]

Rescue missions present some of the most vivid and colorful accounts of Chinese Communists in marine narratives. Many of these operations were later recounted by GIs with a sense of adventure and humor. Compared with the evil Fu Manchu in the colonial era or the insidious brainwashing captors in *The Manchurian Candidate* during the height of Cold War hysteria, Chinese Communists in these personal tales and media reports appeared more human, often shifting between friends and foes, hosts and captors.[91] However, official documents reveal that these encounters often carried high stakes and great risks, especially after the civil war escalated and General Marshall's mediation mission failed. Rescue efforts became more difficult, requiring high-level, lengthy negotiations. For instance, on December 25, 1947, a Christmas hunting party of marines from Qingdao exchanged fire with local Communist forces about thirty miles outside the city. The clash left one marine dead and four captured, who were then held for nearly one hundred days before their release on April 1, 1948. As in previous cases, the captives were subjected to elaborate "educational lessons" through lectures and readings, and by eating, living, and traveling together with their captors. Local Communist authorities did not believe the Americans were on a simple recreational outing so far from their base and accused the marines of supporting the Nationalist war effort and engaging in "aggressive activity of imperialism."[92] They also demanded an apology and admission of responsibility from the Americans, along with acknowledgment of US complicity in the civil war. Rather than seeking ransom, the Communists aimed to negotiate with high-level American officials on terms that positioned the Communists as an equal and legitimate government. Although the American military generally denied these allegations as false, these incidents – along with the resulting personal, military, and diplomatic exchanges – directly questioned the efficacy of the American tactic of deference and claim of dominance in the region.

Not all incidents ended up as harmless "touring" adventures. Communist forces were seen and felt as a real threat to the lives of marines tasked with key occupation duties of guarding munitions, coal mines, bridges, railroads, and warehouses. Some soldiers expressed dissatisfaction that these incidents usually received scant attention and were reduced to "a bland, colorless paragraph in a routine report."[93] Wary of their political implications, high-ranking US officials downplayed such events and remained largely silent in their public statements. In the aftermath of the Anping Incident, for example, General Marshall urged restraint and low exposure on the American side. He was concerned with how both the Communists and Nationalists exploited such incidents for their propaganda purposes.[94] Similarly, following the shooting of two marines in Anshan, an area where "Chinese irregulars previously have fired on marines guarding coal train," General Rockey declared to the news agency that "he believed it had no military significance."[95] Shortly after the second Xinhe dump attack, marines quietly withdrew from the dump and turned the ruins over to the Nationalist army rather than retaliating. In general, the US military did not engage in overt confrontation or retaliation following these clashes. The direct use of force against the CCP was restrained, despite superior American firepower that included a formidable combat force of tanks, fighter aircraft, artillery, and infantry directly from the Pacific. Following clashes with the Communists, marines stationed close to "bandit areas" were often instructed to be on high alert, stay neutral in local confrontations, and open fire only if being attacked or their mission was directly threatened. Instead, the strategy of consolidation was adopted to minimize the exposure of marines to vulnerable positions. This approach involved consolidating forces in more concentrated locations and relocating soldiers from stretched railroad lines and remote areas to major cities under Nationalist Government control. In North China, the American military added barbed wire and extra defenses, increasing regular patrols in barracks and camps, and renewing safety drills including oversized tanks and marine fighters. These practices were meant to be a show of force to the hostile groups watching, but they did not always work.[96]

Despite deliberate silence from the high-level leadership, marine newspapers reported incidents of Communist raids on camps and harassment along train tracks, as well as "kidnapping incidents" when GIs entered areas controlled by the Communists.[97] Back in the United States, news of the dire situation in China and GI casualties reached a wide audience through both mainstream and small-town newspapers. A combat correspondent for the *Tulsa Daily World* in Oklahoma reported that marines barely escaped sniper fire over their heads even while watching movies, as well as faced frequent highway ambushes. The Chinese Communists aimed to "create enough 'incidents' to arouse American public opinion."[98] Another newsman from the *Hickory Daily Record* in North Carolina wrote about Bessemer City native Private First Class William R. Rabb, who was one of the two sentries on guard duty during a well-planned Communist attempt to destroy a large ammunition dump. The explosion was described as producing "a great burst of orange light and a thundering roar that smashed windows for five miles around."[99] Through vivid accounts like these, the American public closely followed developments in China, and many became increasingly alarmed. At home, wives and mothers bombarded their congressional representatives with letters and requests to "bring the boys back home." Leftist media, labor organizations, and citizen groups campaigned for the withdrawal of the US military from China and rallied against America's imperialist stance in postwar Asia.[100] For instance, from November 11 to November 30, 1946, the Division of Public Liaison in the State Department received a total of 182 public letters concerning China, of which 95 percent urged the "withdrawal of troops and termination of all aid to Chiang."[101]

Veterans, now no longer restrained by wartime censorship laws, wrote and protested against their prolonged stay long after WWII had ended. One army officer wrote to his sweetheart back home, lamenting, "Having defeated the Japanese, the troops do not like being played as pawns in this Chiang-Mao political game."[102] Another marine private expressed, "We had survived fierce combat in the Pacific, and now none of us wanted to stretch his luck any further and get killed in a Chinese civil war. We felt a terribly lonely sensation of being abandoned and expendable."[103] Frustrated GIs signed petitions to General Wedemeyer and the Congressional Investigation Committee on Demobilization, asking the pointed question, "Why are we here?" They organized mass meetings outside the China Theater headquarters in Shanghai, "mirroring the same activities in Yokohama, Tokyo, Manila, Guam, Saipan, Honolulu and Frankfort."[104] Around the world, thousands of veterans took to the streets from V-J Day to January 1946, protesting the delayed demobilization. On Christmas Day alone, twenty thousand troops marched in protest in Manila, joined by others from across the Pacific. Ultimately, clashes with Chinese Communists, causing harm to American soldiers and Chinese villagers, exacerbated the already low morale and public opinion back home.[105]

As for the CCP, it remains unclear how much its central leadership at Yan'an knew about the planning of local armed conflicts with the American forces. Most of the smaller skirmishes are still little known today due to a lack of investigations or access to classified records. It seems that CCP forces had orders to avoid open hostilities for the most part, but local troops sometimes acted more aggressively and on their own. In the Anping Incident, for example, Zhou Enlai, who was representing the Party in the ceasefire negotiations in Beijing, only found out that it was a local Communist initiative in the later stages of the investigation but chose to continue the cover-up.[106] An armed direct clash with the

48   1 Occupying China: Mission Impossible

American military in the middle of the peace talks was not in line with the Communist policy, which did not want to provoke the Americans, but rather preferred a neutralized American position. It is thus more likely, as Marshall insightfully pointed out, that the incident occurred because local forces had been energized by the powerful Communist anti-American campaign that linked the American military presence to assisting the Nationalists in the civil war. Once launched, the trajectory of propaganda did not always adhere to the official Party line. Individuals mobilized by the propaganda might take initiative on their own, as in the Anping ambush and the killing of John Birch, an American missionary turned soldier.[107] Overall, the Communist Party had been protesting against the Americans' actions of "interfering with Chinese sovereignty and participating in the Nationalist army's attack of Communist-controlled area."[108] Mao's interview with American journalist Anna Louise Strong in August 1946 also sent a clear message regarding the American show of force: "The atomic bomb is a paper tiger which the U.S. reactionaries use to scare people," and the Americans are terrifying only "in appearance ... but in reality they are not so powerful."[109]

Staging Justice: Juridical Sovereignty and Tensions with the Nationalists

On the Fourth of July 1946 the air arm of the marine garrison celebrated the American national holiday by staging a majestic aerial display over Beijing and adjacent Communist territories. As Graham Peck observed, this "show of force" on America's Independence Day ironically emphasized to the Chinese that "for the time being they did not have full independence to decide their own future."[110] This dramatic demonstration of power, while aimed at hostile groups, also had significant implications for the Nationalist allies, who increasingly saw these spectacles as an infringement on Chinese sovereignty (see Figure 1.9). This sentiment had already surfaced during the American-led Japanese surrender ceremonies, where Chinese leaders felt the Americans had overstepped their roles as invited guests. The sentiment became even more pronounced as Americans took charge of adjudicating Japanese war crime trials on their own, escalating tensions at the governmental level.

Almost immediately after the Japanese surrender, the American military started to arrest and adjudicate war criminals in China, three months earlier than the actions conducted by the Chinese government.[111] The US Military Commission was convened by Lieutenant General Wedemeyer to try "persons, units and organizations accused as war criminals in this theater." Over the course of these proceedings, a total

Staging Justice 49

Figure 1.9 Navy carrier planes in a "show of force" flight over Beijing with the Forbidden City in the background, September 1945. NARA.

of eleven cases were brought against the Japanese involving seventy-five defendants, sixty-seven of whom were convicted and ten sentenced to death. From January to September 1946, forty-seven Japanese war criminals were detained and tried by the US Military Commission in Shanghai.[112] While conducting military operations to liberate the formerly Japanese controlled areas, American forces also performed a "mission of justice" by showcasing war crimes trials in China. In the name of reciprocity, the American military not only enjoyed exclusive jurisdiction over its own members, but also extended its independent jurisdiction over a variety of so-called war crimes cases involving Japanese soldiers, German civilian residents and American civilians in China, and Taiwanese POWs. This lesser-known mission provided a window into the US system of law and order in the postwar world. To achieve American standards of justice, the military staged victory and retribution – but at the cost of China's sovereignty and the Nationalist Government's legitimacy.

Figure 1.10 Japanese defendants in the Hankou trial, featuring Major General Masataka Kaburagi standing, February 1946, Shanghai. *The China Press.*

The American trial in China began in January 1946 with the sensational Hankou trial, in which eighteen Japanese were charged with the torture and murder of three downed American aviators in December 1944 after their bombing mission over Japan. Of these eighteen, five were executed, including Major General Masataka Kaburagi, chief of staff of the 34th Japanese Army headquartered in Hankou (see Figure 1.10). This became the first war crimes trial held in China and attracted attention from major Chinese and English media outlets.[113] The public spectacles took place in the courtroom of the US Military Commission, located on the top floor of Tilanqiao Prison, also known as Ward Road Jail. Built by the British in the early twentieth century, this massive panopticon-like jail was the "largest prison in the Far East," surpassing the infamous Sugamo Prison that housed war criminals from the Tokyo Trial. In a newly whitewashed room, two Chinese witnesses testified that at least one, and possibly all, of the three B-29 crewmen were burned alive by their Japanese captors. These testimonies recounted a harrowing story of beatings, torture, and a "hate parade" during which the victims were stoned and doused with water in the streets before being carried into a crematorium and thrown into the blazing ovens. Grim relics from the cremation were introduced as evidence, including "three charred belt buckles and a good luck charm."[114] General Claire Chennault, who commanded the 14th Air Force in China and directed a retaliatory air raid on Hankou, attended the hearing as a special guest, bringing further spotlight to the case. An American pilot who survived captivity as a POW in China flew back to testify, adding not only strong evidence but also emotional weight to a trial that garnered significant publicity and empathy.

Initially, the appearance of justice seemed well maintained through procedural transparency. In the public trial, both prosecution and defense teams presented a trove of evidence gathered during pre-investigations, and witnesses from all sides were called to testify. Vigorous debates took place over the evidence and testimonies presented. However, one problematic issue was soon raised by the defense, who challenged the US jurisdiction over the Hankou trial. The defendant's counsel, Major Levin, filed a "special plea" questioning the jurisdiction of the Commission, providing the following two reasons: (a) "The United States Government has not established a Military Government in China for the purposes of occupying territory therein." (b) "The United States is not administering Martial Law in China. Second, The United States Government does not have rights of extraterritoriality in the Republic of China." In opposition, the prosecutor claimed, first, that the accused were considered war criminals and therefore the Commission had jurisdiction over them pursuant to the order of the China Theater. Second, citing the examples of the Philippines and Japan, he argued that "neither military or martial law is a prerequisite to the appointment of a military commission." In short, the prosecutor stated that the commission had jurisdiction to try war criminals in the custody of the US military authorities; it was not bound by territories. Consequently, the Commission decided to side with the prosecution and denied the defense's motion.[115]

Prosecuting cases of atrocities against US soldiers might have presented a more straightforward scenario. The punishment of the "Japanese devils" who tortured and brutally murdered American flyers by American judges seemed fair, evoking fresh memories of the Chinese sufferings, for example, in the notorious Nanjing Massacre. However, in the 1946 case of a major German spy ring known as the Ehrhardt Bureau, the issue of jurisdiction was once again brought to the forefront during the trial. This time, it provoked direct scrutiny and questioning from the Chinese side. In this proceeding, twenty-seven German civilian residents in China were accused of espionage and war crimes. Although the Germans allegedly committed their crimes in China and were apprehended in China, they were tried by the Commission on the grounds that they had committed war crimes against the United States.[116] The defense counsel, L. C. Yang, argued that "the War Crimes Commission had no jurisdiction to hold the trial" as these German nationals were still residents of China, and the accused came under Chinese law instead. In response, the prosecutor, Lieutenant Colonel Jeremiah J. O'Connor, stated that "the crimes were against International Law and thus do not fall under the jurisdiction of any local domestic courts," and the trials formed part of military operations undertaken with the complete agreement of the Chinese government. During the exchanges, he added that "it appeared that the Chinese were suffering from lack of facilities and personnel to undertake such trials, but he personally could recommend an able volunteer. (Laughter)."[117] The laughter, as reported by *North China Daily News*, was meant as a reaction to the American officer's "humor." But the accusation of the Chinese "lack of facilities and personnel," and by extension, the overall incompetence of the legal system was offensive to Chinese elites who had made decades-long efforts to reform the system and fight for China's international status. It is true that qualified Chinese personnel trained in international law remained lacking. For example, the Chinese representatives failed to prepare sufficient-quality evidence in the Tokyo Trial convened on April 29, 1946. There was also a shortage of food, coal, medical care, and facilities for Japanese prisoners in China, and more broadly, for nearly all ordinary Chinese people at the time. As a result, the Allied Powers in Japan would not extradite many main culprits to China but preferred to seek justice through American-led trials in Japan.[118] But such a public comment at the historic Tilanqiao Prison, masqueraded as humor, also reflected lingering Western distrust of the Chinese legal system, what some scholars have called "legal Orientalism."[119] Notably, in the Chinese government version of the news report, the American prosecutor's statement of recommending an "able volunteer" was translated as "Mao Sui zijian," referencing the legendary character Mao Sui, a loyal retainer who offered his humble service to his lord during the Warring States period. This translation turned the American into a devoted guest and subordinate.[120]

The American "volunteer" in this case might be more able, but was an uninvited one. Compared with the Hankou case, with which Chinese elites could more easily sympathize, these trials of former Axis Power citizens roused direct critiques of the Americans interfering with Chinese sovereignty. Chinese society saw these German civilian nationals, generally grouped under the crime of espionage, as different from Japanese military personnel who committed brutal crimes against individual American victims, especially heroic flyers. Professionals opined that these Germans accused of espionage should not fall under the jurisdiction of the United States Army Forces in the China Theater, but rather the Allied forces in the China war zone or the Chinese government. Overall, the American military in China during the war, when these crimes were supposedly committed, was under the command of Generalissimo Chiang Kai-shek. If these cases concerned major interests of America or other Allied nations, they suggested, China's Ministry of National Defense could organize a special mixed court consisting of Sino-American military tribunals, with a Chinese judge presiding.[121]

The unresolved legal issues and disregard of Chinese jurisdiction undermined the projected sense of American justice and strained relations with the Chinese government. Tension arose as early as January 21, 1946, when the former German ambassador to Japan, General Eugen Ott, was brought to Tokyo as a friendly witness at the request of the Supreme Commander for the Allied Powers in the war crimes trials. After Adolf Hitler had dismissed him from his post as the ambassador to Japan, General Ott had lived in China since 1943 in an unofficial capacity.[122] In early May 1946, Ott returned to China to visit his ill wife, all arranged by the US military without seeking Chinese permission. On May 6, China's Vice Minister of Foreign Affairs queried the American embassy on Ott's visit to China, expressing "some resentment over failure of American military to comply in this instance with Chinese regulations governing admission of aliens." He stressed that "the fact of German general traveling around country as 'guest' of American army was embarrassing to Chinese Govt." On May 11, Robert L. Smyth, the chargé d'affaires, telegrammed the State Department that "our military have made [a] tactless mistake, perhaps essentially unimportant but certainly unfortunate at this time when [the] Chinese are very conscious of their sovereign rights." Perhaps because he included General Marshall in the correspondence, staff from the United States Army Forces in the Pacific under the command of MacArthur justified their actions by citing previous memorandums from the State Department. The memorandums initially had suggested that the case was not "one of importance requiring any special attention," and after the Chinese government's complaint, explained that "the reported disregard of Chinese regulations was unintentional." Major General Ray T. Maddocks, the chief of staff of the United States Army Forces in the China Theater, also justified the situation by stating, "the Chinese [are] represented on the International Tribunal at Tokyo," and therefore Ott's presence also served their interest.[123]

In fact, the Nationalists had closely monitored the United States' arrest, detention, extradition, and trial of war criminals in China from the very first Hankou trial and the more high-profile Doolittle trial.[124] Official reports documented a range of other cases and repeatedly raised concerns about infringements on China's sovereignty to the Vice Minister of Foreign Affairs. For example, more than one hundred Japanese and Taiwanese POWs were arrested in Taiwan and brought to Shanghai for confinement and adjudication. Five Filipinos in Shanghai were extradited to Manila for trial. Four American civilian citizens living in Shanghai, who had worked for the Nazis and been charged with treason, were detained and returned to the United States for trial before a civilian court.[125] Overall, the detained and accused had different statuses ranging from military personnel to civilians; from Japanese, Taiwanese, Germans, and Filipinos to Americans; and from those residing in China proper to those residing in Taiwan, a former Japanese colony. Their alleged crimes ranged from killing American soldiers to espionage and treason. Each category presented a different legal challenge. Regardless, the US Army Forces in China retained custody of the accused without formal agreements from the Chinese government. Initially and even after official complaints from Chinese authorities, the American military acted on its own without going through the proper diplomatic channels with the Chinese Ministry of Foreign Affairs or Ministry of National Defense.

As cases grew in number and complexity, tensions escalated, making the situation increasingly contentious. But it was not until June 1946 that some formal guidelines were provided. On June 12, China's Committee to Deal with War Crimes (戰犯處理委員會) passed three resolutions stating that the arrest, detention, and extradition of war criminals, including Americans, must be adjudicated through diplomatic channels between the Chinese Ministry of Foreign Affairs and the American embassy, and no other Chinese bureaus or local governments could make any agreement with the American military. For future cases, the US military should advise the local military or police organ, who would make arrests on the Americans' behalf and then follow the proper procedures for extradition. This guideline was issued to local governments throughout China and sent to the American embassy. In August, Lieutenant General Alvan Cullom Gillem, the commanding general of the United States Army Forces in China, conveyed his disagreement through the American embassy. He replied: "It is a fact that agreements in regard to war criminals of enemy nationality were reached at Chungking with appropriate Chinese military officials, concurred in by the representatives of several non-military Chinese Ministries who formed the Chinese-American Committee," and "these agreements continue in effect at present, and the Chinese military authorities continue to advise the United States Army Headquarters that war crimes are within military jurisdiction."[126] In fact, this had been the official stance and rationale that the US military provided for the previous cases. When various Chinese bureaus inquired, the US military claimed that it had notified certain Chinese military authorities, according to certain verbal agreements during the war. However, China's Ministry of National Defense found "no records to investigate" on such a written agreement, and only had a note of an oral discussion in 1945, together with a memo that the American requests of China's formal approval of such an agreement had not been received.

A logical explanation for such conflicting exchanges seems that military officials from both sides had some informal conversation during the war, which the American side took and used as an agreement. But the Chinese side did not respond or agree to the request for a formal agreement, nor did it sign one. The lack of an affirmative answer was certainly not a result of Chinese disinterest in the issue. On the contrary, stacks of memos circulated at a high level, within which the vital importance of such an issue was clearly identified by concerned and frustrated officials from various agencies. But as if they were kicking a ball back and forth, there was no firm reply from any decision-maker, probably because Chiang Kai-shek himself did not officially advise on this issue and held a somewhat ambiguous attitude.[127] As previously discussed, the Nationalist Government was trying to prove its new status as a civilized and leading modern nation following international law and had always been sensitive about the issue of sovereignty.[128] Chiang clearly instructed in some cases that Japanese in Taiwan must first be tried by the Chinese court and then could be extradited to the American authorities. The Chinese administration was caught in an awkward situation: the danger of such American practices interfering with Chinese jurisdiction and sovereignty, potentially setting legal precedents for other foreign powers, coupled with the reality of the US military circumventing the Chinese system to execute justice on its own. Perhaps that was why the problem had been left hanging. It was not a rare practice for Chiang to avoid written agreements of this nature that would infringe on China's sovereignty, but he was keenly aware of such de facto practice.

With no explicit directive from the very top, the problem was largely left unsettled for a year since the American military started to arrest suspects almost immediately upon the end of the war. Finally, on September 27, 1946, the Chinese Ministry of Foreign Affairs, Ministry of National Defense, and Judicial Yuan held a joint meeting devoted to this very issue. Their solution was that China would accept the de facto reality of these American trials while maintaining the principle that Chinese approval must be sought through diplomatic channels for future cases. Such a special arrangement was justified on the grounds that the nature of war crimes differed from regular legal cases, and therefore their handling procedure could be different. Three days after the meeting that laid out the principles and guidelines, the heads of the three ministries presented a letter to Chiang, who then gave his approval in early October.[129] The revised "Measures Governing the Arrest, Extraditions, and Trials of War Criminals by the United States Forces" was then presented to the American embassy in Nanjing, affirming that "pending the establishment of peace, Allied justice would seem more effectively served if the procedure in such matters were left to the competency of the appropriate Sino-American military authorities" – the US proposition General Gillem had raised the previous August.[130] The official diplomatic negotiations, or rather lack of negotiation, ended with virtually a fait accompli of Chinese acquiescence.

These tensions over war crimes dealings again underscore the uneven reciprocity characteristic of Sino-US legal practice at the time, as in the case of extraterritorial protection afforded to US military personnel in China. Ultimately, the "standpoint of justice" and the interpretation of reciprocity between the two allies turned out to be quite different. When the Chinese government requested the extradition of Lieutenant Colonel William K. Evans, a former American officer who stole a large amount of gold bullion from Taiwan upon the end of war, the Foreign Ministry cited the recent Ehrhardt Bureau case in which the crime was "committed in China, was a violation of Chinese law, and involved the property of the Chinese Government," and all the German accused were tried in the US military court.[131] But the Chinese request, appealing to the principle of reciprocity, was not granted. Evans, who had schemed and left China in time, was instead tried in the civilian court of California, where he currently resided, and he later escaped justice because the grand jury could not reach a guilty consensus, influenced by the defense's manipulation of racism against Asians.[132] As if to get even for all these unanswered inquiries, requests, and protests, China, on the grounds of illness, did not extradite General Okamura Yasuji to Tokyo when the US Allied forces in Tokyo made this request through diplomatic channels. This time, Chiang Kai-shek decided to put his foot down and gave personal orders to keep the former commander in chief of the China Expeditionary Army of Japan, who was later acquitted by the Chinese court.

Compared to the Tokyo Trial, the American adjudication of war criminals in China remains little studied, but it actually involved more complex disputes over jurisdiction, international law, and sovereignty. In principle, it was in America's own interest to appear as a true torchbearer of justice in postwar China, both out of liberal ideals and in response to the demands of Cold War realpolitik. Nevertheless, the US military acted without advance authorization from the Chinese government and continued to do so, citing a vague verbal agreement reached during the war by certain unnamed authorities. To attain restitution for Americans in a speedy and efficient way, it solely relied on its military tribunal system, rather than going through the proper diplomatic process or the Chinese legal system. In the eyes of many, allowing the US courts to adjudicate matters related to war criminals in China, just like GIs' exemption from local laws, represented a continuation of the long colonial legacy of extraterritoriality. This American mission of justice, premised on the claim of a superior legal system, disregarded Chinese jurisdiction and sovereignty. It foreshadowed the emerging global law and order under American domination.[133]

The Nationalist Government's official policy of "repaying hatred with benevolence" and its lenient treatment of Japanese officers, condemned by the Chinese Communists at the time, not wrongfully, were motivated by political reasons rather than a desire to provide the justice that Chinese victims long deserved. This forgiving approach was in sharp contrast with the initial attitude of the American military authorities in China – that is, to be ruthless toward the Japanese. But the United States taking things into its own hands also created a huge challenge for the image and legitimacy of the Chinese government. When the US military overstepped its role in war crimes dealings, the Nationalist regime was left in a difficult position, especially when answering to the Chinese elites and people who criticized the American infringement on Chinese judicial sovereignty (*faquan*) by launching its own mission of justice.

***

The staging of American occupation in postwar China aimed to showcase US victory, might, justice, and, ultimately, dominance. This show of force, intended to dominate and deter, achieved mixed results among the Japanese, Communists, and Nationalists. American ritual performance intersected with the everyday world, as Chinese spectators gathered at public surrender ceremonies, military parades, and war crimes trials. While these spectacles enthralled many locals, they also prompted questions about sovereignty; many wondered if America had simply replaced Japan's rule of China. As "invited guests" of the Chinese government, US soldiers demanded legal, political, and social privileges in their operations and daily lives. Within this context of national and systemic inequality, these servicemen carried out their diverse duties and came into contact with the local population. Their expectations of special treatment diverged from American claims of equality and democracy, making the occupation susceptible to political manipulation in the charged atmosphere of the civil war. This discrepancy undermined the legitimacy of the US military's presence, as well as the legitimacy of the Nationalist Government the US tried to assist. Ultimately, the occupation's mission to "help bring about stabilized peace" in China ended up as a destabilizing force.[134] What began as an untenable military endeavor evolved into a fragile and controversial political mission – an impossible task.

2 Sensory Contact
Life in the Orient

When marine Private E. B. Sledge looked out of his train window in September 1945, he saw a "desolate landscape" in North China: "Everything was windswept, dusty, and brown. Different shades of brown, but brown nevertheless." Upon disembarking, he encountered "the imposing ancient multistory tower of the Chien Men Gate" in Beijing, which "stood like a massive fortress atop the huge centuries-old wall around the city." Soon he arrived at his billet, located in the historical legation quarters, where "one could see evidence of repairs on the walls from damage during the Boxer Rebellion in 1899."[1] The so-called Peking siege was broken by foreign troops, including American, making it one of the earliest marine missions in China. For Second Lieutenant John B. Simms, the initial Chinese scene was farmlands with dirt roads, "drab and totally lacking color," and its uniformed people where "one group faded into the next without distinction" because of the "sameness of their clothing, dark blue or black for the most part with a brighter blue or white being almost the only contrast." Shortly afterward, "wandering through the old city" of Tianjin "introduced the American to sights, sounds, and smells that clouded the senses and left him gasping."[2]

This chapter explores the US servicemen's everyday lives in postwar China through their visceral, sensorial experience. The China mission assigned American soldiers a wide variety of capacities, roles, and spaces in their interaction with the Chinese people. Sometimes, this placed GIs in dangerous environments vulnerable to violent attacks. Other times, it enabled American influence to penetrate to places and groups that had been too far to reach, allowing the forging of direct relations with lasting impacts on both sides. While largely maintaining a privileged lifestyle, GIs also engaged in intimate connections with local populations by exchanging goods, services, languages, and cultures. They went on sightseeing trips in the Forbidden City, smelt the "honeydipper" carts on the street, ate water buffalo meat, danced with Chinese women, and learned Pidgin Chinese. Acting as soldiers as well as tourists, consumers, cultural messengers, and everyday diplomats on the ground, they experienced China in ways that both followed and contradicted official policies and popular representations.

Historically, American soldiers' sensory encounters with China were characterized by both fascination and contempt, enchantment and alienation. Their senses were sometimes assaulted by the dust, dirt, noise, and stench of "the Orient," and other times satisfied by its many comforting tastes and gentle touches. Existing Orientalist framing presented GIs with a variety of linguistic, aesthetic, and moral options when conceptualizing Chinese society, ranging from premodern tranquility and a peaceful society to Oriental cruelty, deception, and corruption. The realpolitik of wartime propaganda, assisted by American popular media, spread new positive images of the Chinese allies, from the country's beautiful scenery to its well-educated and democratic people. The GIs' portraits of China consequently often shifted between two opposite poles: Chinese cities and countryside both peaceful and foul; food delicious and poisonous; women elegant and dangerous; people hardworking and dishonest, hospitable and cruel. Racist contempt continued to fill the pages of GI memoirs. However, their sensory experiences and accounts sometimes went against their American "rationality" and military instructions. For example, many indulged in Chinese cuisine and bargained with local hawkers, inventing new Americanisms, foods, and identities that were transferred back to their hometowns. The mental and visceral domains became intricately linked through the exchanges of objects and experiences in quotidian encounters.

Conceptually, the senses provide an analytical lens through which to examine the entangled everyday politics of American military involvement in postwar China. United States servicemen's sensory stereotypes, sensory metaphors, and the construction of the sensory self and otherness reveal the deployment of power in the nexus of diplomatic relations and daily interactions.[3] While their visceral experiences and sensorial narratives were conditioned by preexisting Orientalist beliefs and racist prejudices, as well as the unequal relations between the two nations, GIs' cultural identities were reshaped by intimate interactions involving new sights, smells, tastes, sounds, and touches. Together with their letters, memoirs, photos, souvenirs, reports, and tales sent home, these intimate encounters with Chinese society also helped shape postwar American identities and locals' perceptions of America in profound ways.

Life as an Occupier

> The Marines were the occupying force in this area which made the later entry of Chinese Nationalist forces and officials possible. They – and not the Chinese – disarmed the Japanese.
>
> American Consul in Tianjin, August 27, 1946[4]

American servicemen in China, predominantly white males, belonged to various branches, including the marine leathernecks, the navy bluejackets, and the army doughboys.[5] These groups differed in their historical ties with China, their experiences during WWII, and the perspectives of their senior leadership on the civil war. As their wartime rivalry continued into the postwar era, members of each group took pride in their distinctive identities and often claimed cultural superiority over the others.[6] These service members also varied in experience and background, ranging from "Old China Hands," being officers who had prewar assignments in the country, and WWII veterans from the Pacific battlefield to new recruits fresh out of boot camps. The US military in China had deep roots dating back to the nineteenth century. Between August 1900 and May 1901, approximately twenty-five hundred army soldiers and marines were part of the Eight-Nation Alliance that helped put down the Boxer Uprising and occupied Beijing.[7] A permanent guard was established at the US legation in Beijing, initially consisting of the army's 9th Infantry and later replaced by the marine legation guard, which remained in place until December 8, 1941. To protect American citizens and properties, a near-battalion-sized marine guard and two battalions of the 15th US Infantry were stationed in the nearby city of Tianjin. Additionally, US Navy gunboats patrolled the Yangzi River till the Japanese attack on Pearl Harbor.[8] These historical connections provided US servicemen with a sense of affinity toward China, as their official guides often pointed out, and many of them had actual connections to the country. For instance, Major General Peck, then a colonel, had commanded the 4th Marines in Shanghai in the 1940s, while Major General Rockey and Brigadier General Worton, the IIIAC's commanding officer and chief of staff, respectively, had both served in China before WWII. After spending more than three years in a Japanese prison following his evacuation from Shanghai to the Philippines, Samuel L. Howard also returned to China as a newly promoted major general, replacing General Rockey and assuming command of the 1st Marine Division in September 1946. In total, between three hundred and four hundred US Marine Corps personnel in the subordinate divisions had previously served in China.[9]

Once considered the crème de la crème of US Marine Corps duty, the postwar deployments to China delighted most old China hands.[10] General Worton, who had spent about twelve years serving in the country and mastering the Chinese language during the 1920s and the 1930s, described China to his assistants as a dreamland for assignments.[11] Upon their triumphal return, high-ranking officers stayed in fancy Western-style hotels and beautifully furnished houses seized from citizens of

Figure 2.1 A European-style mansion in Qingdao, serving as the residence of the US Marine Corps commanding general. MCHD.

enemy European nations, many of whom had been longtime residents of China. These homes were equipped with modern amenities, including flushing toilets, bathtubs, heaters, fireplaces, and stovetop kitchens, and a large number of household staff, cooks, and servants – a level of luxury unattainable back home (see Figures 2.1 and 2.2). The Astor Hotel in Tianjin, the first international hotel in modern Chinese history, built in 1863, exuded a Victorian-era atmosphere and had hosted a long list of celebrity guests, including several future US presidents. The Cathay Hotel, located on Shanghai's Bund and owned by Victor Sassoon, boasted a level of luxury that General Wedemeyer called "too doggy for a Nebraska farmboy," and he soon moved out of the British tycoon's flat in the hotel.[12] In Beijing, Brigadier General Gerald C. Thomas, soon to take command of the Fleet Marine Force, Western Pacific, was warmly greeted by the "ancient doorman" at the legendary Wagons-Lits Hotel with "Welcome back, Captain Thomas," a heartfelt acknowledgment of his departure in 1937 from the marine detachment at the American embassy.[13] Local governments formed reception committees for

Life as an Occupier 63

Figure 2.2 A team of Chinese staff, including cooks, servants, drivers, and butlers, providing services at the Marine Corps commanding general's quarters in Qingdao. MCHD.

members of the Allied forces, frequently honoring US officers with lavish banquets and gifts, such as silk, embroidered tablecloths, lacquer vases, ivory figures, and antique screens, as tokens of gratitude and hospitality. Samuel B. Griffith, a former US Marine Corps provost marshal and inspector, recalled that everyone was having "a pretty good time" because the "pressure was off."[14] Similarly, Omar T. Pfeiffer, the former marine commander in Qingdao, noted that Admiral Charles M. Cooke Jr., the commander of the Seventh Fleet and Naval Forces, Western Pacific, replaced senior officers in China because "they were still too much imbued with wartime combat spirit, which is 'eat, drink, and be merry, for tomorrow we die.'"[15] Even in these official oral history interviews, officers – speaking with discretion – admitted that "the division was running like a ship without a rudder."[16]

Most leathernecks from the Pacific were initially thrilled to see civilization again and enjoyed a comfortable life after years of fighting in harsh jungles and brutal battlefields. Given the low cost of living in China and their pay, the lowest of which exceeded fifty dollars a month, all ranks hired houseboys to cook, clean, and run errands.[17] But morale among veterans was low because of the dullness of a daily routine without a well-defined mission and frustration over the lack of a specific date for going home. Many did not feel safe in China, with occasional threats from Communist troops and other local forces. By mid April 1946, nearly all marine veterans originally deployed to China had been sent home or were scheduled to go, having earned enough demobilization points amidst enormous public pressure to release combat veterans. As they were leaving and new recruits were coming, China became "a proverbial swinging door."[18] The personnel situation of the marines was far from ideal, as many rookies lacked basic training and competence but were eager for adventures and glories, without the opportunity to experience actual battles or claim military honors. One fresh enlistee who came to China as a replacement admitted that he felt cheated, as "there was no prospect of action. There were only bars that charged exorbitant prices and coolies who looked to him like a definitely inferior people and girls who fawned and pouted and performed for cash."[19] Short-term sailors were notorious for leisure-seeking activities after extended periods at sea. In late 1945, the Seventh Fleet put ashore between three thousand and seven thousand sailors a night in Shanghai, who had been at sea for years without liberty. They "had pent-up desires to have a lot of fun" and had lots of back pay to afford whatever pleasures they wanted. "It was a hellacious experience."[20]

Shaped by their backgrounds, the experiences of US servicemen in China could also evolve over time. As the initial excitement waned and "their first hangovers have worn off," some were hit by homesickness and China's rampant inflation. The exchange rate plummeted from twenty-seven hundred Chinese yuan per one US dollar when the advance party arrived in Qingdao, to two thousand yuan as the main body of troops landed, and further dropped to twelve hundred yuan within a week.[21] The Oriental paradise of the servicemen's first impression "turned out to be just a glamorous gyp joint."[22] But a lot also depended on where they were stationed. Qingdao, located only two hundred miles south of Soviet-controlled Port Arthur, was the principal Japanese embarkation point and became a major fleet anchorage for the American military in the Far East. Since the end of the nineteenth century, it had been occupied by Germany, followed by Japan, and remained a modern port city known as the Riviera of the Far East. The ice-free port of Qinhuangdao to the north was close to the Manchurian border, where foreign deep draft ships once loaded coal from mines using modern piers built by Herbert Hoover in the early twentieth century. Tianjin, where the IIIAC headquarters were located, impressed most servicemen with mansions inside its former foreign concession, world-class entertainments, and an active social life involving a large European expat community. Beijing, known as China's historical capital, carried the special charms of the ancient culture, while Shanghai attracted a substantial number of troops from inside and outside China as a major liberty spot and a favorite destination for rest and recuperation (R&R) programs and family shopping. Despite the varied features of these cities, the real difference lay between cities and rural areas, where "life was rugged for the Marines on the trains and for the bridge detachments living in substandard housing and standing dangerous and isolated watches."[23] Often these detachments had a billet area consisting of a Chinese compound or a series of huts enclosed within a wire-and-bunker perimeter (see Figure 2.3). But these guards' positions were on rotation, and liberty time was generously granted. Almost all US soldiers maintained a privileged lifestyle while living in postwar China, or at least had a taste of it.

Figure 2.3 Marines posing for a photo while preparing a meal in North China. MCHD.

To maintain soldiers' physical health and morale, the US military had been shipping massive quantities of goods worldwide since Pearl Harbor, establishing a global network of supplies, entertainment, and services. After the war, the military in China moved quickly to establish a variety of recreational and sports facilities for liberty time and training purposes. XABU, the first radio station in China sponsored by the US Marine Corps, was completed on November 10, 1945, to mark the US Marine Corps' 170th birthday.[24] In October 1945, just days after the marines' arrival, two Red Cross clubs opened in Tianjin: the Concordia or the former German Club, located on Woodrow Wilson Road, and the former French Club on Rue de France. These clubs featured canteens staffed by civilian hostesses who arranged dances, snack luncheons, and a variety of entertainment, along with sports facilities such as bowling, billiards, and Ping-Pong.[25] In Qingdao, the Red Cross Club was launched on November 3, taking over the former Qingdao International Club, originally built in 1913 for German colonials. Staffed with American hostesses, the facility was formally dedicated by General Shepherd, in whose honor the building was renamed the Shepherd House. On Christmas Eve, the Enlisted Men's Club opened in the city, featuring "an unlimited supply of Stateside beer, and mural paintings reminiscent of the gayest night spots of the speakeasy era." Additionally, a wide range of sports fields and facilities was established. To bolster "troop morale in the overcrowded Far Eastern city," it was believed that "an active training program amplified by an equally intense athletic schedule" was essential. General Thomas added, "If you feed them and keep them busy, that keeps the trouble down."[26] Tianjin boasted twelve softball fields, five baseball diamonds, a nine-hole golf course, and a track by 1946.[27] In Qingdao, the military converted the Japanese baseball field to an American football field and organized parties at the stunning white sand beach resorts left by their German and Japanese predecessors. In Nanjing and Shanghai, enlisted men played ball games with Chinese amateur or college teams and attended regular dance parties and weekend social events organized by the military.[28] Although the primary goal was to keep the homesick soldiers occupied or away from more dangerous activities, these sports and social events were also used as a type of cultural and public diplomacy to cultivate alliance, showcase postwar peace and prosperity, and represent American democratic and egalitarian ideals. However, in the eyes of locals, American troops' occupation of or exclusive access to privileged residential and entertainment sites continued the colonial tradition of treaty ports, which had used sports to assert masculinity and racial superiority.[29]

American troops resided in designated modern hostels and hotels, former foreign concessions, university campuses, and guesthouses built for them, along with other premier sites equipped with modern facilities. This extensive use placed a strain on local resources. State Department officials reported that anti-American sentiment grew in Beijing and Tianjin as the Chinese were "called on to provide a lot of extra houses" for American military forces, a situation further exacerbated by the recent influx of dependents.[30] A particularly contentious issue involved the marines' acquisition and occupation of former Japanese properties. In heated lease-renewal negotiations over the use of part of the Shandong University campus as marine billets, the US Navy authorities defended the marines' continued occupation – despite sparking student protests – by claiming that "the very existence of the University is in considerable measure due to the presence of those Marines."[31] Similarly, in Tianjin, the marines refused the Chinese request to vacate a former Japanese staff residence that they were using as billets. Marine leadership defended their stance by citing the strategic importance of the location, the scarcity of alternative housing options, and a policy that "Marines pay no rent in conformity with policy of American movements in China relative to use of ex-enemy property." Frederick W. Hinke, the American consul in Tianjin, expressed a clear sense of entitlement in his letters to the embassy: "Cannot perceive how Chinese convenience can be permitted to take precedence over essential American military needs." He further emphasized, "I have yet to learn of any military organization which has ever considered it had to pay for enemy 'military property' requisitioned by it, even after a cessation of hostilities. ... The Chinese seem to regard the Marines as paying guests with emphasis on the 'pay.'" Hinke voiced his "annoyance" with the Chinese Ministry of Economic Affairs for taking the matter directly to the American Foreign Office and pointed fingers at the Nationalists: "Now that the Japanese supply is virtually exhausted, the vultures are looking for more carrion."[32]

In addition to occupying privileged housing, US troops expected and savored extra resources and special treatments. In Qingdao, US military authorities insisted they should not pay for the utilities provided for their servicemen and the harbor maintenance, as they were invited to stay in the city.[33] In Shanghai, where the municipal government imposed feast and hotel taxes at a 20 percent rate and an amusement tax at a 30 percent rate, many GIs refused to pay. In fact, it was not just individual soldiers who refused to pay these taxes, citing inflation and exploitation by local merchants, or due to their "ignorance of Chinese laws and regulations."[34] Authorities of the US Forces in China claimed that United States Army personnel were granted exemption from such levies by Chiang Kai-shek.

This exemption was also justified by the nature of the American military missions in China, whose sole purpose was said to be assisting the Chinese government at its request.[35] While claiming special status, US servicemen also sometimes insisted on "equal" treatment. For instance, when confronted with Shanghai's ballooning prices for food and entertainment, Navy Lieutenant Phil Bucklew, a senior shore patrol officer, took matters into his own hands. Accompanied by two GI investigators – a former Wisconsin football star and a national collegiate wrestling champion from Purdue – and with the support of the Military Police (MP), he declared the luxurious Park Hotel dining rooms "out of bounds" and "stuck to his guns" until the hotel management agreed to cut prices by 50 percent. General Wedemeyer also pledged to "smash this exploitation of Americans."[36] In general, American soldiers saw these demands as legitimate rights rather than special privileges. Like the extraterritorial legal protection and the jurisdiction to try war criminals, American requests for immunities and exemptions were based on the argument of reciprocity.[37]

It seemed a happy ending when *Stars and Stripes* publicly thanked the mayor of Shanghai in March 1946 for granting GIs an exemption from the feast and hotel taxes, with a "Thank You, Mayor" headline.[38] But the American sense of entitlement permeated official communications and affected individual GIs' expectations regarding seeing, smelling, tasting, hearing, and touching China.

In Search of Old China

At the first sight of Shanghai, Elmo R. Zumwalt Jr., then a navy lieutenant, observed: "The river banks were green and beautiful," and "China was one place which lived up to preconceived notions."[39] It was not uncommon to see Westerners project a preindustrial tranquility and a lifestyle free from technological dominance or Western influence onto war-torn China. Through a romanticizing lens, "China was a timeless land," "people were not rushing through life as victims of a timeframe set by machines," and, "on a whole, daily life moved unhurriedly along just as it had for centuries."[40] It was a picturesque land frozen in time, captured by foreign tourists' eyes, and resembling images from *National Geographic*, *Life*, Pearl S. Buck's novels, and wartime propaganda films: "various rice paddies going up the mountain, giant bamboo growing, fast-running mountain streams, little clusters of villages."[41]

Once they got settled into their new duties, GIs, who had ample liberty, went on sightseeing tours of the Forbidden City, the Temple of Heaven, and the Great Wall, among other ancient treasures. Two other sights that featured in GI accounts were rickshaw men and women with bound feet. "It was fascinating to watch the human show pass through and around the station," including "several elderly women hobbl[ing] past with the tottering stiff-kneed gait of those who had their feet bound since infancy."[42] The act of "watching" turned into a fad as GIs looked for these women everywhere and even requested locals' help in finding them. To the initial surprise and disappointment of some newcomers, Chinese streets were not filled with bound feet or pigtails, as portrayed in Hollywood movies. The chances of spotting such phenomena were rendered even slimmer after the Chinese government prohibited local interpreters from taking GIs on trips in search of such scenes in more rural areas, stating that these activities would damage the image of China and harm national dignity.[43] Yet these young men soon found something far more accessible to photograph: the rickshaw. Servicemen routinely took rides while on liberty and also enjoyed racing each other when pulling rickshaw men. The GIs' patronage reenergized the declining business of rickshaw pulling in Chinese cities, which had been threatened both by competing forms of transportation and by repeated government attempts to ban what many reformers saw as a backward social institution and national humiliation.

The exotic old China was not only observed and documented in letters and tales; it was also worn, embodied, and taken home via souvenirs. Sailors came ashore in Shanghai to get dragons sewn onto the cuffs of their blue jackets and underneath the flap.[44] Officers and soldiers alike went out antique hunting for silk, vases, carved wooden cases, embroidered shoes, copper Buddhas, and jade necklaces. The GIs wore old gowns featuring dragon embroidery from the Peking opera, donned traditional silk caps, and held Chinese pipes while sitting straight on tricycles or pulling rickshaws. Led by the so-called old China hands with a touch of "Chinowledge," their younger pals were said to have stormed the burial clothing stores and bought out the entire stock of ingot-shaped pillows for the dead and outdated hookahs, now priced ten times higher, in order to "show off the 'exotic world' to their loved ones back home" (see Figures 2.4 and 2.5).[45]

A popular destination for fine-quality souvenirs, China was also seen as a major hub for cheap and fake goods, with American soldiers learning that "the majority of the confidence rackets originated in China," from hand-carved "antique" wooden chests that split as soon as they were placed in a warm room, to liquor bottles refilled with local concoctions and given Johnnie Walker seals and empty beer cans transformed into beautifully made "sterling" filigree jewelry.[46] Despite the outdatedness of "Oriental products" that GIs demanded, many of which were no longer used in actual Chinese life, businesses happily recreated products and

Figure 2.4 A marine in a Chinese cap checks out goods from a street vendor. MCHD.

services that catered to American tastes. Store names changed to "Alaska, TIPTOP, PEiHAi, GISMO, America, and other sorts of weird names," and were decorated with new Orientalist aesthetics. Stepping into a Qingdao bar, for example, one immediately encountered new vermillion curtains with embroidered yellow flowers reaching the floor, dragons on two fake columns, and four or five palace lanterns in red gauze, all aimed at creating an ersatz "Oriental atmosphere."[47] While encountering the old China for the first time, marines also found themselves "back at the old stand," a place their predecessors had helped shape. At Hempel's – the legendary hangout of the old-time leathernecks of the legation guard, located across from the old polo grounds in Beijing – marines jived to tunes from an ancient jukebox, celebrated hitting the jackpot on slot machines, and enjoyed the merry gurgling of beer, all with "a touch of home."[48]

In their daily encounters, American servicemen's visual representations and imaginings were steeped in overt Orientalist symbolism. Despite their frequent visits to grand restaurants, dance halls, and shopping malls as

In Search of Old China 71

Figure 2.5 Local bumboats cluster around a Seventh Fleet cutter in Shanghai for business, September 1945. NARA.

magnificent as those in New York City, these soldiers made little reference to the modern sensations these sites evoked. Instead, it was the imagined ancient kingdom that showed up on the Chinese screen, which they were constantly and intensely looking at and looking for. Like white visitors touring America's Chinatowns with their fake opium dens and other staged "authentic" scenes, which gave them a feeling of superiority, a display of the old China helped confirm Americans' cultural and moral superiority and justify their postwar occupation.[49]

"Chinks' Stink"

While the peaceful and beautiful Orient was framed and wrapped, ready to be shipped home, China's everyday miasma was revealed to be unbearable and dangerous to both the nose and the mind. Stench, invading the senses with offensive odors, was the strongest sensory experience in GI accounts. City sewage was an utter disaster. No one taking a stroll in Shanghai could avoid the filthy, stinking Suzhou Creek surrounded by thousands of refugees living in little houseboats or junks and using the creek as a garbage dump, sewage disposal, and their sole source of water.[50] In the streets of Beijing, one easily ran into "honeydipper" carts that collected human excrement around the city, which was then sold to farmers as fertilizer. As one marine warned, "on a warm day it was prudent to detour past these carts to avoid the foul odor from the semiliquid contents."[51] The countryside turned out to be even worse. "Whether it was animal or human waste, rotting vegetation or cooking odors, it all seemed to have a certain rank solidity that one had to accept and learn to live with or be constantly on the verge of gagging."[52] Overall, the "whole country smelled."[53]

The GIs' aversion to rancid smells was a result of modern America's own changing notions of odor, disease, and cleanliness. Stench had been increasingly associated with disease, lack of sanitation, and poor public health since at least the nineteenth century as industrialization in the Western world changed the urban landscape.[54] Odors of excrement and decaying human and animal corpses, which had pervaded the public and private spaces of the poor, drew considerable attention from the elites and social reformers. The fear of and policies against odors reflected popular understandings of disease and disease transmission, especially germ theories, which revolutionized understanding of odors. Meanwhile, throughout twentieth-century America, "the drive to bathe, shower, and deodorize spread throughout society," and "soaps, deodorants, and other hygiene products were at the forefront of mass consumer culture," constructing the "sweatless, odorless, and successful middle class."[55]

Notably, American soldiers' portrayals focused not on the industrial stench, but rather on the atavistic filth of old China, particularly the pungent stench emanating from excrement. The sniffers' attention to sewage and filth reflected fears of an archaic population before and outside civilization, rather than the common fear of urban degeneration in the Western world. Smells are subjective, conditional, and markers of Otherness, and one's own smell is rarely regarded as stink.[56] Soldiers seemed to have forgotten that they themselves had recently "looked so filthy and bedraggled in the steaming heat on Peleliu's rugged ridges and in the corpse-reeking morass at Shuri, Okinawa."[57] Instead, they turned all the attention of their nostrils to Chinese odors.

In the accounts of American military men, China's stench and squalor were not only linked to the poor, as begging children, homeless refugees, and ragged urchins filled up modern cities and polluted creeks, but also often went hand in hand with Chinese culture. They were shocked to see "how cheaply human life is sometimes held," ranging from an "often brutal and callous approach to life in China" to "absolute disregard for life" even among friends and families. Horrifying stories included a farmer who, after his donkey cart toppled down an incline, rushed to check on his donkey first before turning to his family. Another account described a mother who tossed an infant under the wheels of a reversing US truck, seeking compensation, as "a girl baby was another mouth to feed." More understanding minds noted the impact of war and violence on Chinese society, such as economic devastation, dislocation, and human suffering, which were rarely experienced in American lives. As one explained, "Survival is said to be the primary driving force in every human life, a fact that is often almost forgotten in our middle class American existence," and "the sanitation a westerner was accustomed to simply didn't exist."[58] But most still linked the stench and suffering of the poor to inherent flaws and human cruelty within local society. In these representations, the Chinese stench became an indication of the country's backwardness, being unaffected by modernity, and was ultimately attributed to racial inferiority.

In fact, "filthy Chinese" had been a powerful narrative since the nineteenth century, as adopted by Western observers and even Chinese reformers.[59] Odors were used as the markings of peoples and civilization. In America, Chinatowns had long been associated with stench, providing further evidence of Chinese "purported racial inferiority" and "grounds for their exclusion."[60] Caucasian noses associated Chinese food with the strange odors of the East, including "squid, rats, and offal, all of which were regarded as embodying the strange and repulsive lifestyle and diet of the Chinese."[61] Befitting a colonial narrative, whiteness signified cleanliness, purity, and health, while Chineseness was marked as inherently repugnant. In postwar Japan, "disgust dominated the affective palette of occupation soldiers," contributing to ways in which boundaries between Americans and the occupied were redrawn in the chaotic aftermath of the war.[62] Despite China's allied status, GIs were also preconditioned to sniff the "Chinks' stink," and stench became a dominant mode through which they experienced the Chinese universe, enforcing preexisting notions of national and civilizational hierarchies. In a way, the Chinese stench continued to spread as a racialized smell in the postwar era.

As Susan L. Carruthers has aptly shown in her study of the American occupation of Japan, "latrines were indeed the measure of men – a yardstick by which civilizational standards could readily be appraised."[63] Discussions on human waste and the toilet were at the forefront of the China stench, including the official guide that cautioned soldiers that "throughout China toilet facilities are by our standards worse than primitive."[64] Indeed, one of the initial assaults GIs encountered in China turned out to be not from armed Japanese troops, but rather from squat toilets. One marine described the toilet on a train from Tanggu to Tianjin as "the subject of much discussion among the troops ... there was no seat, and the toilet bowl was recessed into the floor." But quickly the excitement over "a source of fascination" descended into disgust with the odor, due to "a lack of all types of maintenance" that "was typical of Chinese trains."[65] The exotic turned out to be not so benign, but a menacing cultural shock. While performing their initial task of transporting Nationalist soldiers, American servicemen further encountered the olfactory assault from the Chinese troops, who were described as "urinating on the deck, and even in the scuttlebutts; sitting on urinal troughs to bathe; dipping toothbrushes into water in the heads when cleaning their teeth; taking showers fully clothed; expectorating on decks and bulkheads all over the ship; throwing uneaten rice on the deck; standing instead of sitting on toilet seats, thus distributing fecal material over a wide area; and occasionally failing to use toilets at all."[66]

Americans took pride in their modern plumbing technology. Yet to make a flush toilet work, there were in fact many technological hurdles to cross: water pipes, pumps, screws, many little pieces that made up the miraculous invention. Flushing toilets were found in the modern city of Shanghai as early as the 1880s, but their usage remained limited in the country as a whole. Most of the interior lacked access to running water and the majority of the urban populations still used the traditional system of Chinese latrines, including various types of pit latrines, bucket toilets, and chamber pots. After the war, most people continued to use covered or open-air outhouses and public toilets, or simply resorted to open defecation. Manure collectors gathered feces from people's houses and public toilets and then sold them to farmers.

In urban centers, American officers and soldiers resided in designated places that had access to Western-style toilets linked to running water, indoor plumbing, and an underground sewage system. While they enjoyed modern conveniences and comfort, physically separated from the majority of the locals' living conditions, they remained wary of the potential dangers that the permeating Chinese stench posed to their health and safety. In response, they initiated cleaning campaigns to eradicate the threat and reform local bodies. For mosquito and insect control, the American military conducted aerial spraying in major cities, including Nanjing, Qingdao, Beijing, and Guangzhou, with the consent of Chinese authorities. However, they also initiated actions that were unsolicited and unwelcomed by the local population. In Nanjing, members of the Army Advisory Group requested the municipal government to spray all the farm fields and soil pits surrounding their residence with DDT, as well as remove the soil pits. Angry representatives from the local silkworm industry protested that such unrestricted DDT spraying would kill worms and put peasants' livelihoods in danger. Even the accommodating local officials, who had conducted several on-site investigations, felt that it was impossible to entirely eradicate the more than one hundred soil pits.[67] When GIs shared living space with the Chinese, direct action was often taken. While transporting Nationalist soldiers, US medical officers used DDT powder to delouse them before embarkation. At the same time, a lesson on using the bathroom was given. The war against the Japanese might be over, but another battle needed to be launched against the "Chinks' stench," as "indiscriminate vomiting from seasickness, coupled with the Chinese body odor and the uriniferous atmosphere made this desirable."[68] Though on a much smaller scale, these demands and actions presented a striking resemblance to the sanitizing projects to reform foreign bodies that the American military imposed, in the postwar period, on occupied enemy nations, who were "to experience defeat in the most humiliatingly intimate fashion."[69]

Smells are pedagogical as they demarcate self and other and help justify one's actions to reform others. The Americans were not the only ones who attempted sensory reforms on Chinese bodies. For example, the New Life Movement, officially launched by Chiang Kai-shek in 1934, also propagated rinsing and brushing teeth, cutting nails, and bathing regularly, and forbad spitting on the street or urinating in public as part of living a clean, sanitized, modern, and moral life.[70] However, the smellscapes of China in American servicemen's nostrils were considered uniformly foul and innately backward. Rather than for nation-building, smell was invoked to confirm racial and national hierarchies.

Food Hogs the Limelight

CHAMPAGNE BAR
BEST DRINKS, FRESH FOODS
WITH BEAUTIFUL WAITRESS
RESONABLE PRICE
15 RACE COURSE ROAD
TUNGLOU TIENTSIN
    – Norman G. Albert, *Yohouse from a Boot to a China Marine*, 2011[71]

It is only natural that people far away from home seek familiar cuisine to satisfy their palates, as taste is one of the most enduring sensations humans long for and remember. With the empire's industrial boom and global reach, the US military tried to recreate a healthy and familiar gastronomic world for its servicemen afar, including C and K ration packs of combat food and B rations for field kitchens. The GIs were "the best fed in the world during the Second World War," as "the standard ration provided on military bases contained a staggering 4,300 calories," and "men at the front were allocated 4,758 calories a day."[72]

Interestingly, eating was also one of the few areas of life where American soldiers were more willing to leave their comfort zones, out of necessity, curiosity, or a combination of both. If GIs disdained China's smells, most loved Chinese food, regardless of their rank or status. During the war, Chinese dinner was served once weekly in the US Army headquarters in Chongqing, showing "how popular Chinese food is with these Yanks."[73] After the war, for veterans from the Pacific, who had become fed up with the concentrated packages that left extremely unpalatable aftertastes, fresh food was their top priority upon reentering civilization.[74] American servicemen hired houseboys to cook and clean and ate in restaurants when they had liberty, or had a friend bring takeout while they were on duty. When it came to food and service, they were "living in the splendor."[75] Upon arrival in Shanghai on October 14, 1945, pilot Warren Jefferson Arnett was struck by "the pool of nationalities and types, with its French, Italian and Russian quarters ... at least one restaurant in each where you get the food typical of the country." He tried Viennese food and ate at a restaurant called the White House that was run by Jewish refugees from Germany.[76] Food provided a direct gateway into China and exposed GIs to a new culinary world beyond "the Anglo-Saxon model of meat and two vegetables" as served up in the homogenous American military canteen meals.[77]

There were plenty of banquets for all ranks. The Chinese government promoted cultural diplomacy to enhance Sino-US understanding, and feasting was always a priority (see Figure 2.6). Local elites were encouraged to open their homes to the Americans with the hope that "a taste of the Chinese home-cooked food" and "a glimpse of the Chinese home life" might help eliminate some of the "distorted ideas about Chinese life and views."[78] Chinese officials frequently invited American officers to banquets to show appreciation, and solders also attended various victory parties characterized by long feasts. In fact, both sides used food to create trust and rapport among allies and hostile groups. In the north of Qinhuangdao, a certain Captain Wu of the Nationalist army became an "instant devotee" of a chocolate powder drink a marine detachment

Food Hogs the Limelight 77

Figure 2.6 United States military leadership, including Admiral Charles M. Cooke Jr., accompanied by Chinese hosts, enjoying a Mongolian barbeque at the Summer Palace in Beijing, 1945. MCHD.

officer offered him, which kept the "mutual friendship strong" and "cooperation close," despite the fact that initially neither could understand a word of the other.[79] In a similar story, food provided a safe pathway for marines at risk. Thomas E. Williams, an officer based in Qingdao, attributed the success of his rescue mission of three captured

American aviators from the Communist territory to "the help of quite a lot of chefoo brandy," which had created "the friendliest Chinese communists everyone has ever seen."[80] This food diplomacy predated Richard Nixon's "chopsticks diplomacy" in his successful state banquet that resulted in the historic Sino-US détente.

The ubiquity and everydayness of eating makes it a significant site of sentient interaction, as food cultures are directly shaped by class, race, and nationality. As a powerful way to forge and highlight group identities, food was also used to create connections that blurred divisions. Chinese cuisine provided fresh alternatives to American industrial food as well as novel tastes, experiences, and identities. In 1940s America, Chinese food was still associated with the cheap and convenient, consumed by middle-class and less-privileged groups. As part of the lingering influence of racial prejudice, it had been denigrated by anti-Chinese forces in the nineteenth century and continued to be targeted by white health experts and officials.[81] Many GIs who came to China yearning for chop suey – a stereotypical dish created in America and adapted for American tastes – now realized that "we never had real Chinese food before, although all along we thought so."[82] Although some restaurants in China also sold chop suey during and after the war, the dish was advertised as an "authentic American" food instead.[83] Now among the most popular Chinese dishes were "sweet and sour pork or spare ribs cooked in any provincial style, roast duck Szechwan style, fried eel Shanghai style, and bamboo shoots."[84] Sometimes, the dishes not only went beyond white Americans' usual palate, but also against their knowledge of health and received medical advice. After an inspecting medical service officer objected to its black mold coverage, dry-cured ham from Yunnan was banned from dining tables. After strong protests, the famous Chinese ham triumphantly returned to the GI restaurant run by the Nationalist Government. Eventually, even the inspector was won over by its irresistible taste and took two of the black hams home.[85]

For many American soldiers in China, almost all white, eating fancy Chinese food was a physical and cultural experience of its own, rich in flavors and palate sensations. Together with more affluent Chinese families or at fine restaurants, they "ate, sometimes with hesitation, items strange to the American table but most excellent in flavor. Jellylike, dark green and black 'Hundred Year Old Eggs,' fish stew garnished with chrysanthemum petals, a rice pudding type dish containing nuts and lotus seeds along with other unidentified ingredients, and bird's nest soup rivaled one another for 'most exotic' title, made from the bird's spittle."[86] In contrast to Americans, who were not receptive to the idea of offal even during meat-rationed wartime, the Chinese ate ducks' feet and

Food Hogs the Limelight

Figure 2.7 Two American servicemen on liberty examining raw ducks for their Peking duck dish at a local restaurant. MCHD.

chickens' feet tied with lengths of intestine; pig ears; fish heads; congealed pig, chicken and duck blood; and sea slugs, all of which were considered delicacies (see Figure 2.7).[87] Additionally, their ways of cooking, serving, and eating were also a source of marvel. There was a mix of appreciation and discomfort toward local table manners. One officer described the Chinese art of eating: "Two beautiful pieces of ivory adroitly moved by five slender fingers is a poem in simple movement."[88] In contrast, an army verse vividly portrays the attitude to chopsticks of many an ordinary GI Joe: "Some use them like a pair of tweezers; Some use them like a shovel; But some, preferring tools to teasers, Get in the bowl and grovel."[89]

Although the Chinese were widely celebrated as "famous cooks," the danger associated with food in China could not be overstated. During the first few weeks of their landing, many GIs fell victim to intestinal bugs they dubbed "Genghis Khan's Revenge," reputed to be far worse than the "Montezuma's Revenge" encountered in Mexico.[90] Locals were believed to have developed "an immunity to many of the diseases that kill the white man so easily." Therefore soldiers were to "assume all food and all water is contaminated," as human manure was universally used in China for fertilizer. Counterfeit liquor proved another major threat, at times causing serious hazards.[91] The official marine guide warned: "Probably the liquor poured out in your presence from a bottle bearing a reputable brand name is some horrible mixture that will do more to you than you bargained for. The Oriental dispenser of fire water is a clever hombre, to whom the word conscience is a joke."[92] In response to these risks, inspection teams of officers and doctors evaluated local venues, including kitchens, for sanitary conditions and overall hygiene. Establishments deemed suitable or unsuitable for soldiers' liberty time were marked with "In-Bounds" or "Out-of-Bounds" signs at their entrances, with the system enforced by the shore patrol and MPs. Sometimes, checklists were provided to troops instead of placing signs, as the latter practice was criticized by local authorities for intruding on Chinese sovereignty.

Even so, Chinese liquor presented further hazards, as American servicemen often fell victim to unfamiliar drinks or drinking rituals. The army handbook cautioned the imprudent against engaging in drinking bouts with seemingly mild-mannered Chinese hosts, noting that various local liquors were much stronger than expected.[93] In one incident, a red-haired chief warrant officer, shortly after consuming a second glass of the grain distilled beverage "*bi-gan*," fell over and required ten stitches in the lower rear area.[94] The drinking ritual of "bottoms up," or "*gan bei*" (*gum-bay, kan-pei, gum pei*) also proved particularly risky. Some GIs saw "bottoms up" as a local tradition and an expression of hospitality where forcing liquor and food on reluctant guests was a sign of a successful party, an opportunity for winning friendships, or making business go more smoothly. But others found "this Chinese style of drinking" game difficult to win, especially when outnumbered and consuming local liquor, with some bitterly questioning whether it was a trick to intoxicate them and make them look foolish.[95] Overall, getting drunk in front of the Chinese was seen as a major source of embarrassment or even humiliation.

Food did not just feed people but could also feed mutual grievances. During the Cairo Conference, President Franklin D. Roosevelt met with Chinese official Huang Renlin (Huang Jen-lin), who was responsible for the billeting and subsistence of American soldiers. The president inquired about the troops' well-being, particularly whether they were indeed being fed buffalo meat: "Can you really eat buffalo meat? Isn't it too tough?" In response, Huang explained that beef was not a staple in China, and due to shortages, alternatives like water buffalo and even wild yak were provided. But he assured the president that with proper cooking and an excellent recipe, these alternatives could be quite tasty – so much so that "the boys have not noticed the difference."[96] This amusing personal and diplomatic exchange reflected the drastically different food cultures of beef in the two countries. In the United States, beef was highly valued as a prime source of energy and considered essential for a proper meal. In fact, beef accounted for 65 percent of the designated required meat intake for GIs in China, compared to 30 percent for pork and 5 percent for eggs.[97] In contrast, everyday beef consumption inside China remained uncommon in the 1940s, both for economic and for cultural reasons.[98] The more important unspoken political context, however, was the ongoing Sino-US dispute over American food consumption in China. Huang Renlin was the director of China's War Area Service Corps, which provided for a variety of American servicemen in a hostel network from 1941 to 1946. Based on agreements, China paid for food and lodging for GIs in China, as part of the reverse lend-lease and reciprocal benefit to the United States aid. However, the two sides continued to disagree on the proper outlay and the type of currency for payment. The American military often found Chinese service did not meet US standards and attributed such inadequacy or failure to Chinese graft and incompetency. In contrast, the Chinese side took their payment as a gesture of generosity and took pains to maintain GIs' lifestyles by straining finances and making sacrifices, such as exhausting local beef supplies. During his visit to America in June 1944, Minister of Finance Kung Hsiang-hsi, American educated and Chiang's brother-in-law, complained in a full-dress conference that one American soldier cost as much as five hundred Chinese soldiers, and "very soon there won't be any animals left to help the farmers farm their land."[99] This sentiment was shared by Chinese officials at all levels of government, who believed excessive American consumption and unfair demands were placing a huge financial burden on China and revealed at least partial disregard of Chinese livelihoods. While well-fed and well-dressed GIs had plenty of beef, eggs, milk, alcohol, cigarettes, and candies, Chinese soldiers ate rice, bamboo roots, and pickles and looked small, malnourished, and filthy.[100]

Such food disputes cast a shadow over Sino-US relations throughout the war and continued into the postwar era, when UNRRA clashed with the Chinese National Relief and Rehabilitation Administration over distribution of surplus war supplies and relief goods in China. Food politics extended far beyond the store, kitchen, and dining room, reaching the cattle farmland, the slaughterhouse, and presidential memos and national treaties. The amount of food consumed and what kind were markers of hierarchy. In postwar China, food served as an intimate contact zone where personal and national diplomacy unfolded. Sometimes, it was exchanged as gifts, gestures of friendship, or a gateway to rapport and life. Other times, food became a site of accommodation and tension where issues of taste, health, equality, and fairness were contested.

Despite the long-term American prejudice against Chinese food and military warnings against contamination, food choices that servicemen made revealed how preconceived racial and cultural boundaries were often transcended by actual interactions. As enlisted men tasted a greater variety of food in China, and much more routinely, they began to judge it from culinary rather than merely racial criteria. After the war, the return of US servicemen from China and other parts of Asia led to a boom in Chinese restaurant businesses and the popularity of Chinese food. Thanks to growing sales of frozen and processed products, the cuisine became a major national food in the United States by the 1950s.[101] In 1953, retired Army Brigadier General Frank Dorn, an old China hand who had served as aide to General Joseph W. Stilwell in the China-Burma-India (CBI) Theater, published a cookbook to show his love for food and marveled most of all about Chinese dishes.[102] Julia Child, the famed American chef and author in the postwar American culinary scene, said that she became interested in eating while serving in China, "where the food was so good."[103] She and her husband, Paul Child, had worked for the Office of Strategic Services (OSS) in China, where they enjoyed a variety of authentic Chinese dishes and both became enthusiastic about the cuisine. In addition to Chinese American pioneers, veterans from Asia might be a less visible but important contributor to the transformation of Chinese cuisine from an inferior ethnic food, which a middle-class white family felt culturally or socially embarrassed to embrace, to one associated with metropolitan tastes, global identity, and even fine dining.[104]

Soundscape

No Cuttee, No Savvy
Sign on a Tientsin barber shop:
"Marines heads cut off here.
Ladies heads cut fine."
– *The North China Marine*, November 10, 1945

On September 12, 1945, an American gunboat opened fire at two speeding Japanese PT boats close to the Huangpu shore, marking the navy's triumphal entry into Shanghai. After "our shots broke a tranquil silence," according to Lieutenant Zumwalt, "almost as though it had been prearranged, the Chinese multitudes sent up a cheer and shout of welcome that was a roar. Small steam launches sounded their sirens, their craft twisted and turned like happy animals showing their pleasure. Crowds waved and whistled."[105] The heroic sounds of liberation were full of excitement. Behaving "like a bunch of boys on a weekend outing," the newly arrived marines were "shouting greetings to the curious

Chinese" they saw in the train station. None spoke English, but they "kept smiling and saying 'Ding hao very good.'"[106] Crowds in Qingdao were "yelling and screaming, trying to touch us, and tossing things up to us as a goodwill gesture."[107] In Shanghai, "you walk down the street and people clap and ask for your autograph. Every American is a hero."[108] One old woman combined "the only three words of English she apparently knew into an inane and joyous litany, 'Hello – thank you.' Hello – thank you.' 'Hello – thank you.' It was almost as though this woman, in her withered crackle, was providing the symbolic lyrics for the stark melody of the multitude."[109]

Once US servicemen settled into their billets and camps in the city, they were immediately exposed to a cacophony of unregulated sound. Outside the gates was a blast of honking, grunting, ranting, moaning, prayers, and happy "jabbering and gibberish."[110] There was the "constant murmuring of countless conversations and the shouts of the camel drivers, peddlers and rickshaw coolies," who "all looked and sounded as though time had stood still" since the eighteenth or nineteenth century. Rickshaw pullers yelled at each other in competition over customers, or at passengers to negotiate a price. Vendors, flower girls, and beggars followed rich Americans, constantly shouting, "GI Joe." A Jewish stallholder yelled, "Hot dogs! Hot dogs!" and a suspicious White Russian spoke English "with an accent more Brooklynese than our buddies who were natives of Brooklyn."[111] Overall, Shanghai was home to tens of thousands of refugees after the Russian Revolution and Jews who escaped the Holocaust. These accounts of verbal and nonverbal sounds, familiar or unintelligible, a source of fascination and annoyance, formed the rich soundscape of postwar China, blending elements of premodern chaos with cosmopolitan diversity.

The most common and unique auditory experience for a GI was pidgin English, the lingua franca on the street. A simplified and limited contact language with reduced grammatical structure and vocabulary, pidgin English originally developed in China's southern coasts in the colonial trade era. Postwar cities offered ample opportunities for the patois. Businessmen in urban centers had been serving foreigners for decades, and American soldiers were greeted inside shops by enthusiastic salesmen using fluent yet pidgin expressions. English prep schools became a booming industry, and new pidgin English textbooks kept appearing. Most locals acquired the language in real-life settings, however. Houseboys and workers who had direct and frequent contact with GIs were among the first to learn. A marine's houseboy in Beijing who could not speak a single word of English quickly became "that Chink that speaks English with an Alabama accent," due to his friendship with a Southern soldier. Another houseboy in Qingdao innocently mimicked the marines' impatient calls of "let's go" by saying *lao si gou* (老死狗) in Chinese, which means "old dead dog."[112] Even beggars on the street "who trotted along begging plaintively for a hand out" all started calling "Cumshaw Joe, Cumshaw Joe."[113] A fast learner, one child thief in Tianjin who always waited outside a marine station for a chance could in three weeks curse "in recognizable English... 'Hey Joe. YOU BOO HOW YOU SON-A-DITCH [You no good you son of a bitch]!'"[114] As Chinese civilians utilized their pidgin English, Americans also picked up the lingo and even developed their own version of "pidgin Chinese." For example, instead of the Chinese standard greeting of "Have you eaten?" you would now "often hear these men in khaki say, '*hao pu hao?*' which literally means 'good, no good,' as their translation of the standard English greeting "How do you do?"[115] In a Chinese satire of "pidgin Chinese," a foreigner translated his Chinese friend's title "*dui zhang*" (Captain) as "*bing tou*" 兵頭, but mispronounced it as "*pin tou*" 姘頭, very close in sound, but meaning paramour instead.[116]

These ad hoc everyday communications involved multiple layers of interpretation and misinterpretation from both sides (see Figure 2.8).

Figure 2.8 Cartoon depicting a verbal exchange between a GI and a Chinese man. MCHD.

"*Ding hao*" remained the most frequently used Sino-American phrase, usually accompanied by a thumbs-up. To US soldiers, the Chinese were shouting "*ding hao*" to show their appreciation, and in return, they adopted the authentic Chinese term to show their own goodwill. The American military even recommended using it to build rapport. Yet most Chinese sources attribute the term's origin to wartime allies in the CBI Theater who started using the term, which was later adopted by Chinese civilians. Though *ding hao* appeared to be a Chinese term, it was neither a popular expression for "good," especially compared to alternatives like *hen hao* or *zui hao*, nor did it imply appreciation. Instead, it was a Sino-American co-creation, out of mutual misunderstanding, which became a catchphrase that kept evolving as Americans would modify the phase according to the degree of excitement into *ding hao*, *ding ding hao*, and *ding ding ding hao*, though *ding* already indicates the upmost.[117]

The history of "gung ho," meaning "enthusiastic and eager" in standard English today, further reveals the mixed nature of the Sino-American exchange. The term was introduced into American English in 1942 by Lieutenant Colonel Evans Fordyce Carlson when training a new marine battalion in guerrilla tactics inspired by Chinese Communist forces. Carlson had previously served as the first American military observer with the Chinese Communist army during 1937 and 1938. His remarkable exploits against the Japanese later became the subject of the Hollywood film *Gung Ho! The Story of Carlson's Makin Island Raiders*. However, in Chinese, "gung ho" is "neither a slogan nor a battle cry; it is only a name for an organization," a contraction of Chinese Industrial Cooperatives Movements (the acronym for Industrial Cooperation). In other words, it was mistakenly translated by Carlson, and then mistakenly used by American servicemen to greet the Chinese. This often led to Chinese politely shouting "gung ho" back without knowing exactly what it meant. At other times, the Chinese simply "grinned broadly and bowed," believing marines were saying "*Kung ho fa ts'ai*" instead, which means "Congratulations! May you gather wealth."[118] As one of the terms born during the war as marine slang, "gung ho" survived as an Americanism and kept evolving from "work together" to mean "eager beaver" and "rough indiscipline." But "its several accepted American meanings have no resemblance whatever to the recognized meaning in the original language."[119]

One can only speculate about what the Chinese crowds thought when hearing these "Chinese words." But in these situations, body language, gesture, and context mattered more than the words themselves. To every party, these phrases might all sound like gibberish, but both sides were convinced they were speaking the other's language to show appreciation and friendship. The vocal communication showed a type of entangled relations in which both parties adopted pidgin and introduced new vocabularies into their own. As the two sides pronounced "the same" sounds back and forth, the origins and implications of these phrases remained ambiguous and unsettled. This process differed from a colonial encounter where sound was used to distance the colonizer and the colonized, as in the case of "Cooee," which was adopted and appropriated by Europeans from aboriginal Australian words in the late 1800s to bind the colonialists together.[120] Instead, these pidgin Chinese/English words traveled on a Mobius strip–like path on which it was impossible to locate the beginning or end, and their sounds and meanings continue to evolve in different local contexts.

Beyond the initial greetings of "*ding hao*" and "gung ho," American soldiers engaged in a more complex level of vocal and cultural exchanges using their limited pidgin to shop and live in China. The Chinese market, which often lacked a clearly marked price, was filled with constant bargaining. For instance, on an uneventful day in 1946, Second Lieutenant Simms, then serving in Headquarters Battalion, 1st Marine Division in Tianjin, walked down the street and wanted to buy a water glass in a local stall. His memoir recounts the exchange that ensued:

> "Hey Joe, hen how Joe!"
> "Boo yow." (I shake my head negatively.)
> "Hey Joe, you say how much Joe." (Vendor holds out a glass for inspection.)
> "Boo how, hen boo how!" (I point to an imperfection in the glass.)
> "Hey Joe, hen how! One dollow." (Vendor looks insulted and in a loud voice insists on the quality of his product.)
> "One dollar ... ti quey!" (I look astonished then glare disparagingly at his wares.)
> "O.K. Joe, you say how much Joe." (Vendor starts the pricing.)
> (I hold up three fingers.) "Yuan" (Vendor snorts in disgust and mutters.) "One dollow Joe, hen how!" (Vendor puts glass down as if it is all over.)
> (I pause at the next stall looking at the items displayed there. The second vendor attempts to gain my interest. The first vendor, seeing I'm still in the area, continues rearranging his goods but finally tries again.)
> "Hey Joe, you say how much." (I shrug as if disinterested, then hold up four fingers.) "Yuan" (Vendor mutters some more and I can pick out "boo how" which is evidently his description of all Americans. I start to walk off slowly but repeat the offer once more. Vendor, seeing me move further away makes a counter offer.)
> "Hey Joe." (Vendor holds up five fingers.) "O.K. yuan."
> I walk back counting out the five yuan. He keeps muttering and is likely telling all in listening range that my family is a bunch of tightwads. He hands me the glass with many headshakes to show his unhappiness. I give him the money and receive the glass, then depart.

With a few pidgin words and lots of body language, the sale seemed to have been successfully completed. We do not know how the Chinese vendor felt, but Simms contemplated whether it was worth going to "a lot of trouble" over a ten-cent glass and finally concluded, "But what the heck, I had bargained and my self-esteem had been increased by my brilliant dickering."[121]

In the mundane practice of bargaining, everyday actors like a GI and a Chinese street hawker engaged in creative and loaded negotiations. These routine interactions over "fair trade" did not simply follow the logic of economics or even of the market. Instead, the contested values of these objects and experiences lay in both the material and the symbolic worlds, within which personal, national, and racial dignities were crucial measurements.[122] The "simple" but coded transaction was deeply shaped by different social, cultural, political, and moral systems. There were conflicting scripts to choose from: for example, a mutually beneficial sale among equal allies, an unfair trade between cunning Orientals and innocent Americans, and an imperialist act inflicted upon Chinese victims in a system of unequal treaties. This contingent moment could lead to a small profit, a memorable photo, and a funny story to tell, or to a quarrel, a punitive action, and a nationwide protest. It was precisely in this moment when a local merchant encountered a GI on the street that preexisting scripts were appropriated and turned into deeds, which shaped narratives, memories, and history.

To more sympathetic American participants, both sides walked away satisfied after long and exhausting negotiations, usually over a trivial object, and it was a comical story to share that ended with mutual satisfaction. This tale of success was consistent with the new American middlebrow intellectual representations of the era, highlighting mutually beneficial exchanges between Americans and Asians "within a system of reciprocity."[123] However, the implicit question of "fair trade" never ceased to haunt American narratives of the China trade. Even the marines' official guide included a specific instruction on shopping in China: "We Americans, almost alone among the great peoples of this world, feel a little ashamed about bargaining for things we buy," but we need to "get over that feeling in the Orient," "unless you enjoy being stung every time."[124] The suggestion seemed useful for reducing the losses of innocent servicemen abroad. However, there was only a thin line between a cunning merchant who "scrapes and bows, and bows and scrapes – Then throws the hooks into you" and an evil "Chinese con man" who always cheats.[125]

The era of WWII saw another rise in English idioms associated with China despite having vague or no actual Chinese connections. Terms like

"Chinese whispers," "Chinese fire drill," and "Chinese home runs" emerged to describe situations that were confusing, incomprehensible, messy, or inferior. These phrases were rooted in racism dating back to the nineteenth century, when essentialized portraits of the Chinese characteristics became popularized through the works of missionary-sinologists like Arthur H. Smith and continued to be reproduced in American culture, including marine boot camps.[126] This same racial prejudice also gave rise to the stereotype of the "Chinese con man," a discourse perpetuated by American traders who characterized Chinese as "sly, untrustworthy, cowardly, dirty" and insisted they "must be treated as an inferior race, cowed by gunboats and arms." Theodore H. White, an influential journalist and former student of John King Fairbank at Harvard University, called this, the first of the three most powerful American myths about China, "the Treaty Port legend."[127] Trading is a prominent event in colonial narratives where the natives are either characterized as cheaters or as naive and dumb, ignorant of the real value of things, in both cases separating them from the fair trade model of white civilization.[128] In the larger context of unequal national and racial relations, being taken advantage of by the Chinamen stopped being harmless fun, a comical story to share, or a trivial matter of inconvenience. Instead, it became a personal and national humiliation that required pedagogical and punitive actions, providing justifications for political domination or even military actions. The Opium War, for example, began as a trade dispute and ended with the first of many unequal treaties that brought China into the world of Western imperialist domination. As such, American servicemen also learned that using threats, verbal and physical, seemed the right or only effective way to prevent deceit in business transactions. As one story goes, in a coal sale incident where a Chinese merchant repeatedly tried to cheat on weight, a sergeant finally loaded a "submachine gun with a loud click" and "pointed the muzzle at the manager's face." Afterward, "the manager was shaking with fear, but we had no more cheating."[129] A lesson must be taught.

As a result of such ingrained beliefs about their unreliability and deception, Chinese immigrants rarely achieved justice in the late nineteenth-century American legal system, especially when facing a white opponent, leaving immigrants with a "Chinaman's chance."[130] Half a century later, in the American trials that took place in China, Chinese witnesses still often went unheard or misheard. In the case of Shen Chong, who was raped by an intoxicated marine, a critical misuse of terminology occurred when the MP on duty that night testified that he did not receive any report of a rape accusation. During the trial, it was discovered that the American lieutenant might have misheard and misinterpreted the Chinese police saying "rape" (*qiang jian*) as "intercourse" (*he jian*), two drastically different descriptions set apart by one modifier.[131] After hearing the defendant's claim that the woman was thought to be a street prostitute, many China marines felt the whole thing was just the result of "a language mixup and too much liquor."[132] These hearing patterns show not only the American military's loose discipline and tolerance of sexual misbehavior, but also deep-rooted sociocultural biases and systemic discrimination that directly affected how American soldiers were hearing Chinese speech or talking to Chinese people. What was deemed noise and what was deemed credible information was subject to historical and often biased ears.

Intimate Touches and Violent Contacts

The majority of GIs engaged in extensive material and bodily interactions with the Chinese populace. Officers and soldiers frequently intermingled with locals in ball games, dance parties, banquets, and victory parties organized by both sides, and in everyday settings such as bathhouses, barbershops, restaurants, hotels, entertainment sites, and the streets.[133] Despite prevailing fears over Chinese foulness and diseases, physical contact between American servicemen and Chinese civilians remained common. For just twenty-five American cents, a soldier could indulge in a hot bath, "with the bathing chores performed by an attendant, followed by a manicure and pedicure and a brisk massage," as he lay on a cot in a Turkish bathrobe. The lavish grooming ritual concluded with "a shampoo, haircut and shave."[134] For another twenty-five cents, he could get a shoeshine outside the YMCA or the MP station, or inside bars and restaurants. Occasionally, these interactions led to close relationships. For instance, after saving two drunk marines from missing their curfew one day, a street boy named Liu Chan Deh – who had been shining shoes for his familiar customers in a Russian bar – was adopted as a marine mascot. The nine-year-old orphan then found a new home at the Qingdao air base, living alongside the marines. Over time, the bond grew stronger, and Liu was eventually legally adopted by Sergeant Arthur Jack McCartney in order to bring him to the United States. On February 14, 1949, Liu left China with his new "father" and became Arthur Liu McCartney.[135]

While some of these interactions culminated in happy endings, others proved to be more complex and fraught with tension. Haptic encounters emerged as the most precarious form of everyday interaction and caused significant trouble for Sino-US relations. Sexual relations quickly developed into the most sensitive issue as members of all ranks engaged in intimate involvement with local women. In a country ravaged by war and filled with refugees and prostitutes, brothels quickly became a popular destination for soldiers who enjoyed ample liberty and attractive pay. As in occupied Japan and Korea, American soldiers in China took prostitution for granted and made only halfhearted efforts to contain venereal disease; regulations concerning prostitutes were rarely enforced. The huge discrepancy between the official policy and actual practice revealed the fragile and hypocritical lines that the US military pretended to draw. The proclaimed rigid racial, class, and physical boundaries were easily broken by the gentle and illicit touches. When it came to haptic protocols concerning Chinese women, the military issued conflicting guidelines: They were memorable dolls, on the one hand, and dangerous carriers of disease with hidden agendas, on the other. These ambiguous portraits also applied to the Chinese people in general: They were both allies in arms who shared many traits, and others who had very different bodies, diseases, and physical expressions. For example, "They do not like to be touched. They don't like to be slapped on the back, or even to shake hands," except for some of the "modern ones."[136] In reality, the purported respect for Chinese women and for allied relations often fell flat due to excessive alcohol use, cultural arrogance, racial discrimination, and, ultimately, a hypermasculine military culture that enabled systemic tolerance of sexual misbehavior.

Another major form of violent contact involved physical abuse. Incidents of American soldiers beating, stabbing, and firing at Chinese coolies and civilians were by no means rare. When surrounded by local crowds, unarmed GIs on liberty often felt unsafe, alarmed, and even threatened. This was not only because of the diseases the Chinese were supposed to carry, but also due to the belief that the Chinese formed dangerous mobs that tried to fool people with dishonest business practices, took advantage of foreigners' lack of local knowledge, and intimidated them into submission. Rickshaw pullers, who frequently dealt with American soldiers on liberty, especially drunken ones, became victims of some of the deadliest crimes. As an extension of the physical violence toward Chinese bodies, and often, in avoidance of direct engagements with them, GIs fired at locals who were suspected of theft and black-market dealing of American military goods.

In general, the US military prescribed and policed strict boundaries to safeguard the "American body," drawing sharp distinctions between "China stench" and "Oriental diseases," on the one hand, and American civilization, on the other. These limits were enforced through rigorous sanitation measures and disinfectant sprayed on Chinese locales and individuals, in-bounds and out-of-bounds markers for local sites, and the barbed wire–topped walls of military compounds that were patrolled by armed sentries who could fire at suspected trespassers. Touch, whether sensual or violent, represented the most perilous sensory experience. Serious incidents sparked strong anti-American sentiment and even nationwide protests. Given their significance, these intimate touches and deadly contacts will be discussed in greater detail in the following chapters.

Making Sense of the Senses

In 1947, veteran journalist Harold R. Isaacs, reflecting on his recent experiences with American soldiers in China, painted a grim picture of the tensions that had emerged: "The whole was a snarl of friction, prejudice, and hatred, and it has deepened since the end of the war." He also issued a prescient warning: "The results of it will be felt for a long time to come."[137] That same year, William W. Lockwood, future president of the Association for Asian Studies in the United States, who had served for eighteen months as an army officer in China, wrote that the "first venture in large scale American tourism in China" caused "many sour, even hostile, reactions to the Chinese." He asked: Did millions of returned young GIs "gain a sympathetic and tolerant understanding of that world? Or were their home town prejudices simply confirmed?"[138] These poignant reflections remind us of the lasting impacts of US military operations overseas, both on and through the soldiers who acted as their agents.[139]

In postwar China, US servicemen served both as armed forces performing military duties abroad and as tourists, consumers, cultural messengers, and ambassadors on the ground, there to represent US interests and values. They were also seen as both a military and a diplomatic force representing America by members of the Chinese population, who had rarely encountered Americans in their lives. Similar to their colonial predecessors, GIs largely maintained a privileged lifestyle separate from Chinese society. Orientalist views preconditioned their sensory experiences, shaping how they saw, smelled, tasted, listened to, and touched China; binary framings dominated their sensory narratives. As in other postwar occupied nations, the senses confirmed and reinforced existing sociocultural prejudices and helped maintain inherent inequalities based on race, nation, and civilization. The GIs' mental and sensory worlds were embedded with systemic biases toward the Chinese, sometimes perpetuated by the military itself. But they also "went native," and many embraced local food, touch, language, and culture. The purported physical, racial, and cultural boundaries became blurred through interactions with servants who washed clothes, cooked, and served, as well as elite and professional women who fraternized with foreign troops.

In their daily lives, American servicemen engaged in deeply historical and ideological acts, as when a GI Joe wore a queue on his head or donned "traditional" costumes that no Chinese would want; when a marine pulled a rickshaw with the rickshaw boy riding in it, shouting *"ding hao"* with a thumbs-up to Chinese passersby; and when an officer spent considerable time and energy negotiating with a street vendor over a cheap water glass. It was to experience China in a microcosm through sensory embodiment. They were mimicking "Chineseness," enacting scenes that were embedded in racial imagination, cultural fantasy, and geopolitical hierarchy. This complex exchange of languages, goods, values, and systems in the micro-contact zone of a street embodies the very entangled relations at the core of this study. These transactions did not simply conform to the logic of economics or the dictates of realpolitik. Rather, the contested values of these objects and experiences lay in both the material and the symbolic worlds, within which personal and national dignities were crucial measurements. If these exchanges foreshadowed the coming era of US expansion and global integration, their ultimate aim was to incorporate China into a hierarchical world order full of inequalities.

In China, the tale of postwar Sino-US reciprocity continued to be questioned in the micro-environment of the everyday, as Chinese civilians negotiated prices and payments with GIs, took advantage of the complex economic and cultural exchanges, challenged American pedagogy regarding sensory experiences, and undermined the US version of fairness and justice. In a relation of uneven reciprocity, Chinese soldiers and officers sometimes "listened to" an American officer, "but didn't always do what [he] suggested or asked or recommended that they do."[140] Lip service using pidgin language was paid at almost every level of communication. When the Chinese were shouting the same slogans as the Americans with big smiles, they seemed to be speaking the same language; however, they could also have been pretending – an act that often led to an American interpretation of "mutual satisfaction."[141] In more defiant instances, Chinese boys and girls who begged for cumshaw without success resorted to the "vilest cussing and evil" with their hand and eye movements.[142] A Chinese man gave the marine guards the finger, unzipped his pants, and peed on the compound's electric fence.[143] Perhaps the "real" Chinese were somewhere in between the two prevalent GI narratives: the deceitful business con men sporting disingenuous curiosities and grins, nodding and performing *"gan bei"* tricks; and the naive, comic, and incompetent firemen, who, after their chaotic failed attempts to put out the fire, were finally saved by the Americans with far superior skills and kept cheering, dancing around, and shouting, "*ding hao!*"[144] This, in fact, was the diverse array of ordinary Chinese people that American soldiers encountered – pedestrians, rickshaw pullers, prostitutes, dance girls, black-market customers and dealers, and thieves.

3 Embodied Vehicles
Jeep and GIs

In late August 1945, as marines were beginning their occupation mission, American ambassador Patrick J. Hurley and Nationalist representative Zhang Zhizhong traveled to Yan'an to escort Mao Zedong to the Chongqing Negotiations. All rode together in a Jeep adorned with a large American flag, an iconic moment captured in a widely circulated profile picture (see Figure 3.1). Mao arrived in Chongqing on August 28 aboard a US military C-47 transport aircraft. The arduous negotiations, lasting forty-three days, culminated in the signing of the Double Tenth Agreement, which outlined the common goal of eventually establishing a political democracy in China and plans for a coalition government. However, armed struggles persisted throughout the peace talks, and the military situation in North China rapidly deteriorated. After signing the agreement, Mao immediately returned to Yan'an and delivered a report to the cadres, declaring that the CCP was ready to strike tit for tat.

The determination to counteract any aggression was soon extended to what Mao called the US imperialists who supported the reactionary government of Chiang Kai-shek. Perhaps invoking the principle of "reciprocity," the victorious Communist Party staged its first major military parade at Xiyuan Airport in Beijing on March 25, 1949. The event celebrated the liberation of the historic capital and foreshadowed the imminent liberation of the entire country. In a symbolic gesture – and perhaps a nod to his earlier ride with the Americans – Mao declined an invitation to ride in a more comfortable passenger car, opting instead for a Jeep. With a knowing smile, he remarked, "Isn't it more meaningful to parade in our captured American Jeeps?"[1] This remark, laden with satire, underscored his unmistakable pride and confidence in defeating the mighty Americans. This moment also revealed the uncanny power of the Jeep as both a potent military vehicle and a powerful cultural symbol.

There is perhaps no better visual symbol of the American military presence in postwar China than the iconic Jeep.[2] Communist propaganda targeted the vehicle as the ultimate emblem of US imperialism: Driven recklessly by drunk soldiers, the speeding Jeep ran amok on the streets,

3 Embodied Vehicles: Jeep and GIs   95

Figure 3.1 Mao Zedong getting into a Jeep with Patrick Hurley, Zhang Zhizhong, and David Dean Barrett, en route to the Chongqing Negotiations, Yan'an, August 1945. Photograph by US Army Signal Corps. Image courtesy of Special Collections, University of Bristol Library.

killing innocent civilians while the driver escaped justice. In reality, traffic accidents caused by American military vehicles, which led to frequent injuries and deaths of locals, were indeed the most common trigger of grassroots tensions. Disputes with rickshaw pullers sometimes escalated into physical confrontations, and even manslaughter, sparking massive protests. While existing studies have demonstrated the impacts of these incidents on Chinese anti-American sentiments, the complex social, cultural, and technological dimensions of the Chinese encounter with the Jeep remain little explored. Foregrounding the Jeep's rich materiality and symbolism, this chapter shows that the Chinese experience of the vehicle as a source of modern thrill and as a foreign military object blended early desires for a spectacle and a commodity with increasing nationalist sentiments against the American global empire and all its techno-industrial power, political hegemony, and military prowess.

When the Jeep arrived on postwar Chinese streets, it was an object of enchantment, first as a symbol of Allied victory and prestige, then as a cultural spectacle and popular commodity. However, following frequent incidents caused by drunk driving, speeding, and negligence, the Jeep/GI criminal duo became an instrument of intimidation and destruction, undermining China's existing order. The relationships between GIs and rickshaw men, which mingled fantasy, patronage, rivalry, and conflict, eventually descended into violence and brutality. As disputes over speed limits, economic compensation, moral responsibilities, and legal justice intensified, the American military vehicle embroiled in local street politics became the ultimate symbol of prolonged American occupation trampling Chinese sovereignty.

The Lure of Speed

"A modern knight is a driver behind the wheels. This contemporary cavalier on the road is a young man named 'Jeep Car (*jipu ka*) 吉普卡,'" a transliteration of the newly introduced American military vehicle, the Jeep.[3] As elsewhere in the postwar world, the Jeep featured prominently in Chinese civilians' initial experiences of American soldiers. In the autumn of 1945, residents of areas formerly occupied by the Japanese had their first encounter with the vehicle, as the liberating forces marched through city centers in open trucks and Jeeps. Chinese children's first experiences of the Jeep echoed those of their counterparts in Japan, Korea, Germany, or France, who also chased after the vehicles hoping for goodies. Whether from Allied, defeated, or formerly colonized nations, these children were all war-worn and hungry.

During WWII, the Jeep became one of the most prominent symbols of the American military, what Army Chief of Staff George C. Marshall called "America's greatest contribution to modern warfare."[4] Showcasing the country's superior technological and industrial power, with its world-class quality, design, and production, the Jeep was featured on magazine covers and postcards and in commercials and movie scenes.[5] The iconic vehicle testified to America's global military prowess and appeared in major victories, marches, and advances, together with commanders, soldiers, dignitaries, and stars worldwide: from General Dwight Eisenhower in the iconic Normandy landing and President Roosevelt during the groundbreaking Casablanca Conference to General George S. Patton's legendary marches in North Africa. Chinese leaders also marched in Jeeps, headed by Generalissimo Chiang Kai-shek, as tens of thousands of soldiers shouted slogans of loyalty and devotion in military parades, further enhancing the vehicle's prestige and elite status in China.[6]

On the India–Burma Road, Jeeps and Dodge trucks moved essential supplies to China through rugged mountains and dense jungles that had been cut off by the Japanese encirclement and created a lifeline for the continuing war effort. In 1943, with the help of the Jeep, Joseph Stilwell, the US commander in the CBI Theater, successfully relocated several divisions of the Chinese Expeditionary Force and war refugees through the difficult terrain of the rainforest from Myanmar to India. The ambulance aircraft, nicknamed "Flying Jeep," was known for saving seriously injured soldiers due to its ability to take off from roads and fly at low altitude and speeds.[7] Since the war, the American military had gifted and sold tens of thousands of Jeeps to China. At its peak, the Nationalist army owned more than thirty thousand military vehicles from American surplus supplies. In August 1946, China's Transportation Department approved the use of the Jeep for commercial and private settings, albeit with some restrictions, including the need to show proof of legitimate purchase and the requirement to paint the surface black.[8] From 1947 to 1948, the number of registered Jeeps in Shanghai ranged between 1,000 and 1,460, more than 5 percent of all motor vehicles.[9]

Automobiles remained a novelty to most of the Chinese population, even the intellectual elites. As Jeeps poured into postwar cities, local media introduced the shining invention to its many enthusiastic spectators and consumers. Some reports focused on the technological power of the vehicle, highlighting its origin, design, mechanics, features, and uses.[10] Unlike a regular car, the Jeep did not have fancy equipment or decorations, but was rather depicted as "an unbreakable, unspoilable tough guy."[11] Other advertisements, including those from the United States Information Service, boasted its versatility, calling it the "Omnipotent Jeep" that could be used everywhere, in agricultural tasks like plowing, threshing, and fertilizing, as well as in snow removal, power generation, herding cows, and fire extinction.[12] As readers gazed in awe at the small but formidable vehicle featured in popular periodicals, the Jeep indeed appeared not only undefeatable, but also all-powerful. These descriptions of the Jeep's qualities mirrored those found in American commercials. In postwar America, the Willys-Overland Corporation launched a glamourizing advertisement campaign to pave the way for the Jeep's transition to civilian life. In shiny magazine spaces, Jeeps posed together with long-limbed American beauties drinking Coca-Cola or waving in their bathing costumes to their male friends. The Universal Jeep with narrow and uncomfortable seating, designed for rough driving on bumpy roads, was now celebrated for its versatile performance, economic operation, functional smartness, and ultimately "a brand new thrill in driving."[13]

Associated with the latest technologies, the Jeep became a prestigious commodity on the Chinese market. A comical piece in a Shanghai newspaper supplementary recorded a late-night conversation in a parking lot between "Jeep Big Brother, Ford Tycoon, and Dodge Coolie." Ford, the American passenger vehicle, complains about being fed with charcoal due to shortages of gasoline, as well as the instability of changing bosses frequently – each losing power one after another. The youngest and now most popular Jeep mocks the worn-out coolie truck, which had been working in the city the longest: "You do not look like an American at all!"[14] Chinese perceptions of the vehicle were influenced by racial underpinnings: It was not only linked to an American identity, but also to a white American experience. This mirrors the racial stereotypes prevalent in the portrayal of black truck drivers in the CBI Theater, where such biases were evident. Black drivers were seen as naturally suited for hard labor, capable of enduring extreme heat and harsh environments, and possessing happy-go-lucky personalities who sang, drove, and drank. All of these traits made them excellent truck drivers in the Theater, but not operators of the mighty Jeep.[15]

If the original Jeep embodied American democracy, as commanders and soldiers rode in the front seat in the open air, with minimum comfort but uncontained freedom and limitless possibilities to explore and expand, in its afterlife of civilian use in China, the Jeep was often converted into a fancier passenger vehicle with padded seats and luxurious accessories, in addition to a hired driver. As Marshall McLuhan has shown, in Americans' love affair with automobiles, the car was both technology and media, affecting how people perceived and understood the surrounding world: It charted territory, shaped physical and social landscapes, and "refashioned all of the spaces that unite and separate men."[16] The postwar Jeep, with its redesigned driver-passenger setting and associated hierarchy, not only catered to new owners and usages but also established visible boundaries between owner-passengers, drivers, and those who could not afford such a vehicle (see Figure 3.2). For being not only expensive, but also difficult to acquire, it was an elite vehicle in China that displayed wealth and power.

As technological elements enhanced the Jeep's prestige and allure, its arrival became a cultural event in Chinese society. More than just a military vehicle, the Jeep was a spectacle to behold. In the wake of liberation in August 1945, thousands gathered outside the Park Hotel in Shanghai to catch a glimpse of the first Jeep brought into the city by the United States Military Advisory Group. Newspapers recorded the "crazy scene" where "all day long the rubberneckers milled around and crowded the site," and some even climbed onto the vehicle. Despite not speaking each other's

Figure 3.2 "The Jeep becomes a general-purpose vehicle," 1946. *Min jian.*

language, according to one report, the onlookers and GI drivers smiled at each other and shook hands.[17] Apparently, even residents of the most cosmopolitan city in China could not resist the charm of the Jeep and looked like country bumpkins in front of this newfangled product. Dance stars and movie celebrities posed with Jeeps in photos, and their joyrides in public were reported by local tabloids. Children were also invited to experience this new vehicle. One local publication enthusiastically announced: "Kids! Now you also have an opportunity to ride in a Jeep."[18] Another article taught them how to craft a paper Jeep toy, complete with detailed instructions for cutting and coloring.[19] A twelve-year-old boy's paper Jeep was featured in a magazine alongside a horseracing scene, Christmas tree, wooden rabbit, and goldfish – a mixture of global novelties and Chinese tradition – all to "inspire the minds and intelligence" of children.[20]

Even the Communists, outspoken critics of US military assistance to the Nationalists, were captivated by the Jeep. In the summer of 1944, the United States Army Observation Group, commonly known as the Dixie Mission, arrived in Yan'an to establish the first official relations with the

CCP. Operating from July 1944 to March 1947, the Group made a memorable entrance by plane, bringing several Jeeps loaded with American goods as a replacement for local animal-drawn carts. Having a ride on a Jeep was a novel experience for most Chinese at the time, even more so for the few who could drive one. Decades later, a Communist Party member involved in hosting the mission described his first experience of learning to drive the American vehicle: "The Jeep car was like a frightened savage horse, running wild in a flying speed. I could only hear the sound of wind passing through my ears."[21] During his historic visit to Yan'an in March 1946, General Marshall, standing at the front of a Jeep with Mao at the rear, greeted the crowds at the airport, who cheered and displayed welcoming signs celebrating Sino-American friendship and collaboration. After the Group's departure in 1947, the Americans left these Jeeps to the Communists – together with portable radios, electricity generators, and telegram equipment – and they were immediately put to good use in the civil war.[22]

At the center of the Jeep's enchantment was speed. On the paved roads of modern cities, the motor vehicle's engine provided passengers with fast transportation over long distances. Like the aforementioned Communist driver, when describing Jeeps, Chinese observers almost always used expressions such as "wind-like speed" and "wild run." Speed was the pleasure invented by modernity: The experience of speed became the quintessential way for a person to experience modernity in an age of mass production, a type of "adrenaline aesthetics." Speed also changed concepts of space, distance, chance, and violence.[23] By the 1940s, America, as the industrial powerhouse of the world, had already become a creature of four wheels. Associated with speed, the car symbolized and materialized new freedom, individuality, and agency. In Republican China, city residents had also been trained to see, hear, sense, and admire speed through cinema, advertisements, and fiction. Speed, in the words of New Sensation School writers, was a novel experience that was dangerously exuberating and had permeated the modern Chinese sensorium.[24] If the Chinese awe and fear of the train were more closely linked to the nation-building and colonial expansion of the late nineteenth and early twentieth centuries, focusing on the locomotive's massive power and spheres of influence, the Jeep automobile provided a more independent, flexible, and individualist experience at a fast and controllable speed for travel and transgression, a different type of modern thrill.[25] The Jeep could turn, reverse, and stop whenever and wherever it wanted, projecting an imagined individual self with free will.

The charm of a speedy Jeep also involved intimacy and romance. One college student's "deep friendship" with an American officer

The Lure of Speed

Figure 3.3 "Jeep rhapsody," October 1945. *Zonghe zhoukan*.

began with a Jeep ride. A married, middle-class woman danced happily with her GI boyfriend late into the night, while a Jeep stood by, ready to whisk her home quickly and safely.[26] Visual depictions often highlighted the flying hair or attire of "Jeep girls," who received the title from riding in American military vehicles during the war.[27] In one cartoon titled "Jeep Rhapsody," a GI first drives the Jeep along a steep flight of stairs, picks up a girl who has waved to him seconds before from her window, then drives out of her window in the now-flying Jeep with clouds underneath (see Figure 3.3).[28] Another critic mocked the "Jeep car and Jeep girl" as "the smell of gasoline mixed with face powder scents ... creating an exotic atmosphere."[29] Representations of a GI driving a Jeep in China were highly masculine and often sexual, as the vehicle either carried women or was used to lure them.

The experience of speed and automobility intersected with modern explorations of subjectivity, sexuality, and affect. The typical scene in a Chinese narrative of the GI Jeep began with the sight of a moving vehicle, followed by a view of the foreign driver behind the windshield and a provocatively dressed Chinese woman sitting next to him on their way to restaurants, clubs, and hotels. In the speeding moment, the air would be filled with laughter, smells of perfume and alcohol, and the flaunting girl's evident pity for those less fortunate. It was a multilayered experience featuring the thrill of speed and the danger of transgression in geography, intimacy, and sovereignty. As such, the Jeep was both a material and a cultural object, a manifestation of military, industrial, technological, and cultural power.

The postwar Jeep symbolized a transformative techno-modernity, an American style with supreme speed, mobility, versatility, and commercialization brought about by the liberation. The expanding repertoire of Jeep neologisms such as "Jeep car" (jipu ka), "Jeep soldier" (jipu bing), and "Jeep girl" (jipu nülang) further revealed a type of modern hybridity shaped by sociocultural imaginings of the other. By cleverly playing with a pun on the Chinese character ji 吉, meaning good fortune, Jeep (jipu) acquired auspicious connotations.[30] In its early phase, Jeep conveyed favorable capital that was extended and transferred to other commodities, objects, and endeavors. For example, a new cigarette brand was named "Jeep Car," and the Jeep also functioned as a prominent prop in advertisements for other commodities symbolizing wealth, power, and status.[31] Even a leftist journal adopted the neologism as its title, stating that although it had nothing to do with the vehicle, the journal meant to convey "people's opinions" (minyi), based on the meaning of "general purpose," which many attributed as the origin of the word "Jeep."[32] This prestige and glory associated with the Jeep, however, remained short-lived.

Dangerous Roads: Traffic Accidents and the New Machine Monster

> Jeeps rampaged on the land of China. People became ghosts under their wheels, nowhere to appeal ... Let's learn from our senpai Ah Q's spirit, as if it was still during the war, as if the Jeeps could race even faster, and the innocent drivers could have two more glasses of champagne.
> – *Xinsheng Zhongguo*, 1946[33]

A moving Jeep did not always deliver chocolate, gum, or good fortune – at times, it brought serious accidents. In the wake of the GIs' arrival, traffic accidents became the most common, frequent, and visible form of their misconduct in Chinese cities. American drivers, often drunk or recklessly speeding, injured and killed the elderly, children, women, and other passengers or pedestrians. A glance through local newspapers of the time reveals countless reports of these tragedies. On December 16, 1945, a fast-moving American military vehicle in Shanghai knocked four pedestrians to the ground, injuring three of them, together with another pedicab rider.[34] On August 16, 1946, a Jeep killed a six-year-old on the sidewalk before driving away. When a young Shanghainese jumped onto the Jeep to stop it, he was hit by the driver and fell out.[35] On November 4, 1946, in Tianjin, a speeding Jeep hit a pedestrian, who died from severe brain injury before reaching the hospital; the Jeep disappeared.[36] Two days later, a marine Jeep crashed into another local pedestrian, who succumbed to severe injuries shortly thereafter.[37] On October 16, 1947, a military Jeep in Shanghai crushed two pedestrians to death while injuring a woman, right in front of the headquarters of the Three People's Principles Youth Corps, the Nationalist Party's youth organization.[38]

Traffic accidents involving Jeeps had become a familiar experience for residents who saw, heard, or read about them, leaving a long paper trail in the records of local police departments and the Ministry of Foreign Affairs. According to a police report by the Shanghai municipal government, for example, an estimated 495 traffic accidents involving American military vehicles occurred in the city from September 12, 1945, to January 10, 1946, resulting in 18 deaths and an additional 218 injuries.[39] Even American reporters observed victims of GIs lying in Shanghai hospitals soon after the troops' arrival.[40] It almost felt as if Chinese city streets had turned into another dangerous war zone, where walkers, passengers, rickshaw pullers, pedicab drivers, and even on-duty traffic police frequently fell victim to US military vehicles.

In Chinese critiques, "Uncle Sam's children" and the new automobile were often presented as one and the same: The Jeep was the personified American soldier and the GI was the Jeep in motion; both were masculine, foreign, and dangerous. Jeeps and GIs were blamed for each other's wrongdoings and became an inseparable criminal duo that claimed the lives of innocent pedestrians, bullied rickshaw pullers, and chased and assaulted virtuous young women or carried indecent women around. The Jeep-GI marched without boundaries or restraints, intimidated others with his endless power, and then boasted of his conquests and possessions. In fact, the Jeep-GI duality existed from the time the Jeep was invented. A widely held belief suggests that the name "Jeep" originated from its connection to the GI.[41] More than a versatile and enduring machine, the Jeep was also a loyal comrade on the battlefield, providing assistance, protection, and companionship. In 1943, General MacArthur, who commanded the Southwest Pacific Theater, awarded a wounded Jeep, "the old faithful," a Purple Heart to honor its service in WWII. The Jeep was "an impersonalized common American soldier," newly introduced, going through rigid boot camps, and finally gaining confidence in war, embodying the soldier's three key ideal traits:

optimism, comradeship, and loyalty. Representing the signature spirit of rugged and practical individualism, the Jeep was promoted as an American symbol, burnishing the myth of the iconic figure.[42] In the postwar world, the Jeep quickly became a successful civilian model within the United States and was exported abroad with great success, extending its legendary wartime career.

China first seemed like another remote land where the American hero forged new tales. The vehicle's wartime reputation and surrounding myths greatly enhanced its early appeal. Yet as frequent traffic accidents occurred and news of these spread, the Jeep became a new villain in disguise as a war hero gone wild. After the initial curiosity and excitement, the Chinese populace was struck by the risk, danger, and failure of its technology and its human agents. The accident was a negative indicator, not only of human flaws or negligence, but also of technological failure: The vehicle threw people out on a sharp turn or in a bad collision and failed to stop in front of a playing child. The higher the speed, the greater the severity of the accidents and the lack of control. Earlier expressions of modern thrills about speed, sensation, and freedom were already mixed with a fear of chaos. In fact, Chinese perceptions of the Jeep featured a curious ambivalence from the beginning, even among enthusiastic consumers of foreign goods and experiences. The Jeep journey was felt to be uncannily easy, fast, and full of thrills and excitement, much like flying. At the same time, the journey entailed a sense of violence and potential destruction. In cartoons, "Jeep girls" often looked both thrilled and alarmed, fearful of the rampage the vehicle caused on the street, dreading the impending or potential damage and self-destruction. The supreme qualities of the Jeep were accompanied by an ever-present fear of danger.

A moving vehicle meant a living man. Yet the Jeep was more than an ordinary human: It ran amok on the street, breaking every rule and terrifying all. Ultimately, the Jeep/GI became an abhorrent foreign military monster that was part human, part machine, part beast. The GI in the Jeep was more than a "red-haired foreign devil," a phrase that the Chinese traditionally used to describe Westerners out of racial and cultural fear; the GI in the Jeep was a "killing tiger" with giant headlights, shining with animal urges and wild intimidation.[43] This was an ominously different type of monster, one with a machine shield and armor.[44] In a way, the Jeep was a mechanical extension of and addition to a GI's physical body. It allowed him to penetrate into territories that had previously been difficult or impossible to reach, at a new speed and with actual protection and a sense of invulnerability. It enhanced his claims of masculinity and his allure with the thrills of speed and mobility. In the glimpse of motion, the boundary between human and machine became blurred; the Jeep/GI appeared as a technologically enhanced, foreign military beast that could not be tamed and that transgressed proper geographical, cultural, national, and racial boundaries. The Jeep provided speed, mobility, versatility, and physical protection. It was essentially a human enhancement, an embodiment of the massive militarization of technology and high industrialism of the United States. Consequently, the GI transformed into a mechanically enhanced soldier and hypermasculine alien man with supreme technology, strong purchasing power, and insuppressible sexual drives – a hypersexualized body with uncontrollable animal urges.

Reflecting this technologically mediated fear, Chinese media increasingly depicted GI driving as reckless, impudent, or even brutal. A children's magazine recounted a tragic incident when a Jeep struck a child playing on a street in Nanjing, resulting in a broken leg, significant bleeding, and death.[45] Another reporter rushed to an accident scene just steps from the iconic Sun Yat-sen bronze statue that stood at the capital's heart. There, an overturned Jeep and three blood-covered, intoxicated GIs presented a grim spectacle. Writing with a mix of rage and mockery, the reporter described his excitement at witnessing the scene as akin to watching a Japanese plane being shot down, dubbing the Jeep a "big coffin" for the Chinese.[46] In an almost complete irony, Chinese now painted the Jeep as "disorderly, rude, outrageous, and dangerous," the exact opposite of the "self-sacrificing, humble, homely, but willing to get the job done" entity of its creation myth. The common American boy had become an oversexualized and indecent GI. This growing grievance against GI driving solidified into a shared sentiment and concern. Even *The China Weekly Review*, the prestigious first English periodical founded by American newsmen, published Chinese readers' protests. Charles Tsao, a student of St. John's University, China's leading American missionary college in Shanghai, wrote to the editor on September 25, 1946, of the "nuisance of the shameful servicemen of the U.S. Army and Navy" who were killing innocent Chinese every day in Jeep accidents while the American generals explained to the press that "the GI's life is too monotonous." Declaring himself "not a narrow-minded nationalist," and speaking "from a Christian standpoint," Tsao asked: "My Lord, do you Americans kill your fellow citizens for fun in the States?"[47] Another reader, "Lone-Portia," recounted an incident near the American consulate in Chongqing on December 7, 1948, when a ragged little girl "was crushed by a jeep car of military police and had uttered her last cry for help" while the "criminal chauffeur had driven away" and "the constable there paid no attention." The young woman cried: "It is not in this world that Heaven's justice ends."[48]

The Chinese anger over Jeep accidents was understandable, and the fear real. Many of these most sensationalized accounts came from the Communist media, which targeted reckless GI driving in their anti-American campaigns. But this was an easy fight to pick. The CCP seized on the rising tensions, politicizing these incidents to condemn the so-called American brutalities and the Nationalist Government's incompetency and betrayal. As the GI presence became more visible and accidents more frequent, it was easy to frame the situation in the language of American imperialism. And indeed, drunken drivers often fled accident scenes or denied any responsibility. For the few who were caught or identified, legal consequences were minimal or entirely absent. This lack of accountability further inflamed public outrage and led to a shifting perspective on the Jeep. Patriotic students, leftists, and even some pro-American liberals increasingly came to see the Jeep as a symbol of foreign domination: GIs driving this foreign vehicle, which killed citizens on their own soil with no repercussions, represented America's trampling of Chinese sovereignty.

Overall, the Chinese experience of the Jeep was one of dangerous thrill mixed with techno-political fear. The Jeep was a material and cultural manifestation of the new American global empire. Since the nineteenth century, new infrastructure and transportation technologies, such as paved roads, railroads, telegraphs, and telephones, had facilitated American expansion. After WWII, the United States extended its unprecedented territorial influence afar and asserted power over diverse populations through its supreme techno-political capabilities and universalist claims to its values.[49] To Americans, the wartime "military Jeep" turned into the new postwar "Universal Jeep," a new-day vehicle designed for peace that would serve mankind around the world. In the eyes of many Chinese, however, Jeeps took over their streets and penetrated deep into the very center of city life. They appeared unbounded, parking outside of dance halls, hotels, cafes, shops, and movie theaters in downtown alleys, and even encroaching upon sacred spaces such as the Imperial Palace and the Sun Yat-sen Mausoleum. Jeeps harassed innocent women on the street, abducting victims of sexual violence and fleeing crime scenes effortlessly with no trace or consequence. As such, the Jeep became the ultimate metaphor for the masculine American military empire in an age of high industrialism and global hegemony.

Global Speed in Local Terrains: Street Politics

When American global speed met the intricate local terrain, frequent traffic accidents showcased the complex political, social, and cultural clashes between GIs and Chinese society at large. Speed was a thorny issue that needed government intervention through the use of traffic lights, speed limits, police, new rules, and the arbitration of responsibility. To accommodate the American vehicle system, the Chinese government issued new traffic regulations and right-side driving rules at the end of 1945, replacing the existing left-side driving system.[50] At the instigation of the American military, traffic shifted to the right side of the street on January 1, 1946 – marking another way the American presence reshaped the postwar Chinese landscape.[51] Critics lamented that China had abandoned a fifty-year-old practice overnight, just for the Jeep.[52] Meanwhile, new speed limits were set, partly in response to a rise in accidents caused by speeding American vehicles. In Shanghai, for instance, speed limits of twenty and thirty kilometers per hour in the city and suburban districts, respectively, were established for all vehicles.

Chinese cities of the 1940s were at once modern metropolises and uncharted backwaters with narrow, curvy streets, few traffic lights, unobserved rules, and premodern modes of transportation jostling for space. Urban roads, with their busy traffic and not always law-abiding citizens, presented a new challenge for GIs, who were used to broad country roads back home or battlefields in the Pacific, where they drove at fast speeds and in open spaces. Many were overwhelmed and bewildered by the dense and confusing Chinese urban space, from the maze of paved and unpaved roads in Beijing to the winding streets of Qingdao and the tight alleyway neighborhoods of Shanghai, all lacking adequate traffic signs and policing. On these busy streets, American military vehicles were sharing and often competing for the same space, not only with other motorized vehicles, but also with rickshaws, pedicabs, bicycles, wheelbarrows, mules, and horse-drawn carts, a chaotic mixture of premodern and modern transportation types. In a playful irony, the Chinese word for a modern road, *ma lu*, literally means "horse road." The majority of the local population still lived in rural areas in the 1940s and were unused to motor vehicles. The new speed was said to be so alien that they were "totally unable to calculate the speed with which trucks and buses move," and thus failed to "realize the danger of being struck by such [a] vehicle." Visitors to China reported seeing instances "where villagers or farmers, riding for the first time on a truck, simply jump off when they reach their destination without waiting for it to stop. They have not learned to comprehend the speed of such vehicles, having been accustomed throughout their lives to nothing speedier than a buffalo or a bicycle."[53] For many Chinese on the street, encounters with the Jeep and the American military began as an uncanny bodily and sensory experience.

If the Americans often drove speedily, took sharp turns, and parked freely, it is fair to say that failure to follow the traffic rules was common among all those sharing the roads at the time. Shanghai traffic was a mess in 1946, what some called the worst in history. The situation remained chaotic even after the Communist takeover in 1949, "since pedestrians, automobile drivers, and pedicab men all use the streets as if they belonged to them personally, with virtually no regard for anyone else."[54] In short, everyone behaved badly on the streets and no one followed the rules, nor were the rules strictly enforced. Critics commonly attributed the mess to "overpopulation of this metropolis in the wake of peace, bringing with it [the] greatest volume of motorized, man-propelled and pedestrian traffic in the city's history,"[55] as well as a "host of offenders – jaywalking pedestrians, bicyclists, ricksha runners, pedicab pushers, horse carriages and motor car and truck drivers."[56] Others pointed fingers at the local police. One called them "the root of the evil" for only enforcing the rules sporadically and merely for show.[57] Another blamed the existing chaos on the "lackadaisical" and inefficient traffic police, some newly added to the Shanghai police force, completely unaware of the rules or simply not enforcing them.[58] When WWII ended, for the first time since the mid nineteenth century, Shanghai came under a unified Chinese government. Now with heightened nationalist pride and a strong desire to abolish extraterritoriality, the new government faced the challenge of creating a new system to replace those in former foreign concessions while governing a cosmopolitan city filled with a massive influx of groups from the southwest, refugees looking for jobs, and Allied soldiers.

Compared to the elite class who tended to criticize government control and actions, civilian victims were more focused on restitution issues. After serious traffic incidents that resulted in injuries and deaths, the Chinese usually appealed for compensation through local governments, who then transferred the requests to the US authorities in China. Failure to fulfill such requests became a leading source of tension and disputes, centering around two core issues: Who was responsible and what would be the proper compensation? While Chinese usually blamed American negligence or disregard of their lives, GIs attributed accidents to locals' complete disregard of rules. In reality, there was a range of causes of accidents, and it was sometimes difficult for the US military authorities to come to an easy solution; in extreme cases, the desperate poor tossed babies under US trucks, hoping for compensation.[59] But in general, GIs believed that most accidents happened because "Chinese pedestrians and cyclists exhibit great carelessness in their attitude toward the movement of motor vehicles." American soldiers and MPs frequently expressed frustration with Chinese not following any rules, ignoring traffic lights and not using crosswalks, or rickshaws not staying in the same lane. As one marine observed, "pedestrians did not feel compelled to restrict their movement to the sidewalks, by any means."[60] In response, the US military made persistent requests for new traffic lights, signs posted at major intersections, and strict police enforcement of traffic rules.[61] But the Americans did not always adhere to the regulations themselves. On January 7, 1946, a few days after the implementation of the new speed limit in Shanghai, Lieutenant Colonel Sylvio L. Bousquin complained to the mayor that numerous Chinese civilian cars were exceeding the newly established speed limit. This, he argued, made it difficult to justify enforcing the speed limit on American military vehicles. Bousquin deemed the enforcement discriminatory, calling "the singular emphasis placed upon American military vehicles and personnel unfair and unjust."[62]

The American perspective on the problems affected the compensation system. In practice, the policy was said to be quite liberal. The payment that deceased victims' families received ranged from more than a thousand US dollars to zero, depending on whether such claims were deemed meritorious, partially so, or not at all. Occasionally, individual soldiers involved also paid out of their own pockets when such requests were denied by the US claims office.[63] To "standardize the practice," the US Navy issued "instructions to drivers" in case of injury to a person or damage to property, as follows: "a. stop car immediately and render such assistance as may be needed. b. fill out form, on the spot, as far as possible. c. deliver this form properly to your immediate supervisor." American soldiers were advised to wait on site for MPs, rather than talk to locals or privately settle claims that involved the liability of the US government.[64] Overall, while "evidence" was considered crucial in the decision-making, Chinese testimonies were often overlooked or dismissed as nonessential or unreliable within the American justice system. Lack of evidence and procedural issues were commonly cited as reasons for exonerating the accused, even when Chinese witnesses were abundant, leading to a "Chinaman's chance." In accidents where GIs were not deemed "contributing factors," local victims would be denied compensation by US military authorities, given the standard justification that "the claimant failed to exercise a reasonable amount of caution."

The American decisions and rationales were, however, unacceptable in Chinese eyes, for they often held different ideas about who had the right of way and who was responsible when traffic accidents occurred. Generally speaking, the Chinese customarily held automobile drivers culpable under all circumstances, regardless of whether or not the pedestrians had checked for traffic before crossing the road; this was partly due to an ongoing traditional belief that those in power bore more responsibility because of their advantageous position. For instance, in the early phase of motorcars in the 1910s, some Chinese commentators argued that a carriage had the right of way over a motorcar because it was easier for the latter to make a full stop than for the animal. In 1949, after US military vehicles disappeared from the newly captured Chinese streets, the general rule was established that the drivers of motor vehicles were responsible for accidents that occurred to pedestrians and cyclists because rural populations had little experience with motor vehicles and were unaccustomed to their speed.[65] Even today, the disorder on China's roads can be partially attributed to the belief that drivers, equipped with more powerful machines, bear a greater responsibility compared to pedestrians, regardless of whether the latter are breaking traffic rules. Such a mentality and rationale were in sharp contrast with the modern American notion of equal responsibility based on whether or not one follows the rules. Further, the traffic conditions and systems of the two countries were quite different, with China having adopted European road directions. Motor vehicles were still rare in rural areas. Most hawkers, rickshaw pullers, and other coolies had little knowledge of speed limits or the right of way. Similarly, urban pedestrians were not used to using crosswalks, even when they were available.

The numerous petition letters sent to municipal governments further revealed a major gap between the legal and sociocultural understandings of these incidents among Chinese civilians, some of which were also shared by local officials, and those held by the American military. In local petitions, the pursuit of justice was intricately linked to seeking reparations. For the injured survivors and victims' families, predominately from the laboring class, the first and foremost request was recompense. This monetary relief was usually requested based on the cost of medical treatment, funeral expenses, and loss of income to support their families. For instance, after the death of Zhao Xueyao – an eighteen-year-old worker at a Tianjin textile factory who was fatally struck by an American military truck while his bike was crossing an intersection on the night of July 18, 1947 – his brother submitted a plea to the mayor of Tianjin. This appeal was crafted in the standard format used for such letters. It read:

I respectfully petition Your Honor on behalf of my younger brother, Zhao Xueyao, who was tragically killed by an American military vehicle. I implore you to negotiate compensation on our behalf to alleviate our suffering. My parents are elderly and have no means of income, and I am unemployed. Our family, which includes nine members, both elderly and children, relied on my younger brother to survive ... Since his untimely death, we have been plunged into poverty, unable to secure even loans. As winter approaches, we face severe hunger and cold, and fear that we may succumb to starvation.[66]

Traditionally, financial compensation was considered a just and legitimate means of achieving justice. Material redress was an integral part of seeking moral and legal justice, especially for the impoverished. For many victims at the time, it was even a necessity, as the male victims tended to be the only adult laborers working in cities and providing for their families back in the countryside. Family situations, such as having young children and elderly parents, as well as the lost wages of the dead, were usually mentioned in appeal letters to justify their requests. To those involved in these traffic incidents and the observers reading about them, the denial of compensation meant economic devastation to poor victims' families, especially if they lost the only breadwinner.

Invoking a Confucian style of paternalist relations, these letters appealed to benevolent local officials for justice and mercy. Victims were often supported by a network of intermediaries that included hometown organizations, professional associations, and family members who were literate and had more sociopolitical resources. Typically, these petitions began with polite pleas highlighting personal tragedies, then shifted to sharp critiques of GI criminality if initial requests went unaddressed.[67] To make their case, the petitioners often linked the GIs' misconduct and the victims' failure to receive proper compensation to broader issues of national equality. Instead of citing specific traffic laws or legislations, these appeals stressed the political problem of the US military presence in China and highlighted GIs' contempt for the Chinese people. They criticized the US military's procedures and rationales for denial of compensation as unsatisfactory and its dealings as subjective. Moreover, the dismissive responses from American officials – often a terse, standardized letter – coupled with the lack of repentance evidenced by repeat offenses, was condemned as an affront to the national dignity of all.

The intricate street politics of the Jeep in China was a microcosm of the complex Sino-US interactions on grassroots levels. Influenced by national and racial inequality, these everyday struggles involved various factors including negligence, prejudice, misunderstanding, and differences in technological, social, political, legal, and moral systems. In response to rampant traffic accidents involving American military vehicles, local governments sometimes took actions on their own. For example, the Shanghai Police Bureau once issued orders to fire at such vehicles in "extremely grave" situations.[68] However, the Nationalist Government as a whole lacked the practical and legal means to handle these issues. It struggled to reconcile Confucian moral legitimacy with the American legal system, which relied on trial systems, witness testimonies, and proof of evidence. Hindered by extraterritoriality, the Nationalist Government did not possess judicial authority over the accused GIs. The limitation undermined the government's credibility when it failed to secure redress, settle disputes, and provide justice for victims. This pattern of disputes over responsibility and compensation was evident in various street incidents involving Chinese civilians, ranging from traffic accidents to deadly violence against rickshaw men, which became a more prominent headline issue.

Friends and Foes: GIs and Rickshaw Men

On January 24, 1946, Pulitzer Prize–winning author John Hersey wrote from Shanghai, detailing GIs' rowdyism in the city, ranging from deadly traffic accidents caused by drunk drivers to MPs slapping coolies. Born in Tianjin to an American missionary family, Hersey had learned to speak Chinese before mastering English and spent the war years reporting on conflicts in the Pacific and Europe. In his "Letter from Shanghai" for *The New Yorker*, he observed that "Jeep diplomacy" was replacing "Dollar diplomacy," referring to the large number of Jeeps crowding the streets from US surplus aid and sales.[69] One particular social group affected by this Jeep diplomacy was the Chinese rickshaw pullers, who faced multifaceted impacts. While the Jeep taxi became a competitor and threat to the declining business of the rickshaw, pullers also found themselves beneficiaries of GI patronage, with many servicemen routinely using the service while on liberty. At the same time, rickshaw men were among the first and most frequent casualties in the street accidents caused by American military vehicles, as the two shared the undivided lanes and competed, often aggressively, for the right of way. Overall, the actual and symbolic interactions between American soldiers and Chinese rickshaw men, a relationship that mingled fantasy, patronage, rivalry, and conflict, represented the most entangled type of Sino-US relations.

In the newly liberated Orient, American soldiers encountered the labyrinth of Chinese urban life with its social hierarchy and long-existing rickshaw empire, which was in the final phase of its existence. For Chinese society, the rickshaw trade had been controversial for decades. Invented in Japan in the late 1860s, rickshaws (*ricksha, jinrickshaw*) quickly appeared on Chinese city streets, and rickshaw pulling had since become a major type of work for laborers. The rickshaw was also called the "foreign vehicle" (*yang che*) in China because of its technological advances during the time of its introduction and its early association with the modern paved roads of city life. After the technological improvements of a lighter frame and rubber tires in the early twentieth century, which increased both comfort levels and speed, the popularity of the rickshaw rose among city dwellers. The rickshaw had become a new and often superior form of transportation compared to the old sedan chair and walking. In 1946, more than fifty thousand pullers and twenty thousand rickshaws were running on the road of Shanghai.[70] In 1947, there were more than ten thousand rickshaw pullers, 227 rickshaw companies, and more than seven thousand registered rickshaws in Nanjing.[71] Most rickshaw men were rural immigrants to the cities who survived on daily hard labor.

The rickshaw man had occupied a central place in Republican cityscapes and public discussions from the very beginning.[72] Liberals, social reformers, and socialists had long criticized the business for its inhumane treatment of labor. During the New Life Movement, the Nationalist Government attempted to ban or reduce the number of rickshaws, fearing such "inhumane" labor would tarnish China's international reputation as a modern nation. Meanwhile, the industry had been facing increasing competition from trams and motor vehicles. The postwar government continued its earlier unsuccessful campaigns to abolish the rickshaw trade, beginning in 1945 to reissue regulations aiming to gradually reduce and eliminate rickshaws over a three-year period. In 1946, the Executive Yuan issued implementation edicts across the country. However, the rickshaw pullers, as before, strongly opposed the ban and organized collective actions, including a vow to engage in street riots.[73] Concerns about the ban's impact on labor welfare were also raised by some reformers, who warned that the former rickshaw pullers might try to beg, steal, rob, or kill instead. The situation escalated in late September after the death of a Shanghai puller named Zang Yaocheng (Tsang Ta Erh Tsu), who was killed by an American sailor.[74] This incident, which will be discussed in more detail later in this chapter, sparked large protests in the city. In response, the Nationalist Government set out to reduce the number of rickshaws and street peddlers "to promote morality and improve traffic conditions." Nevertheless, critics called the ban motivated by "a desire to please the Americans who thought rickshaw pulling degraded humanity," and warned that as a result of the ban, "100,000 rickshaw pullers and their dependents would be deprived of a livelihood in due time."[75] Another critic in Beijing pointed out that the postwar ban was mostly because America did not have the rickshaw.[76]

The influx of American personnel unfamiliar with local roads and landscapes injected some fresh blood into the declining business. Rickshaw men offered convenient and necessary transportation for these foreign soldiers eager to explore local attractions including scenic spots, restaurants, clubs, theaters, registered and underground brothels, and other places of entertainment. More than mere transporters, pullers traditionally also assumed the role of local guides for outsiders, offering inside knowledge of the hidden nooks and crannies that did not show up in the usual guidebooks. Some pullers even leveraged their roles to act as intermediaries, earning commissions from brothels. As such, American patronage became a vital new source of income for many of them. Ironically, the GI presence both reenergized a business in crisis and accelerated its final diminishment. The flood of American motor vehicles, especially Jeeps, contributed to the steady decrease in the number of registered rickshaws in Shanghai, which went from 23,066 in March 1947 to 11,029 in August 1948.[77] In response, rickshaw pullers' associations protested the government's ban and distribution of Jeeps to the taxi association. They argued that it would lead to the elimination of rickshaws and the loss of the pullers' livelihood.[78]

For the Chinese government, the rickshaw was a backward social institution and practice to be abolished, for it had no place in the new, modern, and now victorious nation. American views toward the rickshaw, however, were mixed. It was a useful or necessary transportation; in one cartoon, a marine driving a Jeep on a flooded street watches with frustration and jealousy as another GI in a rickshaw rides by, staying dry, comfortable, and smoking in leisure.[79] Despite the occasional comical celebration, most comments from GIs' memoirs emphasized pullers' skinny bodies, harsh labor, poverty, and what they saw as human beasts of burden. Even to more sympathetic eyes, "the average farm mule in Alabama had a far easier life than a Chinese rickshaw coolie."[80] As four-wheeled industrialization democratized road usage among Americans and reshaped their urban landscape and social relations, GIs found in rickshaw men the very embodiment of an inferior civilization of the Orient.

Racism was inherent in GI perceptions of Chinese rickshaw pullers and structured their daily interactions. Being pulled by another human being was an exotic experience, a must-have on the Oriental menu for a GI tour. Pictures of and with pullers were among the most popular China souvenirs sent home. Fueled by "the combination of the troops' high spirits and the Chinese alcoholic spirits," American soldiers also raced each other by pulling rickshaw men down the street, causing expressions of "abject terror on the faces of the ricksha runners as they held tightly to their precarious perches in the passenger seats."[81] This act of apparent role reversal, presumably amusing to the GIs and their audiences back home, had deep roots in racism. Similar to white performers in blackface in American minstrel shows, who performed eccentric "black" songs and dances, this role reversal was a mockery and conveyed to the audience mixed feelings of fascination, desire, and fear.[82] It lampooned Chinese society and culture as exotic and backward for still treating humans as animals while reinforcing notions of white superiority. More broadly, the rickshaw experience validated existing racial and national hierarchies

Friends and Foes: GIs and Rickshaw Men   115

both inside and outside the United States, as in the use of "colored" porters in Pullman train cars. As a Chinese critic noted, the sight of American soldiers pulling rickshaw men was not merely a comedy or a joke because, "unfortunately, we ourselves are the characters in this comedy, or objects of mockery."[83]

Besides routine rides, the enlisted men invented "some spectacular amusements" involving the rickshaw, in Hersey's words, to "take their exuberance out on the town." An official Stars and Stripes rickshaw derby was held in Shanghai on December 1, 1945, in which nineteen "jockeys," girls from the Allied forces, were pulled by Chinese coolies "known as 'horses'" (see Figure 3.4). This event attracted ten thousand GI spectators who gathered at the destination of a stadium originally built for greyhound racing in the former French Concession. Amidst their cheering roar, number seventeen puller, Jiang Ermao, finished the four-mile race first with a twenty-minute ride. The winning jockey was crowned "Rickshaw Queen" by General Wedemeyer, the commander of the

Figure 3.4 United States Army Air Force officer riding in a rickshaw during a race in Shanghai, December 1945. NARA.

American forces in China, and "the winning horse was given a floral horseshoe" and a prize of about seven American dollars.[84] As the smiling Rickshaw Queen held her trophy facing the camera, Jiang stood beside her and "looked strangely at the garland of flowers placed around his neck, like a horse that had won the derby ... His face exhibited curiosity framed with a cross between a smile and dismay."[85] While Chinese media criticized the implicit dog/horse analogy, a few months later, the winning rickshaw man was reportedly invited by the chairman of Madison Square Garden to compete with a famous American runner in New York City. The invitation was supposedly a result of the enthusiastic response to this GI creation, leading to the proposal of a Sino-US sporting event designed to recreate the spectacle to thrill audiences back home. However, it later emerged that the news was an April Fools' Day prank orchestrated by American servicemen.[86]

Such entertainment events, supposedly for pure fun, went beyond simple cultural insensitivity and were instead rooted in the history of colonial hierarchy. The Western world had long associated rickshaws with the Other, particularly its inhumane, preindustrial usage of labor and animal-like behavior. The phrase "beasts of burden" frequently appeared in Westerners' descriptions of Chinese laborers from the nineteenth century and was also commonly spotted in Allied newspapers. American soldiers rode rickshaws in Calcutta and in the Himalayas, where the interesting characters of Mongolian "rickshaw-wallahs" appeared to them as "rough-looking, likeable villains" because of their habit of "laughing and joking as they drag[ged] their unwieldy vehicles up and down Darjeeling's steep and hilly roads."[87] In postwar Hong Kong, British sailors would take time off for races in rickshaws pulled by Chinese coolies while a shipmate acted as a traffic policeman.[88] In South Africa, "Zulu rickshaw 'boys'" who were considered "magnificent physical specimens" were said to "maintain an amazing pace with their vehicles" and to consider it "a special honour to carry a British serviceman, which they did with gay shouts and palpitating capers."[89] The rickshaw scene was in these ways so ingrained in the Western popular imagination of the Orient that children enacted such plays on the streets of London, pulling each other through the old Chinatown of the East End of the city, the Limehouse Causeway. This picture of old Chinatown captured "all the mystery of the glamorous East": "The slant-eyed rickshaw boy pads silently through the burning streets – 'Hold it, you dope, you're off on the wrong tack! It's the East all right, but the East End of London. And old Chinatown is Limehouse Causeway!'"[90]

The concept of China as a rickshaw-pulling nation was deeply embedded in the colonial discourse and Orientalist affects. The rickshaw and the

Jeep represented contrasting forms of speed, power, race, culture, and civilization. Rickshaw queens and Jeep girls were the flip sides of this dualistic hierarchy. Just as American girls rode Chinese rickshaws for a leisurely outing or a fun race, Jeeps carried Chinese girls for GIs' pleasure, to experience modern speed, entertainment, and adventure. Similar to how American tourists posed in staged opium dens in the alluring Chinatowns, taking home an apparent memento of white superiority, photographs of Chinese rickshaw men also helped confirm the superior values of democracy and equality that postwar America was proclaiming. As such, China became not only a nation newly liberated by white GIs from Japanese occupation, but also an Oriental country to be liberated from its own backwardness.

As in a typical colonial imaginary, American soldiers' views of rickshaw men mixed fantasy of the exotic with fear of danger. They saw Chinese pullers both as exotic beasts of burden and as a distinctive sociological group that was "touchy and itching to quarrel" and requiring special talents to tame.[91] Disputes over fares were a common trigger of conflict, with verbal arguments sometimes escalating to physical violence. With their salary and the low Chinese cost of living, marines could maintain comfortable lifestyles with servants, restaurant food, and luxury purchases, as well as a rickshaw ride that cost from three to fifteen American cents in Beijing.[92] Most Americans were willing to pay extra for the novelty, comfort, convenience, or necessity of rickshaw rides. But some were more reluctant. While doing business, GIs found rickshaw men difficult to deal with, especially the endless bargaining. They complained about paying more than Chinese customers, sudden changes in predetermined prices, and frequent price increases by the collective group of pullers. Because of their unfamiliarity with local environments, confusion over the exchange rate, or experiences of dishonesty, they often felt taken advantage of, or even grew angry with pullers who persistently demanded fees, especially when alcohol was involved. When disputes with rickshaw pullers occurred, US servicemen on liberty without their guns sometimes felt vulnerable, outnumbered by huge crowds and overwhelmed by a mixture of verbal and physical aggressions. In designated parking areas and popular entertainment sites, pullers seemed to yell in unintelligible angry voices, determined to get what they were promised or deemed fair, and quickly resorted to their collective group power when tensions arose.

The rickshaw men had traditionally maintained a strong group identity for self-protection and competition with other groups. As one character in Lao She's *Rickshaw Boy* explains, an individual rickshaw puller is like a grasshopper easily caught by a child, tied with a thread, and unable to fly. But when they come together as a group, they can devour an entire field of crops in a second, and there is nothing anyone can do about it.[93] After the war, the pullers' associations organized protests against the government's plans to ban or reduce their numbers, as well as against owners' attempts to raise rickshaw rents. They continued to clash with competitors such as city buses by damaging them in the streets.[94] They also stood together when facing American soldiers, collectively raising fares and addressing disputes. Some pullers were connected to local gangs that solicited GIs into dubious businesses through a mix of lures and threats. On occasion, they openly insulted and assaulted GIs, even in the presence of local police, who themselves held grievances against these foreign soldiers.[95]

Overall, the American forces were confronted with a highly resilient and powerful group that was not easily swayed, as well as a problem that lacked clear macropolitical solutions (see Figure 3.5). After disputes, which sometimes became serious, the US military usually informed Chinese officials in protest, urging them to take actions, such as regulating fares and preventing cheating. Dissatisfied with the results of local intervention or lack thereof, the US authorities also tried to take matters into their own hands. In Qingdao, they designated some places "out of bounds" and considered prohibiting the use of rickshaws altogether. As they came to learn the organizational power of Chinese pullers, marine authorities proposed that "the U.S. Provost Marshal approach the president of the Rickshaw Pullers' Association, warning him of the possibility of measures against the rickshaws and requiring him to make efforts to reduce 'incidents' against the Marines."[96] Another successful tactic solved the problem of inflated rickshaw ride prices for GIs in Beijing, perhaps temporarily, when an old China hand banned all rides until a better group rate was negotiated.[97] But still much of the daily maneuvering was left in the hands of individuals, and how each dispute ended depended on individual circumstances and judgments, which were directly informed by their education, peer wisdom, and beliefs. In the eyes of many, conflicts with Chinese pedestrians, drivers, and rickshaw pullers were a clash of civilizations. They saw these civilians as cunning street mobs who tried to fool them with dishonest business practices, exploited their lack of local knowledge, and intimidated them into paying unfair rates for fares or huge compensation after accidents. Many enlisted men believed that an unarmed GI facing a dangerous coolie mob called for the use of strong force or even violence. Such perceptions were deeply shaped by America's own history of racism and new experience of global occupation. These biased beliefs shed light on why rickshaw men often became victims of some of the most serious crimes and legal injustice.

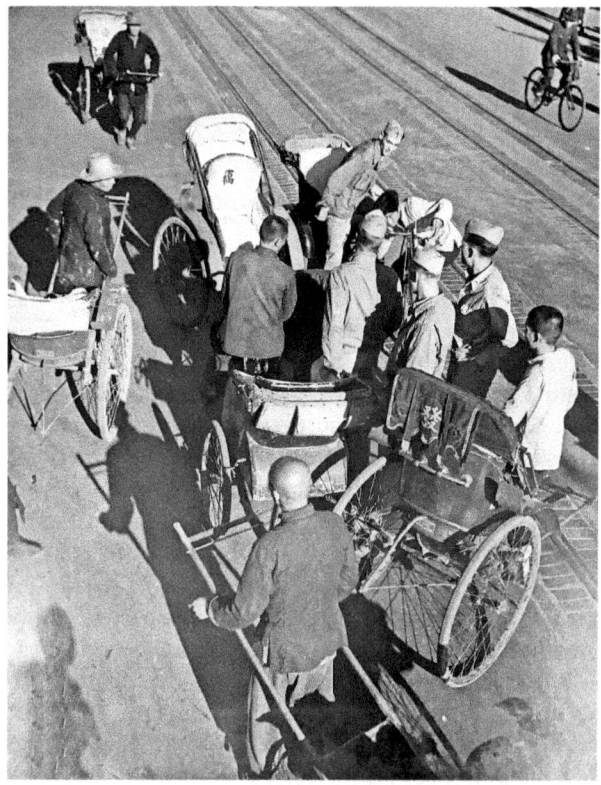

Figure 3.5 American soldiers, along with local rickshaw pullers and pedicab men, gather around the scene of a traffic accident. MCHD.

Tale of the Everyman

At around 10:00 p.m. on September 22, 1946, Shanghai rickshaw man Zang Yaocheng pulled Julian Larrinaga, a Spanish sailor, from an American ship to a club, whereupon Larrinaga walked inside without paying. Zang waited outside until midnight, when Larrinaga finally came out with American sailor Edward Roderick after hours of drinking. Zang persistently requested his fare, and, surrounded by a group of pullers and pedicab riders during the dispute, Roderick hit Zang on the head, who then fell into a coma. Zang was diagnosed with a concussion and died at 5:00 a.m. the following day. After the incident, Zang's only surviving child, a twelve-year-old girl, acted as the appellant, with her uncle serving as her guardian. Her letter, titled "American troops scorned the countrymen and killed my father," was submitted to the mayor of Shanghai by members of the municipal representative council. In it, she requested compensation totaling 145,100,400 *fabi* yuan from the American side, equivalent to several thousand US dollars. The amount was calculated based on her father's projected daily income from age forty-two until age sixty, and also included funeral expenses, the costs of her education and future wedding, and relief for the mental anguish she endured.[98]

In November 1946, a US Navy court-martial acquitted Roderick of the manslaughter charge and Zang's family received no compensation. The decision resulted from a deep distrust of and legal discriminations against Chinese witnesses, especially rickshaw coolies, whose testimonies were deemed "unsatisfactory," both "in establishing the identity of the accused and the offense of which he was accused." An additional reason given was that "there was no American witnesses."[99] After the American decision on the Zang Yaocheng case, the Shanghai municipal government and the Chinese Foreign Ministry contended that the US government had failed to fulfill its obligations to ensure justice and had infringed on China's sovereignty by taking a Chinese witness to its base for testimony without informing the Chinese authorities.[100] On multiple occasions, the government tried to persuade the American navy to reopen Roderick's case, arguing that it had failed to keep the Chinese side adequately informed, violating the terms of the jurisdiction agreement on handling criminal offenses committed by US service personnel. But these official inquiries and protests had no impact on the final legal decisions and did little to quell the anger of the Chinese people. Despite believing Roderick was guilty, Rear Admiral W. A. Kitts remained committed to "protecting what he saw as the established policy of his government, the interests of his service and, like most commanding officers, taking care of his man, even when guilty."[101]

The Zang case was far from unique. Six months later, around 8:00 p.m. on March 30, 1947, a rickshaw puller named Su Mingcheng was killed by a US sailor in Qingdao in a similar situation. Petro Abarra, a US Navy steward's mate second class, took a taxi ride to a "Prime Club" in downtown Qingdao. He refused to pay the agreed fare upon arrival and was ready to leave without solving the matter. Surrounded by his driver and several dozen rickshaw pullers waiting for customers at the site, Abarra took out a pocketknife and stabbed twenty-two-year-old Su Mingcheng in the thigh. Su managed to chase Abarra into the club before collapsing. Moments later, he was pronounced dead at the scene. Other pullers continued to pursue Abarra, who was finally caught by Chinese police officers after running several blocks. As in the Zang case, the offending soldier was taken from the scene by American MPs and later brought before a court-martial. The American court in Qingdao found Abarra guilty and sentenced him "to be reduced to the rating of steward's mate third class, to be confined for a period of ten years, to be dishonorably discharged from the U.S. naval service and to suffer all the other accessories of said sentence." The sentence, however, was reduced to five years confinement shortly afterward. Su's mother was awarded US$1,500 as compensation for the death of her son.[102]

The two cases share striking similarities. Both incidents involved intoxicated soldiers who, late at night and during fare disputes, committed acts of violence against rickshaw pullers while surrounded by fuming, rock-throwing local crowds. In the aftermath, both victims were represented and assisted by rickshaw pullers' unions, which petitioned the mayors for compensation from the Americans and demanded severe punishment for the sailors, an apology from US authorities, and assurances that such incidents would not reoccur. Leaders of rickshaw associations applied pressure on local labor affairs departments, warning that if their demands were not met, a strike involving "thousands of rickshaw pullers" would take place in "defiance of military curfew order and the [municipal officials'] plea to secure friendship between China and the United States."[103] These collective actions and negotiations reveal a strong social network that supported victims and their families in navigating the complex bureaucratic and legal systems. Local pullers' associations, with a tradition of protesting against the killing of pullers by foreigners since the 1910s, played a crucial role in these efforts.

As it turned out, both incidents became political liabilities for the Nationalist Government, drawing protests from local rickshaw pullers, students, and other urban residents. Despite pressure from victims' families, local associations, and the media, the government's attempts to secure fairer sentencing and satisfactory compensation ultimately failed to wield actual influence. In contrast, the CCP quickly capitalized on these sentiments and launched extensive propaganda campaigns targeting these major cases. Coincidently, the Zang incident occurred just as the "US Troops Quit China Week" campaign was being launched in Shanghai, marking an early phase of the anti-American movement. *Wenhui bao*, a major Shanghai newspaper now run by underground CCP members, published more than forty reports on the Zang case from November 24, 1946, to April of the following year. *Xinhua ribao*, a Party organ, featured editorials with explicit titles such as "Protest against the Brutalities of the US Military in China" and "Heinous Murder of Zang Daerzi."[104] A lengthy biography with illustrations, including interviews of Zang's brother and Chinese witnesses, was soon published in a magazine and later turned into a fifty-page pamphlet.[105] Similarly, various Communist and leftist media outlets reported the brutal murder of the innocent young man Su Mingcheng. The tragedy left his elderly mother heartbroken and unconscious beside his cold, blood-covered body, adding another grievance to the US soldiers' growing list of blood debts.[106] Notably, these reports appealed directly to nationalist sentiments against American brutalities. Within them, Zang was portrayed as a Chinese everyman and "citizen of the Republic" (*minguo gongmin*).[107] Su represented the urban poor laborer, "driven by hunger," pulling a yelling American soldier "filled with brandy and whisky," who was abusing, killing, raping, and setting fires" on the "soil of a semi-colonial country." Su's tragic death, deemed "worthless in the eyes of running dogs," became a rallying cry that "united everyone with rage."[108] The Communist narrative transformed the rickshaw puller into a prototype Chinese victim, directly subjected to American violence and left unprotected by the corrupt, betraying Nationalist Government. This powerful image reduced the complex micropolitics and everyday struggles to a simplistic binary between brutal imperialists and defenseless victims, creating a unifying emotional appeal. As leftist broadsheets and CCP media closely followed the incidents, the two cases gained national prominence and later converged into the more vehement Anti-Brutality movement, which would soon shake the entire nation.

The Beijing Jeep

In May 1949, shortly after the People's Liberation Army entered Shanghai, American Vice Consul William Olive was arrested on the street after forcing his way through two rickshaws that blocked his path. He was taken to a nearby police station, where he got into a fight with the police on duty and was subsequently beaten. As a result, Olive spent three days in a cell and was required to apologize in writing before his release.[109] In the new China, the power of the proletariat, like the rickshaw man, triumphed over the power possessed by the American riding in a Jeep. As earlier modern experiences and desires associated with the Jeep faded into fragmented memories, the vehicle's political symbolism as a foreign imperialist criminal became firmly established.

When the Jeep first came to the postwar Chinese streets, it was seen as a symbol of Allied victory, which then turned into a desirable cultural spectacle and popular commodity. But unlike in other places, in China, the vehicle did not smoothly transform into a sign of technology, progress, and, ultimately, postwar modernity.[110] Instead, following frequent traffic accidents and GI crimes, the Jeep turned into a military tool of intimidation, danger, and harassment in the popular perception, a symbol of prolonged American occupation. The Jeep did not become a successfully domesticated commodity easily assimilated into Chinese culture, but remained a foreign machine driven by white soldiers, threatening the existing order of Chinese society and the nation.

While the last US military withdrew from China before the Communist victory and rickshaws finally came to an end in the 1950s, the American Jeep remained running on Chinese streets and subsequently had a long and interesting afterlife. As the Communist army defeated the Nationalists and captured their massive stock of American-made equipment, from weapons to vehicles, the Jeep became commonly used by the Communists in the civil war, and like the American and Nationalist generals, CCP officers also rode in Jeeps when commanding troops at the front lines. Perhaps there is no bigger irony than the "reunion" soon after. In the ensuing Korean War, these captured American military vehicles were again put to good use, this time in fighting the American imperialists directly in order to assist Koreans and protect the homeland. The domestication of the Jeep also took unexpected turns. After the Sino-Soviet split in the 1960s, China began to produce its own famous "Beijing Jeep," a milestone in China's national motor industry. During the Cultural Revolution, Mao, dressed in military uniform, chose to ride in the new Beijing Jeep as he saluted tens of thousands of Red Guards near Tiananmen Square, an iconic image seared into the minds of millions.[111] By a strange twist of fate, the Jeep was again transformed, now into a symbol of Communist victory, pride, and superiority.

4 Intimate Relations
Jeep Girls and Gendered Nationalism

> Flying on twentieth century's wartime street
> A little Jeep of olive green
> Faster than the wind
> Passing over the tram line
> I see
> Uniforms of olive green
> Open smiles on wide mouths
> A red cloud floats past
> A girl's scarf!
> Or is that
> A predator's landscape?
> – Xian Ping, "Panels of an Urban Salon Landscape," 1945[1]

In "Panels of an Urban Salon Landscape," a Chinese poet captures a memorable scene of liberation featuring a swaggering foreign "predator" and a Chinese girl riding in a speeding Jeep. The poem ends with a sour statement: "The world's freedom and peace now depend on this crowd," a satire of both the proclaimed American geopolitical missions in the world and the Chinese female "peacemakers" who fraternize with foreign soldiers.[2] Among all the frictions involving GIs, ranging from daily traffic accidents to brutal murders, sexual relations with Chinese women triggered the strongest anti-American sentiments within Chinese society.[3] Conservatives condemned women for liaisons with American soldiers and acting like whores. The infamous Peking rape incident sparked massive protests and drew an outpouring of support among urban residents, even from some government officials. It astonished many contemporary observers that a single rape case could convulse the entire nation overnight. If the first American Volunteer Group, affectionately dubbed the "Flying Tigers," exemplified the altruistic American heroes during the war, drunken marine rapists became the symbol of American imperialism. Through the injured and maligned bodies of Chinese women, the global US military empire became deeply entangled with China's local politics.

Like other occupied areas, actual and perceived sexual relations between local females and American soldiers often caused social animosity and even vengeful violence. Chinese discussions of women mixed racial, cultural, and sexual anxieties and were formulated along class lines. Critics were mostly concerned about preventing "respectable" middle- and upper-class women from falling into disrepute or from suffering violence, whereas lower-class prostitutes were ignored or seen as a tool to protect the "purity" of the nation.[4] But the Chinese case stands out even more by virtue of the central role occupied by elite women, involving both romance and violence. The Chinese controversy began as a vibrant debate over "Jeep girls," referring to women who socialized, sometimes intimately, with American soldiers during and after WWII.[5] The contemporary translation "Jeep girls" combines the "girl," a social and representational category "largely delinked from biological age,"[6] and "Jeep," a multivalent symbol, as discussed in the previous chapter, of American military victory, industrial and commercial success, and white masculinity. The early discussion, centering on modernity and Westernization, attracted a diverse group of conservatives, liberals, leftists, feminists, and the women themselves. Prevalent hostility toward Jeep girls continued the attacks on "modern women" that had occurred in earlier decades and was deeply embedded in the threats they posed to masculinity, patriarchal gender relations, and hegemonic nationalism. After the Peking rape incident, however, the multivalent debate swiftly gave way to a predominantly nationalist message of reclaiming sovereignty against American imperialism, accompanied by nationwide anti-American demonstrations. In this hypernationalist environment, little space remained for the modern Jeep girls, and Chinese women existed only as whores to be condemned or victims to be defended.

This chapter foregrounds the key role of gendered nationalism in Sino-US relations. Simmering beneath the national alliance and harmonious relations were long-standing dissatisfactions with and resentments toward American superiority since wartime, from the highest levels of the Chinese leadership to ordinary soldiers and civilians.[7] As the nation recovered territories in former Japanese-occupied areas and rejuvenated itself after eight years of devastating war, Chinese elites were eager to reclaim both national sovereignty and individual masculinity. Heightened nationalism clashed with the hypermasculine American military over actual and symbolic territoriality.

Modern Women or Parasitic Whores: The Jeep Girls Debate

How proud the Jeep girls, jumping onto the Jeeps, holding tall allies in their arms, and entering grand ballrooms and exquisite bars with their clicking high heels. How lucky the Jeep girls, opening their fat wallets

> filled with American dollars, perfumes and powders, authentic chocolates and chewing gums brought by airplanes. Every one of them has become Westernized and now looks at the Chinese people the way Westerners look at them, with shifty eyes beaming arrogant foreign airs. Everything is so full of an exotic atmosphere that they forget, forget about their black hair.
> – Chen Minzhi, "Cong Yingguo taitai tandao jipu nülang," 1946[8]

The Chinese epithet "Jeep girls" began to circulate during the war when women were seen riding around in Jeeps with GIs, and it was later expanded to describe all types of women who were perceived to have intimate relationships with American soldiers. Contemporaries divided the Jeep girls into three categories based on socioeconomic differences. At the bottom of the social ladder were destitute prostitutes who operated in registered or underground brothels, facing the precarities of economic exploitation, police harassment and arrest, physical violence, and venereal disease. The Nationalist Government had long maintained an inconsistent and ineffective policy toward prostitution, while local governments adopted a variety of approaches, which often had conflicting objectives of revenue generation, morality, and public health.[9] Like elsewhere, prostitution was already rampant during the war near American barracks.[10] Upon Japan's surrender, the influx of American military personnel from wartime bases in southwest China to major cities previously occupied by the Japanese contributed to a boom in the sex and entertainment industries. In Shanghai, known as the "Paris of the East," prostitutes filled the streets and wandered around the hostel buildings. Writer Robert Payne, then serving as a cultural attaché to the British embassy, had his room door suddenly opened from outside one day, revealing a girl and a hotel coolie, who pursued him with relentless questions: "Want girl?" "Want boy?" "You American?"[11] Lou Glist, a US Army officer stationed in Shanghai, observed that White Russians were highly sought after "in a world where white women were scarce." The more fortunate among them became GI companions, while those less fortunate in appearance or age turned to prostitution.[12] Seasoned Chinese journalist Guo Gen gave a detailed account of Beijing brothels servicing American soldiers. Suzhou Hutong in the downtown area had been a prospering district for international whorehouses with a history tracing back to the late Qing period; it now became "a heaven for the 'Allies,'" attracting a diverse range of prostitutes, including White Russians, Japanese, Koreans, and an increasing number of Chinese rural women who were war refugees. The cost per service in 1946 was said to be about one US dollar, while the girls only ended up with 30 percent after paying pimps, interpreters, and madams. When the local police or the US military tightened rules against brothels, these women often resorted to street prostitution instead. Soon they all became "Mary" in the words of a "GI Joe," who found it difficult to tell them apart or pronounce their Chinese names.[13]

A second type worked in cafes, restaurants, cabarets, nightclubs, and hotels, providing entertainment and occasionally sexual services (see Figure 4.1). Many were hired by the sites to attract customers or increase alcohol sales. With some social and cultural capital, such as varying levels of English-language proficiency, dance skills, and familiarity with modern leisure, these women often accompanied GIs to entertainment sites,

Figure 4.1 American sailors in intimate contact with hostesses at the Diamond Bar in Shanghai, 1949. Photograph by Jack Birns. The LIFE Picture Collection/Shutterstock.

creating a public spectacle, and appeared in popular souvenir photos that soldiers sent home. Postwar tabloids reported former dance stars, opera singers, and actresses becoming Jeep girls.[14] The women in this group were not necessarily destitute, but economic interests remained central to their relationships with GIs, and their activities were a highly visible part of the postwar urban economy and tabloid scene. While mocked for their declining beauty, income, and social status, these former "social butterflies" also appeared fashionable and even enviable posing in their Western-style dresses and accessories, gifted by generous GIs.

The third group included upper-middle-class women whose motivations ranged from financial benefit to the lofty idea of "service to the nation."[15] During the war, English-speaking college students worked for the American military as clerks, translators, and volunteers. Members of women's organizations, often including government officials' wives and daughters, facilitated the Allied forces' operations and their daily lives in China by socializing with officers and soldiers.[16] Some of the earliest marriages between GIs and Chinese women resulted from these interactions.[17] In addition to official parties, American-educated notables hosted home gatherings and arranged blind dates for the army men.[18] After the war, the Nationalist Government continued to encourage elite women to host or attend victory parties to ensure that American soldiers would find China a hospitable place. The US military also held regular social events in collaboration with local organizations like the YWCA and War Area Service Corps (see Figure 4.2). As the number of "Jeep girls" increased, the group's composition and perception evolved, encompassing more women who did not fit the stereotype of being prostitutes from the lowest rungs of society.

In addition to a clear class divide, regional differences existed in the distribution of Jeep girls, with more Westernized cities being seen as more open to such relations compared to conservative places. As one journalist teased, Allied soldiers in Beijing must be so jealous of their comrades in Shanghai, who never ran out of female companions.[19] Variations notwithstanding, the "Jeep girl" label carried a negative connotation and even became a social stigma. Jeep girls were subject not only to the voyeuristic gaze, media scrutiny, and state control, but also to actual violence. Women seen in public with GIs were rumored to be prostitutes, regardless of the true nature of their interactions, and "the venom of the crowd" was usually "leveled at the girl," who was insulted, threatened, and even attacked.[20] In April 1945, an angry crowd in the wartime capital of Chongqing threw rocks and spat at women visiting cafes and restaurants with American soldiers, pulled their hair, and hurled curses at them.[21] Mobs in Chongqing, Chengdu, Kunming, and Guiyang targeted

Figure 4.2 American soldiers socializing with Chinese women in postwar Qingdao. MCHD.

women accompanying GIs in public, resulting in Chiang Kai-shek's order to ban local newspapers' "agitative reporting of 'Jeep girls.'"[22] In November 1946, outside a Shanghai cafe, a US Navy soldier and his Eurasian girlfriend were attacked by a local crowd wielding blackjacks and clubs. The assault occurred after the couple refused to buy flowers from two flower girls. The girlfriend suffered abrasions and contusions to her face and head, while the soldier only had minor contusions. According to him, the mob included both the "coolie class and upper class Chinese." The two Chinese police on the corner who saw the incident "made no attempts to help," and even the Chinese MP was "taking sides with the flower girls."[23] In postwar Beijing and Tianjin, American servicemen and Chinese clients, including armed policemen, battled over dance hostesses.[24] The sentiment was clear and simple, as one Chinese officer declared: "I don't want American soldiers to go with Chinese girls!"[25] In 1946, in response to local animosities, General Chen Cheng, chief of the General Staff of the Armed Forces, allegedly banned Chinese women from riding in American Jeeps.[26] The occasional street fights certainly encapsulated the mounting social tensions and made headlines. However, what occupied center stage in the Chinese media was the wholesale malignment of the so-called Jeep girl phenomenon, pertaining to "respectable women's" willingness to fraternize with the Americans.

One distinctive social and representational category – college students – was singled out as the primary target of media attacks.[27] Using various Chinese terms, such as "female college students," "lady of noble birth," and "campus belle and socialite," commentators debated why students from affluent families would aspire to become Jeep girls. One critic claimed that "money is secondary; it is really vanity that harmed them."[28] Another pointed to the corrupting effects of American commodities and lifestyles on Chinese morals; they were "even worse than the Soviet looting of Manchuria."[29] Other lines of criticism were more explicit in unveiling Chinese men's mixed sexual and racial anxieties over those "red-haired wild beasts."[30] One described educated Shanghai women's attraction to Americans as "just like an iron nail towards a magnet" to explain why "the US military has conquered women all over the world," while another retooled a classical poem to mock female students for "spreading their legs wide open."[31] The lure of GIs, in one author's summation, was both physical and material, ranging from the exotic features of curly hair, blue eyes, pale skin, blond body hair, strong limbs, and "tall, big, manly, strong" physique to the material luxuries of perfume, skin powder, lip balm, and US dollars.[32]

These conservative reactions highlighted the perceived danger of the Jeep girl phenomenon: cultural contamination mixed with sexual and racial conquest. One author wryly remarked that mixed-race children, the so-called Jeep babies, were in such demand that charities in Chongqing posted adoption advertisements to make a profit.[33] Another cartoon portrayed a street "auction" scene, in which a Jeep full of babies was surrounded by an enthusiastic crowd, with a front sign proclaiming "'authentic American breed' costs U.S. $100 per head."[34] In reality, the fates of biracial babies could also be grim as they were often subjected to mistreatment by local families, regardless of whether a marriage had taken place. In one extreme case, a twenty-month-old infant suffered a severe beating at the hands of a relative on his mother's side, while his GI father returned home after being discharged and refused to acknowledge the child or send any financial support.[35]

Similar cultural fears and sexual anxieties also existed in other parts of the world, where men resented the sexual rivalry presented by American soldiers, who were deemed "overpaid, oversexed, and over here!"[36] Moreover, these hostile attitudes continued the critiques of "girl students" and "modern women" that had been made in earlier decades, reflecting a persistent Chinese discomfort with rapid Westernization and male intellectuals' identity crisis and anxiety over educated women.[37] While lower-class courtesans were expected to be sexually available, it only became a scandal when "good girls" were in danger of corruption. Late Qing regulators tried to control female students' uniforms with increasing stringency, and critics warned that there was little distinction between girl students looking like prostitutes and prostitutes who dressed like students to incite licentiousness.[38] In 1928, a group of students from Ginling Women's College who visited a cruiser and danced with British soldiers on board were condemned by outraged male students from nearby Nanking University and the public for engaging in a type of lewd, immoral act and causing national humiliation.[39]

In the 1930s, male Chinese elites criticized modern women's superficiality, using terms such as "vain," "parasitic," "indulgent," and "degenerated."[40] Assisted by social conservatives, Chiang Kai-shek's New Life Movement discouraged and even penalized women who "engaged in the 'negative' and 'evil' endeavours of modernity, such as wearing Western-style clothes, purchasing foreign products, or exposing parts of their bodies in public," and promoted a Chinese model of "frugal modernity."[41] As self-appointed enlightened guardians of women and advisors of the nation, reformist intellectuals were concerned with the moral attributes of modern women and saw it as their responsibility to guide women's morals, behaviors, and emancipation.[42] Communists were also critical of what they considered the individualist lifestyle and materialist consumption rampant in Western capitalist society. Their agenda was to transform these women from "parasites of society" into active participants in political movements, achieving true liberation for women. During the war, these different groups converged in their condemnation of the vices of modernity, material pleasure, and moral degeneration. In their view, at a time of national salvation, women should first be patriotic citizens. The representational image of Jeep girls resembled modern girls' shallow appearance, frivolous behavior, and immoral inner qualities. But their scandalous consumption of luxury foreign goods, now unaffordable or inaccessible to most citizens, made them even worse for the national betrayal.

Conservative attacks were quite effective in stigmatizing "Jeep girls," a label that now bore a strong association with prostitutes. But not all critiques were denunciations of Jeep girls alone, and a more nuanced analysis reveals complexities in the critical voices. A fictional admirer wrote "A Farewell Letter to a Jeep Girl" in a Shanghai weekly.

The piece looks like a mockery of the girl, who is full of "exotic stench," kissing an ugly, toad-like foreign soldier and thereby losing the face of "our citizens of the big nation." But quickly the reader realizes that the piece is actually satirizing the Chinese man, who, out of jealousy, threatens to take his own life if the girl does not reply to his letter. He then declares that from now on he will become decadent, and consequently China's revolution will not succeed.[43] An imaginative essay from another Shanghai tabloid begins with a girl's worry that her Allied "darling" is being confined by the MP for his late return to the barrack. But her "love letter" quickly moves on to ask whether he has received this month's pay, as he has promised to buy her more perfume. The letter ends with her Chinglish note, "Tomorrow I still wait you at the door of Cathay Hotel."[44] In both cases, the main target of mockery is in fact the man.

Modern urban men had long expressed paradoxical feelings toward Chinese women, from hidden voyeuristic desires for new female students in the late Qing period whose new dress and public presence they also criticized, to the mixture of longing for and fear of the modern girl in the 1920s and 1930s.[45] Visual representations act out imaginary social scenes and capture such ambivalences. In Chinese illustrations, Jeep girls appear Westernized in their clothing, hairstyle, makeup, and accessories, as if they adorn the latest Hollywood movie poster. Even their physical features are often exaggerated, mimicking the perceived sexy white body.[46] Like the modern Chinese women of earlier decades, they invoke sensational spectacles with their scandalous dress, bodies, and behavior in public, with their seductive looks, feet far apart, arms extended, and body exposed.[47] These spectacles are enhanced by the objects that women carry, from high heels and sharp American uniforms to the attendant Jeep and GI. Jeep girls are depicted not in the distant background, but rather occupy the center of the picture, often looming larger than men (see Figures 4.3 and 4.4). The Jeep girl is not the white man's concubine or his laundress, but rather the center of attention that she intentionally draws. She is aware of being a commodity, consumed by the GI, the street man, and the media; she is also a consumer herself, of commodities, modern thrill and pleasure, and the attention and prestige associated with the ride.

Despite the prevalent conservative attacks, the Chinese Jeep girl discussion was once a vibrant intellectual debate over modernity and Westernization in which liberals, leftists, and feminists all participated. Hong Shen, an American-educated writer and professor, attributed the enmity toward Jeep girls to the sensitive nature of sexual relations and common phenomena of xenophobia, a universal "bias towards a foreign race" in the game of love.[48] Dong Shijin, a Cornell University–educated

Modern Women or Parasitic Whores   133

Figure 4.3 "Shanghai characters: Jeep girls," 1946. *Xing guang*.

Figure 4.4 "A tribute to Jeep girls," 1946. *Zhilan huabao*.

agriculturist and educator, encouraged such interactions because "no other bonds are stronger than the marriage bond," and asked why Chinese students or workers abroad could marry foreign women but

Chinese women could not seek foreign husbands.[49] Luo Jialun, a student leader during the May Fourth Movement and later president of Tsinghua University, called for abolishing the frivolous term "Jeep girls," encouraging educated Chinese men and women to interact more with the Americans to help eliminate the current misunderstanding.[50] Such a suggestion was reiterated in an article in *West Wind*, one of the most popular magazines of the time, which introduced in detail American dating culture as well as the idea of formulating a new "formal upper-class social intercourse" in China.[51]

These liberal voices are not included in existing studies of the Jeep girls or, at best, are regarded as pro-government propaganda. Indeed, as will be shown later in this chapter, Chinese officials did try to educate the populace about the American social custom of interacting with women along a similar line, aiming to promote harmonious diplomatic relations. But these defenders spoke out of conflicting ideological and political positions. While some, like Luo Jialun, were anti-Communist officials who might have had the government's agenda on their mind, others, like Hong and Dong, were leftist intellectuals sympathetic to the Communist Party. What they shared was a defense of individual freedom and cultural cosmopolitanism, echoing the liberal avowal of modernity since the New Culture Movement.

Likewise, feminist critics were also divided on the issue. Some were critical of the corrupting effects of Western materialism on women, as Jeep girls' "fat wallets are filled with American dollars, perfumes and powders, authentic chocolates and chewing gums brought by airplanes," and all are "Westernized" and "forget about their black hair."[52] Others, in contrast, linked the Jeep girls with women's liberation, highlighting the gender inequality and systemic oppression explicit in male critiques. For example, one author wrote in the influential leftist magazine *Modern Women* that Jeep girls were cursed by men out of jealousy, and women were blamed as the primary cause of national and racial extinction only because they were easy to bully. The real oppressor here, they argued, was not men in general, but fascism and feudalism.[53] Another opined that Chinese women were always the ones to blame: "Our police did not try to catch the American soldier who rode a Jeep into a coal station causing a big mess, but everywhere looking for the Jeep girl."[54] These feminist commentators shared the common agenda of gender equality. But their varying stances further underlined the ambiguity of the Jeep girls as symbols, as well as the difficulty of choosing sides when it came to these deeply entangled issues of Jeep girls, American soldiers, Western-style modernity, and women's liberation.

"I Am a Jeep Girl"

One might expect complete silence from members of such a marginalized and stigmatized group. But Jeep girls, either so labeled or self-claimed, did speak out, both in words and in action. In 1945, outraged female students from a missionary college in Chengdu smashed a newspaper office that had published a pornographic poem mocking them.[55] In postwar China, some women "instigated GIs to insult Chinese policemen" who were questioning them.[56] More often, women wrote open letters to journals defending themselves in the name of economic necessity or patriotic service to the nation.[57] One college student explained that the majority of her roommates worked as dance hostesses for GIs at night because they needed additional income to pay off loans.[58] Another student attributed working as a Jeep girl to the sacred cause of serving the nation after her family had rejected her plan to join the army.[59] These voices reflect both the harsh material reality of dislocated students during and after the war and some women's ability to co-opt the official Nationalist agenda for their own narratives. Toward the end of the war, Chiang Kai-shek launched a major recruitment campaign, soliciting college students' direct participation in the war effort. While few would see working-class women's hostessing as a sacrifice for the nation, educated women's wartime service using their bodies remained controversial for China's patriarchal nation-building project.[60]

An analysis of two self-identified Jeep girls' accounts may afford us insights into the experiences and thoughts of women who forged connections with American soldiers on various levels.[61] In 1948, *West Wind* published a letter from a university student named Lu Xi, asking whether a Chinese woman could and should marry an American man. She told the story of how she met an American officer on her way home and soon developed a close friendship with him. Afterward, she noticed a drastic change in the attitudes of her male schoolmates toward her: Admiration became finger pointing, with some calling her a Jeep girl. Though her anguish and plight were unsurprising, her candid self-portrait was nonetheless illuminating:

> I am a twenty-one-year-old sophomore in college. I know my body is strong and pretty, not the Lin Daiyu type of frail beauty. I have an outgoing and carefree manner, earning me many male admirers at school.... I do not really like flamboyant clothing. But my clothes are fitting. I keep them tidy and elegant because I do not like to wear flowery clothes to show off. Meanwhile, I do not want to wear non-fitting clothes to cover up my shapely body either. In middle school, I enjoyed sports and music. My body was thus fully grown and spirit pleasantly developed. I have never restrained my breasts, nor do I like to use yellow cream to enhance leg skin color. I let nature take its course in everything. I am quite tall, neither fat nor skinny.[62]

Lu Xi spent the entire first page of her four-page essay describing her own body. She emphasized her natural and healthy beauty, distinguishing herself from both traditional Chinese frail femininity, represented by the iconic character of Lin Daiyu from *Dream of the Red Chamber*, and the highly commercialized modern women's style fashioned by Western cosmetics, makeup, and other commodities. Almost unabashedly flaunting her unbound breasts, shapely physique, and love for sports, she celebrated a body free from both Chinese traditions and Western accessories. This image illustrated a type of ideal modern Chinese woman, healthy and fit, educated and civilized. She was neither traditional Chinese nor superficial Western, but a "real" modern woman.

The idea of a liberated woman's body aligned well with the May Fourth message of freedom and equality. The modern woman's "robust beauty" (*jianmei*) was also promoted by reformist intellectuals and the Nationalist Government through new physical education curricula and mass sports programs.[63] However, Lu Xi's emancipation remained limited. Having acknowledged strong mutual feelings between her and the GI, she insisted that she had kept her "dignity and only allowed hand holding once but no kisses." Neither did she have the courage to confess to her Confucian father about her American boyfriend. Her initial protest that "I do not accept that I belong to any type of Jeep girl" was eventually undermined by the self-questioning that ended the letter: "Am I a Jeep girl?" This question resonated with the dilemma faced by Chinese women in forging a type of "moderate *Chinese* modernity" between "American depravity (glamorous and oh-so-romantic) and the dull prison of Confucian morality."[64] Despite her declaration of possessing a modern body, Lu Xi remained unsure of the subjective position of a Jeep girl.

Unlike Lu Xi, beset by anxiety and hesitancy, Shen Lusha identified herself as a Jeep girl and openly discussed her "desire to be possessed" by her lover, Harry. An English speaker brought up in a middle-class family, she presented herself as the lonely wife of a Nationalist army officer stationed in India and claimed to have met the American pilot through a female friend who was once a dance hostess. In her account, Harry's "greatness" included both his "body and soul" and the wealth of his material goods, including his rations of chocolate, gum, coffee, and milk, as well as American perfume, lip balm, nylon stockings, and Airstep leather shoes. Lusha was quite frank about the convenience and benefit of her using and sometimes selling these goods in the lucrative black market, while declaring her dislike of those women who focused only on money. Having an extramarital affair with a foreign man while her husband was serving the nation abroad certainly made her an easy target. As she put it, she had already paid the price of being ostracized by her family and social circles, and she was even stalked and reported on by local tabloids. But in the end she decided, "My behavior is my own business." Knowing that Harry would be returning to America soon, "all I need is to enjoy my lover even for a month."[65]

Playing on the Chinese variant of carpe diem, Lusha's insistence on enjoying Harry while the affair lasted should be read as intentionally provocative. Her piece was a direct response to an earlier article published in the same journal that ridiculed Jeep girls' attraction to GIs' exotic physical features and material wealth.[66] The journal's intention in publishing her piece was also suspicious. In the accompanying illustration, she was dubbed "Eve of Chongqing," with an unmistakable biblical connotation of seduction, corruption, and danger. Like most pictorial representations of Jeep girls, Eve of Chongqing sported curly hair, full lips, large eyes, a long nose, and a curvy body against a backdrop of department stores, movie theaters, dance halls, and restaurants. Her completely Westernized features, combined with a hedonistic lifestyle and philosophy, moral and sexual decadence, and unrepentant attitude, were supposed to trigger immediate aversion, fear, or discomfort, to say the least. But apparently not all readers felt this way. One female reader responded with praise for "Mrs. Lusha's courage and frankness" in "wanting and daring to love" as "a modern figure"; this reader asked the rhetorical question, "who would not hope for sexual and spiritual satisfaction?"[67]

In fact, in the accounts by these "Jeep girls," American soldiers were often portrayed as boyish, brash, crude, and fresh, like "kindergarten kids," while Chinese women were the sophisticated ones.[68] Remembering her first GI friend who laughed loudly, flirted constantly, and kissed her goodbye without permission, a college student said, "I really don't know what to do with these over-innocent country bumpkins."[69] These impressions might be informed by stereotypes that had long existed in Sino-US relations, metaphors such as China being the old civilization and the American nation like a young man. But their observations were not without merit: The majority of the soldiers they encountered had grown up in America's working-class suburbs or rural areas and many were indifferently educated and parochial, whereas some of the Chinese women actually hailed from families of wealth and privilege and had been educated at prestigious English-language schools.[70] Such a dynamic was not exclusive to China. Women across the globe described American soldiers in similar language, as being childish, impetuous, boastful, and flamboyant, prone to talk big, and fond of chasing after girls and spoiling them, making the GIs more attractive.[71]

Like the modern girls who emerged around the world in the interwar period, Chinese city girls had learned English, dance, and skating; consumed Hollywood movies, jazz music, stockings, and cigarettes; increasingly dressed according to the latest American fashions; and became conspicuously visible in public spaces.[72] They now met the real Yanks in movie theaters, dance clubs, and roller-skating rinks and at other events hosted by the government, the US military, and organizations like the YMCA and YWCA. American dating was a foreign concept and an adventure, and American dollars and products made these war heroes even more appealing in a time of postwar material dearth.[73] As in other regions around the world, in China, GIs were in demand for their sacrifice during the war, possession of material goods, and embodiment of the modern West. Meanwhile, such attractions also revealed prevailing racial and sexual perceptions and fantasies about American men. One woman described her GI dance partners as having "blue eyes, blond hair, and long nose," like "animals liberated from the lonely desert," "thirsty for new things."[74] Another said she was attracted to her lover's red hair, thick eyebrows, straight tall nose, short beard, and handsome and strong body, better than any Chinese man, reminding her of a fictional medieval European knight or Douglas Fairbanks Jr. on the silver screen.[75] Through popular magazines, movies, and real-life interactions, Chinese women encountered American men, whom many saw as more romantic, chivalrous, and attractive than their Chinese counterparts.

The limited voices from Jeep girls show a level of agency that has not been taken into account in previous studies of Sino-US encounters. These women fought conservative accusations, justified their relationships with foreign white men in the language of individual freedom and patriotism, and presented themselves as enlightened modern women. Some used their romantic encounters with GIs to explore social and sexual freedom, which was largely restricted by traditional moral codes or the new conservative gender norms of the Nanjing decade. Others defied Orientalist fantasies about Chinese women popularized in Hollywood movies, such as bound-feet concubines or sexualized dolls. And yet most did not want to be called Jeep girls and insisted these interactions were romantic rather than materially driven; many who had actual romantic relationships or even married GIs did so quietly. Thanks to the GI War Brides Act of 1945 and the War Fiancées Act of 1946, Chinese women were able to enter the United States in large numbers for the first time. However, most of the more than five thousand women admitted between 1945 and 1950 did not marry white soldiers. Instead, they reunited with Chinese American veterans, many of whom they had met or married long before the war.[76] In November 1947, *South China*

Morning Post reported an all-time record for new marriages in Hong Kong, as Chinese American ex-servicemen were in a hurry to tie the knot by the end of the year, believing the War Brides Act would soon come to an end.[77] These veterans included both Chinese Americans who were born and raised in America and recent Chinese students who joined the US military while studying in the country. There were exceptions, including the high-profile marriage between Chen Xiangmei, also known as Anna Chennault, and General Claire Lee Chennault, the acclaimed leader of the "Flying Tigers" in China. Despite their elite status, their marriage was deemed illegal in the general's home state of Louisiana. As a result, the general had his will probated in Washington, DC, instead, to ensure its legal recognition and validity.[78]

"China Doll" or "Chinese Rot": GIs' Views of Chinese Women

China Doll
When memories dim, and fade, and soften
Our hard years in the army,
We'll think about the coolie often –
More often still, the warmie.
  – A. L. Crouch, *China Sketchbook: A Book of Army Verse*, 1946[79]

And take to heart the words in the section on Sanitation about disease.
The wine and the women are both loaded.
Stick to song.
  – *A Marine's Guide to North China*, 1945[80]

World War II extended the size and reach of American power around the world, enabling its access to local women "ranging from marriage to prostitution, and a range of relations and interactions in between."[81] The rich corpus of studies on the American military has demonstrated the significant role of sex in reconfiguring the postwar power structure in both domestic and international contexts.[82] Hierarchies of gender, race, and class informed attitudes, policies, and practices on both sides that can be traced to earlier imperial traditions and colonial institutions. Old patterns of cultural bias and racial discrimination continued to structure the asymmetrical power relations between America and other nations, whether defeated, newly independent, or Allied, and deeply shaped GIs' daily interactions with local societies.[83] These resemblances reveal the imperialist origins of the American empire, on the one hand, and the intimate links between military prostitution and sexual violence, on the other, which often transcend political agendas and military objectives.

As Cynthia Enloe argues, such "militarized masculinity" enabled specific kinds of sexual encounters in the shadow of military presence, promoted the image of a hypermasculine soldier, and legitimized the military's supportive attitudes toward prostitution and lack of disciplinary actions against sexual violence.[84]

Upon landing, most American soldiers had only a foggy idea of China. As former army officer William W. Lockwood recalled, back home, China meant "the end of the world," "a lonely laundryman down the street, an occasional bowl of chow mein, a headline with unpronounceable names in the evening paper."[85] Army soldiers in the CBI Theater had been looking forward to girls in China long before stepping on the soil; prostitution in India was a routine recreation set up by the US military, which soldiers felt entitled to.[86] For officer Elmo Zumwalt Jr., the initial experience of entering the city of Shanghai included "a bevy of young girls" who "threw themselves on the car shouting, 'Hey Joe, Meg Wa (American) can do for free,'" being "a fitting tribute to the amorous generosity of the prewar U.S. sailor."[87] Marine veterans of the Pacific War were thrilled to learn of their new mission in China, rather than in Japan, because of their knowledge of the US Marine Corps' historical ties and of what China missions usually entailed.[88] If the leathernecks had supposedly "enjoyed a reputation with the Chinese" since the nineteenth century, according to General DeWitt Peck, China also had a positive reputation among them.[89] Senior members passed down their wisdom about what the decadent East could offer, from affordable and easily available entertainment in cosmopolitan cities to hospitable locals and light military tasks. But they also gave timely warnings. "I knew that venereal disease hits the white man harder than it probably does anyone else," said General William Worton, referring to various diseases that could not be cured by Western medicine, malaises conveniently dubbed "Chinese Rot" and "Chinese Crud."[90]

Besides peer wisdom and popular knowledge, military publications were another major source of GI education. Special China guides repeatedly informed soldiers that the Chinese were "much more reserved," especially in relationships: Except in a limited circle in Tianjin and Beijing, "You just don't have dates, you don't go to social dances, and parties with girls are few and far between."[91] The term "cultural differences" was often used to account for friction over sexual relations and became a convenient catch-all that trivialized conflicts, freeing GIs from any responsibility. In his memorandum to Chiang Kai-shek, General Wedemeyer, who commanded US forces in China from 1944 to 1946, attributed criticisms of GI misbehavior to different social customs and protested against the Chinese term "Jeep girls," emphasizing Americans' high respect for Chinese women.[92] Meanwhile, in official guides, these "reserved" people were also said to be warm and attractive, like "the modern Chinese girl, in her long, closely fitting gown, her bare arms and short hair."[93] Military publications and popular media continued to perpetuate the image of hypersexualized Oriental women in erotic bodies, with racially and sexually charged stereotypes commonly plugged in official publications like *North China Marine* and *Yanks*.[94] During WWII, American soldiers were seen as "red-blooded men" whose sex drive could only be channeled, not suppressed. The media promoted images of (over)sexualized women to motivate soldiers in their liberation missions, and "pinups" were developed to a new level. This hypermasculine culture within the military induced sexual promiscuity and aggression and profoundly changed its young white soldiers.[95]

Overall, when it came to Chinese women, the US armed forces had conflicting messages for its troops: They were both memorable "warmies" and dangerous carriers of diseases. Race informed how the military managed sexual relations with local women and affected how servicemen related to them. Since the nineteenth century, Asian women had been linked to the duality of lure and danger, such as the self-sacrificing Madame Butterfly and the devious Dragon Lady stereotypes. The ultimate embodiment of the Yellow Peril, they entrapped white men with sex and drugs, seducing them into a life of obscenity and violence and endangering the white race by giving birth to racially mixed children.[96] The assorted racial stereotypes and sexual fantasies were best represented in the supporting characters that the likes of Anna May Wong played on the big screen in the 1920s and 1930s, images of women as exotic and erotic, cunning and cruel.[97] Many politicians and even medical professionals in the late nineteenth century believed that Chinese immigrants carried distinct germs that would be transmitted to white men through Chinese prostitutes, leading to the Page Act of 1875, the first restrictive immigration law in the United States, which effectively prevented the entry of Chinese women.[98] The subsequent Chinese Exclusion Act of 1882, which prohibited all immigration of Chinese laborers, was not repealed until 1943, when an annual quota of 105 was set for Chinese immigration. Until after WWII, most US states enforced a range of "antimiscegenation" laws that prohibited intermarriage between individuals deemed white and those of other races, particularly black or Chinese. These laws began to be modified by postwar legislation such as the War Brides Act of 1945 or overturned at the state level, but were not invalidated at the federal level until the 1960s. Within these legal confines, Chinese brides faced persistent racial discrimination and continuing immigration restrictions in America.[99]

As the Chinese changed from inadmissible aliens to wartime allies after Pearl Harbor, a more positive China image emerged thanks to American propaganda. Chinese women now included modern, educated, English-speaking, and Christian women represented by Madame Chiang Kai-shek, as well as kind, hardworking, and resilient peasant women like those depicted in Pearl S. Buck's novel *The Good Earth*.[100] However, the seductive and dangerous Oriental woman by no means disappeared from the American psyche. Military guides advised a GI Joe to stay away from the traditional solaces of "wine and women," for both were "loaded."[101] Through the prism of an ordinary American soldier, the army newspaper *Stars and Stripes* cautioned soldiers on the various Chinese women in the entertainment industries, such as "the bar girl known as Lou" who made the GI act "like a fool" and spend all his nine-month pay in one night at the bar.[102] Even Madame Chiang, who conquered Congress with her Wellesley-educated eloquence, could not completely shed the shadow of the Dragon Lady.[103] The mixed messages about Chinese women existed in parallel with the overall American view of China: a new and modern democratic nation as an ally, on the one hand, and a conservative and corrupt country requiring mentorship, guidance, and even occupation, on the other.

For marine veterans who saw civilization for the first time after years of hardship, "women came second," only after fresh, non-GI food.[104] Soon, some soldiers complained about the limited opportunities for dating due to China's conservative social atmosphere. The first group of 221 army wives did not arrive in China until September 18, 1946, while the first group of marine wives arrived about two months earlier. Dependents made up approximately 10 percent and 20 percent of American navy and marine personnel throughout China in September 1947 and January 1948, respectively.[105] Some officers dated white women, including expatriates from both Allied and enemy nations.[106] Jewish officer Lou Glist, who was assigned to oversee the approval of marriages between GIs and foreigners, observed that American soldiers were highly sought after. He noted that some women in Shanghai were willing to pay GIs several thousand dollars for what they saw as a ticket to the "promised land," leading to a phenomenon of "marriages of convenience" arranged "strictly for financial gain."[107] More commonly, however, China was "experiencing the exuberance of soldiers and sailor unleashed," as the "dissipation of money, energy and sperm, accumulated over these many months away from home, has excited sellers of all sorts of merchandise."[108] American military pay was undoubtedly attractive in war-torn China, which was filled with refugees and prostitutes. During and after the war, commanding officers and soldiers openly frequented brothels and brought women back to the barracks.[109] At the beginning of the occupation mission, General Worton requested that 1 million condoms be shipped.[110] When one private reported he was "always unexposed," his officer scoffed with a questioning, "I do not believe that. Aren't you a man?"[111] Decades later, one commander admitted in an interview that there was "all kinds of misbehavior" and "it was not America at its best."[112]

In contrast with Japan and Korea, where the US military relied on regulated military prostitution, there was no separate system for GIs in China. In the middle of the civil war, a camp town structure as adopted by its Asian neighbors would certainly threaten the Nationalist regime's claims of sovereignty, legitimacy, and new status as a world leader. Instead, US troops were located in the very center of Chinese cities and relied on existing systems of prostitution, sharing space and competing with local customers. As in Japan and Korea, the American military made halfhearted efforts to contain venereal disease. Prior to their arrival in China, marines had been shown educational videos about the dangers of venereal disease. To ensure soldiers' health, the MPs labeled hotels, nightclubs, and dance halls "In-Bounds" and "Out-of-Bounds" and occasionally raided brothels and hotels. Some commanding officers asked soldiers to be inspected and take prophylactics upon their return after liberty.[113] But in general, regulations over prostitution remained loose, and no punishments were enforced as long as exposures and infections were reported. The wonder drug penicillin provided a safety net for soldiers on the ground, and how they spent their liberty time was "one of complete tolerance."[114] Regarding local collaboration, the military took an inconsistent approach. On the one hand, it pressured the Chinese government to ban unauthorized brothels and control the rampant problem of venereal diseases among prostitutes. On the other hand, it requested local authorities' cooperation to satisfy soldiers' material, physical, and sexual needs, such as tax exemptions on restaurant and bar checks and the opening of special entertainment sites for servicemen, despite existing local bans or restrictions on cabarets and nightclubs.[115]

Officially, military publications like *A Pocket Guide to China* and *A Marine's Guide to North China* were meant to prepare a young GI for his new mission in the foreign land. They instructed him to distinguish between "the average Chinese girl," who "will be insulted if you touch her, or will take you more seriously than you probably want to be taken," and "Chinese girls in cabarets and places of amusement who may be used to free and easy ways."[116] These nuggets of wisdom were confusing and impractical at best, if not misleading; their language mixed danger and attraction. In reality, the pronounced respect for Chinese women and harmonious relations often came to naught because of excessive consumption of alcohol, cultural arrogance, racial discrimination, and, ultimately, a toxic military culture that allowed or even enabled systemic tolerance. Americans' long-term racism toward the Chinese had a powerful impact on GIs' perceptions of their mission in the country and their attitudes toward the locals. American servicemen's descriptions of Chinese women and China at large, from commanders to soldiers, showed not only a feeling of national superiority, but also an enduring colonial mentality.

The Peking Rape Incident and the End of Jeep Girls

> I am a quintessential nationalist when it comes to sexual relations, and I cannot bear to see our beautiful female compatriots being trampled by foreign bastards ... if I had tens of millions in gold, I would buy some white slaves for the enjoyment of Chinese rickshaw pullers, coolies, and menial workers!
>
> – Yu Dafu, *Suzhou yanyu ji* [*Suzhou in a misty rain*], 1923[117]

The actual and imagined romance between Chinese women and American GIs coexisted with the harsh reality of sexual violence toward women from all walks of life. On November 1, 1945, two working-class girls in Shanghai narrowly escaped assault by two GIs and one sailor, who stabbed local policemen with knives. The assailants fled only after spotting a group of Chinese soldiers stationed nearby, "armed with pistols, rifles and Thompson sub-machine guns." They happened to be members of the American-equipped New 6th Army, famed for their training and heroism in fighting the Japanese.[118] On September 1, 1946, a civil servant's wife in the capital of Nanjing was chased by GIs on her way home from a late show, where she was raped outdoors and sustained injuries.[119] On August 1, 1947, a factory worker in Qingdao was gang-raped by four American servicemen and pushed down a hill after they had driven away her eleven-year-old son, who had been calling desperately for help.[120] On August 7, 1948, an orchestrated gang rape took place at the end of a farewell dance party in Wuhan, perpetrated mostly by American merchants and officers.[121]

These seemingly isolated incidents show a familiar pattern: drunken soldiers on liberty seeking pleasure and behaving badly, followed by the American military's disappointing legal maneuvers and inconsistent compensation policies. Even major American media acknowledged the severity of the problem and its impact on bilateral relations. On October 13, 1946, a *New York Times* correspondent reported a public statement by Zhang Dongsun, a renowned philosophy professor and leader of the liberal "third force." Zhang condemned American servicemen for being guilty of "drunkenness, gambling, seeking women, smuggling, illegal sale of government properties, robbery, manhandling, killing through reckless driving, insulting and violating Chinese women."[122] Despite numerous official complaints and public warnings of this nature, the US military's response was dismissive, with Lieutenant General Alvan C. Gillem calling them mere political propaganda. Also in October, Nathaniel Peffer, a veteran China journalist and then a professor at Columbia University, wrote a memo at the request of Ambassador Leighton Stuart. In it, he pointed out that "for the first time America begins to occupy a new role in Chinese thought, and it is a role that denotes a loss of moral prestige."[123] By the end of the year, when the American left-wing magazine *Amerasia* warned "GI Welcome Wears Out in China" and "American policy in China is transforming our soldiers into ambassadors of ill-will," a new type of anti-American sentiment was fermenting, a portent that a serious incident was about to break.[124]

On Christmas Eve 1946, Peking University student Shen Chong was raped by an intoxicated Corporal William Gaither Pierson, assisted by Private Warren Pritchard. On her way to watch a Hollywood wartime romance, the nineteen-year-old encountered the two marines, who proceeded to "escort" her to a nearby freezing-cold open field in downtown Beijing and held her there for three hours until she was rescued by the patrolling Joint Office Sino-American Police. In the wake of the rape, accumulated Chinese anger exploded. On December 30, a large number of university students in Beijing joined a demonstration against the reported rape, and the protest quickly expanded nationwide to more than twenty-five cities (see Figure 4.5).[125] Like the earlier incident involving the killing of rickshaw puller Zang Yaocheng, protesters demanded apologies from the American military, punishment of the perpetrators, and the complete withdrawal of US forces from China. A general court-martial held in Beijing found Pierson guilty of rape and sentenced him to fifteen years of confinement in January 1947. But the verdict was overturned by the Judge Advocate General of the US Navy in June, a recommendation approved by the Acting Secretary of the Navy in August. Pierson was exonerated, an outcome that led to further demonstrations.

Ultimately, such legal injustice was enabled by the system of extraterritoriality that granted the United States exclusive military jurisdiction over its service members in China. Furthermore, American rape law at the time demanded that women's physical struggles must be corroborated by medical evidence or witness testimonies, and proving rape was a burden that women had to carry.[126] The court-martial in Beijing, though

Figure 4.5 Tsinghua University students protesting "American brutalities" in Beijing, January 1947. *Lianhe huabao*.

appearing transparent, objective, and fair, actually revealed deep-seated prejudices against the Chinese as well as pervasive suspicions of women in rape cases, both within the American military and the wider society.[127] Before the trial, one marine officer expressed fear that if Shen received compensation, many "girls of loose morals" who associated with GIs would cry rape. During the trial, the defendant questioned Shen's plan for filing claims for compensation. After the initial guilty verdict, many marines in China thought the sentence was unfair, as Pierson had had too much liquor and mistook Shen for a prostitute; he was only a political scapegoat.[128] One GI captured the prevailing mentality: "We put our arms around the girls' shoulders, thinking, as their attitude implied, that they were just friendly street girls," until the girls' crying brought a group of Chinese police and soldiers.[129] Never did it occur to these marines that sexual violence was more than a mere verbal mix-up, an innocent cultural misunderstanding, or a simple "mistake" that could "cause a lot of trouble."[130] Military authorities had long maintained distrust of "ill-intentioned" foreign women trying to take advantage of innocent American boys abroad, seeing them as prostitutes, gold diggers, or alleged rape victims for American government compensation. Many commanders believed that sexual violence was unavoidable, and even General Wedemeyer seemed puzzled as to why this incident had caused such

The Peking Rape Incident and the End of Jeep Girls 147

a big stir.[131] Facing violence on the street and injustice in court, women like Shen Chong had little chance of winning. Her elite family background and educational status might have made her case a national headline in China.[132] But they did not shield her from the trauma of sexual violence or the injustice of the American legal system, infused with racist biases and intricately linked to the military's systemic tolerance of sexual promiscuity and misbehavior.

Despite the victimization of Chinese women, both the Nationalist and Communist Parties prioritized the student protests and political campaigns, disregarding women's experience in their own hegemonic nationalist discourses. The Nationalist Government insisted that the Peking rape was merely an isolated event caused by a drunk low-ranking soldier, in sync with the usual rhetorical strategy of the American military. Further, Chiang Kai-shek called the student protests a result of "instigation by the evil Party" and instructed his officials to attack the Communists rather than address the underlying issues.[133] This was a consistent approach from May 1945, when disturbances over "Jeep girls" in Chongqing were said to be "promoted by 'enemies and traitors,'" with government propagandas accusing Japanese collaborators and Communists for spreading rumors to create Sino-US friction.[134] In the ensuing months after the rape, the Ministries of Foreign Affairs and Education handled diplomatic and student affairs with much trepidation, and both directly reported to Chiang and the Executive Yuan on their progress. Local officials, tasked with controlling demonstrations, resorted to closely monitoring student protesters, occasionally leading to arrests and injuries.[135] Meanwhile, the Nationalist Government launched a propagandistic counter campaign portraying "Soviets' atrocities" in Manchuria as much worse. Pro-government student groups openly confronted the protestors and accused Shen Chong of being a Communist agent.[136] Ultimately, in the regime's desire for harmonious Sino-US relations, there was no place for victims of sexual violence.

Since wartime, the Nationalist Government had faced a dilemma in dealing with such sexual matters: On the one hand, it called on women to practice informal diplomacy and be good hosts, while on the other hand, it persistently promoted a conservative gender ideology. Like the US military, it also tried unsuccessfully to downplay GI sexual misbehavior, framing it as a cultural problem or an isolated legal incident. During the 1945 crisis involving Jeep girls, for example, the mayor of Chongqing lectured the community on American values concerning freedom and public interactions of the two sexes.[137] Anticipating social tensions with the arrival of new American forces after the war, the Nationalist Government distributed "Guiding Principles for Enhancing US-China

Military-Civilian Relations" to local administrations. The pamphlet took pains to explain the cultural distinctions between the two countries, especially how the two genders interact, urging that locals "should not make a fuss about Americans dancing with Chinese women, a common practice for them, and the act should not be seen as promiscuous."[138] While China's official ideology on gender relations remained conservative for decades, the desire to make US troops "feel at home" created an urgent need to educate its people on American customs, especially those connected to the sense of tactility. This also led to ambiguous and even contradictory policies. For instance, the Nationalist Government had attempted to control prostitution and even ban cabarets in the previous two decades, though inconsistently and ineffectively.[139] During the war, general orders prohibited dancing, yet large dance parties were still organized for American troops, who also frequently held their own events.[140] After the war, the government continued to shut down and limit commercial dance halls in newly liberated areas. But exceptions were made to accommodate American guests' needs, with many establishments kept open or reserved exclusively for GIs, barring local entry. Hampered by such conflicting goals and legal restrictions in prosecuting American servicemen, the Nationalists tolerated GIs' sexual promiscuity and denied or trivialized their sexual violence, an approach that eventually backfired. To many of its critics and supporters alike, the regime failed in its mission to protect women and defend the nation. As an ally that had helped win the war, the Chinese had high expectations for the American "liberators," which were drastically different from those of their East Asian neighbors. They also had renewed hopes for their own government, which had been actively promoting the new image of China as one of the "Big Four" nations in the world.

In contrast, the Communists were determined to turn the case into nothing but a political matter of American imperialism, intensifying their propaganda campaign amidst the escalating civil war. Party leaders in Yan'an instructed local organs in Nationalist-controlled cities to actively participate in demonstrations and blamed the Chiang Kai-shek regime for encouraging the American military's continued presence through "secret treaties." The goal was to lead the mass movement in the direction of isolating America and Chiang and resisting American attempts to colonize China.[141] Notably, the timing of the incident was perfect for the launch of a larger anti-American, anti-Chiang movement, part of Mao Zedong's major strategy of "opening the Second Battlefield." The rape occurred the day before the new constitution was formally passed in the National Assembly. Chiang had convened the Assembly in November 1946, but both the CCP and the Democratic League refused to participate, deeming it a facade rather than a genuine representation of coalition and democratization.[142] While maximizing anti-American sentiments inflamed by the rape, the CCP called for the withdrawal of US troops, protested against American aid to the Nationalists during the ongoing civil war, and opposed American interference in China's internal affairs. Not unlike the Nationalists, who used the case to fire at the enemy, the CCP also sought to leverage the situation for its own agenda and did not view the incident as a women's issue.

To the surprise of many, including the Communists, the protest movement following the Peking rape attracted a wide range of support among urban residents, from outspoken leftist and liberal intellectuals to businessmen, government officials, and American professors in China who expressed sympathy or participated in the protest.[143] The case caused nationwide uproar and received supporting letters from overseas Chinese communities in Southeast Asia and America. Popular grievances against GI misbehavior had been accumulating since wartime. But none of the other American "atrocities" led to the same level of public outcry as the Peking rape case, including the two aforementioned cases: the killing of rickshaw puller Zang Yaocheng in Shanghai and the gang rape of dance girls and middle-class wives in Wuhan.[144] Effective Communist organization certainly contributed to the success of the Anti-Brutality movement. But more importantly, gendered nationalist sentiments brought together a variety of groups across geographical and ideological divides. Sex inflamed patriotic passions and provided an emotional bond to all, transforming a private matter into a national event overnight, while race and class provided the principal framing for viewing the incident.

University students, more than 80 percent of whom were male, largely cast Shen Chong as a "virtuous elite woman." Replying to an American provocation that Chinese soldiers also committed rape, the students said bluntly, "They bothered only the peasants and did not molest intellectuals."[145] A Tsinghua University student denounced GIs as being armed with American dollars, emasculating Chinese officials, and corrupting urban women.[146] Women's groups actively participated in the movement, albeit following the overall male-dominated nationalist agenda. Female students' organizations highlighted Shen's special status as a "holy university student," different from prostitutes who asked for it and housewives who, despite enduring multiple assaults, did "not have the strength to resist."[147] Newspaper commentators attributed American soldiers' misbehavior to racial discrimination and "colonialist mentality." Some questioned why a white person who raped a Chinese woman could walk free, while black rapists of white women in America faced the death penalty, noting that "Shen Chong was not black."[148] Others challenged the notion of "American justice," asking whether the outcome would be the same if a man with "yellow face" had raped a white woman, and pointing out that the Chinese were not "slaves living in America's black slums."[149] A long-standing Chinese racial discourse on barbaric "foreign devils" also found its way into the new rhetoric, calling them beastly "red-haired bandits," and shouting, "Go home – American devils, beasts, and drunken soldiers!"[150] Overall, critics directly juxtaposed the rape, a national shame, with China's honor of being a victor of WWII.[151] In these representations, in which Shen and China were violated by aggressive foreign soldiers, Chinese sovereignty was understood and defined in highly gendered terms shaped by prevailing hierarchies of class and race.

In its "Guiding Principles" concerning the social interactions of GIs with local women, the Nationalist Government advised its people not to "treat American servicemen with an 'inferiority complex or discriminative mindset.'"[152] This directive captured the mixed sentiments and somewhat paradoxical attitudes prevalent among the Chinese. On the one hand, Chinese officials and intellectuals were highly sensitive to and critical of American racism. Visitors from China almost never failed to report the prevalent racial issues in American society, especially discrimination against the Chinese. Similarly, Chinese coworkers of American military personnel in China frequently voiced resentment at being treated as inferiors. As one interpreter noted, even someone like him, who had always "worshipped American civilization," was shocked by the racism displayed by GIs, including Chinese American soldiers who adopted the racist attitudes of white men and acted even worse.[153] Another administrative staff member felt that American pity toward China – whether stemming from sympathy or mockery – was the most emotionally difficult attitude for him to endure as it showed how inferior his nation was.[154]

On the other hand, China had its own biases, and society at large was wary of GIs' intimate relations with Chinese women. Street mobs attacked women seen in public with GIs, and many elite families forbade their daughters from dating or marrying foreigners. According to an American army officer, Chiang Kai-shek refused to allow black troops in postwar China because of "his fear of miscegenation," believing "the white soldier already excited the Chinese enough."[155] An old China hand put it more bluntly: "The upper-class Chinese are racists," calling themselves the "Central Kingdom," and although "you will never hear it said," they "feel that unlimited social contact between their women and us, for example, could lead eventually to a mixture of the races."[156] If the controversy surrounding Jeep girls merely simmered with these paradoxical attitudes, they converged and erupted with intense fever after the nineteen-year-old Peking University girl student was raped by a white soldier who ended up walking free.

Casting China as a victimized young elite woman was a powerful nationalist trope that enabled the Communists to successfully propagate their political message of American imperialism, muffling and eventually replacing earlier intellectual debates over modernity and Westernization. After the Peking rape incident, sexual relations with American soldiers ceased to be a heated topic for serious intellectual debate or social gossip, and instead became a political battleground in the civil war. There was little coverage of Jeep girls in popular periodicals or tabloids that had previously published editorials, readers' letters, op-eds, and sensational news related to the topic. Earlier defenders of Jeep girls became silent or turned into outspoken critics of the American military. For example, Hong Shen, then a professor at Fudan University, publicly supported the protests and clashed with pro-government students.[157] The Huang brothers, known for introducing Western culture and ideas to China through the popular journal *West Wind*, participated in the Anti-Brutality movement.[158] This reflected the larger political atmosphere of the late 1940s, when many Western-educated intellectuals grew increasingly skeptical of American claims to justice and liberalism. If sexual romance with the Americans had already triggered the conservatives' fear of white soldiers in China and attacks on Jeep girls, the lack of justice shook the liberals' belief in the American system and certainly put them in a difficult position to defend Jeep girls. As one prominent legal scholar asked, how can America use liberalism to lead the world while not even trying to maintain basic legal justice?[159] While Chinese intellectuals had been enticed by the American ideals of democracy, freedom, and self-determination for more than a century, some now felt betrayed by its realpolitik, such as assisting a corrupt government despite neutrality claims, prolonging the civil war and Chinese people's suffering, and what Communists called the imperialist intervention into Chinese affairs.[160] Amid this hypernationalist attitude toward sexual relations with American "beasts," Chinese women could exist only as rape victims or prostitutes. There was little actual or symbolic space left for the modern Jeep girls, some of whom previously could speak for themselves, albeit in a limited way. Women's sovereignty over their bodies was now displaced by exclusive claims of nationhood by elite men and the ascending Communist Party, which would soon take over the entire country and the destiny of Chinese womanhood.[161]

Shadow of Jeep Girls

On November 5, 1986, the US Navy returned to China for the first time in nearly four decades, docking for a week-long port call in Qingdao. As the navy band played "Happy Days Are Here Again," one thousand sailor-ambassadors were issued a thirty-two-page booklet titled "A Sailor's Liberty Guide to China." The guide "admonished them not to pursue Chinese women or drink too much." During interviews occasioned by this visit, an elderly local man reflected on past interactions, noting that some US sailors and marines had "left an extremely bad impression" after 1945. A younger shipyard worker, who was barely two years old when the last marines departed, also commented that the Americans back then "grabbed women and didn't follow traffic signs."[162]

Sexual dynamics, whether fraternization or violence, deeply shaped Chinese perceptions of the American military presence and formulations of anti-American narratives. Nationalism is a gendered discourse, entailing both gender power within a nation and gendering of different nations. Scholars have long shown the intimate connections between masculinity and nationalism and how the production of new national identities relies on gendered constructions.[163] As WWII drew to a close, China's revival included the reclaiming of both masculinity and sovereignty. Facing the American military, a hypermasculine institution, citizens projected their collective sexual, racial, and cultural anxieties onto the bodies of women as symbols of nationhood. Elite women, particularly university students, became a cultural fixture of desire and derision and a key arena of power contestations between genders, parties, and nations. Chinese women were divided between the Jeep girl, the fallen woman causing racial and cultural contamination, on the one hand, and the rape victim of a white soldier, the symbolic bearer of the violated nation, on the other. Such gendered nationalist discourses, however, rarely take into account women's diverse experiences and their interests, but rather further subordinate them to masculine domination. As Enloe has pointed out, "nationalism typically has sprung from masculinized memory, masculinized humiliation and masculinized hope."[164] Conservatives and the Nationalist Government portrayed women as frugal and virtuous dependents as well as patriotic pawns for promoting harmonious Sino-US relations. Communists targeted American imperialism for its assistance to the Chiang Kai-shek regime and were equally hostile to the Jeep girls. As such, women remained voiceless, and their stories continued to be filtered through patriarchal nationalist agendas. They were victims of both the US military's hypersexualized and racist culture and China's domestic party politics.

As the American military occupation became bygone history in the People's Republic of China, memories of Jeep girls and the Peking rape endured. In Lao She's famous 1957 play *Teahouse*, American soldiers appeared as villains on the streets of postwar Beijing, together with Nationalist spies and local hooligans who wanted to corral all dance hostesses, prostitutes, waitresses, and Jeep girls to establish a grand syndicate to serve the Americans.[165] During the Cultural Revolution, individuals were forced to play the roles of landlords, Jeep girls, reactionary politicians, and conspiracists in public struggle sessions, enduring humiliation and torture.[166] Shen Chong, who had adopted a new name, identity, and path, was also abused by the Red Guards, ironically, because of her alleged fraternization with American soldiers.[167] Mao's wife, Jiang Qing, who was in charge of creating new revolutionary arts, removed a scene from the propagandistic movie *Sea Eagle* (*Hai ying*). The scene depicted a People's Liberation Army officer driving a Jeep with his wife, which Jiang criticized for depicting a "Jeep girl" style.[168] Madame Mao denounced Jeep girls as prostitutes for foreigners and claimed she had once slapped someone who suggested she should become one.[169] In Communist propaganda and literature, the Jeep girls remained stigmatized, and their portraits were deeply shaped by new political agendas in the Cold War era.

Whore or victim? The dichotomous portrayal of Chinese women reveals how their experiences were marginalized in hegemonic nationalist historiographies. In contemporary China, gendered nationalist discourse, deeply ingrained with racism, sexism, and classism, continues to play a prominent role in national and international politics. The trope of Jeep girls morphed into other forms as miscegenation fears persisted in the presence of foreign men, stoking national pride.[170] Meanwhile, the prototype of the Chinese female victim continued to be invoked during periods of Sino-US tensions. Upon entering the Korean War, the Communist Party launched another successful propaganda campaign against American imperialists, featuring the Peking rape incident on the front pages of publications decrying the Americans' "brutalities" and "beastly behavior" in China.[171] Even recent publications highlight scenes of Chinese girls being chased by "monstrous Jeeps" among all the other unforgettable "victory experiences" of 1945.[172] Accompanied by the menacing specter of the GI rapist, the shadow of the Jeep girls continues to loom large and unsettling.

5 Entangled Goods
American Charms and Harms

> Americans come, there is bread and freedom; Soviets come, there is bread but no freedom; Communists come, there is no bread, no freedom.
>
> – Hu Shi[1]

> A noble child is completely fed and raised on American products. From the moment when he is born, assisted by a midwife wearing American-made gloves, to his death, he does not need to eat a grain of rice grown by Chinese farmers, nor wear a piece of cloth woven by Chinese peasants. What he eats are imported milk powder, fish oil, vitamin ABCD, and all kinds of canned food. What he dons are foreign wool sweaters, suits, and jackets.
>
> – *Xinmin wanbao* (*Xinmin Evening News*), February 21, 1947[2]

As exemplified by the first epigraph often attributed to Hu Shi – though likely by mistake – pro-American elites echoed the views of the acclaimed leader of Chinese liberalism, lauding the country's material progress and postwar aid to China, along with its political and economic systems. At the same time, leftists warned against the pervasive American influence on Chinese everyday life, like the cautionary tale told by Shanghai's *Xinmin Evening News*. Regardless of one's attitude, American products (*Meihuo*) remained a key component of Chinese urban residents' memories of the end of WWII. That moment began with the unforgettable scenes of GIs and Nationalist elite units parading in victory, clad in American khakis, leather shoes, weapons, and equipment, through the streets of jubilantly crowded, newly liberated cities. Soon afterwards, American commodities filled up window displays in fancy shops and tens of thousands of street stands: Quaker oatmeal, Listerine toothpaste, Camel cigarettes, American oranges, chocolate, instant coffee, milk powder, ice cream mix, and peanut butter, as well as colorful English-language pictorials depicting American defeats of the Japanese in heroic battles.[3] Everything was for sale and on sale. The American "spiritual aid" also went hand in hand with this material aid.[4] Hollywood movies

5 Entangled Goods: American Charms and Harms 155

banned for decades in Japanese-occupied areas made a full comeback with huge advertisements and posters everywhere, and Shanghai imported nearly two thousand new American films.[5] Popular magazines such as *West Wind* brought every facet of the American culture to the households of middle- and upper-class urbanites, housewives, and youth, emphasizing its quotidian and trivial practices. John King Fairbank, the new director of the US Information Service and later a founding figure of China studies in the United States, observed that "reoccupied China was intellectually starved for much of what we had to offer ... the need for information seemed to me just as urgent as the material supplies being brought in by UNRRA."[6]

In 1946, a Shanghai reporter identified five major sources for the "ubiquitous invasion of American goods": first, those obtained with proper procedures; second, surplus goods distributed as relief or sold on the market; third, smuggled products; fourth, black-market goods from American soldiers through scalpers; and fifth, items from Jews, who sold their own quotas or counterfeits.[7] Average citizens received free items from UNRRA and bought surplus war supplies at reduced prices from government or agency distributers as well as on the rampant black market. For some, encountering American products was like a "reunion with an old lover" who had departed after Pearl Harbor.[8] But for many more, these goods were a necessity during a time of material shortage and high inflation, or an absolute novelty that had only been a privilege for the wealthy. As one author described it, "while dignitaries enjoyed their cocktail parties, ordinary people could eat American canned food to quench their cravings."[9] In comparison to Jeeps and Jeep girls, goods became the most prevalent encounter with America for both Chinese elites and commoners, offering a bittersweet experience of victory, survival, prosperity, and despair.

American military and economic aid to China played a crucial role in China's war against Japan and was equally crucial in its postwar reconstruction. After the war, lend-lease aid continued in China, reaching another US$781 million, while UNRRA distributed massive quantities of war surplus supplies.[10] Scholars today continue to debate over the exact nature and scale of the actual American aid to China, as well as its impacts on China's national economy and the outcome of the civil war. Most focus on the military supplies gifted or sold to China, ranging from arms and munitions to heavy equipment and industrial goods.[11] While these questions remain crucial to our understanding of the civil war period, this chapter shifts the focus from battlefields to the territory of urban residents' households, city warehouses, street stands, and deep valleys, linking the macrohistory of national and global politics to the microhistory of civilian daily lives. It delves into how American goods influenced the Chinese experience and perceptions of the country by highlighting entangled objects within the context of Sino-US relations. Rather than narrowly defined military supplies, my focus lies on the everyday products that had a prominent presence in Chinese lives and fueled debates. In the eyes of Chinese consumers and critics, household items like canned food, coffee, Coca-Cola, DDT, and penicillin, which will be explored in detail later, were all associated with the American military – whether originating from wartime military inventions, acquired from the surplus sales and UNRRA relief efforts, introduced or sold by US soldiers, or distributed and guarded by them.

In the postwar era, American goods reached all echelons of society, from elites to the destitute, affecting rickshaw pullers who began their days with instant coffee, Jeep girls who flaunted the latest fashions, street vendors who dealt with legal and illegal merchandise, young thieves and local gangs who frequently pilfered from US military warehouses, farmers who saw their fields sprayed with DDT, owners of local businesses who competed with imported products, and tens of thousands of residents who consumed or rejected American wheat, flour, and rice. As a result, American products became a familiar experience, as a necessity, a popular commodity, and a cultural spectacle that influenced Chinese consumption, tastes, and views. Some locals were drawn closer to the "Beautiful Country" (*Mei guo*), while others were alarmed by the risks of "Americanization" (*Mei hua*), fearing the impacts of its material and spiritual aid to Chinese industry, society, and morality.[12]

The influx of foreign industrial goods created significant difficulties for local businesses, engendering fears of capitalism crushing the Chinese economy. Riding the tide of the National Goods Movement, the Communists orchestrated anti-American boycotts as a strategic measure to mobilize urban populations in their wider struggle against the Nationalist Government. However, the movement turned out far less successful than the one triggered by the Peking rape incident. In the end, it was the US military's mishandling of goods-related matters that lent the Communists a more compelling and unifying narrative in their opposition against US imperialism. The military's stringent policies against theft and black-market activities made everyday encounters with American goods increasingly dangerous and sometimes fatal. Its "halt or shoot" policy, implemented to protect US properties, led to frequent civilian deaths, followed by a series of legal disputes and political frustrations as Nationalist officials lodged complaints and protests to no avail. These incidents became another major source of Chinese grievance, alongside traffic accidents and sexual relations. Together, the three signature causes, serving as rallying points, coalesced into a powerful campaign led by the Communist Party against American brutalities.

Bitter Sweet: Tastes of America

Not poetic or romantic, but it [coffee] is a comfort for the masses.
– Zhou Nan, 1946[13]

She is sweet like Coca-Cola.
– Er Yi, 1946[14]

Food remained a vital aspect of daily life in postwar China, providing essential nutrients as well as new tastes. Thanks to rampant inflation, dislocations after years of brutal wars, and natural disasters, the era was known for major famines, a refugee crisis, and an economic breakdown. UNRRA carried out emergency food and medical relief in the famine areas of Hunan and Guangxi, levee repairs in the Pearl River delta and the Qiantang River of Zhejiang, and agricultural rehabilitation projects in Henan where the humming of Ford Ferguson and other imported tractors was replacing the centuries-old hand-plowing methods. Large quantities of staple foodstuffs such as flour, wheat, and rice poured into the cities of Beijing, Guangzhou, Nanjing, Shanghai, and Tianjin. Relief food was not only essential for starving peasants, urban refugees, and the unemployed, but also important for civil servants, office workers, teachers, and students who had a higher social status and yet remained economically vulnerable. During his grueling return trip from the southwest back to his former campus in Beijing, a Tsinghua University student was thrilled to receive a five-pound can of milk powder and a five-pound can of bacon. This moment of relief came just before he and his peers boarded empty coal ships heading north from Shanghai. Similarly, another student from Wuhan University developed a fondness for two new favorites: ice cream mix and Klim, a brand of powdered milk initially adopted as part of the US Army ration – Klim being the word milk spelled in reverse. Even decades later, he remembered them as a "delicious snack and superior nourishment after years of malnutrition."[15] In his memoir, English writer J. G. Ballard recalled his experience of the Japanese surrender in Shanghai. On that hot August day in 1945, the teenager watched from the roof of the Japanese prison, where he had been interned for more than two years, as parachutes descended from the bomb doors of a B-29, dropping a line of canisters carrying American relief supplies. The "cargo of treasures" included "tins of Spam and Klim, cartons of Lucky Strike cigarettes, cans of jam and huge bars of chocolate."[16]

Chinese journals introduced a garden variety of nutritious American surplus combat food packages, especially the popular canned food. The C ration pack contained beef stew, pork and beans, and meat hash, plus biscuits, coffee, and sugar. The K ration for soldiers on the front line provided three meals of three thousand calories in total – with veal for breakfast, Spam for lunch, and dried sausage for dinner, in addition to a fruit bar, crackers, cheese, a bouillon cube, malt-dextrose tablets, and a packet of lemon crystals, chewing gum, cigarettes, toilet paper, soap, and water purification tablets. The additional "Ten-in-One" provided more varieties including more types of canned meat, dehydrated potatoes, onion and vegetable soups, and dried milk. The B ration for field kitchens aimed to include three different sorts of meat, four vegetables, a dessert, and canned fruit or fruit juice in the five pounds of food allocated to each man for a day.[17] After sampling these rations, Chinese customers often shared their exhilarating experiences. Many could not believe how huge American potatoes were, acknowledging that although these canned foods might not have been great by American standards, they tasted very delicious to those with hungry stomachs. One customer commented that canned turkey from the US cost the same as local fresh chicken, yet it was boneless and four times larger.[18] Another noted that within a year following the victory, these imported provisions were everywhere, spreading "from the metropolis to the villages and from the wealthy to the poor." Initially driven by curiosity, consumers now embraced these products partly for their cheaper prices.[19]

In addition to satisfying hunger, American food was a novelty to be seen, touched, smelled, and above all, tasted. One of the newly popularized products and tastes was coffee, also included in the ration meal. The US War Department considered coffee an essential element of the troops' diet, as it provided a stimulus for their physical stamina and morale. The wartime demand further accelerated the development of instant coffee, such as the one by Nescafé. Describing his first impression of Shanghai, one college student wrote that he was so jealous of the local customers who could taste American coffee and milk, made fresh from powders on the street market.[20] It was probably an exaggeration that all Shanghainese now loved to drink coffee with its strong taste, bitterness, aroma, and "romantic sentiment."[21] Overall, coffee was more of an acquired taste, a foreign one to begin with. The first known coffee was sold as "cough syrup" in a British drug store in Guangzhou several decades earlier.

But the unfamiliar bitter taste did not prevent the dark drink from becoming popular in China. Coffeehouses had been a familiar urban and cultural space since the second half of the nineteenth century for Western customers as well as an increasing number of affluent, middle-upper-class Chinese urban consumers. In the 1920s and 1930s, New Sensation School writers often wrote in Shanghai's cafes and set many of their stories in similar, Western-style urban spaces, including coffeehouses, dance halls, and Western restaurants. Cafes were also known and projected as sites for romantic and sexual encounters with alluring waitresses and prostitutes.[22] Due to material shortages, coffee consumption during wartime became restricted and even banned in Chongqing as a luxury product. After Japan's surrender, the number of cafes quickly increased. From June to October 1946, for example, coffeehouses in Shanghai increased from about 50 to 186, not counting Western restaurants that also served coffee.[23] Despite being associated with a Western style, China's cafes in the 1940s also accommodated Chinese tastes by adding familiar entertainments such as music, dance, and even traditional Chinese operas. Local customers, mostly male, expected to be entertained.[24] As one observer noted, coffeehouses in Shanghai became filled starting from 9:00 p.m., when customers sought a modern foreign experience after dinner and enjoyed watching traditional operas while drinking coffee served by showy waitresses.[25] Many sites also served Chinese cuisines together with Western drinks and food. For the majority, the coffeehouse was a venue for entertainment and socializing rather than a public space intended to spark or spread revolutionary ideas.

A sudden and major change to Shanghai's coffee culture occurred in the late 1940s when new open-air coffee shops (露天咖啡館) and coffee stands (咖啡攤) sprang up on every street and corner like mushrooms after a rain (see Figures 5.1 and 5.2). As one journalist from *The China Weekly Review* put it, China's masses discovered coffee in the year 1946: "Once sipped only by the well-to-do, coffee today delivers its exhilarating 'lift' to the laboring classes; to the ricksha coolie, pedicab man, domestic servant, and even occasionally to the lowly beggar out to celebrate a bumper crop of alms."[26] In the morning, these brand-new wooden coffee and toast stands, equipped with stools or chairs, served Maxwell House coffee with Carnation milk to tram drivers, conductors, and other early risers. Within three minutes, hot breakfasts with food and coffee were served, as customers washed down their set meals and quickly vacated their seats. During summer, it was common to spot "a perspiring pedicab or ricksha coolie halt" to down two or three glassfuls of iced coffee served in plastic glasses. On a hot day, one sidewalk merchant sold more than one hundred glasses of iced coffee in thirty-five minutes, not including the two unpaid glassfuls, given for "the price of his silence," to the policeman on the corner who came over. Although the coffee tasted weak and iced coffee was even more feeble, these affordable coffee stands

Figure 5.1 Drawing of a streetside coffee vendor in Shanghai, 1946. *Luobinhan*.

Figure 5.2 Drawing of an outdoor coffee stand in Shanghai, 1946. *Guoji xinwen huabao*.

were so popular that they could be found on "virtually every busy street corner and on the sidewalks of lesser roads."[27] Due to their affordability and convenience, canned instant coffees became a new favorite among the working class, even winning over the coolie customers who traditionally sought tea in street stands or low-cost teahouses. American-style snack stands that sold milk, coffee, hot chocolate, and bread with butter were also said to be winning the street competition over the traditional Shanghai-style breakfast featuring beef noodles and sticky rice balls.[28]

Coffee not only brought a novel taste to China, but also created a new social space. One sketch made of the new coffee stands emphasized the freedom unavailable in other fancy foreign restaurants, calling these stands the best at combining Western material and Eastern spirit.[29] Another noted how these coffee stands were a place for everyone. Because of the minimal cost of this American drink, coffee became popular for all, even among coolies who could not have possibly ever "dreamed of enjoying American drinks every day!"[30] In these new stalls, young office workers in suits and sweating rickshaw pullers sat next to each other, drinking coffee and having buttered toast. Thanks to the thousands of street stands, "the noble drink was brought to the street, and the philistines stormed the salon."[31] Lu Xun, a leading leftist writer, who famously mocked intellectuals for their lack of concern about the masses by saying that "I don't drink coffee, and green tea is better," could not have predicted the huge popularity of coffee among Shanghai's working class after the war.[32] Coffee finally fell off its sacred altar, turning from a luxurious foreign drink to a commonplace commodity. As one observer lamented, even this small amount of machine-produced goods from capitalist America had changed the lifestyle of the entire population of Shanghai residents and those beyond.[33]

Not everyone was a convert to coffee. After being offered a canteen cup of coffee by a marine officer in the field as a gesture of friendship, a Nationalist captain only sipped once and never asked for it again. But he became an instant devotee of Toddy, a chocolate drink, and enjoyed pogey bait, a term covering all types of sweets.[34] Compared to the taste of coffee, sweetness appealed to a more universal palate. Like elsewhere in the world, a common scene of liberation included seeing children chasing after American Jeeps and trucks for candies and chewing gum. Chinese newspapers advertised Eskimo Toffee, frozen suckers, and brick ice cream as being "always safe" and able to "protect your children's health."[35] But the most popular American "sweetheart" remained the classic Coca-Cola. During the war, American post exchange (PX) stores on military bases maintained a well-stocked supply of small treats – candies, cigarettes, and drinks – and were a powerful force in "establishing Coca-Cola as the archetypal American beverage."[36] Part of General Marshall's troops welfare policy, these supplies of small luxuries were supposed to ensure soldiers had a little piece of home with them while living abroad. After the war, technicians from the Coca-Cola Company were sent to open plants across the world, including in occupied Germany and Japan, and the company monopolized soft drink markets for US servicemen. Through both veteran consumption and local emulations, "the sale of the drink to American soldiers acted as 'the greatest sampling program in the history of the world,'" and as a result, "by 1950, Coca-Cola had become a preferred drink among veterans returning home as well as among European youths."[37]

The American Armed Forces in China took the Coca-Cola supply seriously. In Qingdao, the US Navy Port Facilities contracted with the Laoshan Iltis Mineral Water Co., Ltd. to produce bottled Coca-Cola for their exclusive consumption.[38] In Shanghai, urgent and imperative requests were repeatedly made to ensure the production of sufficient Coca-Cola. On May 15, 1946, Lieutenant Colonel Sylvio L. Bousquin, Adjutant General, Headquarters United States Army Forces in China, wrote to the Shanghai municipal government to request extended time for the electricity supply of the Far Eastern Import and Export Company that produced CO_2 gas. He stated the "imperative requirements" for CO_2 gas, at 230 kilograms daily, as "failure to obtain this gas will jeopardize 38,000 barrels of Coca Cola Syrup which is now in United States Army stocks." On May 17, they made another request for electricity, this time to increase the allotment for their warehouse electricity consumption limit to 90,000 KWH per month for cold storage protection of perishable food stocks due to the anticipated hot weather in the next few months. Such exception should be made, they argued, despite the electricity shortage in the city and existing restrictions, "due to the fact that our mission in Shanghai is a non-profit making one, but one solely and exclusively for the assistance of the Chinese government, and at the invitation of the Chinese government."[39] As we have seen, the US military expected special privileges, and similar arguments were made in many other situations, such as seeking exemptions from taxes on food, drinks, and hotel stays, as well as waivers for water bills for their residences.

For commercial use after the war, Watson's Mineral Water Company, the licensed bottler in Shanghai, produced Coca-Cola by mixing imported concentrate with carbonated water, using powerful bottling machinery also imported from the United States. In fact, the magic drink was not an immediate hit when it first arrived in China in the early twentieth century. Most people found its phosphoric acid taste strange, resembling a Chinese fever syrup. Sales were not even as successful as for its British or Chinese counterparts due to Coca-Cola's shorter history in China and price disadvantage compared to local soft drinks.[40] The business was subsequently closed during the Japanese occupation. However, when it reopened after the war, Watson's Coca-Cola had a completely new life. It launched a successful marketing campaign including huge billboards that lined the streets, as well as posters, calendars, and flyers everywhere, often paired with female celebrities. More importantly, like elsewhere around the world, GIs became a moving advertisement for the cool American drink as they were seen drinking Coca-Cola everywhere and all the time, in real life and in representational space.

In wartime advertisements, Coca-Cola was frequently portrayed as "a symbol of good will" shared among allies. The message was conveyed through imagery that featured Chinese officers drinking Coca-Cola alongside American pilots, evoking a sense of camaraderie by appealing to the successful operations of the "Flying Tigers" over the hump.[41] After the war, Coca-Cola continued to shine as a global commodity, serving not only to quench thirsts and refresh minds, but also as a cultural symbol to bridge differences and bring peace, freedom, and democracy to the world. Just as some Chinese soldiers tried to emulate the lifestyle of the American allies, so did civilian populations. By the late 1940s, Coca-Cola, with its new postwar prestige and availability, had become the best-selling beverage in Shanghai, defeating competing Chinese carbonated drinks as well as beer and orange juice. Demand was so high that Watson had to increase its production to two hundred and forty thousand bottles a day, and by 1948, Shanghai became the first foreign market to exceed annual sales of more than 1 million cases.[42] As one critic explained, the surging popularity of the "tart Coca-Cola" after the war, while "no one could explain why it was so attractive," had to do with the Chinese worship of the Allies – that is, it was a transfer of admiration of the country to the drink.[43]

Like Coca-Cola and coffee, US goods became both cheaper and tastier to the Chinese after the war, thanks to sales of surplus supplies and America's rising global prestige (see Figure 5.3).[44] An encounter with American food involved a variety of experiences ranging from a sense of curiosity and anticipation in figuring out how to open a can of surplus food to the thrill of discovering supersized potatoes and boneless turkey and the fizz of drinking cold Coca-Cola on a hot summer day. After receiving compressed biscuits and two oversized woolen coats distributed by UNRRA in 1946, two siblings in Shanghai wrote thank you letters to the American children who had donated them, remembering "our English greatly improved during that time." Sometimes the excitement could be puzzling. One individual drank up a cup of coffee in one big gulp

164 5 Entangled Goods: American Charms and Harms

Figure 5.3 American canned food on window display in a Shanghai store, featuring a Coca-Cola poster on the outside wall, 1947. Digital Image Collections of Republic of China (1911–1949).

without knowing to add sugar; another was nervous about how much and what kind of water to mix with the milk and chocolate powder, at which temperature, and for how long.[45] These new experiences took place at home where food was exchanged with families and friends, and in public in open-air food stands, coffeehouses, and Western restaurants, as well as in the representational space of newspaper columns, fiction, and plays as many recounted their personal encounters with American food. To watch and to be watched, tasting these novelties was as much about national prestige and socioeconomic status as about flavor, no matter whether the fare was bitter coffee, sweet Cola, or bittersweet America.

The Fight Goes On: Chemical Weapons of Mass Consumption

In October 1945, *National Geographic* ushered in a new era with its feature article "Your New World of Tomorrow." The piece extolled groundbreaking inventions poised to revolutionize health and medicine, shining a spotlight on two exceptional "wonder drugs" that emerged from wartime technological advancements: DDT and penicillin.[46] During the war, the US military had effectively utilized DDT to control malaria, typhus, body lice, and plague. Following the conflict's end, it quickly gained worldwide popularity as an essential pesticide, seamlessly integrating into the fabric of everyday life.[47] Yet, far more than just another American product, DDT engendered a sense of national pride for its contributions to the double war against the Axis and mosquitos. Its promise of control, health, and prosperity positioned it not merely as a commodity but also as a cherished gift to the world during the crucial period of postwar reconstruction. Accompanying this narrative were pesticide commercials that employed a striking "shoot to kill" messaging, evoking a distinct militaristic undertone. This rhetoric mirrored the approach the United States took in its global initiatives, where the application of potent "weapons" against perceived threats – be they insects, microbes, or humans – showcased America's technological, industrial, and military superiority and dominance in the postwar era.

Like elsewhere, DDT was widely used in China after WWII for insect and pest control. The American military often facilitated the application or requested its use (see Figure 5.4). In Tianjin, American military aircrafts targeted areas where reservoirs were concentrated.[48] In Nanjing, Qingdao, Beijing, and Guangzhou, the American military provided assistance to the Nationalist Government by conducting multiple air spray operations that covered entire cities. Even Chiang Kai-shek's

Figure 5.4 Weekly DDT spraying by a C-47 transport over US military accommodations in Shanghai, September 1946. *Xinwen bao*.

residence in the capital received the attention of American medical officers who applied DDT for pest control.[49] To promote the general use of DDT, a variety of Chinese scientific and popular journals enthusiastically introduced this novel chemical and its associated commercial products. They celebrated its remarkable benefits and versatility, as it could be applied to body, food, animals, bedsheets, and clothes. Hailing it as a "nuclear weapon against insects," Chinese news, books, pamphlets, and advertisements eagerly showcased its prowess, often drawing upon the reputation of American military might. The battle against pests and diseases became another frontier where the extraordinary power of this "wonder drug" was trumpeted on the home front.

Despite DDT's overwhelming official and media acclaim, when the Chinese had direct and close contacts with the new chemical product, its foggy sprays, strong smells, and massive reach also caused discomfort and concerns. Some asked, "Aren't such indiscriminate attacks on enemy and friendly insects leading to the elimination of all?"[50] Witnessing the air spray's devastating effects on bees, one reader from Qingdao warned about DDT killing huge numbers of bees during their breeding season, and called to protect beneficial insects.[51] In Nanjing, locals protested against imposed DDT treatments, especially the unrestricted spraying of all farmland and soil pits surrounding the US Army Advisory Group's residence.[52] The public already knew DDT's toxicity. One cartoon depicts the mixed allure and danger of the chemical, portraying a Chinese man kneeling before a human-sized DDT bottle, while a thinly dressed woman leans against the bottle and holds a spray hose with her one arm and covers her eyes with the other. The begging man, now with chemical spray all over his face, appears to be in pain. In another cartoon, a young male dressed in a suit is swallowing a bottle of DDT, as a Westerner tries to stop him. The accompanying script reads: DDT has turned into a suicidal tool upon arriving in Shanghai.[53] Overall, an encounter with DDT was a direct and physical experience for local residents. Whether watching military aircraft spraying across the city or individual soldiers delousing their houses, clothes, hair, armpits, and even their faces, this constituted an intimate contact with America through chemicals, science, and technology; spectacles of occupation; and civilization. Before boarding navy ships, US medical officers used DDT powder to delouse Chinese soldiers as well as the Japanese. Around the world, foreign children and families were profiled in news photographs, educational pamphlets, and advertisements, shown gratefully receiving a dousing of DDT powder spray from a uniformed American man, "evoking paternal notions of U.S. interests abroad."[54] Whether the recipient was grateful or not, the American servicemen were here to kill, control, and teach, all at once.

If DDT was dubbed the chemical to kill all germs, the other wonder drug, penicillin, held an esteemed reputation in China as the cure for all diseases. Discovered by a British scientist in 1928, penicillin was introduced as a therapeutic agent by American scientists in 1942. As part of the war effort in response to Japanese biological warfare, penicillin was only manufactured on a small scale and monopolized by the armed forces to treat injured soldiers. While it cured many bacterial diseases during the war, including otherwise fatal battle wounds, it gained particular acclaim for its sensational results for curing syphilis. After the war, the "wonder bullet" was put into mass production for commercial and civilian use. It quickly became a major export to the world, representing both a potent American "weapon" that helped win the war and a miracle drug that could now cure everyone.[55]

Penicillin, known in Chinese as *qingmeisu* (青霉素), *pannixilin* (盤尼西林), and *peinixilin* (配尼西林), was first introduced in professional journals in the early 1940s. But it was not until the middle of the decade that it became widely known to the general public. In June 1944, Vice President Henry Wallace travelled to Chongqing, becoming the highest-ranking American official to visit modern China. During his visit, Wallace conveyed personal messages from President Roosevelt to Chiang Kai-shek and also presented a gift of penicillin.[56] Together with this historic visit, the new drug appeared in major Chinese news reports. Its status as an official American gift added diplomatic and political prestige to this groundbreaking medicine. The first sample drugs arrived in August of that year, thanks to the Lend-Lease Act.[57] Sensational stories added to the allure of the new American drug. One popular tale recounted how Tojo Hideki, the former Japanese prime minister who had shot himself in the chest, quickly recovered after receiving penicillin injections, enabling him to stand trial.[58] Chinese scientific, medical, health, and educational magazines introduced penicillin's powerful effect and versatility to a variety of children, youth, and general readers. It was almost universally celebrated as a savior for humankind, a "legendary" or "sacred medicine."[59]

Penicillin's reputation was so powerful that it became a political metaphor for democracy among leftist critics, transforming this panacea for diseases into a remedy for China's political ills. On October 10, 1944, the national day of the Republic of China, Tao Xingzhi, a prominent educator and former student of John Dewey at Columbia University, wrote a poem calling for "true democracy" as the "political penicillin" to eradicate all political germs. He emphasized that while the medical penicillin brought by Vice President Wallace was commendable, it alone could not save the entire population.[60] Less than a month later, Tao presented Jian Bozan, a Marxist scholar educated at the University of California, with a gift of Camel cigarettes, symbolizing a "cure-all elixir" from Roosevelt's country, with the hope that it would "puff out the political penicillin" ignited by the eminent historian's wisdom.[61] After the high-stakes 1945 Chongqing Negotiations, Chairman Zhang Lan of the China Democratic League bid farewell to Mao Zedong at the airport and once again employed the metaphor when responding to a journalist's inquiry about the objectives of the marines' landing, which was taking place in North China. While welcoming the Americans' contribution to disarming the Japanese forces, he also expressed the desire for their increased support of Chinese democracy, stressing that "'democracy' is the political 'penicillin' that can cure China's long ills."[62]

Due to its high demand, imported and black-market penicillin coexisted with surplus distributions and government purchases. Said to be another type of gold for its universal status and enduring value, penicillin was sought after by stocking merchants and black marketeers. Sales and demand were further boosted by commercials, which appeared in major newspapers such as *Shen bao*, promoting the various imported and local products, including injections, creams, new types of treatments, and even odd products like penicillin ice cream and gum. Although its most common clinical uses in Chinese hospitals were treating pneumonia, meningitis, and other serious infections, advertisements primarily targeted venereal diseases, especially gonorrhea and syphilis. On the postwar black market for American military supplies, penicillin was frequently spotted next to condoms and pro-kits.

As in the Nationalist areas, penicillin was well received among the Communists headquartered in Yan'an. Their initial exposure to this American drug came through the Dixie Mission. An American physician within the United States Army Observation Group used penicillin to treat not only his own team members but also some Communists in need. In the words of one Chinese observer, "Penicillin, Hollywood movies, and General Patrick Hurley represented American science and technology, culture, and politics respectively," and more broadly, the "Army Observation Group became a window through which Yan'an learned about the outside world."[63] Members of the propaganda department frequented the American group to collect English publications. Some of the hosts began wearing American military boots and using DDT for mosquito control; learned how to drive a Jeep and perform mechanical repairs; and had their first tastes of Coca-Cola, gum, American alcohol, chocolate, cigarettes, and canned tomato beans. Yang Shangkun, a CCP leader who later became the fourth president of the People's Republic of China, was said to have three passions: Mao Zedong, his wife, and American cigarettes – the latter being "his only vice," which he consumed in monstrous proportions.[64] Before the Observation Group's departure, their Jeeps were packed with the famous Yan'an wool rugs featuring animal patterns, their favorite souvenir. They also left the Communists with plenty of gifts, including penicillin, Jeeps, portable radio stations, hand-cranked generators, and transmitters, all of which were put to good use in the fight against the Chiang Kai-shek regime.[65] Building on American-gifted mold, the first Communist production of penicillium was attributed in 1945 to Richard Frey, an Austrian physician and foreign member of the CCP. Toward the end of the fierce civil war, Communists also fought to secure greater access to UNRRA goods in their occupied areas, including the precious penicillin.[66]

American Goods versus National Goods

> Don an American hat
> Dress in American clothes
> Mouth full of ABC
> Open with God's punishment
> Close with SON OF A BITCH
> Dream an American dream
> Wake up yellow face skin
> Listen to the American words
> Obsessed with America
> Firing an American gun
> Aiming at her own brothers...
> – Ma Fantuo, "Meiguo mi (American obsessions)," 1947[67]

American goods, though not a panacea for all of life's ills, were a highly desirable part of Chinese daily life, sought after by tens of thousands residing on the coast and in the hinterland. While American commodities had been present in China for more than a century and a half, it was only in the late 1940s that commoners and the poor had direct access to these products and experiences, sparking the phenomenon of "American obsessions." These goods formed the American world that directly affected their lives and views of a country that had been too remote to reach. It was also through these iconic and everyday items, together with GIs who visibly consumed, represented, and advertised them, that Chinese society at large saw, felt, and understood the American military presence.

Food stood at the frontline of the debate over American goods as it concerned both the individual body and the national strength on biological, cultural, and psychological levels. Those who had worked for the American military frequently discussed food in conjunction with US soldiers' bodies.⁶⁸ One Chinese college student who had done office work highlighted the American menu, which included a high-calorie diet of eggs, vitamins, and unlimited supplies of butter, bread, and coffee. He pointed out that in order to understand Americans' superior fighting power and emotions, in their work and in their sex drive, one had to understand that they had larger bodies, a result of what they ate.⁶⁹ Huang Shang, once an interpreter for the Allies, also commented on how American food and bodies were much bigger. He couldn't believe how huge their potatoes were and observed that the enormous physical contrast between American and Chinese soldiers was between one who was well fed and well dressed, and the other who was small, malnourished, and "all emaciated." Calling the American Service of Supplies a "fairy treasure chest" filled with everything anyone could want, Huang also commented that this "gigantic and complex organization" was "a miniature of the American Dollar culture" that spread to every corner, from "peach, apricot, beef, ham, to women's legs on Broadway." He argued that without their supply system, "American soldiers could not even fight." In another more exaggerated version attributed to General Chen Cheng, the top Nationalist military commander remarked, "American soldiers cannot fight without coffee," thus highlighting the superior spirit of Chinese troops who, though only sustained by rice porridge, could still fight courageously.⁷⁰

For the Nationalist Government, there was an awkward discomfort in admitting American generosity and superiority and preserving individual and national dignity. Whether during wartime collaboration or postwar reconstruction, Chinese elites tried to maintain a subtle and difficult balance during everyday encounters, from the very top leadership to young employees. Chiang Kai-shek had been promoting a superior Chinese culture and morality for decades and was critical of Western individualism and materialism. Even in a propagandist pamphlet to educate the Chinese about how to properly interact with American soldiers, the Generalissimo reminded them that American officers and soldiers "mostly do not give up their individual material comfort."⁷¹ During the war, Nationalist propaganda celebrated China's heroic "Big Sword Unit," who won a major battle against the Japanese in defending the Great Wall, and the superior Chinese troops who supposedly walked in straw sandals and only had two frozen buns to eat compared to America's "dandy troops" who always had their mouths filled with candies, toffee, gum, or cigarettes. However, Chinese soldiers' belief in the superiority of the big sword over tanks and porridge over coffee was said to be shaken after witnessing their American allies in action at the front line.⁷² In reality, Chinese troops, like the majority of the local population during the war, suffered from severe malnutrition, though some benefited from American military rations as a nutritional supplement.[73] Even worse, those who had grown accustomed to American coffee while working in India now began to request the "common drink" in Chinese teahouses after the war.[74]

As previously discussed, the two sides clashed over the appropriate allocation and payment for feeding and accommodating US troops in China. Nationalist officials voiced concerns about the huge costs incurred in supporting GIs' excessive lifestyle, which strained their finances and exhausted local resources. They also expressed frustration over the apparent lack of respect and appreciation from the American side for the sacrifices made by the Chinese people. Conversely, many Americans felt that the Chinese were ungrateful for US aid and assistance, especially in light of anti-American protests. The critical question of who provided for whom, and under what terms, became a testament to the power relations between the two nations, whether paternal, brotherly, or humanitarian. The mutual feeling of ingratitude was a persistent theme and an underlying source of tension in a relationship of uneven reciprocity.

More broadly, Chinese critics saw food as a bridge to discuss the larger issues of cultural, social, and racial differences and hierarchies. One author explained that American cuisine was very different from the more elaborate Western dishes that had been served in Shanghai restaurants. Typically, breakfast in America consisted of only bread with butter and cereals, occasionally with two eggs in more generous servings. Lunch was simple and dinner was more elaborate, featuring a combination of meat and vegetables. He further commented that, in America, no one enjoyed rare delicacies, nor did anyone eat tree bark, and ordinary people were all healthy. Even the president's food was not much different from an ordinary worker's, with the best meals being beef steak, pork steak, chicken legs, and lamb chops.[75] Commentaries like this approached food as a representation of American culture, which embodied equality and prioritized nutrition over taste, looks, and quantity. Those who held more critical views, however, questioned whether American food was indeed better or actually suited for Chinese bodies. A *Shen bao* article refuted the charge that Chinese physiques were not as strong as Westerners' due to the rice diet, citing a recent American study that linked milk and red meat consumption to higher blood pressure. The author then argued that every nation had its own habits, including dietary practices, and American staple foods were unsuitable for Chinese national habits, as rice had been a staple food for millennia and milk did not fit into most people's daily habits.[76]

Such debates continued the earlier controversy over Western and Chinese food, which had been intimately linked to racial strength and national revival since the late nineteenth century. Reformers and revolutionaries had criticized the Chinese character for obsessing over eating and for having unscientific and ancient dietary habits. These customs, such as the preference for vegetables over red meat, supposedly led to differences in Sino-Western bodies and even in national and racial strengths. In the following decades, commentators continued to debate over milk versus soy milk, flour/bread versus rice, and beef over non–red meat diets. In practice, Western cuisines had been localized to adapt to Chinese tastes and ways of eating. For example, restaurants serving Western food added chopsticks instead of knives and forks to allow customers to eat them the Chinese way, and many created a type of "reformed Western food" (*gailiang xican*) or changed the way certain dishes were typically cooked, such as serving well-done steak and adding soy sauce.[77] While some critics linked discussions of food to national differences or racial hierarchies, others focused on Chinese consumption and Westernization instead. One commentator mocked Western-educated students for acting more Western than "real Westerners." He gave a vivid portrait of such a fictional character, Mary Ma: She eats a sandwich and doesn't even look at Chinese pancakes and fried dough. To her, although coffee and the famous Dragon Well tea are both bitter, the former has a "tasty bitterness" while the latter is "bitter for no good reasons." She never watches Chinese movies and only listens to operas, even without understanding much. She chews gum, eats chocolate, and wears clothes emulating American movie stars and models seen in magazines.[78] Like in the case of Jeep girls, many of these critiques targeted women, whose consumption of imported nylon stockings, perfumes, cosmetics, clothes, and movies attracted disproportionately large media attention. Their purchases were said not to be a result of increasing gender equality or economic independence, but rather of women selling their bodies for the sake of vanity.

Food was the most common, vibrant, and revealing topic in public discussions on American everyday goods. It occupied the forefront of the debate not only because of its physiological necessity but also because of its unparalleled ability to exert direct and intimate influence. By entering one's body and altering the inside and outside through nourishment, contamination, or toxicity, food could pose an immediate, visible, and ultimate threat to Chinese individuals and to the national body. As American food and commodities increasingly dominated the Chinese market, critiques shifted focus from national strength and modernization to political discussions centered on socioeconomic impacts. Particularly, attention turned to the devastating impacts of American imports on Chinese industries, including driving national industries into bankruptcy, leading to massive unemployment, and draining precious foreign currency reserves. Critics from different political backgrounds expressed shared concerns regarding the enormous economic pressure local industries faced due to low-cost American surplus and industrial goods (see Figure 5.5). For example, canned food, cigarette, medical, dairy, and textile companies were all crushed by cheaper American manufactured goods that dominated the market.[79] Leftist leader Ma Yinchu, a prominent socialist economist educated at Columbia University, emerged as a leading critic, squarely blaming American goods and the global capitalist markets for destroying local workers, businesses, and industries.[80] Even pro-government commentators echoed concerns about the perilous nature of "American goods as American disasters," employing the pun *Meihuo* to describe these commodities as "sugar-coated poisons." Many attributed the "invasion of American goods," together with rampant smuggling and the black market, to the Nationalist Government's erroneous economic policy that was endangering the entire nation.[81]

Beyond news media, business associations took these debates to official meetings and policymaking sessions, petitioning local and national governments to ban or restrict foreign products to protect national industries.

Figure 5.5 "How many coins for a pound of American goods?" Shanghai, 1946. *Hai xing*.

They stressed the distinctions between Chinese and American products and argued that the latter were luxuries and therefore should be prohibited from import during a time of material shortage and foreign currency drain.[82] One owner of a canned food business, for example, made three requests: First, the government must limit foreign imports; second, the Chinese must not be infatuated with Western commodities despite their cheaper prices; and third, workers in an industry should cooperate with the owners and endure temporary pain for a better future.[83] The Shanghai stocking industry, with the slogan "cherish your country and your skin, please give up nylon stockings," repeatedly petitioned the government to ban the importation and smuggling of American nylon stockings.[84] The results of these petitions varied. Nylon stockings, said to be "luxury goods," were banned as of August 1948, and even the Shanghai mayor appealed to Chinese women to wear domestic stockings instead.[85] Nevertheless, due to pressure from Hollywood, the mayor's attempt to set up ticket prices for American movies in order to protect the Chinese film industry proved unsuccessful.[86] The Shanghai city council discussed a proposal to limit the import of Coke concentrate, but later accepted Watson's argument that Coke was a regular summer drink, rather than "luxury goods."[87]

Business communities in China had been working with Western imported goods for decades and had developed highly adaptive strategies. After the war, some quickly capitalized on American prestige and status, translating this brand power into innovative products. For example, one company advertised a new cigarette brand called "Jeep Car," while another named a traditional food product "American Guangzhou Mooncake."[88] The "nuclear power" of products "made in the U.S.A." was transferred to local firecrackers, which were renamed "nuclear crackers," and to the newly popularized ballpoint pen as the "nuclear pen."[89] However, as competition intensified during an economic crisis, local enterprises began to change gears. Penicillin advertisements now highlighted domestic versions, brands, and even treatments. Soft drink companies added China to their product names, such as "China Prospers" and "Great China," while others included iconic symbols such as the Great Wall in their trademarks, with slogans like "Chinese people should drink Chinese soft drinks." Watson's Coca-Cola commercials, which in the earlier period emphasized Coca-Cola's "authentic American" identity, now featured "Chinese company" (*Hua shang*) in big characters to highlight the product's Chineseness. Ironically, even though it was a company fully owned by the Chinese and had always been seen as a Chinese entity, Watson's was now attacked by local competitors as being American.[90]

In a global capitalist system, the divisions between Chinese and American companies and between national and American goods, like these companies' business interests, remained ambiguous and shifting. The so-called national goods were in fact the result of an "active process of indigenization" pursued by modern Chinese entrepreneurs who mixed the foreign and modern with the Chinese and domestic.[91] Even avid promoters of these national goods relied on American raw materials, out of either necessity or choice. For instance, Chinese canned food companies, facing domestic material shortages, used American iron cans and emulated Spam from the surplus supplies to create new "Chinese" products. All local beverage manufacturers used imported concentrated flavor essences for their bottled drinks. These ambiguities reflect Chinese businessmen's multifaceted relationships with American goods, characterized by both dependency on their sales and challenges posed by competitive pressures.[92] This entangled relationship also sheds light on why the Communist campaign against the sale and purchase of American products achieved mixed results.

The national products movement had been a driving force behind the spread of nationalist sentiment since the late nineteenth century. It also provided the foundation for numerous anti-imperialist boycotts against foreign goods, such as the 1905 anti-American boycott that began as a reaction to the Chinese Exclusion Act.[93] This time, the campaign served to mobilize urban populations against the Nationalist regime, which was accused of corruption and betrayal. On November 4, 1946, the Treaty of Friendship, Commerce, and Navigation, known as the Sino-American Commercial Treaty, was signed. The negotiations began almost immediately after the victory over Japan, and the two sides disagreed on many issues, particularly the national treatment and most-favored-nation status for American businesses in China. After its signing, the Chinese press was generally critical of the treaty, chastising it for jeopardizing China's economic independence and national integrity. The Communists compared the treaty to the notorious "21 Demands" proposed by the Japanese in 1915, calling it a sellout of Chinese interests by the Nationalist regime in exchange for US aid. The treaty created an uproar among a wide range of groups, from leftists and intellectuals to industrialists and businessmen, and elicited protests across major cities.[94] The friction continued as China's economic situation worsened, exacerbated by the influx of American commodities. Rallying under the slogan of "Love using national products, boycott American products," the Communist Party organized a movement targeting the bulk sale of American surplus property. In Shanghai, underground CCP members convened a meeting on February 9, 1947, inviting prominent leftist intellectuals such as Guo

Moruo and Deng Chumin to lecture on the devastating impacts of the American dumping of goods in China. The meeting drew workers from major shopping malls across four districts before being violently broken up by Nationalist-backed worker groups and plainclothes police, resulting in one death and thirteen injuries. Although invitations were widely distributed, owners of national industries who had similar but less radical slogans did not participate in the protest or boycott, nor did many unemployed workers. Overall, the economic stakes were high for many business owners, who were "fed by the American military," and for the more than ten thousand urban poor who earned their livings as street vendors of American goods.[95] Their participation in the cause would have jeopardized their livelihoods. As one scholar has pointed out, local Communist organizers overestimated the workers' "political consciousness" and the power of patriotism. The event, remembered today as the February Ninth incident in CCP history, failed to attract a substantial number of national capitalists and middle-roaders.[96]

Despite such setbacks, the American military's mishandling of issues concerning US goods, which often resulted in excessive violence toward Chinese civilians, raised tensions to another level. This in turn gave the Communists a more compelling cause and a more unifying agenda in their fight against American imperialism as well as the Chiang regime as its running dog.

Halt or Shoot: Guarding US Property

When Brigadier General Omar T. Pfeiffer took command of the marine forces in Qingdao in May 1947, their primary objective was to ensure the security of United States naval training activities. However, the mission was immediately overshadowed by a pressing issue – the "continuing, almost nightly theft of supplies and material from storage areas" (see Figure 5.6).[97] By then, marine activities had been terminated in Beijing, Tanggu, and Qinhuangdao, leaving the 1st Marine Division a mere skeleton force. As of September 1, 1947, Qingdao stood as the sole marine duty station in China, with several thousand troops housed in Shandong University buildings and grounds. The small but balanced force, including infantry, artillery, communications, and supporting and service troops, was ready for both offensive and defensive actions. In a revealing account from Pfeiffer's Marine Corps oral history interview, he recounted an incident he witnessed one night.

Upon hearing a commotion, the general stepped outside the French doors of the second floor sitting room. From the balcony he saw a Chinese man attempting to steal his personal automobile from the garage below,

Figure 5.6 United States soldiers guarding supplies on deck in Qingdao, December 1949. Carl Mydans/The LIFE Picture Collection/Shutterstock.

only to be chased and pistol-whipped by his driver, eventually collapsing in a bloody heap. The thief disappeared from the hospital at three the next morning and was never seen again. "My opinion," General Pfeiffer expressed, "[is that] this man was a Communist thief." He concluded that these Communist thieves drove American vehicles from the Nationalist areas into Communist-occupied areas, and "that's why none of these stolen vehicles were ever seen again." Consequently, Pfeiffer, as the new commanding general, Fleet Marine Force, Western Pacific, gave the following orders to sentries: "When they saw a theft of U.S. Government property taking place [they] were to shout, 'Halt,' once in English and once in Chinese and if there was no halt, to let them have it, meaning to fire, and to fire to maim, that is, not to kill but to hit." As a result, he continued, "in addition to the almost nightly thefts, we had almost nightly killings because of our high velocity and power weapons."[98]

Archival records and news reports offer ample information on shooting incidents across various locales before and after Pfeiffer's orders. The

5 Entangled Goods: American Charms and Harms

Tianjin municipal archive reveals a sequence of serious events involving locals suspected of theft, which unfolded within days and months of each other.[99] On August 26, 1946, a laborer named Wu Liusuo (Wu Liu-so), employed by the 7th Service Regiment in Tianjin to load goods with six other workers, was shot dead by American guards. The GI sentries reported that some stationery supplies had been thrown out of the window of the warehouse to other Chinese on the street. A private first class on duty attempted to stop the workmen at the gate and ordered them to halt but was unsuccessful. He then fired one shot over their heads. Since none stopped, he fired another shot, which instantly killed Wu. "Eleven cartons of pencils were recovered" from the street. About two months later, on the morning of October 24, 1946, seventeen-year-old Hao Wenqing (Ho Wen-ching) was shot in the Tianjin Rifle Range area. While the Chinese police report included testimonies that Hao and another seventeen-year-old were picking up firewood near the compound, the American military authorities claimed that Hao was part of a band of more than twenty armed Chinese who left the camp with US government property, and some appeared to be carrying rifles. The following justification was given: "They were ordered to halt, both in English and in Chinese, but failed to comply with the order, so fire was opened on them." On the night of November 2, 1946, twenty-year-old Sun Yugui (Sun Yu-kuei) was fatally shot by two marine sentries for attempting to steal an overcoat from a garage. The garage had lost six pieces of clothing in the past and therefore had added sentries on the roof. Earlier in the evening, Sun had been scared off by passersby during his initial attempts. He returned later, managed to pull an overcoat through the garage window, and was shot. Six bullet wounds were found, all in Sun's upper body. According to the American military investigation report: "The sentries then shouted for SUN to halt," but he "did not take any heed. The sentries then fired three (3) rounds into the deck, but SUN did not stop. The sentries then fired six (6) rounds into SUN's body, thus, killing him instantly." The halt-or-shoot policy continued after these repeated fatal incidents, and in such a rigid environment, even the innocent became casualties. In the early evening of November 13, a Chinese patrolling policeman named Yang was on guard duty in the Chinese Customs Compound where ten American freight cars were parked. Mistaking Yang for a thief in the dark, an American sentry fired a first shot, after which Yang ran away out of fear, and a second .30-caliber bullet was fired, hitting him in the shoulder. The American report explained that the shooting of Yang by Private Boudreau was the result of Boudreau being "unable to identify Yang as a Chinese policeman, in the dark," as well as Yang's "failure to understand or to obey Private Boudreau's command to halt."

Due to the high demand for American goods, rampant stealing and looting became a major headache for the US military in China. Brigadier General Thomas Gerald noted that the refugees in Qingdao were destitute, "living on what they could scrape together including the bark of trees," and that "guarding our vast amount of supplies and equipment from a group of hungry refugees presented many problems."[100] Simms, once in charge of billeting and materiel in Tianjin, remembered "the eyes of beggar children and the street thieves" and "the homeless, ragged urchins who had to rely on their sharpness, fleetness of foot and ability to disappear into the crush of the crowd after nipping off with some item of salable nature ... there wasn't much that we Americans had that wasn't of value to someone."[101] Even though General Pfeiffer was convinced that the nightly thieves were Communists, and the Nationalist media tended to blame them as well, the reality was that there was a mixture of pickpocketing by destitute refugees, impromptu theft by opportunistic coolies and employees, and organized looting by gangsters with sophisticated networks of transportation, money laundering, and sales. But the vast majority remained small-scale civilian thefts and the loot was quickly sold on the black market.

Inside and outside the military compounds, stealing seemed to go on everywhere and could occur at any time. American GIs on the street lost watches, telescopes, gasoline, food, American dollars, guns, and munitions to pickpockets. Packages mailed home were stolen from post offices. Stolen parked vehicles ranged from staff cars, Plymouths, and Willys Jeeps to ambulances.[102] To make things worse, in an instant, "obedient servants" transfigured into thieves and were gone in the blink of an eye.[103] A laundry boy absconded with the uniforms he had been washing diligently for months. Another cleaning boy stole lightbulbs, torches, a typewriter, a bicycle, and a speaker. A prostitute left the inn with her GI customer's personal belongings. A typist employed by the American military brought a bag of medicine home "by accident." After a hard day of work, Chinese laborers threw a few bags over the compound wall. Other contracted coolies who helped the US soldiers clean, sweep, and collect garbage hid a few items in their dump trucks. More organized thieves dug holes in walls or made tunnels leading into warehouses. Even large items, such as 542-pound bombs or 55-gallon drums of aviation fuel, would mysteriously disappear.[104] At times, Chinese guards also acted as culprits or coconspirators. A port policeman in Qingdao, in collaboration with workers at the storage house, stole large quantities of American goods during his night shift.[105] In a time of collapsing order and harsh living conditions for most, even Nationalist soldiers occasionally stole and robbed, as shown in long lists in the Qingdao municipal archive.

As early as January 1946, Chinese sentries challenged marine guards within the same area in the wharf area and "pointed loaded rifles at them whenever they approached," preventing them from "effectively patrolling their post."[106] Misgivings that these Chinese soldiers could have been involved in suspicious activities were not completely ungrounded. In May 1946, three port policemen who had bought cigarettes, leather shoes, and blankets were shot and wounded by American guards as they were leaving the port.[107] Things got even worse on the eve of the American military's complete withdrawal. In March 1948, more than ten armed Nationalist soldiers attempted to steal from a warehouse while cursing the local police on site: "Why do you intervene in our stealing of American goods?" One of them held a grenade, threatening aggressively.[108] A month later, unidentified units of Nationalist troops threatened American guards with guns, broke the locks, and looted the warehouse. They fired toward Chinese guards at the port and escaped in a truck.[109]

There was no uniform command to fire at Chinese thieves. The army theater's judge advocate in China during the war had ruled that, in certain cases, GIs could shoot unarmed Chinese individuals suspected of theft, as any theft of American military goods was considered a felony. In response, the Nationalist Government objected to the ruling, questioning whether Chinese sentries could use the same method against US soldiers suspected of burglarizing military warehouses.[110] In practice, some US commanders were more cautious about the consequences of such a policy, while others saw it as the sole means to stop or discourage rampant thefts. For example, Pfeiffer's superior, Admiral Cooke, instructed that the use of firearms against local civilians was intended only as a last resort. He reminded Pfeiffer of the deadly consequences of his shooting orders and the Chinese government's potential reaction. Known for his close relationship with Chiang Kai-shek and strong opposition to reducing American forces in China, the admiral was said to "take the Chinese side of the thing" "whenever Marines clashed with the Chinese"[111] In reply, however, Pfeiffer, who was not "perturbed" by the consequent nightly killings, said, "that was the only way that I knew I could possibly cope with the situation," adding, "my responsibility was still to the United States and the security of its property."[112]

Commander Pfeiffer was not alone in thinking this way. His successor, General Thomas, shared the stance that "a Marine on post with a rifle is told to protect his post, and when somebody busted in there and started to steal something, they'd shoot 'em."[113] When municipal governments raised concerns about these shooting incidents or requested changes of action, the US military's response, replete with similar rationales, was typically couched in standardized bureaucratic language. First, they cited "the loss of a vast amount of property and supplies" as justification for why "stringent regulations regarding the safeguarding of United States Government property must be rigidly enforced." Second, they emphasized that the Chinese continually failed to obey the American order to halt. In April 1947, General Howard, Commander of the 1st Marine Division, defended the existing policy in his reply to the mayor of Tianjin. He noted that American goods worth tens of thousands of dollars had been and continued to be at risk. Therefore, marines must protect American property and, when "all other means failed," would continue to issue firing orders. He further emphasized that the Chinese must halt when ordered by American guards: "If they had halted, they would not have suffered from injury or death." The number of casualty cases, he further explained, was a result of the linguistic difficulties of American guards as well as the Chinese not following orders.[114]

These justifications and official replies from high-level American military leadership in China were telling. To borrow the words of Wilma Fairbank, who served as the cultural attaché of the American embassy in China from 1945 to 1947, for the Chinese population, about 70 percent of which was illiterate, "American practice, developed in a very different society half way around the world, required interpretation."[115] Yet, in such life-and-death scenarios, "all other means" simply meant giving an order to halt once in each language. Interestingly, the marine commander acknowledged the "linguistic difficulties of American guards" but failed to address the linguistic and cultural difficulties Chinese civilians faced in understanding the American order in the American way. Notably, the Chinese word for halt that the American sentry presumably memorized was transliterated and pronounced as "Donge-Donge."[116] However, to Chinese ears, this pronunciation was confusing, if intelligible at all. "Donge-Donge," which sounds like "Dongzhe" (凍着), was not an accurate transliteration to begin with, not to mention how far its many variations pronounced by American soldiers might depart from the original. It actually sounds closer to the word "Dong" (動), which means "move," the exact opposite of "freeze." More importantly, "Dong" (凍) was a literal translation of "freeze," which the Chinese do not use to mean stop.[117] Further, there were no comparable legal and cultural contexts in China for understanding the concept of halt or the consequence of being shot even after warning shots had been fired or the suspect had already been hit. This case again illustrates how deeply ingrained sociocultural prejudice and systemic discrimination affected everyday and sensory interactions between American servicemen and Chinese civilians. In other words, in order for the suspect to comply, this individual had to first actually hear the order, irrespective of their physical surroundings, and then linguistically, culturally, and legally comprehend the meaning of the GI's order to halt. This was a lot to expect from the local suspects who, at that time, were most likely from lower socioeconomic backgrounds, lacking education or even basic literacy. Despite being deemed unreliable by the US military justice system when providing testimonies against their soldiers, Chinese civilians were still held fully responsible for failing to halt or to follow American orders in American terms.

In reality, not all American-guarded goods were "American," even if they were conveniently labeled "US government property." Upon arrival, the marines immediately took over the Japanese supplies in the locations they occupied. As Walter Curley, a Yale graduate and aide to General Worton, noted: The Japanese army "had huge stocks of all military supplies – ammunition, clothing, vehicles, weapons, explosives – and the largest cache of food in North China. It operated mills, engineering projects, plants, [and] distribution centers, and carried enormous inventories of fuel, engines, [and] spare parts, and 'employed' thousands of people." In 1946, Curley took the position of Japanese Equipment and Material Control Officer, a new position created solely for the purpose of dealing with the confiscated assets "worth $400 to $600 million, in 1946 dollars."[118] These honeypots of former Japanese supplies attracted a variety of Chinese characters, from local officials to criminals and scavengers. One Chinese thief in Shanghai was shot dead for digging holes in the wall of a warehouse and stealing three packages of sugar, after failing to halt. The former Japanese warehouse for daily necessities and food used to be guarded by the Nationalists and was now temporarily used by the American aviation regiment.[119] Regardless, sites now occupied by the American military, whether borrowed, leased, or simply taken, were seen as American properties. Part of the Shandong University campus in Qingdao was used as a marine barracks, hospital, and drilling ground; therefore, entrance to this area by students and the general population was prohibited. A former German resident's house in Tianjin was now occupied by the marines, with a wooden sign stating "U.S. Gover't Property, Unauthorized Persons Keep out."[120] In Shanghai, the army and navy authorities set up "no entry" traffic signs outside a theater, the same location where the Japanese had once posted an identical sign. The exclusion of Chinese individuals from entering the navy and army YMCA in Shanghai, in the eyes of a Chinese Christian critic, bore simply too much of a resemblance to the notorious British signpost that allegedly read: "'No dogs and Chinese allowed.'"[121] This evolving political symbol represented not just a personal insult but also direct evidence of Western imperialism.

Smuggling and theft were not monopolized by the Chinese; American personnel actively participated in the lush black market, along with other foreign nationals including Russians, Koreans, Jews, Czechs, and the British. Well known by both sides at the time, GIs routinely traded their supplies while officers also smuggled goods for personal profit. As described by one Chinese interpreter, the "Service of Supplies" was nicknamed "Service of Squeeze" due to its known corruption.[122] Many sold "moonlight requisitions," ranging from basic necessities like food, socks, and uniforms, to even Thompson submachine guns.[123] An American officer concluded that the black market for US Army supplies in Kunming "could not have flourished without American help," a realization that "did not fit well with U.S. criticism of Chinese corruption" or with their own self-portrait.[124] In reality, some soldiers sold their own supplies or stolen ones to make extra spending money, while the more resourceful ones worked with Chinese laborers, merchants, and officials to carry out larger operations.[125] In November 1945, Major General Shepherd signed an order for "military police to seize and confiscate" all the "non-taxed American cigarettes, liquors, articles of clothing, and food stuffs" sold by local merchants and street venders because they were "identified as United States Government property and are intended for the use of the United States personnel."[126] While the American military pointed fingers at Chinese criminals, rarely were their own personnel court-martialed, nor did these black market dealings draw high-level attention.[127] One exception was the case of Marine Colonel Leslie F. Narum and Warrant Officer Burton E. Graham, who smuggled significant quantities of American medicines and pharmaceutical supplies, Chinese furs, and foreign exchange currencies. The case drew American attention not only due to the large scale of the smuggling operation and the involvement of a high-ranking officer, but also because the perpetrators managed to evade customs on both sides, thereby harming American interests as well. Despite these implications, the American military initially tried to keep the case under wraps and requested that Chinese officials handle it as a confidential matter.[128]

The American policy of taking "stringent actions" to protect its properties had real consequences. It enabled excessive use of force, resulting in deadly shooting incidents across the board, ranging from thieves and suspects to the innocent. Because this policy gave soldiers orders to fire at Chinese civilians, excessive violence also went beyond the sentry-guarded military compounds to other sites where American government properties were supposedly identified: from Chinese streets, stores, and stalls to individual households and bodies. As a result, even consumers of American goods were sometimes put in danger. On September 5, 1946, a marine MP fired two shots while apprehending Cao Guiming (Ts'ao Hui-ming), a student from the Catholic University in Beijing, for wearing American uniform pants. One bullet struck his left leg.[129] About three months later in Shanghai, another college student, Gao Ruofan, was forced off his bicycle by American MPs, who then attempted to strip off his American parka. As local crowds gathered, Gao was taken to the American barracks in a Jeep where his coat was removed.[130] In reality, used American clothes, including military uniforms, suits, and coats made from military blankets, were highly prized. Known as a "gospel for the literati," these garments were especially popular among students and teachers who often received them as relief goods or purchased them from stores and vendors.[131] American authorities regarded these "U.S. properties," whether contraband or not, as items to be confiscated on sight. As Provost Marshal Frank R. Harding explained in a letter to the Shanghai Municipal Police Bureau: "I had instructed the military police to check all Parkas worn by civilians as none had been sold by the U.S. Army in the Shanghai area and it would be reasonable to assume that possession would be illegal."[132] As such, any Chinese individual found in possession of American military goods was by default an offender. American soldiers could enforce the order of halt or shoot, and many took the liberty of doing so.

Like in the case of traffic accidents, which I discussed earlier in the book, injured survivors and families of victims in these shooting incidents prioritized financial compensation as one of their first and foremost demands, and such requests were often done through various intermediaries such as professional or hometown associations. Also similarly, legal and sociocultural understandings of these incidents differed significantly between the Chinese and American sides. For instance, the traditional concept of "a life for a life" still held strong among the Chinese people, even in cases where victims might indeed be stealing.[133] In their minds, it was clear that the fault lay with the Americans when soldiers armed with high-velocity weapons killed an unarmed civilian for stealing or attempting to steal, just as drivers were to be blamed in cases when Jeeps ran over pedestrians, regardless of whether they were jaywalking. From the American side, however, the suspect had to prove that he was not responsible or at fault in order to justify any compensation requests, because it was not the policy of the United States to award compensation in cases "where attempts are made to frustrate the operation of governmental departments" – for example, if the injury or death of the suspected thieves was "caused in whole or in part by their own wrongful acts."[134] Even when some were able to make such arguments, victims' families still had to cross many bureaucratic and legal hurdles in order to receive a penny from the US government. In most of the aforementioned cases, the US military rejected the requests for compensation or accountability from families of the victims. Instead, they issued a standardized brief statement to the municipal government, asserting that since the GI was carrying out his orders as a sentry on watch, acting within the scope of his authority, and the deceased individual was attempting to escape "under very questionable circumstances, the United States Government cannot accept any responsibility for his death."[135] Only a small portion of claims were found meritorious after extended periods of investigation. The number of successful complaints ranged between five hundred and six hundred annually, resulting in total compensation exceeding US$50,000. Notably, the American bureaucratic costs for handling these cases were apparently higher than the actual compensation paid out.[136] The stark contrast between Chinese and American perspectives on the stealing problem and its solution was symptomatic of the larger Sino-US tensions of the time. While the US military blamed the Chinese for not following orders and insisted on taking stringent actions against offenders to protect American properties, victims' families, local police handling these cases, and the general public tended to view these deadly shootings and their aftermath as emblematic of injustice and unequal relations.

If the poor focused on compensation, the elite population was more concerned with personal and national dignity. The student community, being a vulnerable social group subject to economic inflation, was also particularly sensitive to these incidents because of their heightened nationalist sentiments after the war. They had been at the forefront of political, economic, and cultural debates about American goods and now directly addressed affronts to China's sovereignty. Like cases of sexual violence, incidents involving university students received extensive media coverage because of their elite status in China. The two aforementioned cases of students wearing purchased GI uniforms were met with sensational newspaper headlines, such as "American soldiers forced removal of students' pants."[137] This narrative, which inaccurately turned the coat into pants, illustrated the perceived dual loss of sovereignty and masculinity. American force had penetrated into the most intimate part of the body, again linking personal and national humiliation. In his own account, college student Gao Ruofan described his exchange with the two American MPs who ordered him to remove his jacket. He said, "If I break the law wearing this piece of clothing, it should be our own Chinese police who handle this." The statement showed the student's sense of violation and the perceived overreach of American authority. His fellow students all became outraged at such treatment and made explicit comparisons of Americans in China with colonial rule: How could this happen in China's reclaimed territory of Shanghai, something that was worse than the "past atrocities of the Japanese toward Korea and Taiwan, the French toward Vietnam, and the British toward India"? "Isn't it obviously contempt for our nation that 'now claimed to be one of the Big Four nations?'"[138] In 1947, after rickshaw puller Su Mingcheng was killed by an American sailor, Shandong University students protested against the American military's continuous occupation of their campus in Qingdao. It was more than mere hypocrisy to the students that when their peers were insulted, violated, and shot at simply for wearing GI uniforms – some of which were sold by American servicemen who underwent no disciplinary actions – the US Marine Corps refused to return part of the university campus, instead using it as barracks and billets, and treating it like American property. As major beneficiaries of relief goods, students increasingly rejected these goods, driven by their patriotic fervor and political activism. Some called for a boycott by appealing to people's political and moral consciousness, arguing that purchasing American goods out of "curiosity and vanity" would make one guilty of betraying the brothers and sisters who had died from American firearms.[139] Others saw that China had "become an American colony," with its political and economic colonialism being worse than that of the Japanese.[140]

In reality, many American servicemen showed empathy toward the impoverished and hunger-stricken population in China. They understood that survival was the driving force behind these Chinese behaviors, many of which were shocking to the sensibilities of middle-class Americans. Some approached these complex and evolving interactions with a touch of humor and tried to come up with tactical solutions. One marine officer recalled a child thief who always waited outside the station for a chance. One day after being stopped from carrying off a seabag larger than himself and twice his weight, the boy stood "calling out names and epithets that I'm certain described my forebearers with undue frankness."[141] To put an end to frequent group thefts of supplies, including "spotters, markers, and other items," in a rural area, his unit set up an ambush one night and successfully caught a thief and a donkey using bird shot. The following day, they negotiated with a delegation of Chinese villagers, and "after many loud and lengthy speeches, each totally incomprehensible to the other side," the donkey was returned, the message of no stealing was clearly conveyed, and this plot "ended the organized raids on the camp."[142] Other service members, however, believed that China was a nation overrun by thieves and criminals and saw coolies and merchants as con men who deserved punishment. Therefore, only severe measures could curtail such activities to protect American property and interests. These deeply ingrained prejudices regarding China and the Chinese were evident in GIs' everyday interactions with locals, including thieves and suspects, street vendors, rickshaw pullers, and even police and officials.

Individual beliefs aside, it was the US military's policy that perpetuated racism and injustice against Chinese civilians through its policing and judicial system. These biased procedures enabled and encouraged violent actions, and their rationales further undermined the military leadership's own efforts to enhance allied relations. In May 1947, Admiral Cooke addressed the troubling issue of repeated deadly shootings of individuals suspected of stealing, stating that "the use of firearms is to be resorted to only... under circumstances that would justify shooting if the incident had occurred in the United States." However, despite expressing caution and sending reminders to local commander Pfeiffer, Cooke justified the policy in response to inquiries from Chinese authorities. He explained to them that in America, "it is lawful for the owner of private property to take such steps as may be necessary to protect his property from loss or danger through theft; and if the violation of his rights amounts to a felony, the use of firearms for such protection is justified."[143] Despite the fact that most cases did not involve self-defense in dangerous situations, nor was reasonable force used against "intruders," the American military felt justified in implementing the halt-or-shoot policy and stood firm in their legal and compensation systems. Even in instances where excessive force was clearly employed, local commanders often shielded the perpetrators – both legally and, at times, physically – keeping them from the reach of local police.[144]

Since WWII, the American military had tried to educate its soldiers on treating the Chinese equally. But in reality, these sporadic and inconsistent statements on fostering mutual respect turned into empty talk that few took seriously in action, just like the official preaching that the Chinese were "most like Americans" who shared many traits with us.[145] The explicit halt-or-shoot instruction became the standing order to follow, and soldiers were exempt from responsibilities for shooting intruders or suspects, if they failed to stop. As seen in the repeated bloody incidents, there was a profound disconnect between American rhetoric and the actual treatment of Chinese individuals. The purported ideals of equality and reciprocity before the law concealed the larger systemic injustices that persisted. Back home, deadly force was supposed to be used only when police believed that they had no other choice in order to protect human lives in dangerous interactions. However, even in America today, unarmed African American suspects are still disproportionately stopped, frisked, shot, and subject to police violence. In 1992, a Japanese student with limited English was fatally shot in Louisiana after going to the wrong house for a Halloween party and failing to stop after the owner told him to "freeze." The shooter was acquitted of manslaughter.[146] Ultimately, the frequent and fatal shootings of locals were not only the result of individual bias and misjudgment. They also stemmed from the American military's flawed policies that provided legal shields for GIs who easily, quickly, and unjustly resorted to deadly force against unarmed civilians – a practice rooted in America's pervasive racism in both domestic and foreign settings.

When an American soldier was given the order to shoot any suspect to protect American property, he could hardly contemplate distinctions between ally and occupied, between American and Chinese sites, and between reasonable and excessive use of force. Instead, he would likely see a Chinese individual as a suspect or criminal who failed to comply when being ordered by a US authority, a narrative that would later be documented in the official report. The fatal decision on how to proceed was left to the judgment of the individual soldier on site, and these split-second decisions took many Chinese lives that were quickly forgotten, if ever acknowledged. Even American authorities admitted that some of these shootings exhibited excessive violence. In Qingdao, a group of children who had gone to an American ship at night to steal were chased into sewage by armed soldiers, who then fired many shots, leading to one death.[147] In the aforementioned case of Sun Yugui, who was shot with six bullets to his upper body, the American investigators acknowledged that "it was not necessary for the sentries to use rifle fire in preventing the theft and apprehending the thief, in that from their position on the roof of the garage it would have been a simple maneuver to have dropped to the ground and to have surrounded the subject during one of the three trips he made to the windows."[148] In a mission that began as an occupation endeavor but eventually became far more intricate and protracted, American soldiers found themselves inadequately trained and ill prepared to handle such complex scenarios. These challenges encompassed a broad spectrum, ranging from impromptu acts of theft by civilians to well-organized robberies, smuggling, and criminal operations. In this relentless and disintegrating urban jungle, Americans confronted a different type of guerrilla warfare amidst the chaotic postwar Chinese environments. As it turned out, these quotidian encounters proved to be even more hazardous and damaging than the deadly but infrequent clashes with armed Communist forces.

American Gifts, American Disasters

In the early fall of 1947, General Pfeiffer, a staunch anti-Communist, concluded his time in China and returned to the United States. By that point, the Nationalist Government faced a dire situation marked by social disintegration, demoralization, and military vulnerability. The Chinese economy continued to deteriorate while student protests and urban unrest surged. Struggling with ammunition shortages without continued support from the United States, the Nationalist army turned toward defensive measures. Despite his "effective" measures against theft, General Pfeiffer harbored the mistaken belief that all the perpetrators were Communists who "moved all their loot through the Nationalist Army lines."[149] In reality, American goods were stolen by individuals of various streaks and colors, including cooks, laundry boys, prostitutes, laborers, gangsters, and even local police, and for different reasons, ranging from profiteering to sheer survival. For instance, General Marshall's Jeep was actually stolen on Christmas Day 1946 by a local criminal, who was caught just before selling the completely remodeled vehicle to a Nationalist officer on the black market. Pfeiffer also held two other erroneous notions: First, the Nationalist Government "never lifted a finger to prevent theft or apprehend a thief," and second, Chiang Kai-shek never kept a record of the number of Chinese killed by the marines or requested indemnity for the victims' impoverished families because he had also decided that the thieves were Communists.[150]

In fact, the Chinese government made various efforts to control black-market activities. Local authorities issued repeated bans on the sales and purchases of American military goods, warning sellers and customers of potential loss and punishment. As early as October 1945, the Shanghai Police Bureau had issued a notice prohibiting the sale or purchase of these goods.[151] Chinese police cracked down on gangs near the wharfs where American navy ships were docked and popular clubs where pickpocketing and robbing were most active. They targeted the so-called leech gang (*mahuang dang*), a group of local hooligans who lured GIs into shops and brothels to earn commissions and also engaged in theft, robbery, or bullying when opportunities arose.[152] Following the notorious 1946 shooting incident in which a student wearing a GI uniform was targeted, the Tianjin government banned its citizens, especially students and nonmilitary personnel, from wearing any American military uniforms. This notice was widely publicized through major Chinese and English newspapers.[153] Later, local authorities also banned peddler stalls from selling American military supplies of household products and prohibited civil servants from purchasing them.[154] In response to ongoing thefts, the Qingdao government set up patrols near American military warehouses and assigned the Chinese wharf police to guard these facilities after investigations showed that many local residents were making a living by stealing from them.[155]

Unsurprisingly, these measures were not effective during a time of economic crisis and sociopolitical chaos. The black market was never easy to eliminate, especially with active participation from some American personnel and Nationalist officials who also made profits from it. The boundaries between legal and black-market goods were not always clear either, as even policemen received confiscated American goods as bonus pay. But the Chinese government did respond to the complaints, requests, and demands from the American military authorities about the rampant theft. They offered various proposals to address the issue, such as measures to reduce the presence of the urban poor, children, beggars, and stall hawkers near the barracks. But not all of the suggestions were taken, particularly those regarding Sino-American collaborations. In a letter to the mayor of Tianjin, Du Jianshi (Tu Chien-shih), a former classmate of Commander Thomas from Army Command and General Staff College at Fort Leavenworth, General Howard rejected the suggestion to add a local police patrol because Chinese police were "not allowed within the American compounds."[156] Similarly, Li Xianliang (Lee Sien-liang), the mayor of Qingdao, proposed that Chinese and American sentries patrol together in order to reduce frequent shootings. Again this was rejected due to the US policy that aimed to avoid the appearance of American involvement in Chinese military affairs or vice versa.[157]

In March 1948, things became so bad that Defense Minister Bai Chongxi, on behalf of Chiang Kai-shek, asked the Ministry of Foreign Affairs to investigate ways to improve legal proceedings and dealings in response to the frequent shootings and killings of Chinese individuals by American military personnel. On April 14, 1948, Mr. Chu (Qu Jinpei) 渠金培, the director of the Foreign Affairs Department at the municipal Police Bureau, met with Major F. H. Vogal from Provost Marshal's headquarters in Qingdao. They produced a memorandum stating that the American authorities would henceforth not directly arrest Chinese offenders, summon Chinese witnesses, or carry out searches of Chinese suspects in possession of American government property. Instead, they agreed that when conducting investigations involving Chinese military personnel or citizens, "the American authority should immediately notify and request the Chinese military police or Chinese police force to conduct a prompt action on the former's behalf."[158] Afterward, the Executive Yuan issued a four-measure instruction to local police and military units on "how to prevent criminal cases involving American military personnel." First, to prevent misunderstandings, local police should exhort people not to stay in or near American compounds. If encountering drunken or misbehaving American soldiers, the police should persuade locals to disperse quickly rather than remain as onlookers. Second, Chinese MPs should be deployed to sites frequented by American soldiers, and in cases of drunkenness and misbehavior, immediately notify the American military, providing detailed reports and memos. Third, top military leaders in each region should maintain close contact with American military officials and use their personal relationships to request restraint in the arbitrary use of firearms against Chinese civilians to protect innocent individuals. Fourth, when incidents occur, police authorities, along with victims' families and local headmen, should investigate the sites, collect evidence and testimonies, and promptly report the cases to the American authorities.[159]

Lacking legal options and authority to regulate American military personnel in China, Nationalist officials were left with limited recourse. They resorted to negotiating memoranda or petitioning their American guests to exercise restraint in the arbitrary use of arms. Even these requests were often made by leveraging personal rapport with US leadership. Rather than developing a systematic approach to curb or end the excessive use of force by American servicemen, the government focused on controlling and educating its own people. The Executive Yuan instructed local officials to minimize the direct contacts between locals and US soldiers.[160] Instances where local officials took a more active role in addressing GI misconduct typically involved elite victims. For example, after the shooting of college student Cao Guiming, Beijing officials visited the hospital the following morning and met with the head of the American MP, requesting an apology, punishment, compensation, and a commitment to prevent similar incidents in the future. Tang Yongxian (Tang Yung Hsien), the city's chief of police, explained that immediate "emergency measures" were taken "in case miscreants see an opportunity to wreak havoc" during the current "special time."[161] Overall, the government was more concerned about whether these cases would be exploited for Communist propaganda than justice or protection for the victims, the majority of whom were from the urban poor.

The Generalissimo himself, wanting to keep the American allies in China for as long as possible, might not have personally addressed the subject of indemnities for the Chinese lives lost. But municipal governments, which were directly involved in the investigations of these incidents and faced pressure from grieving family members and local organizations, repeatedly raised their concerns. Confidential internal reports, typically from the Police Bureau or the Bureau of Foreign Affairs, voiced widespread dissatisfaction. Some officials questioned, "If American soldiers were merely 'firing at the air' as a warning, how come the Chinese victims ended up dead?" They emphasized that all these gunshots were lethal, despite many other options for capturing or stopping the perpetrators, suggesting an intent to arbitrarily kill the victims.[162] Others went as far as urging the Nationalist Government to launch formal protests against the American government. They felt that the statements from American authorities were nothing but excuses accompanied by insincere apologies that merely referred to the deadly killings as "regrettable" – a standard formula repeated after each tragic incident. Moreover, municipal officials expressed frustration over the American failure to adhere to the agreed terms outlined in official memos. Specifically, the US military refused to turn over its members to be questioned by Chinese courts, failed to answer inquiries about the trial process or requests to review judgments before and after their issuance, and searched, detained, and questioned local witnesses and confiscated goods from Chinese citizens without notifying or soliciting permission from Chinese authorities.

While noting the American disregard for Chinese jurisdiction, local officials' complaints and requests to higher authorities were usually justified by invoking the official line of maintaining Sino-US friendship and preventing Communist sabotage, which remained the predominant political agenda. Chiang Kai-shek's concerns about thwarting Communist instigations were well founded. But his tolerance and acquiescence proved counterproductive. The CCP's emphasis on American shootings of civilians became an effective weapon to fire at the American imperialists, thanks to their damaging and imprudent halt-or-shoot policy and the Nationalists' failure to address the issues. Communist media consistently portrayed these shooting incidents as arbitrary acts of violence committed by American forces against innocent civilians. Although the wounded also included organized or armed criminals engaged in munitions raids, such details were conveniently omitted. Alongside traffic accidents and instances of sexual violence, victims of American shootings incidents were depicted as representatives of the collective Chinese populace, including children, laborers, students, and consumers, who endured everyday brutality at the hands of American soldiers with no protection from a corrupt government. In a twist of fate, American gifts and aid turned into American disasters – exacerbating the troubles for the Nationalists already mired in deep military, economic, and political crises.

Sacred Death: Rejecting American Flour

On May 30, 1948, during the Memorial Day services honoring fallen US military personnel, John M. Cabot, the American consul general in Shanghai, criticized student protests led by St. John's University, a "great university supported by contributions from the United States." He warned that "students getting their education through the beneficence of Americans who have contributed their mites to knowledge and understanding – students whose very food depends upon the labor of the American farmer and the generosity of the American taxpayer – should not spread calumnies against the United States." Otherwise, the aid program to China might end.[163] His comments came in the middle of the "Opposing the US Support of Japan" movement, which developed in reaction to American plans to rehabilitate Japanese economy and military capabilities within the evolving Cold War geopolitical dynamics. On May 4 – a date highly significant in modern Chinese history that marks the anniversary of the patriotic May Fourth movement nearly three decades earlier – more than ten thousand representatives from 120 local schools had gathered in Shanghai to form a protest association. Protesters adopted slogans such as "Anti-American aid to Japan," "Opposing American dumping of goods," "Love using national products," and "Anti-hunger, Anti-oppression."[164] The movement quickly spread to other cities, drawing support from a wide political spectrum united by a shared resentment toward Japan, the former enemy responsible for recent atrocities, and concerns over its potential resurgence as a threat.

This wave of dissent showed a growing disillusionment among the intellectual community and the general public with America, which they felt had betrayed China's alliance and disregarded Chinese interests. In Beijing, more than a hundred university professors issued a public statement protesting American support of Japan and refusing to accept American relief materials. The event subsequently was immortalized by Mao Zedong's famous article "Farewell, Leighton Stuart!" which depicted Zhu Ziqing, head of the Chinese department at Tsinghua University, as having, "though seriously ill, starved to death rather than accept U.S. 'relief food.'"[165] This imagery of a sacred death was so powerful that it soon overshadowed other quotidian encounters with American food and aid.

The rejection and denunciation stood in stark contrast to the desires and demands of many Chinese who sought American goods out of necessity, curiosity, or a combination of both. In the postwar era, Chinese civilians drank surplus coffee, emulated GIs by drinking Coca-Cola, used DDT to spray their houses and soil pits, and received penicillin shots for treatment. The influence of the United States extended beyond the elite class and cosmopolitan centers, permeating individual bodies, households, streets, soil, and water, as well as shaping consumption, sensibilities, and values within the intimate and public spheres of Chinese society. Cultural and economic elites in the late 1940s had mixed views of American goods: They celebrated America's material affluence and technological advancement while critiquing its culture of consumption and pleasure-seeking. There was also growing serious concern about the socioeconomic impacts on local industries. Like in the debates over Jeep girls, Chinese nationalist discourses concerning American goods encompassed a variety of conservative, leftist, and industrialist groups, reflecting ongoing discussions over Westernization and modernization from earlier decades. Nevertheless, as the economy collapsed, the civil war escalated, and Communist propaganda intensified, these multivalent debates grew increasingly politicized. American food and goods were no longer seen as neutral nutrients, but rather as toxic agents of imperialist penetration that needed to be rejected and denounced, making for a direct battleground for political struggles.

Ultimately, the Chinese rejection of American goods, as epitomized by the case of Zhu Ziqing, became a rallying cry for the anti-American movement. The highly symbolic imagery of a Chinese individual refusing to eat American flour in order to maintain his personal and national

Figure 5.7 Marines exit China, giving thumbs-up and "ding hao" farewells in Beijing, 1947. Superstock/Alamy Stock Photo.

dignity illustrated the Communist narrative of moral superiority and self-reliance. Although the Communist Party itself received American aid and Soviet weaponry, it promoted the key origin myth that within a war of justice, Communists' "millet plus rifles" were able to defeat Chiang Kai-shek's "bread plus cannon" equipped by the American government.[166] Such a claim of legitimacy began as early as the victory against the Japanese invaders and was amplified during the Korean War, when the CCP asserted its triumph against American aggression. Overall, under the leadership of the Party, the power of the Chinese people, including progressive intellectuals like Zhu, oppressed rickshaw pullers, boycotting workers, and protesting students, prevailed over the power possessed by American goods, military might, and brutal imperialists at large. As Mao put it clearly on the eve of victory: "We are not only good at destroying the old world, we are also good at building the new. Not only can the Chinese people live without begging alms from the imperialists, they will live a better life than that in the imperialist countries."[167] In the turn from American charms to American harms, we find the changing destiny of modern China (see Figure 5.7).

Epilogue
Revisiting the Lost Era

When President Jimmy Carter greeted Deng Xiaoping at the White House during the latter's historic visit to the United States in January 1979, he shook hands with Deng and said to the Chinese vice premier with a smile, "we almost met before."[1] In April 1949, Carter had first landed in China as a young naval officer serving on a submarine visiting Qingdao, while Deng was leading a massive force of the People's Liberation Army in the decisive campaign of crossing the Yangzi River and capturing the Nationalist capital. By early June, the last American marine had evacuated from Qingdao under siege, as the surrounding Communist forces marched into the city unopposed – just four months before the founding of the People's Republic of China. This was truly the end of an era, to put it mildly.

Decades later, President Carter told the story not to lament the fall of China, but to celebrate the beginning of a new relationship. He had since repeatedly stressed a personal connection with China and his "love for the Chinese people." Growing up a Southern Baptist from Plains, Georgia, the seven-year-old farm boy received from his seafaring uncle, who was in the US Navy, a special souvenir – a delicate model of a wooden Chinese junk, which Carter kept in his boyhood home for decades. When he turned ten or twelve years old, his number one hero in the world was Lottie Moon, a Baptist missionary who had devoted her life to China. Finally in 1949, when he was in the navy, Carter toured the same seaports his uncle had visited – Hong Kong, Shanghai, and Qingdao – and was "intrigued with the people of China."[2]

We do not know how much his involvement with China shaped the future American president's view of the country, and it would be a stretch to connect such familiarity to the normalization of bilateral relations under his watch in any tangible ways. Nevertheless, Carter's personal experience was part of the long history of Chinese-US relations since the eighteenth century, what many Americans saw as a special bond forged by generations of missionaries, traders, journalists, politicians, travelers, and soldiers.[3] Notably, this experience was shared to highlight the "people-to-people diplomacy" that Carter famously championed during and after his presidency. In 2011, when attending a ceremony to celebrate the fortieth anniversary of Ping-Pong Diplomacy in the Great Hall of the People in Beijing with Vice President Xi Jinping, Carter restated: "It was that breakthrough just with ping-pong players – that is people-to-people – that was really more important than the decisions of political leaders. And I think that is a stability that is going to prevail in the future."[4]

In many ways, US servicemen in China, which an official army guide called "ambassador[s] of the American people to the Chinese people," formed a direct force of grassroots engagement in the aftermath of WWII.[5] Their quotidian interactions with local civilians from all walks of life embodied a type of informal diplomacy, which played a pivotal role in Sino-US relations during a defining historical moment. These exchanges affected the political dynamics during the Chinese civil war and shaped the sociocultural identities of both sides. The micropolitics of the everyday provided a unique lens through which to better understand the so-called loss of China, leaving behind lasting legacies that remain to be recovered and reevaluated.

A New Script for Anti-Americanism: Everyday Abuse and Resistance

Since the reform movement of 1978, Chinese historiography of WWII has experienced some major changes, especially in reevaluating the Nationalists' contribution to the war effort and the United States' assistance.[6] But discussions of the postwar period between 1945 and 1949 remain fixated on the civil war's outcome. This era is widely considered a pivotal juncture in Sino-US relations, marking the beginning of a profound divergence between the two countries during the Cold War. Yet there is a lack of critical study of the American military presence beyond operational levels. Dominant historiographies, from both the Communist and Nationalist sides, have reduced the chaotic and volatile experiences of encounters to a tidy, sequenced chord concerning national destiny – China's victory over Japan and the triumph of the Communist Party – while disagreeing on whether this occurred despite American support for the Nationalists or because of its lack. Following the end of WWII, both parties sought to capitalize on the prevailing nationalist sentiment and heightened patriotism. The Nationalist Government faced a political quandary: It needed to promote nationalism while also maintaining rapport with the United States. Consequently, it chose to downplay Chinese grievances against GI misconduct, dismissing these incidents as isolated accidents or merely legal matters. This strategy backfired when the CCP seized upon these grievances, launching a powerful propaganda campaign that recast the narrative of anti-American imperialism in terms of everyday brutality. They focused on emotionally charged accounts of the violence US forces perpetrated on Chinese civilians, which resonated deeply with the populace. This incisive propaganda undermined the legitimacy and credibility of the Nationalist leadership. Eventually, the Communists emerged triumphant in this critical battle for public opinion and popular support, alongside the military front.

This American occupation has left behind a toxic legacy that continues to be exploited in Chinese nationalist politics. There were previous anti-American demonstrations. But the late 1940s movement introduced new prototypes and powerful imagery that forged an emotional bond among supporters that transcended socioeconomic, political, and geographical boundaries. As discussed in the book, the Communists developed an effective formula that profiled American racism, sexual aggression, and everyday abuse to denounce American imperialism and encroachment on China's sovereignty. The portrayal of ordinary victims, featuring rickshaw pullers, women, and children being abused or killed by American GIs, evoked the strongest sentiments in the Chinese psyche, especially during times of tension.[7] Sensitive sociocultural issues surrounding race and sex became the foundation for popular anti-American nationalism, providing insight into why such a narrative remains compelling long after the US military presence ended in China.

Upon entering the Korean War, the CCP organized another fierce political campaign for mass mobilization against American imperialists. There is a direct link between the upgraded Korean War campaign and the Anti-American Brutality movement several years earlier. First, the new propaganda war employed similar techniques of mass rallying, petitioning, parading, and performing on the street. Wall posters, cartoons, and editorials appeared on college campuses, in the streets, and in the countryside. More importantly, the mass campaign directly inherited the themes of "'beastly' behavior of U.S. servicemen in China, the unholy alliance between the imperialist America and the Chiang Kai-shek regime, and the American 'rearming' of Japan."[8] Urging the public to hate (*choushi*), despise (*bishi*), and disdain (*mieshi*) US imperialism, propaganda materials republished or recycled materials from previous literature of the late 1940s, refreshing people's memories or educating them on American atrocities against the Chinese people.[9]

Even by 1950, Chinese animosity toward the United States was not as intense as the Communist Party had hoped, hampering its efforts to mobilize the public for a fierce war to "Resist America and Assist

Korea." In its mass propaganda initiatives, the Party tried various affective strategies and found that grassroots audiences responded most strongly to accounts of the harms inflicted by the United States upon the Chinese people, as well as to depictions of anti-Chinese discrimination.[10] Visual materials proved particularly effective, such as "Unsavory Images of American Troops in China" that featured the everyday brutality inflicted upon ordinary citizens. Some visuals reproduced prominent past incidents to evoke a sense of reality and authenticity, including deadly encounters with American military vehicles on the street, the killing of Shanghai rickshaw puller Zang Yaocheng, the rape of Shen Chong in Beijing, and the shooting of a Qingdao workman near a wharf by American guards (see Figures E.1–E.4). Other visuals recast iconic fictional characters in fresh roles to align with the Party's new historical agenda.

Zhang Leping's Sanmao comic strips were among the most popular works of the time. The legendary child-hero, Sanmao, whose name derives from the "three hairs" sticking out on his head, first appeared in the early 1930s as a critic of Chinese society. Misbehaving American GIs

Figure E.1 Illustration of an American military truck rampaging down the street, killing innocent people, part of the "Brutalities of American Troops in China" series, drawn by Ding Hao, 1951. Hunter Collection, Center for Research Libraries, USA.

Figure E.2 Illustration of two drunk American sailors assaulting a rickshaw puller outside a nightclub, part of the "Brutalities of American Troops in China" series, drawn by Ding Hao, 1951. Hunter Collection, Center for Research Libraries, USA.

Figure E.3 Illustration of the rape of a Chinese woman by an American soldier, with a Nationalist official bowing to the American authority who exonerates him, part of the "Brutalities of American Troops in China" series, drawn by Ding Hao, 1951. Hunter Collection, Center for Research Libraries, USA.

A New Script for Anti-Americanism

Figure E.4 Illustration of a Chinese workman shot by an American guard outside a military compound, part of the "Brutalities of American Troops in China" series, drawn by Ding Hao, 1951. Hunter Collection, Center for Research Libraries, USA.

already figured significantly in the artist's work in 1947, *Adventures of Sanmao, the Orphan* (*Sanmao liulangji* 三毛流浪記). In 1951, Zhang created two new series, *Sanmao's Indictment* (*Sanmao de kongsu* 三毛的控訴) and *Sanmao Stands Up* (*Sanmao fanshen ji* 三毛翻身記), and refigured the character into a victim of American brutality to serve the new mission of fighting American imperialists.[11] In one story, Sanmao tries to sell flowers on the street and runs into an American sailor who casually picks a flower from his basket without paying and walks away with a fashionable Jeep girl in his arms. Upon chasing the big American man, the emaciated Sanmao is knocked to the ground with one slap. After trying to reason with the sailor, his grandma is punched and falls, run over by a speeding American Jeep. The GI driver, who has one hand over another Chinese girl next to him, then picks up the man and woman and drives away without even a glimpse of the grandma's body (see Figure E.5). In another story, Sanmao attends an emotional mass denunciation meeting to "oppose the US arming the Japanese." He bursts into tears after hearing a female victim share her experience of being abused by Americans. Sanmao then jumps at the chance to speak of his own traumatic experience (see Figure E.6). The scene provides an educational

202 Epilogue: Revisiting the Lost Era

Figure E.5 "Indifference to life," *Sanmao Stands Up* by Zhang Leping, 1951.

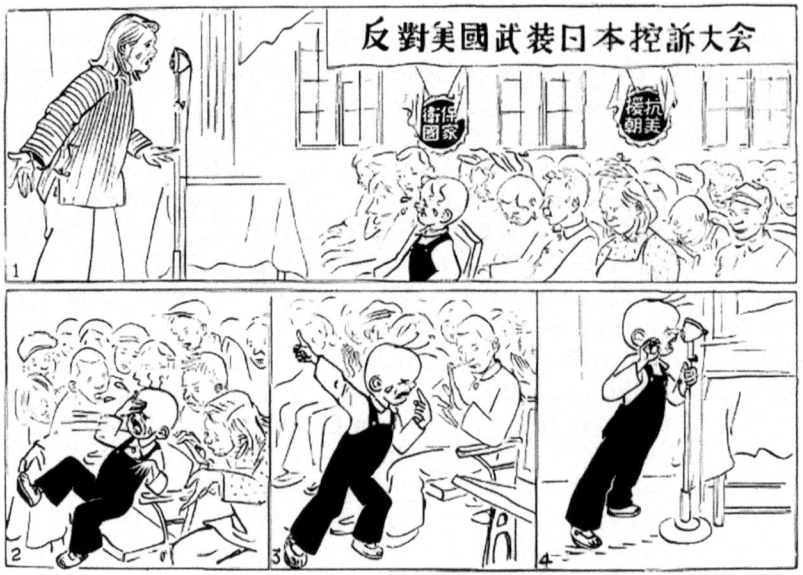

Figure E.6 "Mass denunciation meeting," *Sanmao Stands Up* by Zhang Leping, 1951.

session on American violence and an affective script for actual collective sharing in the tens of thousands of denunciation meetings throughout the country.[12] Supposedly based on true stories, Sanmao's experience foregrounds the daily abuse of the Chinese poor.[13] Sanmao, the well-liked prototypical Chinese child-hero who used to be a middle-class city kid, a boy soldier in the Second Sino-Japanese War, and an orphan wandering the streets of Shanghai after the war, now becomes a victim and witness to American atrocities and aggression. He is no longer satirical or funny, but evokes strong emotions of anger, hatred, and disdain toward America.

After peaking during the Korea War, anti-American sentiments continued in the Cultural Revolution and into the reform era. Although the direct military and political context has often been forgotten, the theme of American brutality has remained ingrained in national memory, perpetuated through popular works like comic strips, history books, and newspaper features, as well as government publications and scholarly works. For instance, mandatory secondary school history textbooks included the Peking rape incident at least until the 1980s, ensuring its longevity as a collective national memory for future generations.[14] Despite his tragic death, rickshaw puller Zang Yaocheng has lived on, with his biography reprinted twice in the 1980s and 1990s and included in the local histories of Shanghai.[15] In the midst of the student protest movement in 1989, a comprehensive eight-hundred-page collection of historical materials was published, documenting the Anti-American Brutality movement that had occurred more than four decades earlier.[16] In 1986, Jet Li, who grew up in mainland China in the 1960s and 1970s, made his directorial debut and starred in a Hong Kong action movie called *Born to Defend* (*Zhonghua yingxiong* 中華英雄).[17] It tells the heroic story of Little Jie, a young veteran from the Nationalist Army who valiantly battles American soldiers. When WWII finally ends, he returns to Qingdao and finds his hometown occupied by imperious GIs. Chinese civilians fall victim to their violence, hit by speeding vehicles, sexually assaulted, and clubbed by both American MPs and Chinese authorities. Little Jie's senior colleague in the army, now a rickshaw puller, and the latter's daughter, who becomes a bar hostess out of poverty, die from these violent assaults. Little Jie goes on to pursue revenge and eventually defeats and kills the GI criminal. The film, titled *Chinese Hero* if translated literally, builds upon the trope of everyday abuse and belongs to the genre of the Chinese folk hero narrative, featuring national humiliation and salvation.[18] But the Chinese protagonist in *Born to Defend* is fighting a more powerful and recent imperialist figure, the American soldier. Little Jie represents the ordinary hero, a poor Chinese laborer and common man who defeats GIs with strength and wit and helps his countrymen through loyalty, friendship, and collective resistance. The story centers around the literal and symbolic fights between Chinese veterans and American soldiers, with the latter calling the former "castrated by the Japanese." It deals with a question different from traditional anti-imperialist folk hero movies. As a character puts it: Who are the real "anti-Japanese heroes," the American soldiers as often claimed or the nameless Chinese men?

The recurring persona of the Chinese victim facing American brutality, as seen in the characters of Sanmao and Little Jie, testifies to its enduring appeal and longevity within Chinese nationalism. The more recent anti-Americanism since the 1990s conjures up eerie parallels with that of 1945–1949, as perceptions of America once again become filled with contradiction, mixing fantasy and hostility. Despite the strengthening of economic and cultural ties between the two nations, popular animosity toward America could rapidly grow with great intensity. During times of tension, the powerful trope can be easily evoked. For example, following the 1999 North Atlantic Treaty Organization bombing of the Chinese embassy in Belgrade, which killed three Chinese journalists and wounded at least twenty, student protesters stoned the US embassy in Beijing and converted the Statue of Liberty into the "Demon of Liberty."[19] Two years later, mass demonstrations again occurred in major cities following the collision of an American surveillance plane with a Chinese navy fighter jet over the South China Sea, which killed the Chinese pilot. Enraged university students and the public demanded an American explanation, apology, and compensation. Previous anti-American narratives were quickly revived and key messages of American aggression and victimization of Chinese resurfaced. Abstract concepts of national humiliation and sovereignty infringement again became embodied by the killing and suffering of the innocent, and infused with emotional appeal and moral justification.

Emotional intensity, polarizing perceptions of America, and high volatility remain key features of Sino-US relations. Like a ticking time bomb, explosive anti-American sentiment can be triggered overnight by a single event, damaging China-US relations that have been built over decades. It takes only one "accident," rather than missile strikes or tanks rolling, to shake up the entire relationship. The "ordinary victim" fans the biggest flames among a wide Chinese base. Once unleashed, the weapon of the everyday does not always adhere to the official party line and can take on a life of its own.

A Forgotten Occupation

For the American side, the mission in China in the aftermath of WWII stands as a minor episode in the history of its global military empire.

Partly because of the relatively small number of troops stationed in the country and the brevity of their presence, existing studies of postwar US occupations often overlook China. The mission's vague objectives and mixed results, difficult to define and evaluate, have further contributed to its obscurity in US diplomatic and military history. There is equally a shortage of popular literature on American veterans after the war compared to their predecessors known for adventures and heroism, such as the renowned Flying Tigers in wartime China or even the old China hands of the early twentieth century.[20] In reality, there is no lack of reports, agreements, or correspondence on the China mission in military and national archives. The images, artifacts, and tales about American soldiers' experiences are also preserved in personal letters, family heirlooms, and private collections. Many intimate stories remain skeletons in the closet or have been buried for nearly eighty years, while others can be spotted in veterans' oral history recordings, reunion pamphlets, news reports, and online forums. Unlike the more coherent narratives of victories, bravery, and sacrifices during WWII, the postwar stories about American soldiers in China are often told in ambiguous and diverse ways. Against the background of shifting geopolitics across the Pacific, these accounts shift among the different themes of liberation, occupation, assistance to an ally, and fights against communism.

Unlike the rich scholarly accounts of US occupation of Japan and Korea, the China story remains comparatively underexplored – particularly the extensive noncombat duties performed by American servicemen, as well as their intimate exchanges with local society. This lack of attention also has to do with the difficulty of situating this chapter within the normative narrative of WWII as "the Good War," a just war that not only brought prosperity to the American nation, but also peace, progress, and democracy to the occupied people.[21] The GI misconduct and subsequent anti-American sentiment, especially in an allied country, do not fit into the triumphalist tale of the occupation in East Asia, but rather speak of the "failures" that have consumed American minds for decades. In the heated environment of the early Cold War, the US government attempted to play the role of a liberal, benevolent leader of the free world. Nevertheless, soon after the Allied victory, nationwide protests erupted in China, becoming what a *Time* magazine piece called the "most conspicuous demonstrations of ill will" against America globally. This realization came as a painful surprise, as Americans became acutely aware that "much of the rest of the world intensely dislikes them," particularly given their record of "staggering charities" to the world.[22] One year after their complete withdrawal, American forces, including veteran officers and divisions that had previously served in China during and after

WWII, were deployed to Korea. There they once again encountered Chinese troops, armed with American equipment that had been captured during the Chinese civil war.

Caught between the monumental conflicts of WWII and the subsequent Korean and Vietnam Wars, American operations in postwar China seem to occupy an awkward and insignificant position. However, they established important precedents and patterns for global engagements during and after the Cold War while providing comparative insights into the workings of US military empire. Operation BELEAGUER marked "the end of a decade-long Marine presence in China but represented a postwar beginning for American foreign policy and the Corps." It served as the debut of "a series of sometimes frustrating MOOTW missions" undertaken by the Marine Corps as "America's force-in-readiness," encompassing all three major types of Cold War operations: humanitarian assistance, nation assistance, and peacekeeping.[23] The operations in China provided a preview, an experimental testing ground, and a dress rehearsal for this new style of warfare, shedding fresh light on its strengths and limitations during the era of limited wars.

In particular, US soldiers in China faced significant challenges due to ambiguous and sometimes conflicting objectives. Their mission impossible – to maintain peace and neutrality while providing assistance to the Nationalist Government – was fraught with the risk of deep entanglement in a violent civil conflict. This precarious balance was epitomized by incidents in Anping, Guye, and elsewhere, where US forces were ambushed by local Communist troops employing guerrilla tactics in a Maoist "People's War" that would later become widely used around the world. As noted by Richard Bernstein, a seasoned journalist with extensive experience in China, "they were the first such confrontations between American forces and a new kind of enemy, one that was going to become familiar over the succeeding decades in Vietnam and, still later, in Iraq and Afghanistan, in the kind of confrontation that gave rise to the term 'asymmetric warfare.'"[24] The operation's key challenges were further highlighted following marines' shelling of Anshan, which led to intensified American criticism over the killing of civilians and the perceived recklessness of placing soldiers in unnecessary danger. This growing public unease with overseas military engagements and demands for the return of American troops would also become a persistent theme. Despite the limited scales of direct confrontations, US military involvement, intended to stabilize and assist a friendly allied nation, ended up becoming a source of instability within Chinese society. These military and political risks foreshadowed similar patterns in later US interventions, such as those in Korea, Vietnam, the Dominican Republic, and the

Middle East. For example, in 1958, invited by its prime minister, US troops were deployed to Lebanon to protect its independence and contain communism following growing instability. In 1965, US troops were sent to the Dominican Republic in response to a civil war outbreak. In both cases, what began as neutral, benign peacemaking operations quickly escalated into combat missions. These actions drew both local and international charges of US imperialism and failed to resolve the underlying domestic and regional issues.[25]

In the legal domain, the United States' practices in China have also established important precedents. For instance, the renewed Sino-US agreements regarding the status of US military personnel in China in 1946 marked "the subtle yet fundamental shift in the legal foundation of U.S. troops' extraterritorial privileges," from "the expediency of temporary wartime combat missions to a potential prerequisite for long-term military presence." This new justification, now based on mere presence rather than active combat duty, became the "foundational doctrine that governed the legal status of U.S. troops abroad for the next several decades," setting a precedent for the Status of Forces Agreements between the United States and various allies during the Cold War.[26] After the Nationalist Party decamped to Taiwan, the small Military Assistance Advisory Group was sent to the island and formally operated as part of the US embassy; it therefore enjoyed diplomatic immunity. With the growing number of the group members and other US military personnel in Taiwan, together with a rise in criminal cases, the Agreement between the Republic of China and the United States of America on the Status of United Armed Forces in the Republic of China was reached in 1965. It was in effect until 1979, when the United States terminated diplomatic relations with the Republic of China and all US military personnel left Taiwan.[27]

In terms of local animosities, postwar Chinese protests against American soldiers' misconduct and the US military presence reflect patterns similar to contemporary anti-base movements in alliance partners such as Japan, South Korea, and the Philippines.[28] For instance, in June 2002, the tragic deaths of two Korean schoolgirls, crushed by a US Army armored vehicle, ignited nationwide demonstrations characterized by the familiar rallying cry, "Yankee go home!"[29] In Okinawa, recurring incidents of sexual violence committed by American servicemen continue to be a major trigger for protests. On Christmas Eve 2023, a local girl was allegedly kidnapped and raped by a member of the air force. In the Philippines, public outcry over toxic waste contamination, environmental destruction, human trafficking, and the abandonment of Amerasian children continues to fuel movements against the US military presence following the successful closure of US bases in 1992.[30] These incidents highlight the unintended consequences of American overseas bases, transforming them into "embattled garrisons" that are strategically important but politically vulnerable.[31] As Andrew Yeo, a scholar in international politics, has pointed out, local protests cannot be simply dismissed as "a form of blanket anti-Americanism." Instead, the political contestation surrounding these military bases blurs the lines between "high and low politics," reflecting deeper societal concerns and national sentiments.[32]

Today, many of these institutional, conceptual, and personal connections between American soldiers and Chinese civilians remain unacknowledged due to the deepening Cold War conflicts that immediately followed. Nor are the sustained sociocultural impacts that quotidian encounters exerted on American society at large duly recognized. The US military presence after WWII exposed tens of thousands of servicemen to lives beyond their comfort zones back home. While performing assigned missions, determined by high-level diplomatic exchanges, political negotiations, and military strategies, US soldiers on the ground often forged intimate connections with local populations by exchanging goods, services, languages, and cultures, an encounter that both followed and contradicted official policies and popular representations. Christina Klein, for example, has identified the late 1940s and 1950s as a distinct cultural moment during which Americans became fascinated with Asia and the Pacific through the proliferation of popular cultural productions. Thanks to the empire's unprecedented reach during the Cold War, Americans produced and consumed a surge of new plays, movies, novels, and nonfiction books about Asia.[33] If these new representational works, often fictional, helped propagate the new ideology of global integration with mutual understanding and benefits, the presence of US troops formed a direct force of everyday diplomacy. China was embodied, enacted, and brought home via GIs' letters, keepsakes, spouses, tastes, vocabularies, and memoirs. Together with the larger body of troops who served in Taiwan, Japan, Korea, Vietnam, and other areas in the region, they helped reshape American identities in the new age of global expansion.

Perhaps there is no better illustration of such intricate relations than the story of Anna Wong. In 1947, General George Marshall left China to assume his new position as the US secretary of state. He invited a beloved maid, Anna, to America, and she agreed. A few years later, when the US Congress approved legislation that allowed twenty thousand Chinese to enter the country, Anna reunited with her family, who were among the first to be admitted. But the beautiful story of friendship and reunion is not without a twist. The patriotic Chinese woman "without much education," who won Marshall and his wife's highest praise for her service, also had issues with the general, not over pay or work hours, but rather the harsh measures that Marshall supposedly took in dealing with the Nationalist Government during his mediation mission. She once burst out, "General Marshall! You no help China, Anna no work for you!" The general, who had chosen China as his duty station from 1924 to 1927 and learned some Chinese while leading the 15th Infantry as a lieutenant colonel, often ignored Generalissimo Chiang Kai-shek's requests and complaints. But on this occasion, he sat down to hear Anna's protest, and it finally took Mrs. Marshall several days and some personal diplomacy to persuade Anna to stay.[34] Stories like this have escaped most scholarly attention. But they help us better understand the potent force of Chinese nationalism, the distinctive position of China within the American global order, and the deep ties that the two sides have forged through an entangled relationship.

Where to (Re)Turn

No one here seems remotely aware of Kunming's past. Amazingly, the travel agents here have almost no maps. "And Kweiyang?" I ask. I remember Kweiyang as being 500 km or so to the east, eighteen hours away by jeep – but the town appears to have fallen down a deep ravine. A place which I considered my war-home has apparently been excised from [the] foreigner's itineraries and local memory.

– Barney Rosset, 1996[35]

When Barney Rosset, an influential American publisher, returned to China for the first time in 1996, he felt disappointed. But it was not just the disappearance of Guiyang (Kweiyang), where he had worked as an army photographer in the 1940s, that he lamented, but also the erasure of the entire history of American contributions to China. Rosset's story is far from unique. Many US veterans returned to China after the country reopened in the late 1970s and found little trace of the old scenes that they had vividly remembered. Their Chinese interpreters, associates, and colleagues in mainland China also largely remained silent on this history, even to their own families, due to the harsh treatments they received during the Cultural Revolution or the fear of being accused as American spies in the future. This significant era, though quite recent, seems a lost one in both the United States and China.

In hindsight, the quotidian encounter between American soldiers and Chinese civilians seems to speak of a doomed loss. Systemic racism and sexism within the US military, as well as the unequal dynamics of uneven reciprocity between the two allied nations, planted not only the seeds of tension, but also the roots of outright conflicts. In the immediate term, the American military occupation, intended to assist the Nationalist Government, ended up contributing to its downfall. As one marine researcher put it, the mission impossible was a military success but a political failure.[36] Communist propaganda campaigns successfully linked everyday grievances against the American military to the Party's political maneuvers against the Nationalist Government. In the long run, this direct encounter transformed Chinese views of Americans, which shifted from admiration to hostility. All of these speak to the potential perils of an occupation mission in a foreign nation.

But this extraordinary encounter also created new connections as seen in stories like Rosset's. The former soldier-turned-publisher maintained his lifelong interest in China, and his long-standing wish was to share his photos with younger Chinese generations – a wish that finally became reality in 2014 at Kunming Municipal Museum. Jeno Paulucci, who had served in the armed forces in Asia, converted his fellow GIs' love for Chinese food into a successful empire of ready-prepared Chinese food for the mass market, with the famous Chun King brand of chow mein with a similar-sounding name to Chongqing, China's wartime capital. By the 1950s, sales of frozen and processed Chinese food had increased 70 percent since the war, making it a major national food.[37] Across the ocean, the famous "Beijing Jeep" was born in 1969, co-opting the design and symbolism of the United States and showcasing China's newly developed industrial power and material progress. As the country embarked on reform and opening-up policies in the late 1970s, the first Sino-American automobile joint venture was formed, which manufactured a new Beijing Jeep model.[38] These stories are testaments to the profound bonds that were forged, suggesting that even in a brief moment of intimacy and estrangement, military missions should also be understood as actual encounters, which often have longer-lasting and more significant legacies than the pursuit of immediate strategic objectives.

Perhaps not all is lost. The postwar era was a precarious time in Sino-US relations, followed by bloody conflicts. But it was also a transformative period that ushered in many new beginnings. During this critical juncture, the two groups – from commanders and statesmen to laborers and servants – engaged in unprecedented human, socioeconomic, and cultural exchanges that would not recur until the door to China reopened in the late twentieth century. When I trace Anna Wong's family history across the Pacific Ocean, track the loss of General Marshall's Jeep on the streets of Nanjing, and zoom in on Shen Chong's body in the Beijing courtroom, I am shown a much larger and different world – one defined by quotidian practices and politics. While state policy and ideological differences may have set the tone for bilateral relations, everyday encounters determined the texture, individual notes, flats and sharps, half beats and pauses, and occupational hazards and opportunities of the era. Only by focusing on these micro-level human interactions can we truly understand this pivotal chapter in Sino-American relations and the underlying dynamics at play. Within these entangled relations were racial prejudice, failed national policies, radically changed perceptions, and lost chances of accommodation; there were also newly forged connections that shaped history and the present world, together with lost lives, unresolved tensions, unfulfilled justice and promises, unrecognized injuries and agonies, and overdue recognition and recollection.

Today we stand at another major crossroads of Sino-American relations. With the unraveling of the symbiotic relationship known as "Chimerica," a term first coined by Niall Ferguson and Moritz Schularick, one critical question remains: What role do everyday interactions play in shaping the great power rivalry and the evolving global order?[39] Grassroots interactions have reached new heights, with the US issuing "105,000 new student visas to Chinese citizens in 2023, the highest since before the pandemic," solidifying their status as the largest group of international students in the country.[40] Yet the two governments are embroiled in an ugly trade war, bitter propaganda battles, intensifying military competition, and high-stakes geopolitical posturing. Tragically, it is ordinary people who bear the brunt of these conflicts. Against the backdrop of the Covid-19 pandemic, Chinese students, Chinese immigrants, and Chinese Americans have faced racial profiling, verbal abuse, and physical attacks in the United States. Conversely, anti-American sentiment has also spilled into violent incidents in China, such as the June 2024 stabbing of four Iowa college instructors in an exchange program by a Chinese man in a Jilin public park, apparently because of a minor collision while walking.[41] These ostensibly "mundane frictions" reveal deep systemic biases, lingering grievances, and the toxic effects of propaganda on both sides – forces that continue to shape perceptions and fuel the broader China-America conflict.

If one lesson can be learned from this entangled history of encounter, as we are again in an extremely volatile period of Sino-US relations, it is that everyday practice and politics matter. As tensions between the two nations rise alongside an unprecedented level of grassroots interactions, we must bring back to the center of our study the everyday exchanges, which have suffered a particular type of historical erasure and political distortion in the loaded discussions of American imperialism and Chinese

Communism. These exchanges provide key opportunities for fostering understanding and building rapport amidst large nationalist struggles and global conflicts. Ultimately, it is the ordinary actors who, wittingly or unwittingly, by coercion or by choice, have always endured at the heart of history, conflict, and reconciliation. They form the core of this study, and it is to the forgotten history of everyday occupation that this book is devoted.

Notes

Introduction

1. "Maxieer diu jipu" 馬歇爾丟吉普 [Marshall lost the Jeep], *Da di* 大地 39 (1946): 10.
2. See Chunmei Du, "Jeep Girls and American GIs: Gendered Nationalism in Post–World War II China," *Journal of Asian Studies* 81, no. 2 (2022): 341–363.
3. For discussions on the loss of China or the lost chance in China, see e.g. Dorothy Borg and Waldo H. Heinrichs, *Uncertain Years: Chinese-American Relations, 1947–1950* (New York: Columbia University Press, 1980); "Symposium: Rethinking the Lost Chance in China," *Diplomatic History* 21, no. 1 (1997): 71–115, especially Warren I. Cohen, "Introduction: Was There a 'Lost Chance' in China?"
4. See Suzanne Pepper, *Civil War in China: The Political Struggle, 1945–1949* (Lanham, MD: Rowman and Littlefield, 1999); Odd Arne Westad, *Decisive Encounters: The Chinese Civil War, 1946–1950* (Stanford, CA: Stanford University Press, 2003); Hans van de Ven, *China at War: Triumph and Tragedy in the Emergence of the New China 1937–1952* (Cambridge, MA: Harvard University Press, 2018).
5. Zuo Shuangwen 左雙文 and Liu Shan 劉杉, "Lengzhan chuqi Sulian de 'zhanlipin' zhengce ji Sujun zai zhanlingqu de junji wenti" 冷戰初期蘇聯的 "戰利品"政策及蘇軍在佔領區的軍紀問題 [Soviet "spoils of war" policy and military discipline problems in occupied areas during the early Cold War], in Du Chunmei 杜春媚, ed., *Lengzhan shiqi de Meiguo yu dongya shehui* 冷戰時期的美國與東亞社會 [*The United States and East Asian societies during the Cold War*] (Taipei: Showwe, 2023), 213–233; Edwin W. Pauley, *Report on Japanese Assets in Manchuria to the President of the United States* (Washington, DC: United States Government Printing Office, 1946), 37.
6. Christian Hess, "Sino-Soviet City: Dalian between Socialist Worlds, 1945–1955," *Journal of Urban History* 44, no. 1 (2018): 9–25.
7. Although the size of the US military was declining because of demobilization in the immediate postwar era, the American empire's global reach and influence continued to expand. On America and postwar East Asia, see Ronald H. Spector, *In the Ruins of Empire: The Japanese Surrender and the Battle for Postwar Asia* (New York: Random House, 2008) and Marc Gallicchio, *The*

Scramble for Asia: U.S. Military Power in the Aftermath of the Pacific War (New York: Rowman and Littlefield, 2008).

8. Existing accounts of the number of Japanese people in China vary due to several factors, including those who died before repatriation, women who chose to remain in China, and units that served in either the Nationalist or Communist armies. For the estimated total number, which ranges from 2 to 4 million, see *Zhongguo zhanqu Zhongguo lujun zongsilingbu shouxiang baogaoshu* 中國戰區中國陸軍總司令部受降報告書 [*Report on the acceptance of the Japanese surrender*] (Zhongguo lujun zongsilingbu 中國陸軍總司令部, 1946), 9–10; US Department of State, *The China White Paper, August 1949* (Stanford, CA: Stanford University Press, 1967), 690; Donald G. Gillin and Charles Etter, "Staying On: Japanese Soldiers and Civilians in China, 1945–1949," *Journal of Asian Studies* 42, no. 3 (1983): 497–518.

9. American troops in China, the majority from the army, reached sixty thousand before Japan's surrender. See US Department of State, *The China White Paper*, 694; Henry I. Shaw, *The United States Marines in North China, 1945–1949* (Washington, DC: US Marine Corps, 1968).

10. The 1905 anti-American boycott movement, which occurred as a reaction to the Chinese Exclusion Act and the discriminatory treatments of Chinese laborers, was more limited in objectives and impacts. See Sin Kiong Wong, *China's Anti-American Boycott Movement in 1905: A Study in Urban Protest* (New York: Peter Lang, 2002); Guanhua Wang, *In Search of Justice: The 1905–1906 Chinese Anti-American Boycott* (Cambridge, MA: Harvard University Press, 2001).

11. See Hong Zhang, *America Perceived: The Making of Chinese Images of the United States, 1945–1953* (Westport, CT: Greenwood Press, 2002). For Chinese elites' shift from enthusiasm to disillusionment with American ideals of global justice and equality after the Treaty of Versailles, see Erez Manela, *The Wilsonian Moment: Self-Determination and the International Origins of Anticolonial Nationalism* (New York: Oxford University Press, 2007), 177–196.

12. "Friendship Lost?" *Time* Magazine 49, no. 6 (October 2, 1947).

13. Graham Peck, *Two Kinds of Time* (Seattle: University of Washington Press, 2008), 684.

14. For an overview of the American empire, see Daniel Immerwahr, *How to Hide an Empire: A History of the Greater United States* (New York: Farrar, Straus and Giroux, 2019) and Charles S. Maier, *Among Empires: American Ascendancy and Its Predecessors* (Cambridge, MA: Harvard University Press, 2007). For studies that focus on the global US military networks since the Cold War, see Maria Höhn and Seungsook Moon, eds., *Over There: Living with the U.S. Military Empire from World War Two to the Present* (Durham, NC: Duke University Press, 2010); David Vine, *Base Nation: How U.S. Military Bases Abroad Harm America and the World* (New York: Henry Holt and Company, 2015); Catherine Lutz, ed., *The Bases of Empire: The Global Struggle against U.S. Military Posts* (New York: New York University Press, 2009).

15. Zach Fredman, *The Tormented Alliance: American Servicemen and the Occupation of China, 1941–1949* (Chapel Hill: University of North Carolina Press, 2022), 169.

16. See Gallicchio, *The Scramble for Asia*, 138–140. A small number of colored troops were present as an advance group in North China, but their deployment was later discontinued. See Vincent Tubbs, "Chinese Welcome Marines," *The Baltimore Afro-American*, October 13, 1945; DeWitt Peck, oral history transcript, 158, Archives Branch, US Marine Corps History Division, Quantico, Virginia (MCHD).
17. See T. Christopher Jespersen, *American Images of China, 1931–1949* (Stanford, CA: Stanford University Press, 1996); Gordon H. Chang, *Fateful Ties: A History of America's Preoccupation with China* (Cambridge, MA: Harvard University Press, 2015), 130–167.
18. See Höhn and Moon, "The Politics of Gender, Sexuality, Race, and Class in the U.S. Military Empire," in *Over There*, 12–20.
19. Christina Klein, *Cold War Orientalism: Asia in the Middlebrow Imagination, 1945–1961* (Oakland: University of California Press, 2003), 1–17.
20. See Rana Mitter, "State-Building after Disaster: Jiang Tingfu and the Reconstruction of Post–World War II China, 1943–1949," *Comparative Studies in Society and History* 61, no. 1 (2019): 176–206.
21. Chiang Kai-shek, *China's Destiny*, trans. Wang Chung-hui (New York: The MacMillan Company, 1947), VII–VIII.
22. Rear Admiral C. W. Styer, of the Office of Chief of Naval Operations, to the Director of the Office of Far Eastern Affairs (Butterworth), January 8, 1948, *Foreign Relations of the United States (FRUS), 1948, The Far East: China, Volume VIII* (Washington, DC: Government Printing Office, 1973), Document 257.
23. Following the British, the United States and the Qing Dynasty in 1844 signed the unequal Treaty of Wanghia that granted extraterritoriality to American citizens, who would be tried and punished only by American authorities for crimes committed on Chinese soil. A more comprehensive and definitive version of legal rights than the British had won in the Treaty of Nanking, this provision became the model for other foreign powers and had long-term impacts on China's diplomatic history. See Yanqiu Zheng, "A Specter of Extraterritoriality: The Legal Status of U.S. Troops in China, 1943–1947," *Journal of American-East Asian Relations* 22, no. 1 (2015): 17–44.
24. In international law, the concept of unequal treaties remains vaguely defined and practically ambiguous. In China, the issue of unequal treaties (*bupingdeng tiaoyue*) has attracted considerable attention, mixing historical, academic, and diplomatic concern and political interest from various entities claiming legitimacy based on the abolishment of unequal treaties. See Matthew Craven, "What Happened to Unequal Treaties? The Continuities of Informal Empire," *Nordic Journal of International Law* 74 (2005): 335–382; Shahrad Nasrolahi Fard, *Reciprocity in International Law: Its Impact and Function* (London: Routledge, 2016); Dong Wang, "The Discourse of Unequal Treaties in Modern China," *Pacific Affairs* 76, no. 3 (2003): 399–425.
25. See Zhang Longlin 張龍林, "Kangzhan houqi zhuHua Meijun zhuanshu guanxiaquan yanjiu" 抗戰后期駐華美軍專屬管轄權研究 [Research on the

exclusive jurisdiction of US forces in China during the late war period], *Xibei daxue xuebao* 西北大學學報 42, no. 1 (2012): 80–86.
26. The Ambassador in China (Gauss) to the Secretary of State, January 30, 1943, *FRUS, 1943*, Document 627.
27. "ZaiHua Meijun zhaoshi chuli banfa" 在華美軍肇事處理辦法 [Procedures for handling incidents involving US military personnel in China], 020-050204-0011, Academia Historica Archives (AHA) 國史館, Taipei, Taiwan.
28. The Chinese Ministry for Foreign Affairs to the American Embassy in China, October 13, 1943, *FRUS, 1943*, Document 632.
29. "Gaishan zaiHua Meijun renyuan xingshi anjian shenpan chuli chengxu banfa" 改善在華美軍人員刑事案件審判處理程序辦法 [The instruction for improving the judicial procedure of criminal cases involving US military personnel], M041-003-005524-0005, June 1948, Sichuan Provincial Archives (SPA) and J0002-3-007261-055, Tianjin Municipal Archive (TMA).
30. For an influential debate on the issue, see Zhang Zhenkun 張振鵾, "Zaishuo 'ershiyi tiao' bushi tiaoyue: Da Zheng Zemin xiansheng" 再說"二十一條"不是條約: 答鄭則民先生 [Again on "Twenty-one Demands" are not a treaty], *Jindaishi yanjiu* 近代史研究 1 (2000): 238–252; Zheng Zemin 鄭則民, "Guanyu bupingdeng tiaoyue de ruogan wenti: yu Zhang Zhenkun xiansheng shangque" 關于不平等條約的若干問題: 與張振鵾先生商榷 [Some questions on the unequal treaties: A discussion with Mr. Zhang Zhenkun], *Jindaishi yanjiu* 近代史研究 1 (2000): 215–237. For revisionist histories, see Wang Qi 王淇, "Yijiu sisan nian 'ZhongMei pingdeng xinyue' qianding de lishibeijing jiqi yiyi pingxi" 一九四三年《中美平等新約》簽訂的歷史背景及其意義評析 [The historical background and analysis of the 1943 Treaty between the United States and China for the Relinquishment of Extraterritorial Rights in China], *Zhonggong dangshi yanjiu* 中共黨史研究 4 (1989): 9–15; Wang Jianlang 王建朗, "Zhongguo feichu bupingdeng tiaoyue de lishi kaocha" 中國廢除不平等條約的歷史考察 [A historical investigation into China's abolition of unequal treaties], *Lishi yanjiu* 歷史研究 5 (1997): 4–18; Hou Zhongjun 侯中軍, "Jindai Zhongguo bupingdeng tiaoyue jiqi pingpan biaozhun de tantao" 近代中國不平等條約及其評判標準的探討 [An investigation of unequal treaties in modern China and their qualifying criteria], *Lishi yanjiu* 1 (2009): 64–84; Wu Lin-Chun 吳翎君, "1946 nian ZhongMei Shangyue de lishi yiyi" 1946 年中美商約的歷史意義 [The historical significance of the 1946 Sino-American Treaty], *Guoli zhengzhi daxue lishi xuebao* 國立政治大學歷史學報 21 (May 2004): 41–66.
31. See Ministry of Foreign Affairs, *Treaties between the Republic of China and Foreign States (1927–1957)* (New York: AMS Press, 1974), 676–792; "320.3 Commercial Treaty (I) Sino-American Treaty, 1943–1946," The Chinese Civil War and US-China Relations: Records of the US State Department's Office of Chinese Affairs, 1945–1955, Archives Unbound, Gale Primary Sources, US National Archives and Record Administration, College Park, Maryland (NARA).
32. For a study of the Philippines' special relationship with the US, especially how Philippine leadership after independence used "nonconfrontational resistance" in its dealings with the Americans, see Nick Cullather, *Illusions*

of Influence: The Political Economy of United States–Philippines Relations, 1942–1960 (Stanford, CA: Stanford University Press, 1994).
33. "Painful Surprise," *Time* magazine 49, no. 2 (January 13, 1947).
34. Philip West, *Yenching University and Sino-Western Relations* (Cambridge, MA: Harvard University Press, 1976), 181.
35. William Henry Chamberlain, "Post War Ironies," *Wall Street Journal*, January 14, 1947, 4.
36. See Jeffrey N. Wasserstrom, *Student Protests in Twentieth-Century China: The View from Shanghai* (Stanford, CA: Stanford University Press, 1991).
37. Mao Zedong, "The Chiang Kai-shek Government Is Besieged by the Whole People," in *Selected Works of Mao Tse-tung*, vol. IV (Beijing: Foreign Languages Press, 1961), 135–139.
38. Zhonggong zhongyang dangshi yanjiushi 中共中央黨史研究室, *Zhongguo gongchandang lishi (diyijuan)* 中國共產黨歷史(第一卷) [*History of the Chinese Communist Party*, vol. 1] (Beijing: Zhonggong dangshi chubanshe, 2010), 673–780.
39. Jon W. Huebner, "Chinese Anti-Americanism, 1946–48," *Australian Journal of Chinese Affairs* 17 (1987): 115–125.
40. Mao Zedong, "Manifesto of the Chinese People's Liberation Army," in *Selected Works of Mao Tse-tung*, vol. IV, 147–153.
41. Pepper, *Civil War in China*, 42–93.
42. Xixiao Guo, "The Anticlimax of an Ill-starred Sino-American Encounter," *Modern Asian Studies* 35, no. 1 (2011): 240; Zhonggong Beijing shiwei dangshi yanjiushi 中共北京市委黨史研究室, ed., *Kangyi Meijun zhuHua baoxing yundong ziliao huibian* 抗議美軍駐華暴行運動資料彙編 [*Collected materials on the Anti-American Brutality movement*] (Beijing: Beijing daxue chubanshe, 1989), 3–8.
43. Charles J. Canning, "Peiping Rape Case Has Deep Social, Political Background," *The China Weekly Review* (January 11, 1947): 166; Pepper, *Civil War in China*, 42–93.
44. "Anti-Americanism, Communist Attitude," December 5, 1946, RG 84: Records of Foreign Service Posts of the Department of State, Box 19, NARA.
45. See Chen Weimin 陳衛民, "Shilun 'erjiu' douzheng de jingyan jiaoxun" 試論"二九"斗爭的經驗教訓 [A tentative argument on the lessons from the "February ninth" struggles], *Shi lin* 史林 2 (1996): 68–74.
46. See e.g. Jinan Shudian 冀南书店, ed., *ZhuHua Meijun baoxinglu* 駐華美軍暴行錄 [*Record of brutalities by US Forces in China*] (Weixian: Jinan shudian, 1946); *Meiguobing gunchuqu* 美國兵, 滾出去 [*American soldiers, get out*] (Aiguo yundong chubanshe, 1947); Fang Ke 方克, ed., *Jiang Jieshi maiguo zhenxiang* 蔣介石賣國真相 [*The truth about Chiang Kai-shek selling out the country*] (Harbin: Dongbei shudian, 1947); Dongbei junzheng daxue zhengzhibu 東北軍政大學政治部, eds., *Meijun zaiHua baoxinglu* 美軍在華暴行錄 [*Record of American soldiers' brutalities in China*] (Heilongjiang, Beian: Dongbei junzheng daxue zhengzhibu, 1947); Huabei xuesheng yundong xiaoshi bianji weiyuanhui 華北學生運動小史編輯委員會, eds., *Huabei xuesheng yundong xiaoshi* 華北學生運動小史 [*A brief history of student movements in North China*] (Beijing: Huabei xuesheng yundong xiaoshi bianji weiyuanhui, 1948).

47. See e.g. *Kangyi Meijun zhuHua baoxing yundong ziliao huibian*, 109–123; Communist anti-American propaganda materials collected by the Nationalist Government Ministry of Justice, "Guanyu fanMei gongzuo de zhishi" 關於反美工作的指示 [Instructions on anti-American work], 1946, 530-01-07-061, Archives of the Institute of Modern History (AIMH) 近代史研究所檔案館, Taipei, Taiwan; "Gongfei fanMei huabao" 共匪反美畫報 [Communist bandit anti-American pictorials], 1948, 530-01-12-085, AIMH; "Gongfei fanMei huakan" 共匪反美畫刊 [Communist bandit anti-American illustrated publications], 1948, 530-01-12-086, AIMH.
48. Maurice Blanchot, *The Infinite Conversation*, trans. Susan Hanson (Minneapolis: University of Minnesota Press, 1993), 238.
49. For existing studies on grassroots interactions between American serviceman and Chinese civilians, see Fredman, *The Tormented Alliance*; Xixiao Guo, "Climax of Sino-American Relations, 1944–1947," PhD diss., University of Georgia, 1997; Zhiguo Yang, "United States Marines in Qingdao: Military-Civilian Interaction, Nationalism, and China's Civil War, 1945–1949," PhD diss., University of Maryland, 1998. For the military operational side, see Katherine K. Reist, "The American Military Advisory Missions to China, 1945–1949," *Journal of Military History* 77, no. 4 (2013): 1379–1398; George B. Clark, *Treading Softly: U.S. Marines in China, 1819–1949* (Westport, CT: Praeger, 2001); Shaw, *The United States Marines in North China*; Edward John Marolda, "The U.S. Navy and the Chinese Civil War, 1945–1952," PhD diss., George Washington University, 1990; Joseph G. D. Babb, "The Harmony of Yin and Yank: The American Military Advisory Effort in China, 1941–1951," PhD diss., University of Kansas, 2012; Jonathan Blackshear Chavanne, "The Battle for China: The U.S. Navy, Marine Corps and the Cold War in Asia, 1944–1949," PhD diss., Texas A&M University, 2016.
50. For the approach of everyday life in historical studies, including its relationship with German *Alltagsgeschichte* and Italian microhistory, see Alf Lüdtke, "Introduction: What Is the History of Everyday Life and Who Are Its Practitioners?" In Alf Lüdtke, ed., *The History of Everyday Life: Reconstructing Historical Experiences and Ways of Life* (Princeton, NJ: Princeton University Press, 1995), 3–40; Paul Steege, Andrew Stuart Bergerson, Maureen Healy, and Pamela E. Swett, "The History of Everyday Life: A Second Chapter," *Journal of Modern History* 80, no. 2 (2008): 358–378.
51. Cynthia Enloe, *Seriously! Investigating Crashes and Crises as If Women Mattered* (Oakland: University of California Press, 2013), 39–48.
52. Although the study of international relations is a field that by tradition focuses on macro-level patterns and high-level national and supranational agents, more recent scholarship has increasingly turned to micropolitics, attending to the ways in which locally grounded agents have engaged with and influenced world affairs. For the recent shifts toward the study of everyday and micropolitics in international relations, see special issue, *Cooperation and Conflict* 54, no. 2 (2019): 123–309, especially Annika Björkdahl, Martin Hall, and Ted Svensson, "Everyday International Relations: Editors' Introduction," *Cooperation and Conflict* 54, no. 2 (2019): 123–130; special issue "Everyday Diplomacy: Insights from Ethnography," *Cambridge Journal of Anthropology*

34, no. 2 (2016): 2–139, especially Marsden Magnus, Diana Ibañez-Tirado, and David Henig, "Everyday Diplomacy: Introduction to Special Issue," *Cambridge Journal of Anthropology* 34, no. 2 (2016): 2–22.
53. Harry Harootunian, "Shadowing History: National Narratives and the Persistence of the Everyday," *Cultural Studies* 18, no. 2–3 (2004): 181–200.
54. For studies of everyday lives that challenge the traditional historiographies of Europe during and after WWII, see e.g. Paul Steege, *Black Market, Cold War: Everyday Life in Berlin, 1946–1949* (New York: Cambridge University Press, 2007); Lindsey Dodd and David Lees, eds., *Vichy France and Everyday Life: Confronting the Challenges of Wartime, 1939–1945* (London: Bloomsbury Academic, 2018). For studies on everyday lives in modern Chinese history, see e.g. Madeleine Yue Dong and Joshua L. Goldstein, eds., *Everyday Modernity in China* (Seattle: University of Washington Press, 2006); Diana Larry, *The Chinese People at War: Human Suffering and Social Transformation, 1937–1945* (New York: Cambridge University Press, 2010); Jeremy Brown and Matthew D. Johnson, eds., *Maoism at the Grassroots: Everyday Life in China's Era of High Socialism* (Cambridge, MA: Harvard University Press, 2015).
55. In his influential study *Critique of Everyday Life*, Henri Lefebvre shows us the omnipresence of the everyday and its potential for resistance and subversion. See Henri Lefebvre, *Critique of Everyday Life*, vols. 1–3, trans. John Moore (London: Verso, 2008).
56. See Du, "Jeep Girls and American GIs."
57. See Zach Fredman and Judd Kinzley, eds., *Uneasy Allies: Sino-American Relations at the Grassroots, 1937–1949* (Cambridge: Cambridge University Press, 2024); J. Megan Greene, *Building a Nation at War: Transnational Knowledge Networks and the Development of China during and after World War II* (Cambridge, MA: Harvard University Press, 2023); Charlotte Brooks, *American Exodus: Second-Generation Chinese Americans in China, 1901–1949* (Oakland: University of California Press, 2019); Jack Neubauer, *The Adoption Plan: China and the Remaking of Global Humanitarianism* (New York: Columbia University Press, 2025). For people-to-people diplomacy in the People's Republic of China, see Terry Lautz, *Americans in China: Encounters with the People's Republic* (New York: Oxford University Press, 2022); Pete Millwood, *Improbable Diplomats: How Ping-Pong Players, Musicians, and Scientists Remade US-China Relations* (Cambridge: Cambridge University Press, 2023); Kazushi Minami, *How Americans and Chinese Transformed US-China Relations during the Cold War* (Ithaca, NY: Cornell University Press, 2024).
58. Michel de Certeau points out the agencies of the ordinary man as he reappropriates the preexisting material of language, symbols, and material goods in everyday situations of "dwelling, walking, spelling, reading, shopping, cooking." These "tactics" in everyday practices are influenced by the law of external forces but never wholly determined by their rules and products. See Michel de Certeau, *The Practice of Everyday Life* (Oakland: University of California Press, 1984); Michel de Certeau, Fredric Jameson, and Carl Lovitt, "On the Oppositional Practices of Everyday Life," *Social Text* 3 (1980): 3–43.

1 Occupying China

1. Minjian yingxiang 民間影像, ed., *Wo de 1945: Kangzhan shengli huiyilu* 我的1945: 抗戰勝利回憶錄 [*My 1945: Memoirs of victory against Japan*] (Shanghai: Tongji daxue chubanshe, 2017), 305.
2. "Paul Child to Charles Child, March–October 1945," Julia Child Papers, 1925–1993. MC 644, box 4, folder 57. Schlesinger Library, Radcliffe Institute, Harvard University.
3. Zhang Xianwen 張憲文 and Zhang Yufa 張玉法, eds., *Zhonghua minguo zhuantishi* 中華民國專題史 [*Special history of the Republic of China*], vol. 16 (Nanjing: Nanjing University Press, 2015), 21.
4. Gallicchio, *The Scramble for Asia*; Spector, *In the Ruins of Empire*.
5. Shen Yunlong 沈雲龍, ed., *Zhongguo zhanqu Zhongguo lujun zongsilingbu chuli Riben touxiang wenjian huibian* 中國戰區中國陸軍總司令部處理日本投降文件匯編 [*Compilation of Japanese surrender documents handled by the Chinese Army General Headquarters in the China Theater*] (Taipei: Wenhai chubanshe, 1945), 56.
6. Yu Huamin 于化民, "Dui Ri shouxiang quan zhengduan beijing xia de Zhonggong yu Mei guanxi" 對日受降權爭端背景下的中共與美關係 [CCP-American relations amid disputes over the right to accept Japan's surrender], *Shixue yuekan* 史學月刊 12 (2011): 64–78.
7. See Van de Ven, *China at War*, 209–215.
8. Ronald H. Spector, "After Hiroshima: Allied Military Occupations and the Fate of Japan's Empire, 1945–1947," *Journal of Military History* 69, no. 4 (2005): 1121–1136; Gillin and Etter, "Staying On," 497–518.
9. Communists claimed that they alone pursued justice and proper punishments of the Japanese war criminals in their liberated areas, rather than the Nationalists or the Americans. See "Zhen shouxiang yu jia shouxiang" 真受降與假受降 [Real and fake acceptance of surrender], *Xinhua ribao* 新華日報, December 25, 1945; Barak Kushner, *Men to Devils, Devils to Men: Japanese War Crimes and Chinese Justice* (Cambridge, MA: Harvard University Press, 2015).
10. Shaw, *The United States Marines in North China*; Clark, *Treading Softly*, 131–165.
11. Lori Watt, *When Empire Comes Home: Repatriation and Reintegration in Postwar Japan* (Cambridge, MA: Harvard University Press, 2009), 51–52.
12. Michael Parkyn, "Operation BELEAGUER: The Marine III Amphibious Corps in North China, 1945–49," *Marine Corps Gazette* 85, no. 7 (2001): 32–37; United States Joint Chiefs of Staff, *Joint Publication 3–0* (Washington, DC: US Government Printing Office, 1995), vii.
13. See Melvyn Leffler, *A Preponderance of Power: National Security, the Truman Administration, and the Cold War* (Stanford, CA: Stanford University Press, 1992), 128; The Secretary of State to the Secretary of Defense (Forrestal), August 4, 1948, *FRUS, 1948*, Document 205; Reist, "The American Military Advisory Missions to China, 1945–1949"; Babb, "The Harmony of Yin and Yank."
14. United Nations Relief and Rehabilitation Administration, *UNRRA in China, 1945–1947* (Washington, DC: UNRRA, 1948), 34–35; Irving Barnett,

"UNRRA in China: A Case Study in Financial Assistance for Economic Development (with Emphasis on Agricultural Programs)," PhD diss., Columbia University, 1955.
15. Weizhen Zhang and Tao Peng, "The Qingdao Pattern and U.S.-Chinese Crisis Management: The KMT, the CCP, and the U.S. Marines in Qingdao during the Chinese Civil War (1945–1949)," *Journal of Cold War Studies* 25, no. 2 (2023): 150–178.
16. See Nancy Bernkopf Tucker, *Patterns in the Dust: Chinese–American Relations and the Recognition Controversy, 1949–1950* (New York: Columbia University Press, 1983); Niu Jun 牛軍, *Cong Heerli dao Maxieer: Meiguo tiaochu guogong maodun shimo* 從赫爾利到馬歇爾: 美國調處國共矛盾始末 [*From Hurley to Marshall: A history of the American mediation between the Nationalists and the Communists*] (Beijing: Dongfang chubanshe, 2009).
17. Shaw, *The United States Marines in North China*, 25.
18. Shaw, *The United States Marines in North China*, 5.
19. John B. Simms Memoir, COLL/3308, 59–60, MCHD.
20. Shaw, *The United States Marines in North China*, 9.
21. Henry Aplington, "Sunset in the East: A Memoir of North China, 1945–1947," *Journal of American–East Asian Relations* 3, no. 2 (1994): 161.
22. Parkyn, "Operation BELEAGUER," 34–35; Peck, oral history transcript, 155; Benis M. Frank and Henry I. Shaw Jr., *Victory and Occupation: History of U.S. Marine Corps Operations in World War II*, vol. V (Washington, DC: US Marine Corps, 1968), 576–578. Frank, the chief historian of the Marine Corps and a China marine in 1945, conducted oral history interviews with several commanders referenced in this book, including General Peck.
23. Simms Memoir, 4.
24. Curley Papers, 117.
25. E. B. Sledge, *China Marine: An Infantryman's Life after World War II* (Oxford: Oxford University Press, 2002), 40–41.
26. Robert H. Barrow, oral history transcript, session 2, MCHD.
27. For example, see Curley Papers, 117; Lemuel C. Shepherd Jr., oral history transcript, 96, MCHD.
28. Curley Papers, 124.
29. Curley Papers, 124.
30. Shepherd, oral history transcript, 96.
31. Gillin and Etter, "Staying On."
32. Barney Rosset, "12 September 1945 Letter to Parents: Page 2," *Columbia University Libraries Online Exhibitions*, https://exhibitions.library.columbia.edu/exhibits/show/rosset/item/7665.
33. Sledge, *China Marine*, 32–34.
34. Curley Papers, 131.
35. Curley Papers, 135.
36. Elmo R. Zumwalt, *On Watch: A Memoir* (New York: The New York Times, 1976), 10–14.
37. Uchida Ginnosuke was later tried by the Nationalist Government and eventually executed in Sugamo Prison by Allied authorities in 1951.

38. Chen Zhanbiao 陳占彪, ed., *Sandao quanfu riyue chongguang: kangzhan shengli shouxiang xianchang* 三島蜷伏日月重光: 抗戰勝利受降現場 [*Islands coiling, sun and moon remerge: Scenes of accepting surrender after victory in the War of Resistance*] (Beijing: Sanlian shudian, 2015), 406–407; Oral history of Bill Hook, transcript, Old China Hands Oral History Project Collection, California State University, Northridge (OCHOH).
39. Curley Papers, 142. But seen from the site pictures, American representatives wore casual khakis with ties.
40. Chen Songqing 陳松卿, "Qingdao shouxiang jianwen" 青島受降見聞 [Impressions of the Qingdao surrender ceremony], in Zhongguo renmin zhengzhi xieshang huiyi Qingdaoshi weiyuanhui wenshi ziliao yanjiu weiyuanhui 中國人民政治協商會議青島市委員會文史資料研究委員會, eds., *Qingdao wenshi ziliao di 9 ji* 青島文史資料第9輯 [*Historical literature of Qingdao*, vol. 9] (1992), 196–198.
41. Shepherd, oral history transcript, 98–99.
42. Chen, *Sandao quanfu riyue chonguang*, 406–407.
43. Chen, "Qingdao shouxiang jianwen," 196–198.
44. See Shen, *Zhongguo zhanqu Zhongguo lujun zongsilingbu chuli Riben touxiang wenjian huibian*, 100–101. The Nationalist Government also sent a representative to Hong Kong, where Chiang initially insisted on Chinese accepting the surrender but later agreed to a British-held one. Although Chiang's initial instruction stated no formal ceremonies were to be held, except in Taiwan and northern Vietnam, in reality many took place, though varying in scale and complexity.
45. Shepherd, oral history transcript, 96.
46. Although the Nationalist Government rejected the Japanese officers' request to keep their swords, the Japanese forces were permitted to carry weapons for self-protection until they arrived at the repatriation ships. For Sino-Japanese negotiations over the sword arrangement and the ceremony program, see the accounts by two key figures involved: Gangcun Ningci 岡村寧次 (Okamura Yasuji), *Gangcun Ningci huiyilu* 岡村寧次回憶錄 [*Memoirs of Okamura Yasuji*] (Beijing: Zhonghua shuju, 1981), 47–55; and Leng Xin 冷欣, *Cong canjia kangzhan dao mudu Rijun touxiang* 從參加抗戰到目睹日軍投降 [*From joining the war of resistance to witnessing the Japanese surrender*] (Taipei: Zhuanji wenxue chubanshe, 1967), 190–213.
47. On these different maneuvers, see John W. Dower, *Embracing Defeat: Japan in the Wake of World War II* (New York: W. W. Norton & Company, 2000), 41; Werner Sollors, *The Temptation of Despair: Tales of the 1940s* (Cambridge, MA: Belknap Press, 2014), 187.
48. Marc Gallicchio, *Unconditional: The Japanese Surrender in World War II* (Oxford: Oxford University Press, 2023), 169.
49. Curley Paper, 142.
50. Shepherd, oral history transcript, 99.
51. Directive by President Truman to the Supreme Commander for the Allied Powers in Japan (MacArthur), August 15, 1945, *FRUS, 1945*, Document 390.

52. See Lemuel C. Shepherd Jr., personal papers, COLL/1113, Box 2, MCHD; Bevan G. Cass, ed., *History of the Sixth Marine Division* (Washington, DC: Infantry Journal Press, 1948), 234–235.
53. Lü Wenzhen 呂文貞, "Zhongguo dishiyi zhanqu huabei dui Ri shouxiang gailüe" 中國第十一戰區華北對日受降概略 [Overview of the Japanese surrender to 11th Chinese War Area in North China], *Jornal San Wa Ou* 新華澳報, September 10, 2015. Original written in 1954.
54. See Lü, "Zhongguo dishiyi zhanqu huabei dui Ri shouxiang gailüe."
55. Robin Wagner-Pacifici, *The Art of Surrender: Decomposing Sovereignty at Conflict's End* (Chicago, IL: University of Chicago Press, 2005), ix–x, 59.
56. Curley Papers, 31.
57. Shepherd, oral history transcript, 99.
58. Shepherd, oral history transcript, 98.
59. Sledge, *China Marine*, 36; Shepherd, oral history transcript, 96–103.
60. Shaw, *The United States Marines in North China*, 8.
61. Shepherd, oral history transcript, 98–99.
62. Shaw, *The United States Marines in North China*, 8.
63. Clark, *Treading Softly*, 135. Another CCP official could have been mistaken as Zhou, as this meeting is not mentioned in the *Zhou Enlai nianpu* [Zhou Enlai Chronicle] or Zhou's major biographies.
64. Frederick W. Mote, *China and the Vocation of History in the Twentieth Century: A Personal Memoir* (Princeton, NJ: East Asian Library Journal in association with Princeton University Press, 2010), 36–39.
65. Peck, oral history transcript, 150–151; Shaw, *The United States Marines in North China*, 9–10.
66. Incidentally, the total number of navy and marine personnel casualties is same as in the Boxer Movement from June 1900 to May 1901. See "Casualties: U.S. Navy and Marine Corps Personnel Killed and Wounded in Wars, Conflicts, Terrorist Acts, and Other Hostile Incidents," U.S. Navy Naval History and Heritage Command, www.history.navy.mil/content/history/nhhc/research/library/online-reading-room/title-list-alphabetically/c/casualties1.html.
67. Yang Kuisong 楊奎松, "1946 nian Anping shijian zhenxiang yu Zhonggong duiMei jiaoshe" 1946年安平事件真相與中共對美交涉 [The truth about the 1946 Anping Incident and CCP-US negotiations], *Shixue yuekan* 史學月刊 4 (2011): 60–74; Zuo Chengying 左承穎 and Yang Yuqing 楊雨青, "Hequ hecong: Anping shijian hou guogongMei sanfang dui zhuHua Meijun de yinying" 何去何從: 安平事件后國共美三方對駐華美軍的因應 [What next: Communist, Nationalist, and American responses to US forces in China post-Anping Incident], *Junshi lishi yanjiu* 軍事歷史研究 34, no. 1 (2020): 76–86.
68. Final Report on the Anping Incident, October 8, 1946, *FRUS, 1946*, Document 168.
69. The two were assassinated, potentially with guns supplied by the US Navy to the Nationalist secret service. See Peck, *Two Kinds of Time*, 723.
70. "Wei dui Anping shijian yao weiwen xiang Meijun shoushang shibing dengshi gei shishehuiju de miling" 為對安平事件要慰問向美軍受傷士兵等

事給市社會局的密令 [Confidential order to the Municipal Social Bureau concerning condolences for injured US soldiers in the Anping Incident], J0002-3-007364, TMA; President Chiang Kai-shek to Major General Keller E. Rockey, USMC, at Tientsin, August 2, 1946, *FRUS, 1946*, Document 725.
71. See Zuo and Yang, "Hequ hecong."
72. Theodore H. White and Annalee Jacoby, *Thunder Out of China* (New York: William Sloane Associates, Inc., 1946), 296.
73. General Marshall to President Truman, August 16, 1946, *FRUS, 1946*, Document 20.
74. Frank and Shaw, *Victory and Occupation*, 625–627; Waijiaobu zhu PingJin tepaiyuan gongshu 外交部駐平津特派員公署 [Office of the Commissioner of the Ministry of Foreign Affairs in Beijing and Tianjin], "Xinhe Meijun beiji'an" 新河美軍被擊案 [The attack on the US Army at Xinhe], J0010-1-000616. April 1947, TMA; Wu Hong 武宏, "Yexi Meijun danyaoku" 夜襲美軍彈藥庫 [Night raid on US ammunition dump], in Zhengxie Tianjinshi Ninghexian weiyuanhui wenshi ziliao weiyuanhui 政協天津市寧河縣委員會文史資料委員會, eds., *Ninghe wenshi ziliao di 2 ji* 寧河文史資料第2輯 [*Historical literature of Ninghe*, vol. 2] (1991), 137–138; Yang Bingheng 楊秉亨, "Yexi Meijun danyaoku de qianqianhouhou" 夜襲美軍彈藥庫的前前後後 [The complete story of the night raid on the US ammunition dump], in Zhengxie Tianjinshi ninghexian weiyuanhui wenshi ziliao weiyuanhui, eds., *Ninghe wenshi ziliao di 3 ji* 寧河文史資料第3輯 [*Historical literature of Ninghe*, vol. 3] (1995), 87–93.
75. Frank and Shaw, *Victory and Occupation*, 618–619; "Attack by Dissident Forces on First Marine Division (Reinf) Ammunition Supply Point at *HSIN-HO*, Report of October 9, 1946," General George C. Marshall's Mission to China, 1945–1947, Archives Unbound, Gale Primary Sources, NARA.
76. Frank and Shaw, *Victory and Occupation*, 576–577.
77. Simms Memoir, 59.
78. Sledge, *China Marine*, 35–38.
79. White and Jacoby, *Thunder Out of China*, 289.
80. "U.S. Marines Shell Village after Chinese Shoot 2 Yanks," *St. Louis Post-Dispatch*, December 8, 1945; "Chinese Shelled by U.S. Marines: Village Attacked after Killing of Private, Wounding of Corporal 'in Cold Blood,'" *The New York Times*, December 9, 1945.
81. "Semper Fidelis," *The Washington Post*, December 12, 1945.
82. "400.3001 US Armed Forces in China (Jan–Jun 1946)," The Chinese Civil War and U.S.-China Relations: Records of the U.S. State Department's Office of Chinese Affairs, 1945–1955, Archives Unbound, Gale Primary Sources, NARA.
83. "Semper Fidelis."
84. "U.S. Marine Is Shot by Chinese Civilians," *The New York Times*, December 11, 1945.
85. Thomas E. Williams Memoir, COLL/575, 14–31, MCHD.

86. Robert F. Burford, "7 Marines Unharmed in 11-Day Detention by Communists," *The China Weekly Review* (August 24, 1946), 301.
87. Shaw, *The United States Marines in North China*, 16–17; Clark, *Treading Softly*, 152–153.
88. Norman G. Albert, *Yohouse from a Boot to a China Marine* (Bloomington, IN: Trafford, 2011), 60–63.
89. Burford, "7 Marines Unharmed in 11-Day Detention by Communists."
90. Albert, *Yohouse from a Boot to a China Marine*, 60–63.
91. See John Pomfret, *The Beautiful Country and the Middle Kingdom: America and China, 1776 to the Present* (New York: Henry Holt and Company, 2016).
92. Efforts Leading to Release of United States Marines Captured by Chinese Communists, *FRUS, 1948*, Documents 288–297.
93. Sledge, *China Marine*, 42.
94. Guo, "The Anticlimax of an Ill-Starred Sino-American Encounter," 218–225; Yang, "1946 nian Anping shijian zhenxiang yu Zhonggong duiMei jiaoshe."
95. "Chinese Shelled by U.S. Marines," 23.
96. Sledge, *China Marine*, 41.
97. See e.g. Albert, *Yohouse from a Boot to a China Marine*, 49–63.
98. Jack Murphy, "Ambush New Bullet-Studded Invitation for U.S. Marines to Pull Out of China," *Tulsa Daily World*, August 4, 1946.
99. John Roderick, "Bessemer City Marine Hero in China Attack," *Hickory Daily Record*, April 9, 1947.
100. See e.g. Roi Ottley, "GI Protests Seen Cause for Alarm to Imperialists," *The Pittsburgh Courier*, February 2, 1946; "Wants American Troops in China Brought Home," *The New York Times*, September 6, 1946; Frederick Field, "The Record of American Imperialism in China," *Political Affairs* 25, no. 1 (1946): 31–41.
101. Letter to the US Embassy in Nanjing, December 18, 1946, RG 84, Box 19, NARA.
102. Lou Glist, *China Mailbag Uncensored: Letters from an American GI in World War II China and India* (Houston, TX: Emerald Ink, 2000), 236.
103. Sledge, *China Marine*, 40.
104. Glist, *China Mailbag Uncensored*, 236.
105. James R. Compton, "Marines and Mothers: Agency, Activism, and Resistance to the American North China Intervention, 1945–46," *Marine Corps History* 8, no. 1 (2022): 21–40.
106. See Yang, "1946 nian Anping shijian zhenxiang yu Zhonggong duiMei jiaoshe."
107. Birch, who later became the figurehead for the famous right-wing John Birch Society during the heyday of the Cold War, was killed by Communist guerrillas in Shandong shortly after the end of WWII. See Terry Lautz, *John Birch: A Life* (New York: Oxford University Press, 2016).
108. Yu, "Dui Ri shouxiang quan zhengduan beijing xia de Zhonggong yu Mei guanxi," 77.

109. Mao Zedong, "Talk with the American Correspondent Anna Louise Strong," in *Selected Works of Mao Tse-tung*, vol. IV (Beijing: Foreign Languages Press, 1961), 97–102.
110. Peck, *Two Kinds of Time*, 723–724.
111. The Nationalist Government formed ten military courts for adjudication of war crimes in December 1945 and held the earliest trials in April 1946. See Liu Tong 劉統, "Guomin zhengfu shenpan Riben zhanfan gaishu (1945–1949)" 國民政府審判日本戰犯概述 (1945–1949) [Overview of the National Government's trial of Japanese war criminals (1945–1949)], *Minguo dang an* 民國檔案 1 (2014): 72–84.
112. Philip R. Piccigallo, *The Japanese on Trial: Allied War Crimes Operations in the East, 1945–1951* (Austin: University of Texas Press, 2021), 68–74; Xu Jiajun 徐家俊, "Tilanqiao jianyu: Zhongguo jingnei diyige shenpan Riben zhanfan de changsuo" 提籃橋監獄：中國境內第一個審判日本戰犯的場所 [Tilanqiao jail: China's first venue for the trials of Japanese war criminals], *KangRi zhanzheng yanjiu* 抗日戰爭研究 4 (1998): 215.
113. Waijiaobu 外交部, "Mengjun zongbu yaoqiu yindu zhanfan Gangcun Ningci Songjing Taijiulang dengren" 盟軍總部要求引渡戰犯岡村寧次松井太久郎等人 [Allied headquarters requests the extradition of war criminals Okamura Yasuji, Matsui Takurō, and Others], 052–073, 1945–1948, 020–010117–0023, AHA.
114. "Fliers Burned Alive by Japs, Court Is Told," *The Washington Post*, February 12, 1946; "Tells How Japs Stirred Chinese to Strike Yanks," *Chicago Daily Tribune*, February 13, 1946.
115. "Prosecution's Brief in Opposition to Defense 'Special Plea' on Lack of Jurisdiction," *United States of America v. Masataka et al.*, Shanghai, China, February 14, 1946. United Nations War Crimes Commission, www.legal-tools.org/doc/0b3a09; "Meijun xushen Rizhanfan" 美軍續審日戰犯 [US military continues the trial of Japanese war criminals], *Shen bao* 申報, February 12, 1946.
116. The major spy ring was led by Lieutenant Colonel Lothar Eisenträger (alias Ludwig Ehrhardt), chief of Nazi intelligence, including headquarters in Shanghai and branches in Beijing and Guangzhou. He was sentenced to life imprisonment for conducting espionage for the Japanese after Germany's surrender. The investigation was led by journalist-turned-marine captain and Office of Strategic Services field commander Frank Farrell, who was awarded a Legion of Merit for the service. See Henry R. Lieberman, "Ehrhardt, German Spy in Orient, and 20 Aides Sentenced in China; Leader Gets Life Term from United States Army Commission for Aiding Japanese – Two Receive Thirty Years," *The New York Times*, January 18, 1947.
117. Waijiaobu, "Mengjun zongbu yaoqiu yindu zhanfan Gangcun Ningci Songjing Taijiulang dengren," 0193.
118. Kushner, *Men to Devils, Devils to Men*, 69–107.
119. America's continuing insistence on extraterritoriality was also "justified" by the long-existing belief that China was under lawless corrupt governments, a discourse of "legal Orientalism" that continued well into the Cold War

era. See Teemu Ruskola, *Legal Orientalism: China, the United States, and Modern Law* (Cambridge, MA: Harvard University Press, 2013).
120. Waijiaobu, "Mengjun zongbu yaoqiu yindu zhanfan Gangcun Ningci Songjing Taijiulang dengren," 0192.
121. Waijiaobu, "Yindu zhanfan fagui" 引渡戰犯法規 [Extradition laws for war criminals], 020–010117–0002, 106–7, September 16, 1946, AHA.
122. Germany maintained extensive commercial investments in China for decades and enjoyed close relations with the Nationalist Government, which admired German advisors. This partnership continued until Hitler shifted support to Japan. Significant German communities were established in major cities, particularly in the former German colony of Qingdao.
123. "Ott, Eugen and Ott Files," General George C. Marshall's Mission to China, 1945–1947, Archives Unbound, Gale Primary Sources, RG 59: General Records of the Department of State, Lot Files 54 D 270, NARA.
124. The trial centered on the killing of three American flyers involved in the famed Doolittle Raid over Tokyo in 1942, who had bailed out or crash-landed in eastern China. In Shanghai, four Japanese army officers were found guilty and sentenced to five to nine years of hard labor. These sentences, justified on the ground that the officers were simply obeying orders from higher up, were deemed unexpectedly lenient. See "4 Get Jail Terms in Doolittle Case," *The New York Times*, April 16, 1946.
125. Waijiaobu, "Mengjun zongbu yaoqiu yindu zhanfan Gangcun Ningci Songjing Taijiulang dengren," 0134–140; Waijiaobu, "Yindu zhanfan fagui."
126. Waijiaobu, "Mengjun zongbu yaoqiu yindu zhanfan Gangcun Ningci Songjing Taijiulang dengren," 0175–0177, 1946.
127. For more details on the conflicted claims and confusing exchanges as well as Chiang's silence on this issue, see Liu Ping 劉萍, "Zhanhou Meijun zaiHua chuzhi zhanfan wenti chutan" 戰後美軍在華處置戰犯問題初探 [Preliminary study on postwar American military's handling of war criminals in China], *Minguo dang an* 民國檔案 3 (2016): 128–138.
128. For Chinese trials of Japanese war criminals, see Kushner, *Men to Devils, Devils to Men*, 137–184.
129. Waijiaobu, "Yindu zhanfan fagui."
130. Waijiaobu, "Mengjun zongbu yaoqiu yindu zhanfan Gangcun Ningci Songjing Taijiulang dengren," 0175–0177, 1946. The two sides also agreed to pursue the arrest and extradition of non-enemy war criminals through regular diplomatic channels.
131. Waijiaobu, "Meijun Zhongxiao William K. Evans (Ai Wensi) an (yi)" 美軍中校 William K. Evans(艾文思)案(一) [Case of US Lieutenant Colonel William K. Evans (1)], 020–050210–0032, 25, AHA.
132. See Zach Fredman, "Smuggling, Military Jurisdiction and the Remaking of US Empire in Postwar China," in Fredman and Kinzley, eds., *Uneasy Allies*, 254–270.
133. For the legacies of war crimes trials and postwar justice in East Asia, see Barak Kushner, *The Geography of Injustice: East Asia's Battle between Memory and History* (Ithaca, NY: Cornell University Press, 2024).

134. "Statement by Admiral Charles M. Cooke, Jr.," September 13, 1946, RG 84, Box 19, NARA.

2 Sensory Contact

1. Sledge, *China Marine*, 17–20.
2. Simms Memoir, 2–3.
3. For the usage of sensory history in studying international relations, see Mark M. Smith, *Sensing the Past: Seeing, Hearing, Smelling, Tasting, and Touching in History* (Berkeley: University of California Press, 2007); Andrew J. Rotter, *Empires of the Senses: Bodily Encounters in Imperial India and the Philippines* (New York: Oxford University Press, 2019); Susan L. Carruthers, "Latrines as the Measure of Men: American Soldiers and the Politics of Disgust in Occupied Europe and Asia," *Diplomatic History* 42, no. 1 (2018): 109–137.
4. Correspondences between Consul in Tianjin and Counselor of Embassy in Nanjing, August 1946, RG 84, Box 33, NARA.
5. Female personnel after the war were limited to a small number from the Women's Army Corps. See Mai Tian 邁天, "Meiguo nübing zai Shanghai" 美國女兵在上海 [American female soldiers in Shanghai], *Shen bao*, December 17, 1945.
6. See Louis Morton, "Army and Marines on the China Station: A Study in Military and Political Rivalry," *Pacific Historical Review* 29, no. 1 (1960): 51–73; Marolda, "The U.S. Navy and the Chinese Civil War, 1945–1952."
7. Michael H. Hunt, "The Forgotten Occupation: Peking, 1900–1901," *Pacific Historical Review* 48, no. 4 (1979): 501–529.
8. See Clark, *Treading Softly*.
9. Babb, "The Harmony of Yin and Yank," 228.
10. Clark, *Treading Softly*, 48.
11. Curley Papers, 113–137.
12. John Hersey, "Letter from Shanghai," *New Yorker* (February 9, 1946): 82–90.
13. Gerald Thomas manuscript, folder E17, 43, MCHD.
14. Samuel B. Griffith, II, oral history transcript, 168, MCHD.
15. Omar T. Pfeiffer, oral history transcript, 292–299, MCHD.
16. Griffith, oral history transcript, 169.
17. Oral history of Thomas Nallen, transcript, 14, OCHOH. For 1942–1946 US Military Base Pay Charts, see www.navycs.com/charts/1942-military-pay-chart.html.
18. Clark, *Treading Softly*, 156.
19. "North China Hunting," *China Weekly Review* (April 20, 1946): 161.
20. Barrow, oral history transcript, session 2.
21. Cass, *History of the Sixth Marine Division*, 214.
22. "China," *Outfit* 1 no. 52 (November 19, 1945): 14.
23. Aplington, "Sunset in the East: A Memoir of North China, 1945–1947," 155–175.
24. Cass, *History of the Sixth Marine Division*, 220.

25. "2 Red Cross Clubs Open in Tientsin," *The North China Marine*, November 10, 1945.
26. Thomas manuscript, 57; Gerald Thomas, oral history transcript, 251, MCHD.
27. Xixiao Guo, "Paradise or Hell Hole? U.S. Marines in Post–World War II China," *Journal of American–East Asian Relations* 7, no. 3–5 (1998): 172–173.
28. Minjian yingxiang, ed., *Wo de 1945*, 328–410.
29. For sports and American empire, see e.g. Heather L. Dichter and Andrew L. Johns, eds., *Diplomatic Games: Sport, Statecraft, and International Relations since 1945* (Lexington: University Press of Kentucky, 2014); Gerald R. Gems, *The Athletic Crusade: Sport and American Cultural Imperialism* (Lincoln: University of Nebraska Press, 2006).
30. "Memorandum for General Marshall," January 8, 1947, RG 84, Box 33, NARA.
31. "Memorandum of Conversation with Officials of Shantung University, Tsingtao," June 17, 1948, RG 84, Box 122, NARA.
32. Correspondences between Consul in Tianjin and Counselor of Embassy in Nanjing, August 1946, RG 84, Box 33, NARA.
33. "Guanyu zhuanzhi shuichang mianshou Meijun shuifei de han" 關於轉知水廠免收美軍水費的函 [Qingdao Water Works' reply on exemption of American military personnel's water bills], June 25, 1947, B0031/003/00466/0094, Qingdao Municipal Archives (QMA) 青島市檔案館; Yang, "U.S. Marines in Qingdao," 143–148.
34. "Shanghaishi caizhengju guanyu Meijun renyuan mianshuiwenti wanglaiwenshu" 上海市財政局關於美軍人員免稅問題往來文書 [Correspondence from the Shanghai Finance Bureau regarding the tax exemption issue for US military personnel], 1945–1946, Q432-3-68, Shanghai Municipal Archives (SMA) 上海市檔案館.
35. As if a ghostly echo of the most-favored-nation clause in the Treaty of Wanghia in 1844, the British sought to follow the American example by requesting a waiver of the feast and hotel taxes for their military personnel. However, this request was rejected by the Chinese Foreign Ministry. See Waijiaobu, "ZhuHua shiguan shizheng juanshui huomian" 駐華使館市政捐稅豁免 [Exemption of municipal tax for the embassy in China], 020–990800-0036, 1946, AHA.
36. Joseph Hearst, "One Tough Yank Makes Shanghai Quit Its Gouging," *Chicago Daily Tribune*, November 26, 1945.
37. "Shanghai caizhengju guanyu Meijun renyuan mianshui wenti wanglai wenshu" 上海財政局關於美軍人員免稅問題往來文書 [Correspondence from the Shanghai Finance Bureau regarding tax exemption certificates for American military personnel], Q432-3-54, SMA.
38. "Xiexie ni, shizhang" 謝謝你, 市長 [Thank you, mayor], *Shen bao*, March 9, 1946.
39. Zumwalt, *On Watch*, 7.
40. Sledge, *China Marine*, 51.
41. Barrow, oral history transcript, session 2.

42. Simms Memoir, 5.
43. "Nanjingshi zhengfu xunling" 南京市政府訓令 [Nanjing municipal government orders], November 19, 1945, 10040010127(00)0002, 南京市檔案館 [Nanjing Municipal Archives], Nanjing, China (NMA); "Tianjinshi zhengfu xunling" 天津市政府訓令 [Tianjin municipal government orders], November 15, 1945, J0025-3-002525-001, TMA.
44. Barrow, oral history transcript, session 2.
45. Qu Wen 瞿文, "Haoqi lieyan de zhuHu Meibing" 好奇獵艷的駐滬美兵 [Curious GIs philandering in Shanghai], *ZhongMei zhoubao* 174 (1946): 17–19.
46. Simms Memoir, 18–19.
47. Dongfang Peng 東方朋, "Qingdao Meijun yao chetui zhiqian" 青島美軍要撤退之前 [Before American military's withdrawal from Qingdao], *Xinwen zazhi* 新聞雜誌 [*News magazine weekly*] 2, no. 9 (1949): 16.
48. "Back at the Old Stand: It May Look Like a Butcher-Shop But It's Still Good Old Hempel's," *The North China Marine*, November 10, 1945.
49. Yong Chen, *Chop Suey, USA: The Story of Chinese Food in America* (New York: Columbia University Press, 2014), 99–101.
50. Simms Memoir, 22.
51. Sledge, *China Marine*, 47–49.
52. Simms Memoir, 25.
53. Oral history of Thomas Nallen, transcript, 13, OCHOH.
54. Melanie A. Kiechle, *Smell Detectives: An Olfactory History of Nineteenth-Century Urban America* (Seattle: University of Washington Press, 2017).
55. Mark S. R. Jenner, "Follow Your Nose? Smell, Smelling, and Their Histories," *American Historical Review* 116, no. 2 (2011): 339; Suellen Hoy, *Chasing Dirt: The American Pursuit of Cleanliness* (Oxford: Oxford University Press, 1995), 105.
56. Occasionally, Allied soldiers became aware of their own body smells when the Chinese in the countryside held their noses and dogs bared their teeth whenever they passed. See F. X. Moloney, "They Went to China," *Wings: Official Magazine of the R.A.A.F.* 5, no. 12 (September 18, 1945): 9.
57. Sledge, *China Marine*, 32–33.
58. Simms Memoir, 15–34.
59. Hu Cheng 胡成, "'Buweisheng' de Huaren xingxiang: Zhongwai jian de butong jiangshu" 「不衛生」的華人形象 : 中外間的不同講述 [Image of the "unsanitary Chinese": Differing narratives between foreigners and the Chinese], *Bulletin of the Institute of Modern History Academia Sinica* 56 (2007): 1–43.
60. C. Y. Chiang, "Monterey-by-the-Smell," *Pacific Historical Review* 73, no. 2 (2004): 213.
61. Chen, *Chop Suey, USA*, 82–85.
62. Carruthers, "Latrines as the Measure of Men," 112.
63. Carruthers, "Latrines as the Measure of Men," 112.
64. United States Army Forces, *A Pocket Guide to China* (Washington, DC: War and Navy Departments, 1942), 20.
65. Sledge, *China Marine*, 15–16.

66. Guo, "Paradise or Hell Hole?" 168.
67. "Wei pensa DDT quyuxian yishi zhi Meijun guwentuan han" 為噴灑DDT區域限一事致美軍顧問團函 [Correspondence to the US Military Advisory Group regarding the geographical limits of DDT spraying], 1947, 10030060631(00)0005, NMA; "Wei chuli Meijun junguan zhuzhai fujin fengang qingxing de dafu" 為處理美軍軍官住宅附近糞缸情形的答復 [Response regarding the dealings of soil pits near US military officers' residences], 1947, 10030060631(00)0062, NMA.
68. Guo, "Paradise or Hell Hole?" 168.
69. Carruthers, "Latrines as the Measure of Men," 124.
70. See Federica Ferlanti, "The New Life Movement in Jiangxi Province, 1934–1938," *Modern Asian Studies* 44, no. 5 (2010): 961–1000.
71. Albert, *Yohouse from a Boot to a China Marine*, 74.
72. Lizzie Collingham, *The Taste of War: World War Two and the Battle for Food* (New York: Penguin Press, 2013), 415–439.
73. Frank Tao, "'Hao Pu Hao?' 'Ting Hao': Off-Duty Life of U.S. Army Men in China," *The Stars and Stripes* (London Edition), December 9, 1943.
74. Sledge, *China Marine*, 25.
75. Hersey, "Letter from Shanghai," 85.
76. Warren Jefferson Arnett (AFC/2001/001/11032), 101–4, Veterans History Project Collection, American Folklife Center, Library of Congress, Washington, DC.
77. Collingham, *The Taste of War*, 438.
78. Tao, "'Hao Pu Hao?'"
79. Simms Memoir, 30–31.
80. Williams Memoir, 22–31.
81. Chen, *Chop Suey, USA*, 126–152.
82. Tao, "'Hao Pu Hao?'"
83. Haiming Liu, *From Canton Restaurant to Panda Express: A History of Chinese Food in the United States* (New Brunswick, NJ: Rutgers University Press, 2015), 68.
84. Tao, "'Hao Pu Hao?'"
85. Huang Renlin 黃仁霖, *Huang Renlin huiyilu* 黃仁霖回憶錄 [*The memoir of General Huang Renlin*] (Beijing: Tuanjie chubanshe, 2006), 91.
86. Simms Memoir, 14.
87. Collingham, *The Taste of War*, 432.
88. Tao, "'Hao Pu Hao?'"
89. A. L. Crouch, *China Sketchbook: A Book of Army Verse* (Shanghai: Stars and Stripes, 1946), 15.
90. Simms Memoir, 7.
91. Oral history of Thomas Nallen, transcript, 12, OCHOH.
92. United States Army Service Forces, *A Pocket Guide to China*, 18, 20; United States Marine Corps, *A Marine's Guide to North China* (San Francisco, CA: First Marine Division, 1945), 11–13.
93. United States Army Forces, *Here's How: A Handbook for American Troops in China* (China-Burma-India, 1944).
94. Simms Memoir, 6.

95. Huang Shang 黃裳, *Guanyu Meiguo bing* 關於美國兵 [*About American soldiers*] (Shanghai: Shanghai chuban gongsi, 1947), 30–31.
96. Huang Jen-lin, Memoirs, Huang Renlin Papers, Box 1, "China's Number One Meeter and Greeter," chapter 10, 6–7. Hoover Institution Library & Archives.
97. Nonglinbu 農林部, "ZhongMei junxulianxihuiyi youguan roulei beiwanglu" 中美軍需聯席會議有關肉類備忘錄 [Memo on meat requirements for troops], 1945, 20-08-041-19, AIMH.
98. See Poon Shuk-wah 潘淑華, "Huniu yu shaniu: Wanqing ji minguo shiqi Zhongguo niurou jingji yinqi de zhengyi" 護牛與殺牛: 晚清及民國時期中國牛肉經濟引起的爭議 [To kill or not to kill: Controversies over the beef economy and oxen protection in late Qing and Republican China], *Shijie lishi pinglun* 世界歷史評論 3 (2021): 177–203.
99. Arthur N. Young, *China and the Helping Hand, 1937–1945* (Cambridge, MA: Harvard University Press, 1963), 291; Lloyd E. Eastman, "Nationalist China during the Sino-Japanese War 1937–1945," in John K. Fairbank and Albert Feuerwerker, eds., *The Cambridge History of China*, vol. 13 (Cambridge: Cambridge University Press, 1986), 589.
100. Huang, *Guanyu Meiguo bing*, 73–84.
101. Liu, *From Canton Restaurant to Panda Express*, 63–65.
102. Frank Dorn, *A General's Diary of Treasured Recipes* (Chicago, IL: Henry Regnery Company, 1953).
103. Julia Child Papers, 1925–1993. MC 644, box 1.
104. Madeline Y. Hsu, "From Chop Suey to Mandarin Cuisine: Fine Dining and the Refashioning of Chinese Ethnicity during the Cold War Era," in Sucheng Chan and Madeline Y. Hsu, eds., *Chinese Americans and the Politics of Race and Culture* (Philadelphia, PA: Temple University Press, 2008), 173–193.
105. Zumwalt, *On Watch*, 7–8.
106. Sledge, *China Marine*, 15–16, 53.
107. Albert Edward Peck (AFC/2001/001/57459), Memoirs (MS 22), Veterans History Project Collection.
108. Barney Rosset, "12 September 1945 letter to parents: page 1," *Columbia University Libraries Online Exhibitions*, https://exhibitions.library.columbia.edu/exhibits/show/rosset/item/7664.
109. Zumwalt, *On Watch*, 10–11.
110. Barrow, oral history transcript, session 2.
111. Sledge, *China Marine*, 22, 51.
112. Oral history of George Carrington, transcript, 28, OCHOH.
113. Sledge, *China Marine*, 26, 45.
114. Simms Memoir, 4–5.
115. Tao, "'Hao Pu Hao?"
116. "Yangjingbang huayu" 洋涇浜華語 [Pidgin Chinese], *Shen bao*, October 20, 1946.
117. Ju Ying 菊影, "YinMian qianxian huiyi" 印緬前綫回憶 [Memories of the India–Burma front line], *Shen bao*, June 23, 1946.

118. "Excerpts: 'Things Chinese,'" *The North China Marine*, November 10, 1945.
119. Albert F. Moe, "'Gung Ho,'" *American Speech* 42, no. 1 (1967): 19–30.
120. Paul Carter, *The Sound In-Between: Voice, Space, Performance* (Kensington: New South Wales University Press, 1992).
121. Simms Memoir, 19–20.
122. See Nicholas Thomas, *Entangled Objects: Exchange, Material Culture, and Colonialism in the Pacific* (Cambridge, MA: Harvard University Press, 1991).
123. Klein, *Cold War Orientalism*, 1–17.
124. United States Marine Corps, *A Marine's Guide to North China*, 8.
125. Crouch, *China Sketchbook*, 8; Simms Memoir, 18–19.
126. Smith's *Chinese Characteristics* was one of the most widely read books about China at the time. See Arthur Smith Henderson, *Chinese Characteristics* (New York: Revell, 1894); "Marines Finally See a 'Chinese Fire Drill,'" *The North China Marine*, November 17, 1945.
127. Theodore H. White, "LIFE Looks at China," *Life* (May 1, 1944): 99.
128. Thomas, *Entangled Objects*.
129. Sledge, *China Marine*, 96–97.
130. Mae Ngai, *The Chinese Question: The Gold Rushes and Global Politics* (New York: W. W. Norton & Company, 2021), 64.
131. William G. Pierson case, 81–85, RG 59: General Records of the Department of State, Box 4663, NARA.
132. Waijiaobu, "Shen Chong an (er)" 沈崇案(二) [Shen Chong case (2)], 019, 020-050204-0002, AHA.
133. Tao, "'Hao Pu Hao?'"
134. Cass, *History of the Sixth Marine Division*, 218.
135. Because Liu was an underage orphan, a lawyer had to arrange a Chinese man named Liu to pose as his biological father and relinquish his paternal rights to finalize the adoption paperwork in China. See Suzanne Liu Taylor, "The Life of Liu," Old China Hands Unpublished Manuscripts, California State University, Northridge.
136. United States Army Forces, *A Pocket Guide to China*, 4–8, 42.
137. Harold R. Isaacs, *No Peace for Asia* (Cambridge, MA: MIT Press, 1967), 32–33.
138. William W. Lockwood, "The GI in Wartime China," *Far Eastern Survey* 16, no. 1 (January 15, 1947): 9.
139. See e.g. Gallicchio, *The Scramble for Asia*; Akira Iriye, "Contemporary History as History: American Expansion into the Pacific since 1941," *Pacific Historical Review* 53, no. 2 (1984): 191–212.
140. Barrow, oral history transcript, session 2.
141. For further theorizations of symbolic interactions, see e.g. Erving Goffman, *The Presentation of Self in Everyday Life* (Edinburgh: University of Edinburgh, 1956) and *Strategic Interaction* (Philadelphia: University of Pennsylvania Press, 1969); Clifford Geertz, *The Interpretation of Cultures: Selected Essays* (New York: Basic Books, 1973).
142. Glist, *China Mailbag Uncensored*, 268.

143. The man was reportedly shocked by electricity and fled amidst the guards' laughter. See Oral history of Thomas Nallen, transcript, 16, OCHOH.
144. Sledge, *China Marine*, 107–108.

3   Embodied Vehicles

1. Wang Jianzhu 王建柱, "Tiananmen guangchang de shiwuci yuebing" 天安門廣場的十五次閱兵 [Fifteen military parades in Tiananmen Square], *Hongyan Chunqiu* 紅岩春秋 10 (2017): 8–13.
2. In Chinese usage at the time, *Jipu* or *Jipuka* was a convenient catchphrase for American military vehicles. Though most often referring to the original American model of the Willys Jeep, it also included the so-called medium Jeep and large Jeep such as the Dodge truck. See Wei Jun 維浚, "Jipu bushi che" 吉普不是車 [Jeep is not just a car], *Xin guang* 新光 (June 27, 1946): 11.
3. Zhu Junle 祝君樂, "Jeepcar yu Jeep girl" Jeep Car 與Jeep Girl [Jeep car and Jeep girl], *Xinwen tiandi* 新聞天地 3 (February 20, 1945): 16–17.
4. Arthur J. Pulos, *The American Design Adventure, 1940–1975* (Cambridge, MA: MIT Press, 1988), 18–20.
5. Kathleen German, "Economic Convergence and the Celebration of Mass Production: The World War II Advertising Campaign to Sell Jeeps," in Paul M. Haridakis, Barbara S. Hugenberg, and Stanley T. Wearden, eds., *War and the Media: Essays on News Reporting, Propaganda and Popular Culture* (Jefferson, NC: McFarland, 2009), 92–111; Matthew J. Seelinger, "From the Jeep to the Humvee: U.S. Army Light Combat Vehicles, World War II to Present," *On Point* 11, no. 3 (December 2005): 8–13.
6. For example, see "Jiang Zhuxi cheng jipuka xunshi gedui" 蔣主席乘吉普卡巡視各隊 [President Chiang inspects the troops in a Jeep], *Yangzi jiang* 揚子江 1, no. 4 (1946): 3; "Jiang Zhuxi zai Ping yuebing" 蔣主席在平閱兵 [President Chiang holds military parade in Beijing], *Guofang yuekan* 國防月刊 5, no.1 (1948): 1.
7. Luo Luo 羅洛, "Meiguo de jipuche" 美國的吉普車 [America's Jeep], *Dushu zazhi* 讀書雜誌 2, no. 1 (1945): 23; Yi Shi 易石 trans., "Feixing jipu" 飛行吉普 [Flying Jeep], *Shubao jinghua* 書報精華 18 (1946): 25.
8. Yuan Menghong 袁夢鴻, "Faling guizhang" 法令規章 [Laws and regulations], *XiangGuiQian xunkan* 湘桂黔旬刊 1, no. 9 (1946): 5; "Minyong jipuche ying zunshou shixiang" 民用吉普應遵守事項 [Rules to be observed by civilian Jeeps], *Yunshu zhoukan* 運輸周刊 33 (August 25, 1946): 1.
9. "Shanghaishi cheliang dengji" 上海市車輛登記, *Shanghaishi gongwu tongji baogao* 上海市公務統計報告 [Shanghai municipal public affairs statistical report] 2, no. 3 (1947): 74; "Shanghaishi cheliang dengji" 上海市車輛登記, *Shanghaishi gongwu tongji baogao* 上海市公務統計報告 [Shanghai municipal public affairs statistical report] 3, no. 8 (1948): 89.
10. Te Fude 特福德, "Jipuche shi shenme" 吉普車是什麼 [What is a Jeep], *Xinsheng Zhongguo (New China monthly)* 新生中國 1 (1945): 18.
11. Luo, "Meiguo de jipuche."
12. "Wanneng jipuka" 萬能吉普卡 [Omnipotent Jeep car], *Wen fan* 文飯 (1946): 3; Chun Hua 春華 trans., "Wanneng de jipuche" 萬能的吉普車

[The omnipotent Jeep], *Shishi zazhi* 時事雜誌 1 (1946): 18–19; Meiguo xinwen chu 美國新聞處, "Jipuka ke fuzhu nongye" 吉普卡可輔助農業 [Jeep can assist in agriculture], *Guofang yuekan* 2, no. 3 (1947): 1.
13. See The Staff, "The 'Jeep' Post-War," *Scientific American* 173, no. 2 (1945): 102–109; "Do You Remember When Driving a Jeep Was a Brand-New THRILL," *Union Jack* (August 24, 1946): 2.
14. Cheng Zhongyu 成仲於, "Jipu dage" 吉普大哥 [Big brother Jeep], *Xin Shanghai* 新上海, no. 16 (1946): 8.
15. See Huang, *Guanyu Meiguo bing*, 19–20. As in other theaters, black troops were only assigned hard labor jobs in road building, transportation, engineering, and supplies, rather than core military tasks.
16. Marshall McLuhan and W. Terrence Gordon, *Understanding Media: The Extensions of Man* (Corte Madera, CA: Gingko Press, 2003), 292–301.
17. Jin Cao 勁草, "Jipuka: Kuangre jingtou zhi yimu" 吉普卡: 狂熱鏡頭之一幕 [Jeep car: A frenetic scene], *Sheng li* 勝利 4 (1945): 14.
18. Xiao Jizhe 小記者, "Jipuche" 吉普車 [Jeep], *Ertong zhishi* 兒童知識 3 (1946): 26.
19. Yao Jiadong 姚家棟, "Wo jiao ni zuo jipuche" 我教你做吉普車 [Let me teach you to make a Jeep], *Ertong gushi yuekan* 兒童故事月刊 1, no. 1 (1947): 28; Zhang Yanxing 張言行, "Laozuo jiaocai" 勞作教材 [Crafting textbook], *Guomin jiaoyu fudao yuekan* 國民教育輔導月刊 3, no. 1 (1948): 34–35.
20. "Qifa xinzhi de jiantie" 啟發心智的剪貼 [Mind inspiring paper crafts], *Xin ertong* 新兒童 13, no. 4 (1947): 18.
21. Li Yaoyu 李耀宇 and Li Dongping 李東平, "Wo suo zhidao de Yan'an Meijun guanchazu" 我所知道的延安美軍觀察組 [The US Army Observation Group to Yan'an that I know of], *Nanfang zhoumo* 南方周末 1045 (February 19, 2004).
22. Yang Shangkun 楊尚昆, *Yang Shangkun huiyilu* 楊尚昆回憶錄 [Memoir of Yang Shangkun] (Beijing: Zhongyang wenxian chubanshe, 2001), 228–230.
23. Enda Duffy, *The Speed Handbook: Velocity, Pleasure, Modernism* (Durham, NC: Duke University Press, 2009), 1–17.
24. For Chinese modern sensations and speed, see Leo Ou-Fan Lee, *Shanghai Modern: The Flowering of a New Urban Culture in China, 1930–1945* (Cambridge, MA: Harvard University Press, 1999); Wen-hsin Yeh, *Shanghai Splendor: Economic Sentiments and the Making of Modern China, 1843–1949* (Berkeley: University of California Press, 2007).
25. For studies on the experience of the train and modernity, see Wolfgang Schivelbusch, *The Railway Journey: The Industrialization of Time and Space in the Nineteenth Century* (Oakland: University of California Press, 2014); Li Siyi 李思逸, *Tielu xiandai xing: Wanqing zhi minguo de shikong tiyan yu wenhua xiangxiang* 鐵路現代性: 晚清至民國的時空體驗與文化想像 [Railway modernity in China: The temporal-spatial experience and the cultural imagination of trains, 1840–1937] (Taipei: China Times, 2020).
26. Lu Xi 露茜, "Wo shi jipu nülang ma?" 我是吉普女郎嗎? [Am I a Jeep girl?], *Xifeng* 西風 104 (March 1948): 173–176; Shen Lusha 沈露沙, "Wo shi Jeep

Girl" 我是Jeep Girl [I am a Jeep girl], *Xinwen tiandi* 4 (April 20, 1945): 32–34.
27. "Jipu nülang lizan" 吉普女郎禮讚 [A tribute to Jeep girls], *Zhilan huabao* 芝蘭畫報1 (April 21, 1946); Adam Cathcart, "Atrocities, Insults, and 'Jeep Girls': Depictions of the U.S. Military in China, 1945–1949," *International Journal of Comic Art* 10, no. 1 (2008): 140–154.
28. Ji 基, "Jipuka kuangxiang qu" 吉普卡狂想曲 [Jeep rhapsody], *Zonghe zhoukan* 綜合周刊 1, no. 2 (October 1945): 8.
29. Zhu, "Jeep car yu Jeep girl," 16–17.
30. Jian Pa 見怕, "Wei jipu zhengming" 為吉普正名 [Rectify the Jeep name], *Wen fan* 28 (1946): 1.
31. "Jipuka xiangyan" 吉普卡香煙 [Jeep car cigarette], advertisement, *Shen bao*, August 30, 1946, 1.
32. "Jipu yu minyi" 吉普與民意 [Jeep and public opinion], *Ji pu* 吉普 1 (1945): 2.
33. "Hengchong zhizhuang" 橫衝直撞 [Rampage], *Xinsheng Zhongguo* 新生中國 1, no. 5 (January 1946): 8.
34. "Meijunche zhuangshang xingren" 美軍車撞傷行人 [American military vehicle injuries pedestrians], *Shen bao*, December 17, 1945.
35. "Hongmao qiangdao de xuezhai" 紅毛強盜的血債 [Blood debts owed by red-haired foreign devils], *Renmin ribao* 人民日報, October 18, 1946.
36. "Jiangqu zawen" 蔣區雜文 [Miscellaneous essays on the Nationalist-controlled areas], *Renmin ribao*, November 14, 1946.
37. "Jin Meijun jipuche pengshang xingluren, Chen Yongzhen shangzhongzhisi" 津美軍吉普車碰傷行路人，陳永珍傷重致死 [US military Jeep in Tianjin injures pedestrian Chen Yongzhen, who subsequently died], *Yishi bao* 益世報, November 8, 1946.
38. "Junyong jipuche kaishang xingrendao, yasi liangren shang yiren" 軍用吉普車開上行人道, 壓死兩人傷一人 [Military Jeep mounts curb, crushes two and injures one], *Dagong bao* (Ta Kung Pao) 大公報, October 16, 1947.
39. "Meijun cheliang zhaoshi ji sibai yu jian" 美軍車輛肇事計四百餘件 [American military vehicles had over four hundred accidents], *Shen bao*, January 12, 1946.
40. Hersey, "Letter from Shanghai," 82.
41. There are different explanations for the origin of the name Jeep. Another popular version is that GP, general purpose, sounds similar to the word Jeep. See Seelinger, "From the Jeep to the Humvee"; Patrick R. Foster, *The Story of Jeep* (Iola, WI: Krause, 2004), 34–91.
42. German, "Economic Convergence and the Celebration of Mass Production"; The Staff, "The 'Jeep' Post-War," 102–109.
43. Du Yun 渡雲, "Jipuche muzhongwuren, laobaixing xingming jiaoguan" 吉普車目中無人, 老百姓性命交關 [Jeep ignores everyone, people's lives at stake], *Shen bao*, July 23, 1946.
44. In modern warfare, armor and equipment extend soldiers' capacity for violence, provide protection, and allow physical invulnerability. For conceptualizations of a motorized body, see Despina Kakoudaki, *Anatomy of*

a Robot: Literature, Cinema, and the Cultural Work of Artificial People* (New Brunswick, NJ: Rutgers University Press, 2014), 69–113; Donna J. Haraway, "A Cyborg Manifesto: Science, Technology, and Socialist-Feminism in the Late 20th Century," in *Manifestly Haraway* (Minneapolis: University of Minnesota Press, 2016), 3–90.
45. Xu Zisun 徐紫蓀, "Dangxin jipuche" 當心吉普車 [Watch out for the Jeep], *Ertong banyue kan* 兒童半月刊 1 (1946): 3.
46. Xiao Jiang 曉江, "Xue! Zongli tongxiangqian jipu fanshen" 血!總理銅像前吉普翻身 [Blood! Jeep overturns in front of the Premier's statue], *Hai tao* 海濤 2 (March 3, 1946): 1.
47. Charles Tsao, "Kill for Fun?" *The China Weekly Review* (October 5, 1946): 125.
48. Lone-Portia, "Accident," *The China Weekly Review* (December 25, 1948): 79.
49. See Immerwahr, *How to Hide an Empire*; Maier, *Among Empires*.
50. In the late Qing period, both systems were adopted, depending on the locales and which Western country had a larger influence in that part of China. Left-hand driving was used during the New Life Movement in the 1930s, as well as in Manchuria and the Japanese-occupied areas.
51. "Benfu guanyu cheliang gaikao youshi de bugao" 本府關於車輛改靠右駛的佈告 [Notice of change to right-side driving], 1945, Q1-6-217, SMA; Hersey, "Letter from Shanghai," 82.
52. Wan Er 莞爾, "Wei le jipuche" 為了吉普車 [For the Jeep], *Hai jing* 海晶 11 (1946): 12.
53. "Who's Responsible?" *The China Weekly Review* (June 11, 1949): 30.
54. "Who's Responsible?"
55. "Traffic Snarls," *The China Weekly Review* (August 10, 1946): 243.
56. "Shanghai's Traffic Police," *The China Weekly Review* (September 14, 1946): 39.
57. "Shanghai's Traffic Police."
58. "Traffic Snarls."
59. Simms Memoir, 16.
60. Sledge, *China Marine*, 46.
61. "Xianbing diyituan Meijun jianyi" 憲兵第一團美軍建議 [Recommendations from the First Battalion of the American military police], October 20, 1946, 0019/001/00469/0086, QMA.
62. "Guanyu chuli cheliang chuanzhi zhaohuo wenti yu disan fangmian silingbu deng de laiwang wenshu" 關於處理車輛船隻肇禍問題與第三方面司令部等的來往文書 [Correspondence on handling vehicle and vessel accidents with the Third Theatre Command], 1946, Q1-6-638, SMA.
63. "Guanyu chuli Meijun ouru cheliang qichuan zhaohuo deng wenti yu Jingchaju Gongwuju deng de laiwang wenshu" 關於處理美軍毆辱、車輛汽船肇禍等問題與警察局、工務局等的來往文書 [Correspondence on handling US military assaults and vehicle and steamship accidents with the Police Bureau, Public Works Bureau, and others], 1945–1946, Q1-6-415, SMA; "Guanyu Meijun cheliang qishi de wenjian" 關於美軍車輛啟事的文件 [Documents about the notice on American military vehicles], 1946,

J181-010–00289, J181-010–00290, Beijing Municipal Archives (BMA) 北京市檔案館.
64. "Shanghaishi Jingchaju Huangpuqu guanyu Meijun zhaohuo wenjian" 上海市警察局黃浦區關於美軍肇禍文件 [Documents from the Huangpu District Police Bureau of Shanghai on American military incidents], 1946, Q132-2-148, SMA.
65. "Who's Responsible?"
66. "ZhuHua Meijun zhaoshi (wu)" 駐華美軍肇事(五) [American military misconduct in China (5)], 020–050204–0043, 106, 1947, AHA.
67. Yang, "United States Marines in Qingdao," 149–155.
68. "Guanyu chuli cheliang chuanzhi zhaohuo wenti yu disan fangmian silingbu deng de laiwang wenshu."
69. Hersey, "Letter from Shanghai," 82–90.
70. Wei 衛, "Jipuche yu renliche" 吉普車與人力車 [Jeep and rickshaw], *Jingji zhoubao* 經濟周報 3, no. 1 (1946): 4.
71. Yao Han 耀漢, "Shoudu de renliche" 首都的人力車 [Rickshaws in the capital], *Gongshang xinwen* 工商新聞 20 (1947): 8.
72. While leftist literature portrayed rickshaw men as the most vulnerable victims of poverty and a symbol of the oppressive social system, newspapers included tragic and comic incidents involving pullers who were "paupers or beasts of burden" as well as those who stole from passengers and fought in street brawls. See David Strand, *Rickshaw Beijing: City People and Politics in the 1920s* (Berkeley: University of California Press, 1989), 20–37.
73. Yan Changhong 嚴昌洪, "Jindai renli chefu qunti yishi tanxi" 近代人力車夫群體意識探析 [Analysis of the group consciousness of modern rickshaw pullers], *Huazhong shifan daxue xuebao* 華中師範大學學報, no. 6 (2007): 67–68.
74. Reports from the time also referred to him as Zang Daerzi and Zang Dayaozi.
75. Guo, "The Climax of Sino-American Relations," 279–280.
76. Yao, "Shoudu de renliche," 8.
77. "Shanghaishi cheliang dengji," 1947, 1948.
78. Wei, "Jipuche yu renliche."
79. Albert, *Yohouse from a Boot to a China Marine*, 76–81.
80. Sledge, *China Marine*, 46.
81. Simms Memoir, 7.
82. The minstrel show was the most popular entertainment form in nineteenth-century America and remained popular for more than a century beginning in the 1830s. See Eric J. Lott, *Love and Theft: Blackface Minstrelsy and the American Working Class* (New York: Oxford University Press, 1993).
83. Huang, *Guanyu Meiguo bing*, 85.
84. Hersey, "Letter from Shanghai," 86; "Shanghai 'huangbaoche huanghou' jingsai" 上海"黃包車皇后"競賽 [The Stars and Stripes rickshaw derby], *Shanghai tuhua xinwen* 上海圖畫新聞 [*The Illustrated Shanghai News*] 6 (1946): 19.
85. Glist, *China Mailbag Uncensored*, 209.

86. Tang Bo 湯波, "Huangbaoche huanghou" 黃包車皇后 [Rickshaw queen], *Xinhua ribao*, December 2, 1945; "Niuyue juxing renliche bisai" 紐約舉行人力車比賽 [New York holds rickshaw race], *Shen bao*, April 3, 1946; "Jiang Ermao fuMei xinwen nai Hu Meijun ezuoju" 姜二毛赴美新聞乃滬美軍惡作劇 [News of Jiang Ermao going to America is a GI prank], *Dagong bao*, April 5, 1946.
87. "Himalayan He-men," *Victory: The Weekly for India Command* 10, no. 1 (January 29, 1944): 41–44.
88. "R. N. Official Photograph," *Pacific Post*, September 25, 1945. For British leisure activities in Hong Kong, see Mark Hampton, *Hong Kong and British Culture, 1945–97* (Manchester: Manchester University Press, 2016), 72–99.
89. J. Heming, "South Africa as I Saw It," *Union Jack*, April 8, 1946.
90. Untitled photograph, *Good Morning: The Daily Paper of the Submarine Branch*, 653 (1944): 4.
91. "Revelry and Rivalry in Shanghai," *Salt* 11, no. 10 (January 14, 1946): 23; Mark Wilkinson, "American Military Misconduct in Shanghai and the Chinese Civil War: The Case of Zang Dayaozi," *Journal of American–East Asian Relations* 17, no. 2 (2010): 146–173.
92. Sledge, *China Marine*, 27–28.
93. Lao She 老舍, *Luotuo Xiangzi* 駱駝祥子 [*Rickshaw boy*] (Beijing: Renmin wenxue chubanshe, 2019), 220.
94. Shi Jun 施君, "Renli chefu de gongchao" 人力車夫的工潮 [Rickshaw puller's strike], *Kaiming shaonian* 開明少年 10 (April 16, 1946): 56; "Business Foot-Notes," *The China Weekly Review* (June 29, 1946): 109.
95. See e.g. "Cha renli chefu bushou zhixu, bing shiyou ouru Meijun" 查人力車夫不守秩序, 並時有毆辱美軍 [Investigate rickshaw pullers not maintaining order and occasionally assaulting American troops], July 8, 1947, A0019/003/00253/0101, QMA; "Guanyu renli chefu ouji Meijun kache shibing de xunling" 關於人力車夫毆擊美軍卡車士兵的訓令 [Directive on rickshaw pullers assaulting American soldiers in military trucks], B0024/001/00498/0086, QMA; "Guanyu dui Meijun wuxu jiayibaohu de xunling" 關於對美軍務須加以保護的訓令 [Directive on the necessity to protect American troops], April 2, 1946, B0024/001/00676/0072, QMA.
96. See Yang, "United States Marines in Qingdao," 184.
97. Sledge, *China Marine*, 26–28.
98. "Shanghai canyihui guanyu shimin Zang Genbao ji qifu Zang Daerzi bei Meijun jibi qing jiaoshe de wenjian" 上海參議會關於市民臧根寶及其父臧大二子被美軍擊斃請交涉的文件 [Documents from the Shanghai Representative Council on citizen Zang Genbao's request regarding her father, Zang Daerzi, killed by American soldiers], 1947, Q109-1-1742, SMA. Due to the substantial difference between official and black-market exchange rates, the equivalent amount in US dollars is estimated to range from $3,600 to more than $10,000. This sum is considerably higher than the typical amounts requested for similar cases.
99. See "ZhuHua Meijun zhaoshi (er)" 駐華美軍肇事(二) [American military misconduct in China (2)], 020–050204–0040, 1–153, 1946, AHA.

100. See "ZhuHua Meijun zhaoshi (er)"; Chang Tien Fu 張天福, "The Shanghai High Court's Reply," *The China Weekly Review* (June 7, 1947): 24–26.
101. See Wilkinson, "American Military Misconduct in Shanghai and the Chinese Civil War." Meanwhile, a Chinese court in Shanghai held a trial for Julian Larrinaga, convicting him of inciting Roderick to commit the crime and sentencing him to one year and nine months incarceration.
102. "Wei Meijun cisha renli chefu Su Mingcheng yi'an Qingdaoshi jingchaju cheng shizhengfu" 為美軍刺殺人力車夫蘇明誠一案青島市警察局呈市政府 [Qingdao Police Bureau report to the municipal government on the case of rickshaw puller Su Mingcheng, who was killed by an American soldier], April 5, 1947, in Zhonggong Qingdaoshiwei dangshiziliao zhengweihui bangongshi 中共青島市委黨史資料征委會辦公室, ed., *Qingdao dangshi ziliao di 4 ji* 青島黨史資料第四輯 [*Historical materials of the CCP in Qingdao*, vol. 4] (Qingdao: Qingdaoshi chubanshe, 1989), 269–270; "Guanyu zhizhi Shanda xuesheng yin Meijun cisha chefu yi'an faqi fanMeiyundong qingxing de daidian" 關於制止山大學生因美軍刺殺車夫一案發起反美運動情形的代電 [Cable on halting Shandong University students' anti-American movement over the case of a US solider stabbing a rickshaw puller], B0024/001/00502/0070, QMA.
103. "Shanghai difang fayuan youguan Meiguo duoshou dasi Zang Daerzi anjian" 上海地方法院有關美國舵手打死臧大二子案件 [Shanghai District Court case on the American sailor who killed Zang Daerzi], Q185-1-622, SMA; Yang, "United States Marines in Qingdao," 187.
104. See e.g. "Meijun you xingxiong" 美軍又行凶 [GIs commits another act of violence], *Wenhui bao* 文匯報, September 24, 1946; "Renli chefu dui Meijun de kongsu" 人力車夫對美軍的控訴 [Rickshaw puller's accusation against US military], *Wenhui bao*, September 29, 1946; "Shelun: Kangyi zhuHua Meijun de baoxing" 社論:抗議駐華美軍的暴行 [Editorial: Protesting the brutalities of the US military in China], *Xinhua ribao*, September 29, 1946; "Zang Daerzi canan" 臧大二子慘案 [Heinous murder of Zang Daerzi], *Xinhua ribao*, October 12, 1946.
105. Tang Hai 唐海, "Zang Dayaozi zhuan" 臧大咬子傳 [Biography of Zang Dayaozi], *Wen cui* 文萃 2, no. 18 (1947): 19–31.
106. See e.g. Xiao Feilübin 小菲律賓, "Wan Su Mingcheng" 挽蘇明誠 [Mourning Su Mingcheng], *Qing bao* 青報, April 10, 1947; "Qingdao Meijun cansha chefu, quanshi gejie fenqi kangyi" 青島美軍慘殺車夫, 全市各界紛起抗議 [Qingdao GI brutally murders rickshaw puller, citywide protests erupt], *Renmin ribao*, April 22, 1947; Chen Xueyi 陳學毅, "Meiyou chuntian de Qingdao" 沒有春天的青島 [Qingdao without spring], *Qun zhong* 群衆 1, no. 12 (1947): 19–20; "Xue zhang" 血賬 [Blood debts], *Xin wenhua* 新文化 3, no. 5 (1947): 2.
107. Wilkinson, "American Military Misconduct in Shanghai and the Chinese Civil War."
108. "Gei bei cisi de chefu" 給被刺死的車夫 [To the stabbed-to-death puller], in *Qingdao dangshi ziliao di 4 ji*, 410–412.
109. "Racial Tensions," *The China Weekly Review* (July 16, 1949): 138.

110. For the Jeep as a new type of mobile modernity in postcolonial South Korea, see Han Sang Kim, "My Car Modernity: What the U.S. Army Brought to South Korean Cinematic Imagination about Modern Mobility," *Journal of Asian Studies* 75, no. 1 (2016): 63–85. For another example of an automobile's potency as a national cultural symbol and a postwar global commodity, see Bernhard Rieger, *The People's Car: A Global History of the Volkswagen Beetle* (Cambridge MA: Harvard University Press, 2013).
111. While the Jeep stood as an iconic symbol of victory, it was the "Red Flag" (*hongqi*) that later emerged as China's "national car" and became the standard parade vehicle for Communist leaders during National Day celebrations. See Wang, "Tiananmen guangchang de shiwuci yuebing."

4 Intimate Relations

1. Xian Ping 弦平, "Dushi shalong fengjing huipian" [Panels of an urban salon landscape] 都市沙龍風景繪片, *Gong dao* 公道 2 (1945): 8.
2. Xian, "Dushi shalong fengjing huipian."
3. American male soldiers also had sexual relations with Chinese men and visited male prostitutes in China. However, queer sexualities are not included in this chapter because of their lack of visibility in existing sources, which focus almost exclusively on Chinese women and American male soldiers. Such a contemporary framing reflects the long-standing sexual and gender biases within Chinese society. Meanwhile, American policies on soldiers' sexuality in this period were also based on heterosexual white males, while homosexual soldiers' sexuality was largely denied or suppressed. See Allan Bérubé, *Coming Out under Fire: The History of Gay Men and Women in World War II* (Chapel Hill: University of North Carolina Press, 2010).
4. Haunted by defeat, Japanese male elites feared a sexual invasion by Americans and tried to build a "female blood wall" as a buffer zone. Meanwhile, the Korean government ghettoized small villages of camp towns to prevent American servicemen from entering Korean society, while financially benefiting from the sex trade. See Robert Kramm, *Sanitized Sex: Regulating Prostitution, Venereal Disease, and Intimacy in Occupied Japan, 1945–1952* (Oakland: University of California Press, 2017), 29–56; Na Young Lee, "The Construction of Military Prostitution in South Korea during the U.S. Military Rule, 1945–1948," *Feminist Studies* 33, no. 3 (2007): 453–481.
5. The Chinese term was also occasionally used to refer to Chinese women riding with Chinese soldiers, but this was rare. Though not exclusive, the English term "Jeep girls" in American military newspapers was mostly used to refer to Chinese women.
6. Modern Girl around the World Research Group, eds., *The Modern Girl around the World: Consumption, Modernity and Globalization* (Durham, NC: Duke University Press, 2008), 9.
7. See Fredman, *The Tormented Alliance.*

8. Chen Minzhi 陳敏之, "Cong Yingguo taitai tandao jipu nülang" 從英國太太談到吉普女郎 [From English ladies to Jeep girls], *Nü sheng* 女聲 4, no. 1 (1946): 26.
9. Elizabeth J. Remick, *Regulating Prostitution in China: Gender and Local Statebuilding, 1900–1937* (Stanford, CA: Stanford University Press, 2014).
10. Peck, *Two Kinds of Time*, 518–550.
11. Robert Payne, *China Awake* (New York: Dodd, Mead and Company, 1947), 420.
12. Glist, *China Mailbag Uncensored*, 203.
13. Guo Gen 郭根, "Beiping sannian: Cong cansheng dao jiefang de yiduan lücheng" 北平三年: 從慘勝到解放的一段旅程 [Three years in Beijing: Journey from a pyrrhic victory to liberation], in San Mu 散木, ed., *Guo Gen wenlu* 郭根文錄 (Taiyuan: Sanjin, 2013), 94–97.
14. For example, see "Ye Baobao lunwei jipu nülang" 葉寶寶淪爲吉普女郎 [Ye Baobao turns into a Jeep girl], *Hai jing* 41 (1946): 8; Wei Tuo 韋陀, "Bai Guang: Zuo jipu nülang" 白光: 做吉普女郎 [Bai Guang: Becoming a Jeep girl], *Xin Shanghai* 新上海 12 (1946): 1; Feng Chun 逢春, "Chen Lu Qingdao zuo jipu nülang" 陳璐青島做吉普女郎 [Chen Lu becomes a Qingdao Jeep girl], *Hai yan* 海燕 2 (1946): 7; "Wang Wenlan yu Meijunguan tongju" 王文蘭與美軍官同居 [Wang Wenlan lives with an American officer], *Hai tao* 8 (1946): 3.
15. Yang Xiaohui 楊小慧, "Buneng wanquan zebei tamen" 不能完全責備她們 [Cannot entirely blame them], *Minzhu zhoukan* 民主週刊 1, no. 15 (1945): 14; Yun 雲, "Zhaodai mengjun de lianhuanhui shang" 招待盟軍的聯歡會上 [At the GI gala], *Fu nü* 婦女 3 (1946): 15.
16. Peck, *Two Kinds of Time*, 537–538; Huang, *Guanyu Meiguo bing*, 39.
17. See "Kunming ZhongMei nannü shejiao" 昆明中美男女社交 [Social intercourse between American men and Chinese women in Kunming], *Xinwen tiandi* 6 (June 20, 1945): 16–17.
18. Tao, "'Hao Pu Hao?'" 7.
19. Chen Er 陳耳, "Beiping Meijun de yihan?" 北平美軍的遺憾? [Regrets of the Beijing GIs?], *Qiri tan* 七日談 5 (1946): 11.
20. "Criticize GIs, Chinese Girls," *The Stars and Stripes* (London Edition), May 25, 1945.
21. "Chongqing shi jingchaju cheng shizhang dian" 重慶市警察局呈市長電 [Cable from Chongqing Municipal Police Bureau to the mayor], 1945, 0053-0010-00019-0000-099-000, Chongqing Municipal Archives (CMA) 重慶市檔案館.
22. "Guomin zhengfu junshi weiyuanhui xunling" 國民政府軍事委員會訓令 [National Military Council's orders], 1945, 0053-0010-00142-0200-293-000, CMA.
23. "Meihaijun shibing beiou an" 美海軍士兵被毆案 [Case of assault on an American Navy soldier], November 1946, microfilm Q131/-078, SMA.
24. "Tianjin Huanggong wuting jingchaju banshiyuan yu Meijun fasheng chongtu" 天津皇宮舞廳警察局辦事員與美軍發生衝突 [Police Bureau staff clashed with American soldiers at the Palace Dancehall in Tianjin], 1946. J181-024-03258, BMA; "Neierqu baogao Migaomei wuting you

Zhongguoren yu Meibing wei nüwuke fasheng chongtu xingyou" 內二區報告米高梅舞廳有中國人與美兵為女舞客發生衝突形由 [District Two report on the fights between Chinese people and American soldiers over taxi dancers at the MGM Dancehall], 1946, J181-010-00299, BMA.

25. "Chongqing shi jingchaju xunling" 重慶市警察局訓令 [Order from the Chongqing Municipal Police Bureau], September 4, 1945, 0061-0011-00048-0000-019-000, CMA.
26. Lu 魯, "Nanjing jipu jinzai nülang" 南京吉普禁載女郎 [Nanjing bans Jeep riding for women], *Shen bao*, July 19, 1946.
27. A recent product since China opened higher education to women in the early twentieth century, "university student" was more than a credential or indicator of socioeconomic status. As one commentator put it, she will always be called a "female college student" no matter how long she is out of school. See Xi Lin 西林, "'Nüxuesheng' yu 'liuxuesheng'" "女學生"與"留學生" ["Female students" and "students returned from abroad"], *Xiandai pinglun* 現代評論 1, no. 20 (1925): 8–10. The more general group of "girl students" received considerable media attention and male scrutiny beginning in the late nineteenth century. See Pingyuan Chen, "Male Gaze/Female Students: Late Qing Education for Women as Portrayed in Beijing Pictorials, 1902–08," in Nanxiu Qian, Grace S. Fong, and Richard J. Smith, eds., *Different Worlds of Discourse* (Leiden: Brill, 2008), 315–347; Yun Zhang, "The Emerging Modern Woman: Representations of the 'Girl Student' in Early Twentieth Century Urban China," *Harvard Asia Quarterly* 16, no. 3 (2014): 50–59.
28. "Jipu nülang" 吉普女郎 [Jeep girls], *Heibai zhoubao* 黑白週報 2 (1946): 10.
29. Xiao Tian 笑天, "Kangyi Meijun baoxing yundong xiangqing poushi" 抗議美軍暴行運動詳情剖視 [Analysis of the protest movement against American military brutality], *Taipingyang yuekan* 太平洋月刊 2 (1947): 66–68.
30. Hui Feng 迴風, "Jipu nülang de mingyun" 吉普女郎的命運 [The fate of Jeep girls]! *Qiri tan* 11 (1946): 2.
31. Wuming Jizhe 無名記者, "Meijun zhengfu le quanshijie de nüxing" 美軍征服了全世界的女性 [The US military has conquered women worldwide], *Zhongguo wenzhai* 中國文摘 5 (1945): 7; Liao Yuyang 廖宇陽, *Wanqinglou shici wenshi heji* 晚晴樓詩詞文史合集 [*A collection of poetry, literature and history of the Wanqinglou*] (Nanchang, Jiangxi: Jiangxi renmin chubanshe, 2015), 235–237.
32. Zhu, "Jeep car yu Jeep girl."
33. Fang Cao 芳草, "Chongqing shi shang zhenggou jipu nülang dapi sishengzi" 重慶市上爭購吉普女郎大批私生子 [Illegitimate children of Jeep girls on high demand on the Chongqing market], *Hai guang* 海光 9 (1946): 8.
34. Chen Mingxun 陳明勳, "Wei 'Mei' lun" 唯"美"論 ["America" only theory], *Wen fan* 5 (1946): 3.
35. Since the American soldier had already been married to an American woman when he married the Chinese woman, and was now a civilian no longer under the jurisdiction of the Department of Statement or the

Department of National Defense, the legal position of the Chinese woman and her baby remained uncertain. See Correspondences between the China Inland Mission and the American Embassy, 1947, RG 84, Box 83, NARA.

36. John Costello, *Virtue under Fire: How World War II Changed Our Social and Sexual Attitudes* (Boston, MA: Little, Brown and Company, 1985), 230.
37. Louise Edwards, "Policing the Modern Woman in Republican China," *Modern China* 26, no. 2 (2000): 115–147.
38. Chen, "Male Gaze/Female Students"; Zhang, "The Emerging Modern Woman."
39. See Gael Graham, "The Cumberland Incident of 1928: Gender, Nationalism, and Social Change in American Mission Schools in China," *Journal of Women's History* 6, no. 3 (1994): 35–61.
40. Madeleine Yue Dong, "Who Is Afraid of the Chinese Modern Girl?" in *The Modern Girl Around the World*, 214.
41. See Hsiao-Pei Yen, "Body Politics, Modernity and National Salvation: The Modern Girl and the New Life Movement," *Asian Studies Review* 29, no. 2 (2005): 165; Margherita Zanasi, "Frugal Modernity: Livelihood and Consumption in Republican China," *Journal of Asian Studies* 74, no. 2 (2015): 391–409.
42. Edwards, "Policing the Modern Woman in Republican China."
43. Wang Aming 王阿明, "Yifeng gei jipu nülang de juemingshu" 一封給吉普女郎的絕命書 [A farewell letter to a Jeep girl], *Xin tiandi* 新天地 4 (1946): 5.
44. Zhengxing guanzhu 正興館主, "Jipu nülang zhi mengjun shu" 吉普女郎致盟軍書 [A Jeep girl's letter to an Allied solider], *Wen fan* 2 (1946): 7.
45. Chen, "Male Gaze/Female Students"; Dong, "Who Is Afraid of the Chinese Modern Girl?"; Zhang, "The Emerging Modern Woman."
46. Cathcart, "Atrocities, Insults, and 'Jeep Girls.'"
47. Dong, "Who Is Afraid of the Chinese Modern Girl?"
48. Hong Shen 洪深, "Nannü jian" 男女間 [Between men and women], *Chongqing ribao* 重慶日報, May 17, 1945, 45–47.
49. Dong Shijin 董時進, "Guanyu jipu nülang" 關於吉普女郎 [About Jeep girls], *Dagong bao* May 25, 1945.
50. Luo Jialun 羅家倫, "Jipu nülang" 吉普女郎 [Jeep girls], *Nüqingnian yuekan* 女青年月刊 2, no. 1 (1945): 5–6.
51. Yan Jun 燕君, "ZhongMei nannü shejiao" 中美男女社交 [Social intercourse between American men and Chinese women], *Xi feng* 79, no. 35 (August 1945): 35–37.
52. Chen, "Cong Yingguo taitai tandao jipu nülang."
53. Chao 超, "Tan 'jipu nülang'" 談 "吉普女郎" [On "Jeep girls"], *Xiandai funü* 現代婦女 6, no. 1–2 (1945): 2.
54. Guo, "Beiping sannian."
55. Liao, *Wanqinglou shici wenshi heji*, 235–237.
56. "Li Lihua fan youshangfenghua an" 李麗華犯有傷風化案 [The case of Li Lihua offending morality], *Minzhong ribao* 民眾日報, March 26, 1946.
57. Zhu Xia 朱霞, "Woxiang zuo jipu nülang ne" 我想做吉普女郎呢 [I want to become a Jeep girl], *Yue kan* 月刊 2, no. 2 (September 1946): 57–58.
58. Yang, "Buneng wanquan zebei tamen."

59. Cai Huiming 蔡惠明, "Yige kechuan jipu nülang de zishu" 一個客串吉普女郎的自述 [In her own words by an occasional Jeep girl], *Wen fan* 17 (1946): 10.
60. For studies on women warriors and sex spying in 1930s and 1940s China, especially concerning the conflicting calls for female fidelity and national service, see Louise Edwards, *Women Warriors and Wartime Spies of China* (Cambridge: Cambridge University Press, 2016) and "Policing the Modern Women in Republican China."
61. Some of the so-called Jeep girl stories were in fact written by men looking for a good satire. But the two cited in this article do not appear to be so. The first piece includes meticulous details and is not written in the usual sensational style of Jeep girl satires. The intention of the pro-government's journal *Xinwen tiandi* in publishing the second story, a very provocative piece, remains suspicious, perhaps as a cautionary tale. Both authors used pseudonyms, likely transliterations from English names.
62. Lu, "Wo shi jipu nülang ma?"
63. Maura Elizabeth Cunningham, "The Modern Girl in Motion: Women and Sports in Liangyou," in Paul Pickowicz, Kuiyi Shen, and Yingjin Zhang, eds., *Liangyou: Kaleidoscopic Modernity and the Shanghai Global Metropolis, 1926–1945* (Leiden: Brill, 2013), 94–110; Yunxiang Gao, *Sporting Gender: Women Athletes and Celebrity-Making during China's National Crisis, 1931–45* (Vancouver: University of British Columbia Press, 2013), 58–80.
64. Louise Edwards, "The Shanghai Modern Woman's American Dreams: Imagining America's Depravity to Produce China's 'Moderate Modernity,'" *Pacific Historical Review* 81, no. 4 (2012): 568–570.
65. Shen, "Wo shi Jeep Girl."
66. Zhu, "Jeep car yu Jeep girl."
67. Zhu Zhechi 朱者赤, "Du woshi 'JEEP GIRL' zhihou" 讀我是 "JEEP GIRL" 之後 [After reading I am a "Jeep girl"], *Xinwen tiandi* 5 (May 20, 1945): 28–29.
68. Cai, "Yige kechuan jipu nülang de zishu."
69. Cheng Huina 程慧娜, "Jipu nülang yanzhong de Meiguobing" 吉普女郎眼中的美國兵 [American soldiers in the eyes of Jeep girls], *Du zhe* 讀者 2 (1945): 58.
70. Susan Zeiger, *Entangling Alliances: Foreign War Brides and American Soldiers in the Twentieth Century* (New York: New York University Press, 2010), 226.
71. For the attractions of American boys to British girls, see Costello, *Virtue under Fire*, 206.
72. Edwards, "Policing the Modern Woman in Republican China."
73. Affected by the war conditions, dating in America became less committed to long-term fidelity both at home and abroad. Meanwhile, the American courtship rituals were said to be less formal, for example, compared to British customs. See John D'Emilio and Estelle B. Freedman, *Intimate Matters: A History of Sexuality in America* (Chicago, IL: University of Chicago Press, 2012), 240–256; Costello, *Virtue under Fire*, 230–232.
74. Cheng, "Jipu nülang yanzhong de Meiguobing."
75. Shen, "Wo shi Jeep Girl."

76. More than twelve thousand Chinese Americans had been drafted during WWII. See Meredith Oyen, *The Diplomacy of Migration: Transnational Lives and the Making of U.S.-Chinese Relations in the Cold War* (Ithaca, NY: Cornell University Press, 2015), 78–87; Xiaojian Zhao, *Remaking Chinese America: Immigration, Family, and Community, 1940–1965* (New Brunswick, NJ: Rutgers University Press, 2002), 78–83.
77. "Marriage Notices: Over Two Hundred Posted at Supreme Court," *South China Morning Post*, November 22, 1947, 2.
78. Catherine Forslund, *Anna Chennault: Informal Diplomacy and Asian Relations* (New York: Rowman & Littlefield, 2002), 40–41.
79. Crouch, *China Sketchbook*, 9.
80. United States Marine Corps, *A Marine's Guide to North China*, 13.
81. Zeiger, *Entangling Alliances*, 71.
82. For example, see Petra Goedde, *GIs and Germans: Culture, Gender, and Foreign Relations, 1945–1949* (New Haven, CT: Yale University Press, 2003); Höhn and Moon, *Over There*; Sarah Kovner, *Occupying Power: Sex Workers and Servicemen in Postwar Japan* (Stanford, CA: Stanford University Press, 2012); Katharine H. S. Moon, *Sex among Allies: Military Prostitution in U.S.–Korea Relations* (New York: Columbia University Press,1997); Mary Louise Roberts, *What Soldiers Do: Sex and the American GI in World War II France* (Chicago, IL: University of Chicago Press, 2013).
83. The American military displayed a colonial mentality that women of occupied territories should be sexually available, just like women of color in colonial empires. See Kramm, *Sanitized Sex*; John W. Dower, *War without Mercy: Race and Power in the Pacific War* (New York: Pantheon Books, 1986); Yukiko Koshiro, *Trans-Pacific Racisms and the U.S. Occupation of Japan* (New York: Columbia University Press, 1999); Seungsook Moon, "Regulating Desire, Managing the Empire: U.S. Military Prostitution in South Korea, 1945–1970," in Höhn and Moon, *Over There*, 39–77.
84. Cynthia Enloe, *Maneuvers: The International Politics of Militarizing Women's Lives* (Berkeley: University of California Press, 2000).
85. Lockwood, "The GI in Wartime China," 11.
86. Huang, *Guanyu Meiguo bing*, 42.
87. Zumwalt, *On Watch*, 10.
88. Sledge, *China Marine*, 9.
89. See Clark, *Treading Softly*; United States Marine Corps, *A Marine's Guide to North China*, 2–5.
90. Simms Memoir, 7; Guo, "Paradise or Hell Hole?" 159.
91. United States Marine Corps, *A Marine's Guide to North China*, 13.
92. "Guanyu gaishan ZhongMei renmin zhijian guanxi shang Jiang Zhongzheng cheng" 關於改善中美人民之間關係上蔣中正呈 [Memorandum to Chiang Kai-shek on enhancing Sino-U.S. relations], 1945, 0053-0010-00142-0100-235-000, CMA.
93. United States Army Service Forces, *A Pocket Guide to China*, 15.
94. See Huang, *Guanyu Meiguo bing*, 97–101; Robert Shaffer, "A Rape in Beijing, December 1946: GIs, Nationalist Protests, and U.S. Foreign Policy," *Pacific Historical Review* 69, no. 1 (2000): 43.

95. See Costello, *Virtue under Fire*; Enloe, *Maneuvers*; Roberts, *What Soldiers Do*.
96. Gina Marchetti, *Romance and the "Yellow Peril": Race, Sex, and Discursive Strategies in Hollywood Fiction* (Berkeley: University of California Press, 1993).
97. Yunte Huang, *Daughter of the Dragon: Anna May Wong's Rendezvous with American History* (New York: Liveright, 2023).
98. George Anthony Peffer, "Forbidden Families: Emigration Experiences of Chinese Women under the Page Law, 1875–1882," *Journal of American Ethnic History* 6, no. 1 (1986): 28–46.
99. For Asian/white miscegenation in the broader context of America's varied treatment of all interracial, sexual relationships, see Peggy Pascoe, *What Comes Naturally: Miscegenation Law and the Making of Race in America* (New York: Oxford University Press, 2009); Emma Jinhua Teng, *Eurasian: Mixed Identities in the United States, China, and Hong Kong, 1842–1943* (Berkeley: University of California Press, 2013).
100. Madeline Y. Hsu, *The Good Immigrants: How the Yellow Peril Became the Model Minority* (Princeton, NJ: Princeton University Press, 2015), 1–129.
101. United States Marine Corps, *A Marine's Guide to North China*, 13.
102. Crouch, *China Sketchbook*, 34–40.
103. Karen J. Leong, *The China Mystique: Pearl S. Buck, Anna May Wong, Mayling Soong, and the Transformation of American Orientalism* (Berkeley: University of California Press, 2005), 106–154.
104. Sledge, *China Marine*, 25.
105. See "Events in Brief," *The China Weekly Review* (September 14, 1946): 54; American Armed Forces personnel and their dependents, September 22, 1947 and January 31, 1948, RG 84, Box 83 and Box 121, NARA.
106. For example, General Rockey's aide, Captain Frank Gorman, was involved with Ullie Ott, daughter of General Eugen Ott, the former German ambassador to Japan. Walter Curley dated Gisela Jannings, a German woman from an affluent family that had resided in China for decades. See Clark, *Treading Softly*, 143; Griffith, oral history transcript, 179.
107. Glist, *China Mailbag Uncensored*, 248.
108. Glist, *China Mailbag Uncensored*, 179.
109. Fredman, *The Tormented Alliance*, 135–162.
110. Guo, "Paradise or Hell Hole?" 159.
111. Sledge, *China Marine*, 30.
112. Barrow, oral history transcript, session 2.
113. Simms Memoir, 7–8.
114. Sledge, *China Marine*, 31.
115. "Meijun qiuwu" 美軍求舞 [Americans seeking dance], *Shen bao*, October 8, 1947; "Dangju guanzhi jinü wunü zhiding sixiang banfa" 當局管制妓女舞女制定四項辦法 [Government issued four regulations on prostitutes and dance girls], *Yishi bao*, August 9, 1946.
116. United States Army Service Forces, *A Pocket Guide to China*, 15.

117. Yu Dafu 郁達夫, *Yu Dafu sanwen* 郁達夫散文 [*Essays by Yu Dafu*], ed. Yi Qi 亦祺 (Hangzhou: Zhejiang wenyi chubanshe, 1999), 91.
118. "Guanyu Meijun xujiu ouda cheliangzhaohuo deng wenti de baogao" 關於美軍酗酒毆打車輛肇禍等問題的報告 [Reports on American soldiers' misconduct including intoxication, battery, and traffic accidents], 1945, Q1-6-416, SC0025, SMA.
119. Wang Yu 望愉, "Shui neng rongren Meijun zhuHua" 誰能容忍美軍駐華 [Who can stand the American military in China], *Min chao* 民潮 (January 1, 1947): 1.
120. "Qingdao Meijun lunjian shaofu" 青島美軍輪奸少婦 [American soldiers in Qingdao gang raped a young wife], *Yishi bao*, August 12, 1947.
121. Female Chinese attendees included paid dance hostesses and singing girls, as well as middle-class women who were tricked into believing that it was a regular dance party. The so-called Jingming building affair received major media coverage at the time. For example, see "Hankoushi jiti qiangjian an" 漢口市集體強姦案 [Gang rape in Hankou], *Shen bao*, September 26, 1948.
122. Benjamin Welles, "Much China Crime Laid to Our Troops," *The New York Times*, October 13, 1946. In 1951, Zhang was accused of espionage to aid America during the Korean War and later tragically died in prison during the Cultural Revolution.
123. The Ambassador in China (Stuart) to the Secretary of State, October 17, 1946, *FRUS, 1946*, Document 201.
124. "GI Welcome Wears Out in China," *Amerasia* 10, no. 6 (1946): 173–174.
125. The estimated student numbers ranged from four thousand to ten thousand, depending on the political affiliations of the sources. See James A. Cook, "Penetration and Neocolonialism: The Shen Chong Rape Case and the Anti-American Student Movement of 1946–47," *Republican China* 22, no. 1 (1996): 65–97; Shaffer, "A Rape in Beijing, December 1946," 31–64; Zhang, *America Perceived*, 85–86.
126. It was not until the 1970s, in the wake of the women's and civil rights movements, that the archaic American rape law was finally revised. See Susan Estrich, "Rape," *Yale Law Journal* 95, no. 6 (1986): 1087–1184.
127. For an in-depth analysis of how injustice toward Shen Chong was executed in the US justice system, see Chunmei Du, "Rape in Peking: Injured Woman, Microhistory and Global Trial," *Gender & History* 36, no. 3 (2024): 620–638.
128. William G. Pierson case; Waijiaobu, "Shen Chong an (er)."
129. See "Guanyu Meijun xujiu ouda cheliangzhaohuo deng wenti de baogao."
130. United States Army Service Forces, *A Pocket Guide to China*, 15.
131. "Meijun qiuwu."
132. Shen's father, a high official in the Nationalist Government, was in charge of infrastructure to facilitate the American military operations during the war. Her great-grandfather was Shen Baozhen, a powerful viceroy in the late Qing government.
133. Zuo Shuangwen 左雙文, "1946 nian Shen Chong shijian: Nanjing zhengfu de duice" 1946 年沈崇事件: 南京政府的對策 [The 1946 Shen Chong

incident: Nanjing government's policies], *Jindaishi yanjiu* 近代史研究 1 (2005): 65–103.
134. "Say China Traitors Told 'Jeep Girl' Lies," *The Stars and Stripes* (London Edition), May 31, 1945; Nan Ming 南溟, "Jipu nülang" 吉普女郎 [Jeep girls], *Xingqi zhoukan* 星期周刊 1 (June 3, 1945): 2.
135. In practice, local dealings varied. For example, while Chongqing police attacked and arrested student protesters using mobs or the police force, He Siyuan, the Beijing mayor was more sympathetic and tolerant, telling reporters that he would also participate in the protest if he were younger. In general, local police were sent to maintain order and control traffic but refrained from forceful intervention. See Waijiaobu, "Shen Chong an (yi)" 沈崇案(一) [Shen Chong case (1)], 020-050204-0001, AHA and and "Shen Chong an (er)."
136. Wasserstrom, *Student Protests in Twentieth-Century China*, 240–262; Zhang, *America Perceived*, 77–118.
137. He Yaozu 賀耀祖, "ZhongMei nannü shejiao guannian zhi chengqing" 中美男女社交觀念之澄清 [Clarification on Chinese and American conceptions of social intercourse between men and women], *Dagong bao*, May 27, 1945.
138. "Guanyu gaishan ZhongMei renmin zhijian guanxi shang Jiang Zhongzheng cheng"; Guomin zhengfu 國民政府, *Jiaqiang ZhongMei junmin ganqing xuanchuan gangyao* 加強中美軍民感情宣傳綱要 [*Guiding principles for enhancing US–China military–civilian relations*], 5, 1945, Chongqing Library.
139. Introduced into China in the late nineteenth and early twentieth centuries, social dance had become a popular activity among the upper-middle classes and a well-developed business in major cities. Many Nationalist elites continued to dance in their private spaces even during the war, despite the government ban. See Andrew Field, *Shanghai's Dancing World: Cabaret Culture and Urban Politics, 1919–1954* (Hong Kong: Chinese University of Hong Kong Press, 2010), 233–261; Gail Hershatter, *Dangerous Pleasures: Prostitution and Modernity in Twentieth Century Shanghai* (Berkeley: University of California Press, 1999), 271–303; Remick, *Regulating Prostitution in China*.
140. Tao, "'Hao Pu Hao?'"
141. Pang Xianzhi 逄先知, ed., *Mao Zedong nianpu: 1893–1949, xiajuan* 毛澤東年譜：一八九三──一九四九, 下卷 [*Chronological biography of Mao Zedong, 1893–1949*], vol. 3 (Beijing: Zhongyangwenxian chubanshe, 2002), 159.
142. See Westad, *Decisive Encounters*, 57–61; Pepper, *Civil War in China*, 138–140.
143. Wu Shichang 吳世昌, "Lun Meijun shijian" 論美軍事件 [On the GI incident], *Guan cha* 觀察 1, no. 21 (1947): 3–4.
144. Beijing's geographical and symbolic position in China, together with the prestige of Peking University, also help explain why the Peking rape case received so much attention among students and in the media. Being the cultural center of China and less controlled than the capital, Beijing hosted tens of thousands of returning college students after eight years of Japanese occupation, a key demographic among whom patriotic sentiments and national aspirations reached a new height. See Wilkinson, "American

Military Misconduct in Shanghai and the Chinese Civil War"; Wu Wenshi 武文士, "Hankou 'Jingming dalou shijian' zhenxiang" 漢口"景明大樓事件"真相 [Truth of the "Jingming building affair" in Hankou], *Wenshi chunqiu* 文史春秋 4 (1994): 43–46.
145. Shaffer, "A Rape in Beijing, December 1946," 40.
146. Xiao, "Kangyi Meijun baoxing yundong xiangqing poushi."
147. Zhonggong Beijing shiwei dangshi yanjiushi, *Kangyi Meijun zhuHua baoxing yundong ziliao huibian*, 421–423.
148. Zeng Luo 曾珞, "Shen Chong yu Pierxun: 'Heibai fenming'" 沈崇與皮爾遜: "黑白分明" [Shen Chong and Pierson: "Black and white"], *Libai liu* 禮拜六 82 (1947): 11.
149. Shi Lang 十郎, "Gongdao ji qita" 公道及其他 [Justice and others], *Shen bao*, August 20, 1947.
150. "Hongmao qiangdao de xuezhai"; Zhonggong Beijing shiwei dangshi yanjiushi, *Kangyi Meijun zhuHua baoxing yundong ziliao huibian*.
151. See Cook, "Penetration and Neocolonialism"; Zhang, *America Perceived*, 77–118.
152. Guomin zhengfu, *Jiaqiang ZhongMei junmin ganqing xuanchuan gangyao*, 7.
153. Shen Youdi 沈友棣, "Wo zenyang zai Meijun zhong dang fanyiguan" 我怎樣在美軍中當翻譯官 [How I worked as an interpreter in the US military], *Shidai xuesheng* 時代學生 1 (December 1945), 13–14.
154. Ge Liang 戈良, "He Meijun tongguo de rizi" 和美軍同過的日子 [Days that I lived with American soldiers], *Shanghai wenhua* 上海文化 9 (1946): 54–57.
155. Glist, *China Mailbag Uncensored*, 189.
156. Curley Papers, 121.
157. Min 閔, "Hong Shen yu youxing xuesheng fasheng chongtu" 洪深與遊行學生發生衝突 [Hong Shen clashed with student protesters], *Hai tao* 5 (1946): 11.
158. *Xi feng* (*West Wind Monthly*) was founded by Lin Yutang in 1936, and later run by the Huang brothers (Huang Jiade and Huang Jiayin) who also began to publish two new journals of *Guang* (*Light*) and *Jia* (*Family*) after the war.
159. Fei Qing 費青, "Pierxun qiangjian an fan'anshi dawen" 皮爾遜強奸案翻案事答問 [Q&A on the revoked Pierson case], *Guan cha* 3, no. 1 (1947): 13–14.
160. By the 1930s and 1940s, America had become increasingly familiar to literate and urban Chinese through a rising number of students abroad, popular periodicals, and cultural interpreters. Perceptions shifted from "model America" to "flawed America," reflecting a deeper understanding of its history, culture, and issues. See David Arkush and Leo O. Lee, eds., *Land without Ghosts: Chinese Impressions of America from the Mid-Nineteenth Century to the Present* (Berkeley: University of California Press, 1989), 143–200.
161. Tani E. Barlow, "Theorizing Woman: Funü, Guojia, Jiating," in Angela Zito and Tani E. Barlow, eds., *Body, Subject and Power in China* (Chicago, IL: University of Chicago Press, 1994), 253–289; Gail Hershatter, *Women and China's Revolutions* (Lanham, MD: Rowman & Littlefield, 2018).

Notes to pages 152–154

162. Daniel Southerland, "U.S. Navy Returns to China," *The Washington Post*, November 6, 1986; Edward A. Gargan, "After a 37-Year Absence, U.S. Vessels Visit China," *The New York Times*, November 6, 1986.
163. Höhn and Moon, *Over There*; Nira Yuval-Davis, *Gender and Nation* (London: Sage, 1997).
164. Cynthia Enloe, *Bananas, Beaches and Bases: Making Feminist Sense of International Politics* (Berkeley: University of California Press, 2014), 93.
165. Lao She 老舍, *Chaguan* 茶館 [*Teahouse*] (Beijing: Beijing gongye meishu chubanshe, 2018), 45.
166. "Pingnan xian 'wenhua dageming' dashijian" 平南縣"文化大革命"大事件 [Major events of "the Cultural Revolution" in Pingnan County], 1986. Chinese Cultural Revolution Database 中國當代政治運動史數據庫, The Chinese University of Hong Kong (CUHK).
167. While protesters cast her as a virtuous young woman who had been violated, rumors about Shen continued to spread, ranging from her being a Jeep girl who had willingly fraternized with American soldiers to being a Communist spy who was setting a trap to trigger a political storm. After the trial, Shen returned to Shanghai and graduated from Fudan University. She remained silent about the incident until shortly before her death, when she confirmed her identity as Shen Chong. See Ai Qun 艾群, *"Shen Chong shijian" zhenxiang* "沈崇事件"真相 [*Truth of the "Shen Chong affair"*] (Beijing: Zhonggong dangshi chubanshe, 2012), 1–4, 180–194; Chen Guohua 陳國華, "Ding Cong he Shen Jun: Fengyun chuanxing guo" 丁聰和沈峻:風雲穿行過 [Ding Cong and Shen Jun: A journey through history], *Beijing qingnian bao* 北京青年報, June 23, 2016, B5.
168. Jiang Qing 江青, "Guanyu dianying de wenti" 關於電影的問題 [Problems about films], May 1966. Chinese Cultural Revolution collection, Box 15, Folder 13, Hoover Institution Library & Archives.
169. "Jiang Qing zai Qinghua daxue gongchengwulixi de jianghua" 江青在清華大學工程物理系的講話 [Jiang Qing's speech in the Department of Engineering Physics at Tsinghua University], September 29, 1976. Chinese Cultural Revolution Database, CUHK.
170. For contemporary college campus racism against black students from Africa, especially regarding their relationships with female Chinese students, see Yinghong Cheng, "From Campus Racism to Cyber Racism: Discourse of Race and Chinese Nationalism," *The China Quarterly* 207 (2011): 561–579.
171. Zhang, *America Perceived*, 150.
172. Minjian yingxiang, ed., *Wo de 1945*.

5 Entangled Goods

1. See Yue Nan 岳南, *Nandu beigui 3: Libie* 南渡北歸3: 離別 [*Southward migration, northward return 3: Parting*] (Changsha: Hunan wenyi chubanshe, 2015), 9.
2. "Meiguo guantou gungunlai" 美國罐頭滾滾來 [American canned food pours in], *Xinmin wanbao* 新民晚報, February 21, 1947.
3. Minjian yingxiang, ed., *Wo de 1945*, 160–409.

4. Tang Shaohua 唐紹華, "Zhongguo jingshen shiliang huang yanzhong" 中國精神食糧荒嚴重 [China is experiencing a severe shortage of spiritual nourishment], *Shen bao*, June 2, 1946.
5. Wang Chaoguang 汪朝光, "Haolaiwu de chenfu: Minguo nianjian Meiguo dianying zaiHua jingyu yanjiu" 好萊塢的沉浮: 民國年間美國電影在華境遇研究 [Rise and fall of Hollywood films in China], *Meiguo yanjiu* 美國研究 2 (1998): 113–139. American films continued to be shown until China entered the Korean War.
6. John King Fairbank, *Chinabound: A Fifty-Year Memoir* (New York: Harper & Row, 1982), 301.
7. Ji zhe 記者, "Shanghai shi Meiguohuo de tianxia" 上海是美國貨的天下 [Shanghai is the land of American goods], *Zhongguo gongshang xinwen* 中國工商新聞 3, no. 5 (1946): 15–16.
8. "Cong shiji shuodao ditan" 從市集說到地攤 [From market to street stalls], *Shen bao*, May 26, 1949.
9. Xu Jibo 徐季搏, "Tantan guohuo guantou" 談談國貨罐頭 [On Chinese canned food], *Shuichan yuekan* 水產月刊 1, no. 5 (1946): 58–59.
10. See Young, *China and the Helping Hand, 1937–1945*, 350; 440–441; US Department of State, *The China White Paper*, 1048–1051; Wu Jingping 吳景平, "Kangzhan shiqi ZhongMei zujie guanxi shuping" 抗戰時期中美租借關係述評 [A review of Sino-American lend-lease relations during the Sino-Japanese War], *Lishi yanjiu* 4 (1995): 48–62.
11. See Yang Yuqing 楊雨青, *Meiyuan weihe wuxiao? Zhanshi Zhongguo jingjiweiji yu ZhongMei yingdui zhi ce* 美援為何無效? 戰時中國經濟危機與中美應對之策 [*Why is American aid ineffective? Wartime Chinese economic crisis and Sino-American responses*] (Beijing: Renmin chubanshe, 2011).
12. For Europeans' experiences and perspectives on American goods, see Victoria de Grazia, *Irresistible Empire: America's Advance through Twentieth-Century Europe* (Cambridge, MA: Harvard University Press, 2006).
13. Zhou Nan 周南, "Kafeitan de qingdiao" 咖啡攤的情調 [Coffee stands' sentiments], *Guoji xinwen huabao* 國際新聞畫報, 1946.
14. Er Yi 而已, "Shanghai xishi teji" 上海西施特輯 [Shanghai Xishi specials], *Hai tao* 15 (1946): 6.
15. Minjian yingxiang, ed., *Wo de 1945*, 167, 227–228.
16. J. G. Ballard, *Miracles of Life: Shanghai to Shepperton, An Autobiography* (New York: Liveright, 2013), 93–94.
17. UNRRA 聯合國善後救濟總署, ed., "Meijun zuozhan shiliang shuoming" 美軍作戰食糧說明 [Explanation of American combat food], *LuQing shanjiu xunkan* 魯青善救旬刊, no. 17 (1946): 6–8; Collingham, *The Taste of War*, 437–443.
18. "Ziyoutan: Jiujing jianwen" 自由談: 舊京見聞 [Freedom talks: Experience in the old capital], *Shen bao*, December 23, 1947.
19. Xu, "Tantan guohuo guantou."
20. Minjian yingxiang, ed., *Wo de 1945*, 416–417.
21. Zhang Ke 張克, "Kafei zatan" 咖啡雜談 [Coffee miscellany], *Jilian huikan* 機聯會刊 220 (1948): 20–21.

22. For cafe culture in relation to colonialism and modernity, see Lee, *Shanghai Modern*; Laikwan Pang, "The Collective Subjectivity of Chinese Intellectuals and Their Café Culture in Republican Shanghai," *Inter-Asia Cultural Studies* 7, no. 1 (2006): 24–42.
23. Shanghaishi zhengfu tongjichu 上海市政府統計處, ed., *Shanghaishi tongji zongbaogao* 上海市統計總報告 [*Shanghai municipal general statistical report*] (Shanghai: Longchang Printing House, 1946), 31; Xue Liyong 薛理勇, *JiuShanghai zujie shihua* 舊上海租界史話 [*Accounts of old Shanghai's foreign concessions*] (Shanghai: Shanghai shehui kexueyuan chubanshe, 2004), 108.
24. Chen Wenwen 陳文文, "1920–1940 niandai Shanghai kafeiguan yanjiu" 1920–1940 年代上海咖啡館研究 [Studies of Shanghai cafes between 1920 and 1940], Master's thesis, Shanghai shifan daxue, 2010.
25. Li Shui 麗水, "Kafeiguan zai Shanghai" 咖啡館在上海 [Coffeehouses in Shanghai], *Xin guang* 5 (1947): 3.
26. H. C. Mei, "Masses here 'Discover' Coffee, but Sip It in the Streets," *The China Weekly Review* (October 19, 1946): 203.
27. Mei, "Masses here 'Discover' Coffee."
28. Li Qing 李清, "Wo cong Tangshan lai" 我從唐山來 [I am from Tangshan], *Feng xia* 風下 59 (1947): 129, 190.
29. Wu Guifang 吳貴芳, "Chongmanzhe yiguo qingdiao de kafeitan sumiao" 充滿著異國情調的咖啡攤素描 [Sketch of exotic coffee stands], *Yishi bao*, October 9, 1946.
30. Zhou, "Kafeitan de qingdiao."
31. Sima Xu 司馬訏, "Shanghai wuyan xia de kafei qingdiao" 上海屋簷下的咖啡情調 [Coffee sentiments under the eaves of Shanghai], *Shijie chenbao* 世界晨報, August 13, 1946.
32. Lu Xun 魯迅, *Sanxianji* 三閒集 [*Triple leisure*] (Beijing: The People's Literature Publishing House, 1958), 91. In reality, Lu Xun also went to cafes to meet and talk with friends.
33. Wu, "Chongmanzhe yiguo qingdiao de kafeitan sumiao."
34. Simms Memoir, 31.
35. "Display ad," *The China Weekly Review* (August 10, 1946).
36. Collingham, *The Taste of War*, 438.
37. Collingham, *The Taste of War*, 474.
38. "Guanyu yinliaopin qita shixiang" 關於飲料品其他事項 [Regarding other matters on drinks], 1946–1948, B0049/001/00618, QMA. The company was owned by a German firm that opened a Coca-Cola bottling plant in 1932.
39. "Shanghai gongyongju guanyu zhuHua Meijun zongbu qingqiu gongdian ji meiqi dengan shixiang an" 上海公用局關於駐華美軍總部請求供電及煤氣等案事項案 [Shanghai Public Utilities Bureau on the US Army Headquarters in China's request for electricity and gas supply and other related matters], 1946, Q5-3-5321, SMA.
40. Liang Yao, "Nationalism on Their Own Terms: The National Products Movement and the Coca-Cola Protest in Shanghai 1945–1949," *Modern Asian Studies* 51, no. 5 (2017): 1439–1468.
41. Coca-Cola advertising, *Spartanburg Herald*, November 4, 1943.

42. Yao, "Nationalism on Their Own Terms."
43. Hai Ren 海人, "Kekoukele de mimi" 可口可樂的秘密 [Coca-Cola's secrets], *Libai liu* 禮拜六 88 (1947): 8.
44. Another example is the stronger-tasting American cigarette, which was less popular in China than the British or Chinese brands, but came to dominate the market after the war. See Wan Kuiyi 萬揆一, "Minguo shiqi Kunming xiangyan shihua" 民國時期昆明香煙史話 [Accounts of cigarette history in Republican Kunming], in Zhongguo renmin zhengzhi xieshang huiyi Yunnansheng Kunmingshi Panlongqu weiyuanhui wenshiziliao weiyuanhui, eds., *Kunmingshi Panlongqu wenshi ziliao xuanji di 8 ji* 昆明市盤龍區文史資料選輯第8輯 [Historical literature of Panlong District, Kunming, vol. 8] (1993), 83–109.
45. Minjian yingxiang, ed., *Wo de 1945*, 327–420.
46. F. Barrows Colton, "Your New World of Tomorrow," *National Geographic* (October 1945): 385–410.
47. David Kinkela, *DDT and the American Century: Global Health, Environmental Politics, and the Pesticide That Changed the World* (Chapel Hill: University of North Carolina Press, 2011).
48. "Feiji pensa DDT" 飛機噴灑DDT [Airplane sprays DDT], *Dagong bao*, June 19, 1946.
49. "Zhuxi guandi chenshe jianjie" 主席官邸陳設簡潔 [Chairman's official residence furnished simply], *Shen bao*, April 20, 1946.
50. He Qi 何琦, "Mantan feiji pensa DDT" 漫談飛機噴灑DDT [Ramble about airplanes spraying DDT], *Yi chao* 醫潮 1, no. 4 (1947): 30–32.
51. Lü Letian 呂樂天, "Feiji penshe DDT de huiyi" 飛機噴射DDT的回憶 [Memories of airplanes spraying DDT], *Zhongguo yangfeng zazhi* 中國養蜂雜志 5, no. 3 (1946): 4–5; Huang Zigu 黃子固, "DDT yu fengye zhi guanxi" DDT與蜂業之關係 [Relations between DDT and the beekeeping industry], *Zhongguo yangfeng zazhi* 5, no. 1 (1946): 16–18.
52. "Guanyu banli Meijun guwentuan zhuzhai fujin fenkeng ji shuitang qingxing yishi gei shiweishengju de chengwen" 關於辦理美軍顧問團住宅附近糞坑及水塘情形一事給市衛生局的呈文 [Report to the Municipal Health Bureau concerning the handling of soil pits and ponds near US MAG residences], 1947, 10030060631(00)0010, NMA; "Guanyu banli Meijun yisheng deng zhuzhai fujin fengang weizhi de diaochaqingkuang yishi gei shiweishengju de chengwen" 關於辦理美軍醫生等住宅附近糞缸位置的調查情況一事給市衛生局的呈文 [Report to the Municipal Health Bureau on the investigation of soil pit locations near US MAG residences], 1947, 10030060631(00)0011, NMA; "Shiyong chuchongji DDT quanjuan" 施用除蟲劑DDT全卷 [Complete volume on the application of insecticide DDT], 1946, 20-16-002-09, 19, AIMH.
53. He Ji 何基, "DDT yidao Shanghai, biancheng le zisha de yongtu" DDT一到上海,變成了自殺的用途 [DDT arrives in Shanghai, immediately turning into a suicide tool], *Jin bao* (Shanghai) 今報 (上海), August 16, 1946.
54. See Kinkela, *DDT and the American Century*, 41.
55. Robert Bud, *Penicillin: Triumph and Tragedy* (Oxford: Oxford University Press, 2007), 75–96.

56. "Hualaishi xieyou shajun liangyao pannixilin jiang song Jiang zhuxi zhuanzeng woguomin" 華萊士携有殺菌良藥盤尼西林將送蔣主席轉贈我國民 [Wallace brings the antibiotic penicillin to Generalissimo Chiang as a gift to our citizens], *Dagong bao*, May 24, 1944.
57. Mary Augusta Brazelton, "The Production of Penicillin in Wartime China and Sino-American Definitions of 'Normal' Microbiology," *Journal of Modern Chinese History* 13, no. 1 (2019): 102–123.
58. Xi Yangsheng 夕陽生, "'Peinixiling' jiu Dongtiao" "配尼西靈" 救東條 ["Penicillin" saves Tojo], *Xin Shanghai* 新上海 17 (1946): 12. Tojo supposedly recovered after a month, after being nourished by hospital food especially his favorite American juice, cereals, and soup, said to be better than traditional Japanese miso soup.
59. Wang Gaopeng 王高朋, "Qingmeisu zai jindai Zhongguo de chuanbo yu jieshou" 青黴素在近代中國的傳播與接受 [The dissemination and acceptance of penicillin in modern China], Master's thesis, Hebei University, 2018; Xu Dingding 徐丁丁, "Penicilin (Qingmeisu) Zhongyiming de bianqian" Penicillin (青黴素)中譯名的變遷 [The evolution of penicillin's Chinese translations], *Zhongguo kejishi zazhi* 中國科技史雜誌 36, no. 3 (2015): 325–335.
60. Tao Xingzhi 陶行知, *Xingzhi shigeji* 行知詩歌集 [Collection of Tao Xingzhi's poems] (Shanghai: Dafu chuban gongsi, 1947), 384.
61. Tao, *Xinzhi shigeji*, 387–388.
62. "Minzhu shi pannixilin, ke zhiliao Zhongguo zhengzhi: Zhang Lan da jizhe wen" 民主是盤尼西林, 可治療中國政治: 張瀾答記者問 [Democracy is penicillin, and can cure Chinese politics: Zhang Lan answered reporters' questions], in Yuan Donglin 袁冬林 and Yuan Shijie 袁士杰, eds., *Pu Xixiu jizhe shengya xunzong* [Sketches of Pu Xixiu's journalist career] 浦熙修記者生涯尋蹤 (Shanghai: Wenhui chubanshe, 2000), 380–381.
63. Li Yaoyu 李耀宇, *Yige Zhongguo geming qinlizhe de siren jilu* 一個中國革命親歷者的私人記錄 [A private record by a participant of the Chinese Revolution] (Beijing: Dangdai Zhongguo chubanshe, 2009), 172.
64. Payne, *China Awake*, 347.
65. See Li, *Yige Zhongguo geming qinlizhe de siren jilu*, 162–184. The author recalls receiving a Gillette razor marked with "U.S.A. military" and using it until the 1950s. Unable to find a replacement, he eventually threw it away during the Cultural Revolution to conceal his past interaction with American soldiers.
66. Wang, "Qingmeisu zai jindai Zhongguo de chuanbo yu jieshou," 75–79.
67. Ma Fantuo 馬凡陀, "Meiguo mi" 美國迷 [American obsessions], in *Hainei qitan* 海內奇談 [Strange tales of the country] (Harbin: Dongbei shudian, 1947), 6.
68. These American associates' observations resembled those made by Chinese intellectuals who visited America in the 1940s. Among their first impressions was that America was a huge country with abundant land and resources. In their regular travelogues and articles sent home, these writers and scholars also noted the American lifestyle of consuming a large quantity of goods that were often wasted; the obsession over "pleasure of the flesh";

69. Ge, "He Meijun tongguo de rizi."
70. Huang, *Guanyu Meiguo bing*, 48–50, 73–74.
71. "Ruhe zhidao guanbing yu mengjun xiangchu" 如何指導官兵與盟軍相處 [How to guide Chinese soldiers in interacting with Allied forces], 0053-0010-00142-0200-312-000, CMA.
72. Huang, *Guanyu Meiguo bing*, 73–74.
73. Albert Fields, "Medical Officer in China," *The Military Surgeon* 103, no. 4 (October 1948): 292–304; Michael Shiyung Liu, "Eating Well for Survival: Chinese Nutrition Experiments during World War II," in Angela Ki Che Leung, Melissa L. Caldwell, Robert Ji-Song Ku, and Christine R. Yano, eds., *Moral Foods: The Construction of Nutrition and Health in Modern Asia* (Honolulu: University of Hawaii Press, 2020), 89–108.
74. Huang, *Guanyu Meiguo bing*, 81–83.
75. Xiao Fu 蕭夫, "Cong yinshi qiju kan Meiguo" 從飲食起居看美國 [America from the view of everyday living], *Shen bao*, December 5, 1946.
76. Chen Yixian 陳詒先, "Wo yi tan chi" 我亦談吃 [My view on eating], *Shen bao*, March 25, 1948.
77. Zou Zhenhuan 鄒振環, "Xican yinru yu jindai Shanghai chengshi wenhua kongjian de kaituo" 西餐引入與近代上海城市文化空間的開拓 [Introduction of Western food and the expansion of modern Shanghai's urban cultural space], *Shi lin* 史林 4 (2007): 137–149.
78. Shi Jimei 施濟美, "Chunqiu, Mali Ma" 春秋, 瑪利馬 [Spring and Autumn, Mary Ma], *Shen bao*, October 13, 1947.
79. Qian Jiaju 千家駒, "Jingji wencui: yinianlai Zhongguo jingji de zongjie" 經濟文萃: 一年來中國經濟的總結 [Collection of economic articles: Summary of the Chinese economy in the past year], *Jingji zhoubao* 4, no. 2 (1947): 23.
80. Ma Yinchu 馬寅初, "Meiguohuo he guanliao benqian" 美國貨和官僚本錢 [American goods and bureaucratic capital], *Zheng bao* 正報 94 (1946): 4.
81. "Meihuo kuang" 美貨狂 [American goods craze], *Beifang wenhua* 北方文化 2, no. 6 (1946): 21, 23.
82. "Guoneiwai jingji yizhou: Shanghai gongshang daibiao jinjing qingyuan" 國內外經濟一周: 上海工商代表进京請願 [Domestic and international economic weekly: Shanghai business representatives petition in the capital], *Jingji zhoubao* 3, no. 7 (1946): 5.
83. Xu, "Tantan guohuo guantou."
84. "Aihu nide guojia aihu nide pifu, qingni fangqi nilong siwa" 愛護你的國家愛護你的皮膚, 請你放棄尼隆絲襪 [Cherish your country and your Skin, please give up nylon stockings], *Shen bao*, May 31, 1948.
85. "Shizhang xiang nüjie huyu hebi chuan boli siwa" 市長向女界呼籲何必穿玻璃絲襪 [Mayor appeals to women not to wear American stockings], *Shen bao*, December 12, 1947.
86. Wang, "Haolaiwu de chenfu."
87. Ren Huizhi 任晦之, "Meiguo yingpian yu kekou kele" 美國影片與可口可樂 [American movies and Coca-Cola], *Qun zhong* 2, no. 26 (1948): 18.

88. Wei Qin 味琴, "Meiguo yuebing" 美國月餅 [American mooncakes], *Shen bao*, August 24, 1946.
89. Minjian yingxiang, ed., *Wo de 1945*, 214.
90. Yao, "Nationalism on Their Own Terms," 1453–1467.
91. See Yeh, *Shanghai Splendor*, 70–78.
92. For studies on Chinese nationalism and consumerism, see Karl Gerth, *China Made: Consumer Culture and the Creation of the Nation* (Cambridge, MA: Harvard University Asia Center, 2003); Sherman Cochran, *Big Business in China: Sino-Foreign Rivalry in the Cigarette Industry, 1890–1930* (Cambridge, MA: Harvard University Press, 1980).
93. See Gerth, *China Made*.
94. Zhang, *America Perceived*, 63–69.
95. "Kao Meijun chifan" 靠美軍吃飯 [Make a living through the American military], *Zhou bo* 周播, no. 3 (1946): 4.
96. Chen, "Shilun 'erjiu' douzheng de jingyan jiaoxun."
97. Pfeiffer, oral history transcript, 319–322.
98. Pfeiffer, oral history transcript, 319–322.
99. The following three cases come from "Meijun qiangsha ji qiche zhuangshang an" 美軍槍殺及汽車撞傷案 [Incidents of shootings and traffic accidents involving American soldiers], 1947, J0009-1-000107, TMA.
100. Thomas manuscript, 56–57.
101. Simms Memoir, 4–5.
102. "Meijun shiqie cheliang" 美軍失竊車輛 [Stolen American military vehicles], May 1946, 10030082535(00)0007, NMA.
103. "Guanyu zai Zhongguo jiuba xuangua jinzhi huo xuke Meijun runei paishi de tongzhi" 關於在中國酒吧懸掛禁止或許可美軍入內牌示的通知 [Notice about displaying "in-bounds" or "out-of-bounds" signs in Chinese bars], 1947, B0060/001/00003/0001, QMA.
104. Oral history of William Stokley, transcript, 8, OCHOH.
105. "Guanyu junren shushi ming you Meijun huowu touchu de chengwen" 關於軍人數十名由美軍貨物偷出的呈文 [Report on dozens of soldiers stealing from US military supplies], March 4, 1948, B0033/001/000496/0025, QMA; "Guanyu yiyiwu Meijun cangku beiqie de chengwen" 關於一一五美軍倉庫被竊的呈文 [Report on the theft of US military warehouse 115], April 27, 1948, B0033/001/000496/0031, QMA; "Guanyu gangjing Zang Xianzheng tong gongren Yang Quanrong toudao Meijun wupin juxun gongci de chengwen" 關於港警臧賢証同工人楊全榮偷盜美軍物品據訓供詞的呈文 [Report on the interrogation statements of port policeman Zang Xianzheng and worker Yang Quanrong for stealing US military supplies], August 21, 1947, B0033/001/00043/0027, QMA.
106. "Guanyu zhizhi wojun weibing dui Meijun shibing buyouyi xingdong de daidian" 關於制止我軍衛兵對美軍士兵不友誼行動的代電 [Cable on preventing our soldiers' unfriendly actions toward American soldiers], January 26, 1946, B0024/001/00675/0027, QMA.
107. "Gangjing bei Meijun gangbing kaiqiang jishang" 港警被美軍崗兵開槍擊傷 [Port police shot and wounded by American guards], May 9, 1946, B0033/001/00299/0112, QMA.

108. "Guanyu junren shushi ming you Meijun huowu touchu de chengwen."
109. "Guanyu yiyiwu Meijun cangku beiqie de chengwen."
110. Fredman, *The Tormented Alliance*, 122–124.
111. After the CCP's victory, retired Admiral Cooke led a group of informal actors who coordinated unofficial US foreign and military policy, helping sustain the alliance with the Republic of China after officially Washington withdrew its support for Chiang. See Thomas, oral history transcript, 251; Hsiao-ting Lin, "Taiwan's Secret Ally," *Hoover Digest* 2 (2012): 192–203.
112. Pfeiffer, oral history transcript, 319–322.
113. Thomas, oral history transcript, 252.
114. "Wei fangzhi Meijun qiangji qiefan banfa zhi pingyu zhi Du shizhang de cheng" 為防止美軍槍擊竊犯辦法之評語致杜市長的呈 [Letter to Mayor Du on measures to prevent American military personnel from shooting thieves], 1947, J0002-3-007260-047, TMA.
115. Wilma Fairbank, *America's Cultural Experiment in China, 1942–1949* (Washington, DC: US Government Printing Office), 147–148.
116. "Meijun qiangsha ji qiche zhuangshang an."
117. The word used in the Chinese report to describe the American order was 停步 (*tingbu*). See "Wei fangzhi Meijun qiangji qiefan banfa zhi pingyu zhi Du shizhang de cheng."
118. Curley Papers, 142–143.
119. "Shanghai de wuye youmin siren qiangjie Meibing jinbiao" 上海的無業游民四人搶劫美兵金錶 [Four Shanghai vagabonds robbed an American soldier's gold watch], 1947, Q131-5-1962, SMA.
120. "Xinhe Meijun beiji an."
121. Ben Y. Lee, "Race inequality," *The China Weekly Review* (September 6, 1947): 7. The exact sign did not exist, but the messages conveyed were similar. See Robert Bickers and Jeffrey Wasserstrom, "Shanghai's 'Dogs and Chinese Not Admitted' Sign: Legend, History and Contemporary Symbol," *China Quarterly* 142 (1995): 444–466.
122. Huang, *Guanyu Meiguo bing*, 50.
123. Sledge, *China Marine*, 63–64.
124. Peck, *Two Kinds of Time*, 636.
125. "Meibing mai dayi" 美兵賣大衣 [GI selling coats], *Dagong bao*, December 31, 1946; "Qingdao Meijun liang daoan" 青島美軍兩盜案 [Two theft cases involving American troops in Qingdao], *Dagong bao*, June 17, 1947.
126. "Guanyu jinzhi zai malu liangpang fanmai Meijun yanjiu dengwu de tonggao" 關於禁止在馬路兩旁販賣美軍煙酒等物的通告 [Notice on prohibiting street sales of American military cigarettes, alcohol, and similar items], November 5, 1945, B0038/001/01292/0016, QMA.
127. Thomas, oral history transcript, 252–253.
128. "Guanyu Meijunxuguan xiezhu Tianjin Xinshichang yanghang zhiyuan zousi an" 關於美軍需官協助天津新時昌洋行職員走私案 [On the smuggling case involving a US military procurement officer assisting employees of the Tianjin Xinshichang firm], November 26, 1947, B0024/001/00826/0030, QMA.

129. "Guanyu Meixianbing qiangshang Zhongguo xuesheng Cao Guiming zuotui he Meijun jiaoshe qingxing de chengwen" 關於美憲兵槍傷中國學生曹桂明左腿和美軍交涉情形的呈文 [Report on the negotiations following the incident involving an American MP shooting the left leg of Chinese student Cao Guiming], 1946, J001-001-00541, BMA.
130. "Zhongguo xinwen zhuanke xuexiao xuesheng Gao Ruofan bei Meixianbing boqu Mei junyong dayi shi" 中國新聞專科學校學生高若凡被美憲兵剝去美軍用大衣事 [Incident involving Gao Ruofan, a student from China Journalism College, being stripped of a US military coat by an American MP], 1946, Q109-1-1810-9, SMA.
131. Dong Yang 動羊, "Meiguo jiu yifu" 美國舊衣服 [American used clothes], *Yishi bao*, May 20, 1946.
132. "Zhongguo xinwen zhuanke xuexiao xuesheng Gao Ruofan bei Meixianbing boqu Mei junyong dayi shi."
133. Shang Haiming 尚海明, "Shanzhong, xiongsi yu sharen changming: Zhongguoren sixing guannian de wenhua chanshi" 善終、凶死與殺人償命：中國人死刑觀念的文化闡釋 [Good death, violent death and a life for a life: A cultural interpretation of Chinese views on the death penalty], *Faxue yanjiu* 法學研究 4 (2016): 61–78.
134. See Yang, "United States Marines in Qingdao," 158.
135. See "Meijun qiangsha ji qiche zhuangshang an."
136. Because of the high administrative costs, General Wedemeyer corresponded with Chiang Kai-shek in 1946, asking the Chinese government to handle and pay for the compensations on America's behalf, with the cost being counted toward China's surplus sales payments. See "Shanghai gaodeng fayuan guanyu yu zhuHua Meijun zongbu shangyi sunhai peichang xieding juan" 上海高等法院關於與駐華美軍總部商議損害賠償協定卷 [Shanghai High Court files on negotiations with the US military headquarters in China on harm compensation agreements], 1946, Q187-1-5, SMA.
137. "Zhongguo xinwen zhuanke xuexiao xuesheng Gao Ruofan wei bei Meixianbing boqu Mei junyong dayi shi yu Shanghaishi canyihui de wanglai hanjian."
138. "Zhongguo xinwen zhuanke xuexiao xuesheng Gao Ruofan wei bei Meixianbing boqu Mei junyong dayi shi yu Shanghaishi canyihui de wanglai hanjian."
139. "Faqi 'bumai Meiguohuo yundong' xuanyan" 發起"不買美國貨運動"宣言 [Manifesto on launching the "boycotting American goods movement"], *Wen cui* 2, no. 3 (1946): 35.
140. Li, "Wo cong Tangshan lai," 129, 190.
141. Simms Memoir, 4–5.
142. Simms Memoir, 56.
143. Admiral Charles Cooke's Letter to Mayor Li Xianliang, May 23, 1947, collection no. 24, catalogue no. 1, folder no. 499, QMA. Also see Yang, "United States Marines in Qingdao," 159–160.
144. Oral history of William Pinkston, transcript, 4–5, OCHOH.
145. United States Army Service Forces, *A Pocket Guide to China*, 4–8.

146. Rhoda J. Yen, "Racial Stereotyping of Asians and Asian Americans and Its Effect on Criminal Justice: A Reflection on the Wayne Lo Case," *Asian Law Journal* 7, no. 1 (2000): 1–28.
147. "Guanyu Zhongguo xiaohai dao Meijun junjian daoqie bei Meibing jibi shiyi de qiancheng" 關於中國小孩到美軍軍艦盜竊被美兵擊斃事宜的簽呈 [Memo on the incident of Chinese children being shot dead by GIs for stealing from American warships], 1946, B0033/001/00300/0175, QMA.
148. The Foreign Claims Commission awarded fabi 2,223,000 to Sun's mother. See "Meijun qiangsha ji qiche zhuangshang an."
149. Pfeiffer, oral history transcript, 319–322.
150. Pfeiffer, oral history transcript, 319–322.
151. "Shanghaishi jingchaju xiezhu Meijun jidi silingbu xingzhenchu soucha suowei Meijun yongpin zhi jingguo qingkuang" 上海市警察局協助美軍基地司令部刑偵處搜查所謂美軍用品之經過情況 [Details of Shanghai Municipal Police Bureau assisting the criminal investigation department of the US Military Base Command in searching for so-called US military supplies], 1945, Q131-5-294, SC0037, SMA.
152. "Shanghaishi jingchaju guanyu Meijun han" 上海市警察局關於美軍函 [Correspondence from the Shanghai Police Bureau on the US military], 1947, Q131-5-7143, SMA.
153. "Wei qudi Zhongwai ren chuan renhe Mei junyong fuzhuang" 為取締中外人穿任何美軍用服裝 [To ban Chinese and foreigners from wearing any American military clothes], August 1946, J0002-3-007229-041, TMA; "Meijun zhifu fei junren budechuanzhuo" 美軍制服非軍人不得穿著 [Civilians prohibited from wearing US military uniforms], *Dagong bao*, August 14, 1946.
154. "Guanyu qudi ge jiuhuoshang liudong jiuhuotan chushou Meijun riyongpin de xunling" 關於取締各舊貨商流動舊貨攤出售美軍日用品的訓令 [Order banning used-goods vendors and mobile stalls from selling US military daily supplies], May 7, 1947, A0019/003/00174/0090, QMA.
155. "Guanyu yanjia fangfan Meijun cangku fujin jumin xingqie de xunling" 關於嚴加防範美軍倉庫附近居民行竊的訓令 [Order strictly preventing theft by residents near US military warehouses], January 20, 1947, A0019/003/00391/0017, QMA.
156. "Wei fangzhi Meijun qiangji qiefan banfa zhi pingyu zhi Du shizhang de cheng."
157. Admiral Charles Cooke's Letter to Mayor Li Xianliang, May 23, 1947.
158. "ZaiHua Meijun zhaoshi chuli banfa" 在華美軍肇事處理辦法 [Procedures for handling incidents involving US military personnel in China], 020-050204-0011, AHA.
159. "ZaiHua Meijun zhaoshi chuli banfa"; Xingzhengyuan 行政院, "Guanyu fangzhi Meijun renyuan xingshi anjian fasheng ji quebao shouhairen huozhi gongyun caipan zhuyishixiang" 關於防止美軍人員刑事案件發生及確保受害人獲致公允裁判注意事項 [Precautions for preventing criminal cases involving American military personnel and ensuring fair trials for victims], 1948, J0002-3-007261-060, TMA.

160. Xingzhengyuan, "Guanyu fangzhi Meijun renyuan xingshi anjian fasheng ji quebao shouhairen huozhi gongyun caipan zhuyishixiang."
161. Similarly, the US government also paid more attention to this case, perhaps at the request of the Nationalist officials. In his reply, Colonel B. W. Gally of the First Marine Division stated that "the Marine Military Policeman was not authorized to fire in this instance and disciplinary action will be taken as adjudged by a military court, and expenses should be paid by the headquarters." See "Guanyu Meixianbing qiangshang Zhongguo xuesheng Cao Guiming zuotui he Meijun jiaoshe qignxing de chengwen."
162. "Meijun qiangsha ji qiche zhuangshang an."
163. "Student Agitation Causes Concern; US Said Ready to Negotiate," *The China Weekly Review* (June 5, 1948): 27.
164. Pepper, *Civil War in China*, 72–78; Huang Jingshan 黃景山, "1948 nian Beiping diqu fanMeifuRi yundong" [1948 "Opposing the US Support of Japan" movement in the Beijing area] 一九四八年北平地區反美扶日運動, *Beijing dangshi* 北京黨史 5 (1988): 11–19.
165. In June 1948, Zhu signed on the public statement refusing to purchase discounted American flour, shortly before his death from severe stomach ulcers in August. Following his typical satirical style, Mao warned that those who bowed to American alms or relief flour should be wary of stomachaches. See Mao Zedong, "Farewell, Leighton Stuart!" in *Selected Works of Mao Tse-tung*, vol. IV, 433–440.
166. Mao Zedong, "The Situation and Our Policy after the Victory in the War of Resistance against Japan," and "Talk with the American Correspondent Anna Louise Strong," in *Selected Works of Mao Tse-tung*, vol. IV, 11–26, 97–102. In reality, though to a lesser degree, the Communists also received American military supplies during WWII and were an incidental beneficiary of the postwar American supplies to the Nationalist Army when the latter were captured or surrendered. Chiang was even teased as director of the CCP army supplies. Also see Yang Kuisong 楊奎松, *"Zhongjian didai" de geming: Guoji dabeijing xia kan Zhonggong chenggong zhi dao* "中間地帶"的革命：國際大背景下看中共成功之道 [*Revolution in the "middle area": The CCP's road toward success in the international context*] (Guilin: Guangxi shifan daxue chubanshe, 2012), 541–573.
167. Mao Zedong, "Report to the Second Plenary Session of the Seventh Central Committee of the Communist Party of China," in *Selected Works of Mao Tse-tung*, vol. IV, 361–376.

Epilogue

1. Fu Hongxing 傅紅星 directed, *Xuanfeng jiuri* 旋風九日 [*Mr. Deng goes to Washington*]. Beijing: Zhongyang xinwen jilu dianying zhipianchang, 2015.
2. Mike Peters, "Carter Recalls His Lifelong Fascination with China," *China Daily*, December 15, 2011; "Guest Lecture by Former U.S. President Jimmy Carter," Emory University, February 14, 2018, www.cartercenter.org/news/editorials_speeches/carter-emory-lecture-china-north-korea.html.

3. See Gordon H. Chang, *Fateful Ties: A History of America's Preoccupation with China* (Cambridge, MA: Harvard University Press, 2015); Guoqi Xu, *Chinese and Americans: A Shared History* (Cambridge, MA: Harvard University Press, 2014); Pomfret, *The Beautiful Country and the Middle Kingdom*; David A. Hollinger, *Protestants Abroad: How Missionaries Tried to Change the World but Changed America* (Princeton, NJ: Princeton University Press, 2017).
4. Peters, "Carter Recalls His Lifelong Fascination with China."
5. United States Army Service Forces, *A Pocket Guide to China*, 44.
6. See e.g. Rana Mitter, *China's Good War: How World War II Is Shaping a New Nationalism* (Cambridge, MA: Harvard University Press, 2020); Arthur Waldron, "China's New Remembering of World War II: The Case of Zhang Zizhong," *Modern Asian Studies* 30, no. 4 (October 1996): 945–978; Rana Mitter and Aaron William Moore, eds., "China in World War II, 1937–1945: Experience, Memory, and Legacy," special issue, *Modern Asian Studies* 45, no. 2 (March 2011): 379–490.
7. For the role of embodied experiences in Maoist politics of the everyday, see Timothy Cheek, "Attitudes of Action: Maoism as Emotion in Political Theory," in Leigh Jenco, ed., *Chinese Thought as Global Theory: Diversifying Knowledge Production in the Social Sciences and Humanities* (Albany: State University of New York Press, 2016), 75–100.
8. See Zhang, *America Perceived*, 149–150; Fredman, *The Tormented Alliance*, 196–202.
9. See e.g. Mei Yu 梅雨, "Canbao de Meiguo qinlüezhe" 殘暴的美國侵略者 [Brutal American invaders], *Renmin ribao*, November 13, 1950; Liu Danian 劉大年, *Meidi qinHua shi* 美帝侵華史 [*The history of American imperialist aggression in China*] (Shanghai: Jiaoyu chubanshe, 1950); Xinhua shishi congkanshe 新華時事叢刊社, ed., *Meijun zhuHua shiqi de xuezhai* 美軍駐華時期的血債 [*The blood debts incurred by US troops stationed in China*] (Beijing: Renmin chubanshe, 1950); Rong Qun 榮群, ed., *Meijun zaiHua de baoxing* 美軍在華的暴行 [*Brutalities committed by US troops in China*] (Shenyang: Dongbei renmin chubanshe, 1951); Zhuang Lang 莊浪, drawings by Ding Hao 丁浩, *Meijun zai Zhongguo de baoxing* 美軍在中國的暴行 [*Brutalities of American troops in China*] (Shanghai: Dadong shuju, 1951).
10. Sei Jeong Chin, "The Korean War, Anti-US Propaganda, and the Marginalization of Dissent in China, 1950–1953," *Twentieth-Century China* 48, no. 1 (2023): 23–47.
11. Laura Pozzi, "The Revolution of a Little Hero: The Sanmao Comic Strips and the Politics of Childhood in China, 1935–1962," PhD diss., European University Institute, 2014.
12. Zhang Leping 張樂平, *Sanmao jiefang ji* 三毛解放記 [*Sanmao's liberation*] (Shanghai: Shaonian ertong chubanshe, 2020), 108, 122–124.
13. Sanmao's experience stood in sharp contrast to that of Liu, an orphan street boy discussed earlier. Liu shined marines' shoes in Qingdao, grew close to them, and was eventually legally "adopted" by a marine who brought him to America and helped him find a permanent family. See Taylor, "The Life of Liu."

14. *Gaoji zhongxue keben: Zhongguo lishi* 高級中學課本: 中國歷史 [*Senior high school textbook: Chinese history*, vol. 4] (Beijing: Renmin jiaoyu chubanshe, 1957); *Chuji zhongxue keben: Zhongguo lishi* 初級中學課本: 中國歷史 [*Junior high school textbook: Chinese history*, vol. 4] (Beijing: Renmin jiaoyu chubanshe, 1982, 1986).
15. Wilkinson, "American Military Misconduct in Shanghai and the Chinese Civil War," 172.
16. Zhonggong Beijing shiwei dangshi yanjiushi, ed., *Kangyi Meijun zhuHua baoxing yundong ziliao huibian*.
17. Jet Li 李連杰 directed, *Zhonghua yingxiong* 中華英雄 [*Born to defend*] (Hong Kong: Sil-Metropole Organisation, 1986).
18. In fact, Jet Li is famous for portraying folk-hero characters, including Wong Fei-hung, a martial arts master who fought foreigners during the chaotic years of the late nineteenth and early twentieth centuries. Under unequal treaties, American traders sold, bullied, and abducted Chinese coolies and women, transporting them to "Gold Mountain."
19. Peter Hays Gries, "Tears of Rage: Chinese Nationalist Reactions to the Belgrade Embassy Bombing," *China Journal*, no. 46 (2001): 25–43.
20. Exceptions include Sledge's memoir, *China Marine*, and several historical novels such as Jesse Bedwell, *China Marine* (Snowflake, AZ: Cedar Hill, 2005); Harold Stephens, *Take China: The Last of the China Marines* (Bangkok: Wolfenden, 2002); and Paul E. Wilson, *China Marine* (North Charleston, SC: BookSurge, 2008).
21. Richard Polenberg, "The Good War? A Reappraisal of How World War II Affected American Society," *Virginia Magazine of History and Biography* 100, no. 3 (1992): 295–322.
22. "Painful Surprise."
23. Parkyn, "Operation BELEAGUER," 36–37; Andrew J. Britschgi, "Military Operations Other Than War: Coming in from the Cold," in Karl P. Magyar, ed., *United States Post-Cold War Defence Interests: A Review of the First Decade* (New York: Palgrave Macmillan, 2004), 149–164; Leo J. Daugherty III and Rhonda L. Smith-Daugherty, *Counterinsurgency and the United States Marine Corps, Volume 2: An Era of Persistent Warfare, 1945–2016* (Jefferson, NC: McFarland & Company, Inc., 2018), 66–104.
24. Richard Bernstein, *China 1945: Mao's Revolution and America's Fateful Choice* (New York: Alfred A. Knopf, 2014), 320–321.
25. Britschgi, "Military Operations Other Than War."
26. Zheng, "A Specter of Extraterritoriality."
27. See Hungdah Chiu, "The United States Status of Forces Agreement with the Republic of China: Some Criminal Case Studies," *Boston College International and Comparative Law Review* 3, no. 1 (December 1979): 67–88.
28. Fredman, *The Tormented Alliance*, 10, 203–206.
29. "Korean Students Attack US Troops," *BBC News*, July 20, 2002. The two American soldiers were tried in a court-martial in South Korea and later acquitted, which sparked further furious reaction among protestors.

30. Roland G. Simbulan, "People's Movement Responses to Evolving U.S. Military Activities in the Philippines," in Lutz, ed., *The Bases of Empire*, 145–180.
31. Kent E. Calder, *Embattled Garrisons: Comparative Base Politics and American Globalism* (Princeton, NJ: Princeton University Press, 2007), 2.
32. Andrew Yeo, *Activists, Alliances, and Anti-U.S. Base Protests* (New York: Cambridge University Press, 2011).
33. Klein, *Cold War Orientalism*.
34. Huang, "China's Number One Meeter and Greeter," chapter 11, 4–12.
35. Astrid Myers, "Kunming Airport with Barney Rosset," November 1996, *Columbia University Libraries Online Exhibitions*, https://exhibitions.library.columbia.edu/exhibits/show/rosset/item/7578.
36. Parkyn, "Operation BELEAGUER," 35–36.
37. Liu, *From Canton Restaurant to Panda Express*, 63–65.
38. This joint venture was quickly caught in tortuous negotiations but managed to continue into the next decade. Meanwhile the Jeep has persisted in China, evolving into various forms and products, with the Beijing Automotive Group Co., Ltd. continuing to produce Jeep-style models. See Jim Mann, *Beijing Jeep: A Case Study of Western Business in China* (Boulder, CO: Westview Press, 1997).
39. Niall Ferguson and Moritz Schularick, "'Chimerica' and the Global Asset Market Boom," *International Finance* 10, no. 3 (2007): 215–239; and Fan Yang, *Disorienting Politics: Chimerical Media and Transpacific Entanglements* (Ann Arbor: University of Michigan Press, 2024).
40. Jonathan Cheng, "In Rare Rebuke, U.S. Ambassador Accuses China of Undermining Diplomacy," *Wall Street Journal*, June 24, 2024. For American universities' opportunities and challenges in admitting students from China, as well as Chinese universities' efforts toward internationalization, see William Kirby, *Empires of Ideas: Creating the Modern University from Germany to America to China* (Cambridge, MA: Harvard University Press, 2022), 112–395.
41. United States ambassador Nicholas Burns claimed that Beijing has been stirring up anti-American sentiment and expressed concerns over the recent incident. See Cheng, "Rare Rebuke."

Bibliography

Archival Sources

Academia Historica Archives 國史館, Taipei, Taiwan (AHA).
Archives of the Institute of Modern History 近代史研究所檔案館, Academia Sinica, Taipei, Taiwan (AIMH).
Beijing Municipal Archives 北京市檔案館, Beijing, China (BMA).
Chinese Cultural Revolution Database 中國當代政治運動史數據庫, Chinese University of Hong Kong, Hong Kong, China.
Chongqing Library 重慶圖書館, Chongqing, China.
Chongqing Municipal Archives 重慶市檔案館, Chongqing, China (CMA).
Gale Primary Sources, Archives Unbound.

- The Chinese Civil War and US–China Relations: Records of the US State Department's Office of Chinese Affairs.
- General George C. Marshall's Mission to China, 1945–1947.

Hoover Institution Library & Archives, Stanford University, Stanford, CA, United States.
Hunter Collection, Center for Research Libraries, Chicago, IL, United States.
International Criminal Court Legal Tools Database, United Nations War Crimes Commission. www.legal-tools.org.
Marine Corps History Division, Quantico, VA, United States (MCHD).
Nanjing Municipal Archives 南京市檔案館, Nanjing, China (NMA).
Old China Hands Oral History Project Collection, California State University, Northridge, United States (OCHOH).
Old China Hands Unpublished Manuscripts, California State University, Northridge, United States.
Qingdao Municipal Archives 青島市檔案館, Qingdao, China (QMA).
Rare Book and Manuscript Library, Columbia University, New York, United States.
Schlesinger Library, Radcliffe Institute, Harvard University, Cambridge, MA, United States.
Shanghai Municipal Archives 上海市檔案館, Shanghai, China (SMA).
Sichuan Provincial Archives 四川省檔案館, Chengdu, China (SPA).
Tianjin Municipal Archives 天津市檔案館, Tianjin, China (TMA).
US National Archives and Records Administration, College Park, MD, United States (NARA).

266   Bibliography

Veterans History Project Collection, American Folklife Center, Library of Congress, Washington, DC, United States.

Newspapers and Periodicals

Amerasia
Baltimore Afro-American
BBC News
Beifang wenhua 北方文化
Beijing qingnian bao 北京青年報
Chicago Daily Tribune
China Daily
The China Press
China Weekly Review
Chongqing ribao 重慶日報
Da di 大地
Dagong bao 大公報
Du zhe 讀者
Dushu zazhi 讀書雜誌
Ertong banyue kan 兒童半月刊
Ertong gushi yuekan 兒童故事月刊
Ertong zhishi 兒童知識
Far Eastern Survey
Feng xia 風下
Fu nü 婦女
Gong dao 公道
Gongshang xinwen 工商新聞
Good Morning: The Daily Paper of the Submarine Branch
Guan cha 觀察
Guofang yuekan 國防月刊
Guoji xinwen huabao 國際新聞畫報
Guomin jiaoyu fudao yuekan 國民教育輔導月刊
Hai jing 海晶
Hai tao 海濤
Hai xing 海星
Hai yan 海燕
Heibai zhoubao 黑白周報
Hickory Daily Record
Ji pu 吉普
Jilian huikan 機聯會刊
Jin bao 今報
Jingji zhoubao 經濟周報
Jornal San Wa Ou 新華澳報
Kaiming shaonian 開明少年
Lianhe huabao 聯合畫報
Libai liu 禮拜六
Life
Luobinhan 羅賓漢
LuQing shanjiu xunkan 魯青善救旬刊
The Military Surgeon
Min chao 民潮
Min jian 民間
Minzhong ribao 民衆日報
Minzhu zhoukan 民主週刊

National Geographic
The New York Times
The New Yorker
North China Marine
Nü sheng 女聲
Nüqingnian yuekan 女青年月刊
On Point
Outfit
Pacific Post
Pittsburgh Courier
Political Affairs
Qing bao 青報
Qiri tan 七日談
Qun zhong 群衆
Renmin ribao 人民日報
Salt
Scientific American
Shanghai tuhua xinwen 上海圖畫新聞
Shanghai wenhua 上海文化
Shen bao 申報
Sheng li 勝利
Shidai xuesheng 時代學生
Shijie chenbao 世界晨報
Shishi zazhi 時事雜誌
Shubao jinghua 書報精華
Shuichan yuekan 水產月刊
South China Morning Post
The Spartanburg Herald
St. Louis Post-Dispatch
The Stars and Stripes (London Edition)
Taipingyang yuekan 太平洋月刊
Time magazine
Tulsa Daily World
Union Jack
The Wall Street Journal
Washington Post
Wen cui 文萃
Wen fan 文飯
Wenhui bao 文匯報
Wings: Official Magazine of the R.A.A.F.
Xi feng 西風
Xiandai funü 現代婦女
Xiandai pinglun 現代評論
XiangGuiQian xunkan 湘桂黔旬刊
Xin ertong 新兒童
Xin guang 新光
Xin Shanghai 新上海
Xin tiandi 新天地
Xin wenhua 新文化
Xing guang 星光
Xingqi zhoukan 星期周刊
Xinhua ribao 新華日報
Xinmin wanbao 新民晚報
Xinsheng Zhongguo 新生中國
Xinwen bao 新聞報

Xinwen tiandi 新聞天地
Xinwen zazhi 新聞雜誌
Yangzi jiang 揚子江
Yi chao 醫潮
Yishi bao 益世報
Yue kan 月刊
Yunshu zhoukan 運輸周刊
Zheng bao 正報
Zhilan huabao 芝蘭畫報
Zhongguo gongshang xinwen 中國工商新聞
Zhongguo wenzhai 中國文摘
Zhongguo yangfeng zazhi 中國養蜂雜誌
ZhongMei zhoubao 中美週報
Zhou bo 周播
Zonghe zhoukan 綜合周刊

Other Sources

Ai, Qun 艾群. *"Shen Chong shijian" zhenxiang* "沈崇事件" 真相 [Truth of the "Shen Chong affair"]. Beijing: Zhonggong dangshi chubanshe, 2012.

Albert, Norman G. *Yohouse from a Boot to a China Marine*. Bloomington, IN: Trafford, 2011.

Aplington, Henry. "Sunset in the East: A Memoir of North China, 1945–1947." *Journal of American–East Asian Relations* 3, no. 2 (1994): 155–175.

Arkush, David, and Leo O. Lee, eds. *Land without Ghosts: Chinese Impressions of America from the Mid-nineteenth Century to the Present*. Berkeley: University of California Press, 1989.

Babb, Joseph G. D. "The Harmony of Yin and Yank: The American Military Advisory Effort in China, 1941–1951." PhD diss., University of Kansas, 2012.

Ballard, J. G. *Miracles of Life: Shanghai to Shepperton, an Autobiography*. New York: Liveright, 2013.

Barlow, Tani E. "Theorizing Woman: *Funü, Guojia, Jiating*." In *Body, Subject and Power in China*, edited by Angela Zito and Tani E. Barlow. Chicago, IL: University of Chicago Press, 1994, 253–289.

Barnett, Irving. "UNRRA in China: A Case Study in Financial Assistance for Economic Development (with Emphasis on Agricultural Programs)." PhD diss., Columbia University, 1955.

Bedwell, Jesse. *China Marine*. Snowflake, AZ: Cedar Hill, 2005.

Bernstein, Richard. *China 1945: Mao's Revolution and America's Fateful Choice*. New York: Alfred A. Knopf, 2014.

Bérubé, Allan. *Coming Out under Fire: The History of Gay Men and Women in World War II*. Chapel Hill: University of North Carolina Press, 2010.

Bickers, Robert, and Jeffrey Wasserstrom. "Shanghai's 'Dogs and Chinese Not Admitted' Sign: Legend, History and Contemporary Symbol." *China Quarterly* 142 (1995): 444–466.

Björkdahl, Annika, Martin Hall, and Ted Svensson, eds. "Everyday International Relations." Special issue, *Cooperation and Conflict* 54, no. 2 (2019): 123–309.

Blanchot, Maurice. *The Infinite Conversation*, trans. Susan Hanson. Minneapolis: University of Minnesota Press, 1993.

Borg, Dorothy, and Waldo H. Heinrichs. *Uncertain Years: Chinese-American Relations, 1947–1950*. New York: Columbia University Press, 1980.
Brazelton, Mary Augusta. "The Production of Penicillin in Wartime China and Sino-American Definitions of 'Normal' Microbiology." *Journal of Modern Chinese History* 13, no. 1 (2019): 102–123.
Britschgi, Andrew J. "Military Operations Other Than War: Coming In from the Cold." In *United States Post–Cold War Defence Interests: A Review of the First Decade*, edited by Karl P. Magyar. New York: Palgrave Macmillan, 2004, 149–164.
Brooks, Charlotte. *American Exodus: Second-Generation Chinese Americans in China, 1901–1949*. Oakland: University of California Press, 2019.
Brown, Jeremy, and Matthew D. Johnson, eds. *Maoism at the Grassroots: Everyday Life in China's Era of High Socialism*. Cambridge, MA: Harvard University Press, 2015.
Bud, Robert. *Penicillin: Triumph and Tragedy*. Oxford: Oxford University Press, 2007.
Calder, Kent E. *Embattled Garrisons: Comparative Base Politics and American Globalism*. Princeton, NJ: Princeton University Press, 2007.
Carruthers, Susan L. "Latrines as the Measure of Men: American Soldiers and the Politics of Disgust in Occupied Europe and Asia." *Diplomatic History* 42, no. 1 (2018): 109–137.
Carter, Paul. *The Sound In-Between: Voice, Space, Performance*. Kensington: New South Wales University Press, 1992.
Cass, Bevan G., ed. *History of the Sixth Marine Division*. Washington, DC: Infantry Journal Press, 1948.
Cathcart, Adam. "Atrocities, Insults, and 'Jeep Girls': Depictions of the U.S. Military in China, 1945–1949." *International Journal of Comic Art* 10, no. 1 (2008): 140–154.
de Certeau, Michel. *The Practice of Everyday Life*. Oakland: University of California Press, 1984.
de Certeau, Michel, Fredric Jameson, and Carl Lovitt. "On the Oppositional Practices of Everyday Life." *Social Text* 3 (1980): 3–43.
Chang, Gordon H. *Fateful Ties: A History of America's Preoccupation with China*. Cambridge, MA: Harvard University Press, 2015.
Chavanne, Jonathan Blackshear. "The Battle for China: The U.S. Navy, Marine Corps and the Cold War in Asia, 1944–1949." PhD diss., Texas A&M University, 2016.
Cheek, Timothy. "Attitudes of Action: Maoism as Emotion in Political Theory." In *Chinese Thought as Global Theory: Diversifying Knowledge Production in the Social Sciences and Humanities*, edited by Leigh Jenco. Albany: State University of New York Press, 2016, 75–100.
Chen, Pingyuan. "Male Gaze/Female Students: Late Qing Education for Women as Portrayed in Beijing Pictorials, 1902–08." In *Different Worlds of Discourse: Transformations of Gender and Genre in Late Qing and Early Republican China*, edited by Nanxiu Qian, Grace S. Fong, and Richard J. Smith. Leiden: Brill, 2008, 315–347.
Chen, Songqing 陳松卿. "Qingdao shouxiang jianwen" 青島受降見聞 [Impressions of the Qingdao surrender ceremony]. In *Qingdao wenshi ziliao*

di 9 ji 青島文史資料第9輯 [*Historical literature of Qingdao*, vol. 9], edited by Zhongguo renmin zhengzhi xieshang huiyi Qingdaoshi weiyuanhui wenshi ziliao yanjiu weiyuanhui 中國人民政治協商會議青島市委員會文史資料研究委員會. 1992, 196–198.

Chen, Weimin 陳衛民. "Shilun 'erjiu' douzheng de jingyan jiaoxun" 試論 "二九" 斗爭的經驗教訓 [A tentative argument on the lessons from the "February ninth" struggles]. *Shi lin* 史林 2 (1996): 68–74.

Chen, Wenwen 陳文文. "1920–1940 niandai Shanghai kafeiguan yanjiu" 1920–1940 年代上海咖啡館研究 [Studies of Shanghai cafes between 1920 and 1940]. Master's thesis, Shanghai shifan daxue, 2010.

Chen, Yong. *Chop Suey, USA: The Story of Chinese Food in America*. New York: Columbia University Press, 2014.

Chen, Zhanbiao 陳占彪, ed. *Sandao quanfu riyue chongguang: Kangzhan shengli shouxiang xianchang* 三島蜷伏日月重光: 抗戰勝利受降現場 [*Islands coiling, sun and moon remerge: Scenes of accepting surrender after victory in the war of resistance*]. Beijing: Sanlian shudian, 2015.

Cheng, Yinghong. "From Campus Racism to Cyber Racism: Discourse of Race and Chinese Nationalism." *China Quarterly* 207 (2011): 561–579.

Chiang, Connie Y. "Monterey-by-the-Smell." *Pacific Historical Review* 73, no. 2 (2004): 183–214.

Chiang, Kai-shek. *China's Destiny*, trans. Wang Chung-hui. New York: The MacMillan Company, 1947.

Chin, Sei Jeong. "The Korean War, Anti-US Propaganda, and the Marginalization of Dissent in China, 1950–1953." *Twentieth-Century China* 48, no. 1 (2023): 23–47.

Chiu, Hungdah. "The United States Status of Forces Agreement with the Republic of China: Some Criminal Case Studies." *Boston College International and Comparative Law Review* 3, no. 1 (December 1979): 67–88.

Chuji zhongxue keben: Zhongguo lishi 初級中學課本: 中國歷史 [*Junior high school textbook: Chinese history*, vol. 4]. Beijing: Renmin jiaoyu chubanshe, 1982, 1986.

Clark, George B. *Treading Softly: U.S. Marines in China, 1819–1949*. Westport, CT: Praeger, 2001.

Cochran, Sherman. *Big Business in China: Sino-Foreign Rivalry in the Cigarette Industry, 1890–1930*. Cambridge, MA: Harvard University Press, 1980.

Collingham, Lizzie. *The Taste of War: World War Two and the Battle for Food*. New York: Penguin Press, 2013.

Compton, James R. "Marines and Mothers: Agency, Activism, and Resistance to the American North China Intervention, 1945–46." *Marine Corps History* 8, no. 1 (2022): 21–40.

Cook, James A. "Penetration and Neocolonialism: The Shen Chong Rape Case and the Anti-American Student Movement of 1946–47." *Republican China* 22, no.1 (1996): 65–97.

Costello, John. *Virtue under Fire: How World War II Changed Our Social and Sexual Attitudes*. Boston, MA: Little, Brown and Company, 1985.

Craven, Matthew. "What Happened to Unequal Treaties? The Continuities of Informal Empire." *Nordic Journal of International Law* 74 (2005): 335–382.

Crouch, A. L. *China Sketchbook: A Book of Army Verse*. Shanghai: Stars and Stripes, 1946.
Cullather, Nick. *Illusions of Influence: The Political Economy of United States-Philippines Relations, 1942–1960*. Stanford, CA: Stanford University Press, 1994.
Cunningham, Maura Elizabeth. "The Modern Girl in Motion: Women and Sports in *Liangyou*." In *Liangyou: Kaleidoscopic Modernity and the Shanghai Global Metropolis, 1926–1945*, edited by Paul Pickowicz, Kuiyi Shen, and Yingjin Zhang. Leiden: Brill, 2013, 95–110.
Daugherty, III, Leo J., and Rhonda L. Smith-Daugherty. *Counterinsurgency and the United States Marine Corps, Volume 2: An Era of Persistent Warfare, 1945–2016*. Jefferson, NC: McFarland & Company, Inc., 2018.
D'Emilio, John, and Estelle B. Freedman. *Intimate Matters: A History of Sexuality in America*. Chicago, IL: University of Chicago Press, 2012.
Dichter, Heather L., and Andrew L. Johns, eds. *Diplomatic Games: Sport, Statecraft, and International Relations since 1945*. Lexington: University Press of Kentucky, 2014.
Dodd, Lindsey, and David Lees, eds. *Vichy France and Everyday Life: Confronting the Challenges of Wartime, 1939–1945*. London: Bloomsbury Academic, 2018.
Dong, Madeleine Yue, and Joshua L. Goldstein, eds. *Everyday Modernity in China*. Seattle: University of Washington Press, 2006.
Dongbei junzheng daxue zhengzhibu 東北軍政大學政治部, eds. *Meijun zaiHua baoxinglu* 美軍在華暴行錄 [*Record of American soldiers' brutalities in China*]. Beian: Dongbei junzheng daxue zhengzhibu, 1947.
Dorn, Frank. *A General's Diary of Treasured Recipes*. Chicago, IL: Henry Regnery Company, 1953.
Dower, John W. *War without Mercy: Race and Power in the Pacific War*. New York: Pantheon Books, 1986.
Embracing Defeat: Japan in the Wake of World War II. New York: W. W. Norton & Company, 2000.
Du, Chunmei. "Jeep Girls and American GIs: Gendered Nationalism in Post–World War II China." *Journal of Asian Studies* 81, no. 2 (2022): 341–363.
"Rape in Peking: Injured Woman, Microhistory and Global Trial." *Gender & History* 36, no. 3 (2024): 620–638.
Duffy, Enda. *The Speed Handbook: Velocity, Pleasure, Modernism*. Durham, NC: Duke University Press, 2009.
Eastman, Lloyd E. "Nationalist China during the Sino-Japanese War 1937–1945." In *The Cambridge History of China* 13, edited by John K. Fairbank and Albert Feuerwerker. Cambridge: Cambridge University Press, 1986, 547–608.
Edwards, Louise. "Policing the Modern Woman in Republican China." *Modern China* 26, no. 2 (2000): 115–147.
"The Shanghai Modern Woman's American Dreams: Imagining America's Depravity to Produce China's 'Moderate Modernity.'" *Pacific Historical Review* 81, no. 4 (2012): 567–601.

Bibliography

Women Warriors and Wartime Spies of China. Cambridge: Cambridge University Press, 2016.

Enloe, Cynthia. *Maneuvers: The International Politics of Militarizing Women's Lives*. Berkeley: University of California Press, 2000.

——— *Seriously! Investigating Crashes and Crises as If Women Mattered*. Oakland: University of California Press, 2013.

——— *Bananas, Beaches and Bases: Making Feminist Sense of International Politics*. Berkeley: University of California Press, 2014.

Estrich, Susan. "Rape." *Yale Law Journal* 95, no. 6 (1986): 1087–1184.

Fairbank, John King. *Chinabound: A Fifty-year Memoir*. New York: Harper & Row, 1982.

Fairbank, Wilma. *America's Cultural Experiment in China, 1942–1949*. Washington, DC: US Government Printing Office.

Fang, Ke 方克, ed. *Jiang Jieshi maiguo zhenxiang* 蔣介石賣國真相 [*The truth about Chiang Kai-shek selling out the country*]. Harbin: Dongbei shudian, 1947.

Fard, Shahrad Nasrolahi. *Reciprocity in International Law: Its Impact and Function*. London: Routledge, 2016.

Ferguson, Niall, and Moritz Schularick. "'Chimerica' and the Global Asset Market Boom." *International Finance* 10, no. 3 (2007): 215–239.

Ferlanti, Federica. "The New Life Movement in Jiangxi Province, 1934–1938." *Modern Asian Studies* 44, no. 5 (2010): 961–1000.

Field, Andrew. *Shanghai's Dancing World: Cabaret Culture and Urban Politics, 1919–1954*. Hong Kong: Chinese University of Hong Kong Press, 2010.

Forslund, Catherine. *Anna Chennault: Informal Diplomacy and Asian Relations*. New York: Rowman and Littlefield, 2002.

Foster, Patrick R. *The Story of Jeep*. Iola, WI: Krause, 2004.

Frank, Benis M., and Henry I. Shaw Jr. *Victory and Occupation: History of U.S. Marine Corps Operations in World War II*, vol. V. Washington, DC: US Marine Corps, 1968.

Fredman, Zach. *The Tormented Alliance: American Servicemen and the Occupation of China, 1941–1949*. Chapel Hill: University of North Carolina Press, 2022.

Fredman, Zach, and Judd Kinzley, eds. *Uneasy Allies: Sino-American Relations at the Grassroots, 1937–1949*. Cambridge: Cambridge University Press, 2024.

Fu, Hongxing 傅紅星, dir. *Xuanfeng jiuri* 旋風九日 [*Mr. Deng goes to Washington*]. Beijing: Zhongyang xinwen jilu dianying zhipianchang, 2015.

Gallicchio, Marc. *The Scramble for Asia: U.S. Military Power in the Aftermath of the Pacific War*. New York: Rowman and Littlefield, 2008.

——— *Unconditional: The Japanese Surrender in World War II*. Oxford: Oxford University Press, 2023.

Gangcun, Ningci 岡村寧次 (Okamura Yasuji). *Gangcun Ningci huiyilu* 岡村寧次回憶錄 [*Memoirs of Okamura Yasuji*]. Beijing: Zhonghua shuju, 1981.

Gao, Yunxiang. *Sporting Gender: Women Athletes and Celebrity-Making during China's National Crisis, 1931–45*. Vancouver: University of British Columbia Press, 2013.

Gaoji zhongxue keben: Zhongguo lishi 高級中學課本: 中國歷史 [*Senior high school textbook: Chinese history*, vol. 4]. Beijing: Renmin jiaoyu chubanshe, 1957.

Geertz, Clifford. *The Interpretation of Cultures: Selected Essays*. New York: Basic Books, 1973.
Gems, Gerald R. *The Athletic Crusade: Sport and American Cultural Imperialism*. Lincoln: University of Nebraska Press, 2006.
German, Kathleen. "Economic Convergence and the Celebration of Mass Production: The World War II Advertising Campaign to Sell Jeeps." In *War and the Media: Essays on News Reporting, Propaganda and Popular Culture*, edited by Paul M. Haridakis, Barbara S. Hugenberg, and Stanley T. Wearden. Jefferson, NC: McFarland, 2009, 92–111.
Gerth, Karl. *China Made: Consumer Culture and the Creation of the Nation*. Cambridge, MA: Harvard University Asia Center, 2003.
Gillin, Donald G., and Charles Etter. "Staying On: Japanese Soldiers and Civilians in China, 1945–1949." *Journal of Asian Studies* 42, no. 3 (1983): 497–518.
Glist, Lou. *China Mailbag Uncensored: Letters from an American GI in World War II China and India*. Houston, TX: Emerald Ink, 2000.
Goedde, Petra. *GIs and Germans: Culture, Gender, and Foreign Relations, 1945–1949*. New Haven, CT: Yale University Press, 2003.
Goffman, Erving. *The Presentation of Self in Everyday Life*. Edinburgh: University of Edinburgh, 1956.
Strategic Interaction. Philadelphia: University of Pennsylvania Press, 1969.
Graham, Gael. "The Cumberland Incident of 1928: Gender, Nationalism, and Social Change in American Mission Schools in China." *Journal of Women's History* 6, no. 3 (1994): 35–61.
de Grazia, Victoria. *Irresistible Empire: America's Advance through Twentieth-Century Europe*. Cambridge, MA: Harvard University Press, 2006.
Greene, J. Megan. *Building a Nation at War: Transnational Knowledge Networks and the Development of China during and after World War II*. Cambridge, MA: Harvard University Press, 2023.
Gries, Peter Hays. "Tears of Rage: Chinese Nationalist Reactions to the Belgrade Embassy Bombing." *China Journal*, no. 46 (2001): 25–43.
"Guest Lecture by Former U.S. President Jimmy Carter." Emory University, February 14, 2018. www.cartercenter.org/news/editorials_speeches/carter-emory-lecture-china-north-korea.html.
Guo, Gen 郭根. "Beiping sannian: Cong cansheng dao jiefang de yiduan lücheng" 北平三年: 從慘勝到解放的一段旅程 [Three years in Beijing: Journey from a Pyrrhic victory to liberation]. In *Guo Gen wenlu* 郭根文錄 [*Guo Gen's Record*], edited by San Mu 散木. Taiyuan: Sanjin, 2013, 69–205.
Guo, Xixiao. "Climax of Sino-American Relations, 1944–1947." PhD diss., University of Georgia, 1997.
"Paradise or Hell Hole? U.S. Marines in Post–World War II China." *Journal of American–East Asian Relations* 7, no. 3–5 (1998): 157–185.
"The Anticlimax of an Ill-Starred Sino-American Encounter." *Modern Asian Studies* 35, no. 1 (2011): 217–244.
Hampton, Mark. *Hong Kong and British Culture, 1945–97*. Manchester: Manchester University Press, 2017.

Haraway, Donna J. *Manifestly Haraway*. Minneapolis: University of Minnesota Press, 2016.
Harootunian, Harry. "Shadowing History: National Narratives and the Persistence of the Everyday." *Cultural Studies* 18, no. 2–3 (2004): 181–200.
Henderson, Arthur Smith. *Chinese Characteristics*. New York: Revell, 1894.
Hershatter, Gail. *Dangerous Pleasures: Prostitution and Modernity in Twentieth Century Shanghai*. Berkeley: University of California Press, 1999.
———. *Women and China's Revolutions*. Lanham, MD: Rowman and Littlefield, 2018.
Hess, Christian. "Sino-Soviet City: Dalian between Socialist Worlds, 1945–1955." *Journal of Urban History* 44, no. 1 (2018): 9–25.
Höhn, Maria, and Seungsook Moon, eds. *Over There: Living with the U.S. Military Empire from World War Two to the Present*. Durham, NC: Duke University Press, 2010.
Hollinger, David A. *Protestants Abroad: How Missionaries Tried to Change the World but Changed America*. Princeton, NJ: Princeton University Press, 2017.
Hou, Zhongjun 侯中軍. "Jindai Zhongguo bupingdeng tiaoyue jiqi pingpan biaozhun de tantao" 近代中國不平等條約及其評判標準的探討 [An investigation of unequal treaties in modern China and their qualifying criteria]. *Lishi yanjiu* 歷史研究 1 (2009): 64–84.
Hoy, Suellen. *Chasing Dirt: The American Pursuit of Cleanliness*. Oxford: Oxford University Press, 1995.
Hsu, Madeline Y. "From Chop Suey to Mandarin Cuisine: Fine Dining and the Refashioning of Chinese Ethnicity during the Cold War Era." In *Chinese Americans and the Politics of Race and Culture*, edited by Sucheng Chan and Madeline Y. Hsu. Philadelphia, PA: Temple University Press, 2008, 173–193.
———. *The Good Immigrants: How the Yellow Peril Became the Model Minority*. Princeton, NJ: Princeton University Press, 2015.
Hu, Cheng 胡成. "'Buweisheng' de Huaren xingxiang: Zhongwai jian de butong jiangshu" "不衛生"的華人形象: 中外間的不同講述 [Image of the "unsanitary" Chinese: Differing narratives between foreigners and the Chinese]. *Bulletin of the Institute of Modern History Academia Sinica* 56 (2007): 1–43.
Huabei xuesheng yundong xiaoshi bianji weiyuanhui 華北學生運動小史編輯委員會, eds. *Huabei xuesheng yundong xiaoshi* 華北學生運動小史 [A brief history of student movements in North China]. Beijing: Huabei xuesheng yundong xiaoshi bianji weiyuanhui, 1948.
Huang, Jingshan 黃景山. "1948 nian Beiping diqu fanMeifuRi yundong" 一九四八年北平地區反美扶日運動 [1948 Opposing the US Support of Japan movement in the Beijing area]. *Beijing dangshi* 北京黨史 5 (1988): 11–19.
Huang, Renlin 黃仁霖 (Huang Jen-lin). *Huang Renlin huiyilu* 黃仁霖回憶錄 [The memoir of General Huang Renlin]. Beijing: Tuanjie chubanshe, 2006.
Huang, Shang 黃裳. *Guanyu Meiguo bing* 關於美國兵 [About American soldiers]. Shanghai: Shanghai chuban gongsi, 1947.
Huang, Yunte. *Daughter of the Dragon: Anna May Wong's Rendezvous with American History*. New York: Liveright, 2023.
Huebner, Jon W. "Chinese Anti-Americanism, 1946–48." *Australian Journal of Chinese Affairs* 17 (1987): 115–125.

Hunt, Michael H. "The Forgotten Occupation: Peking, 1900–1901." *Pacific Historical Review* 48, no. 4 (1979): 501–529.
Immerwahr, Daniel. *How to Hide an Empire: A History of the Greater United States*. New York: Farrar, Straus and Giroux, 2019.
Iriye, Akira. "Contemporary History as History: American Expansion into the Pacific Since 1941." *Pacific Historical Review* 53, no. 2 (1984): 191–212.
Isaacs, Harold R. *No Peace for Asia*. Cambridge, MA: MIT Press, 1967.
Jenner, Mark S. R. "Follow Your Nose? Smell, Smelling, and Their Histories." *American Historical Review* 116, no. 2 (2011): 335–351.
Jespersen, T. Christopher. *American Images of China, 1931–1949*. Stanford, CA: Stanford University Press, 1996.
Jinan Shudian 冀南書店, ed. *ZhuHua Meijun baoxinglu* 駐華美軍暴行錄 [*Record of brutalities by US forces in China*]. Weixian: Jinan shudian, 1946.
Kakoudaki, Despina. *Anatomy of a Robot: Literature, Cinema, and the Cultural Work of Artificial People*. New Brunswick, NJ: Rutgers University Press, 2014.
Kiechle, Melanie A. *Smell Detectives: An Olfactory History of Nineteenth-Century Urban America*. Seattle: University of Washington Press, 2017.
Kim, Han Sang. "My Car Modernity: What the U.S. Army Brought to South Korean Cinematic Imagination about Modern Mobility." *Journal of Asian Studies* 75, no. 1 (2016): 63–85.
Kinkela, David. *DDT and the American Century: Global Health, Environmental Politics, and the Pesticide That Changed the World*. Chapel Hill: University of North Carolina Press, 2011.
Kirby, William. *Empires of Ideas: Creating the Modern University from Germany to America to China*. Cambridge, MA: Harvard University Press, 2022.
Klein, Christina. *Cold War Orientalism: Asia in the Middlebrow Imagination, 1945–1961*. Oakland: University of California Press, 2003.
Koshiro, Yukiko. *Trans-Pacific Racisms and the U.S. Occupation of Japan*. New York: Columbia University Press, 1999.
Kovner, Sarah. *Occupying Power: Sex Workers and Servicemen in Postwar Japan*. Stanford, CA: Stanford University Press, 2012.
Kramm, Robert. *Sanitized Sex: Regulating Prostitution, Venereal Disease, and Intimacy in Occupied Japan, 1945–1952*. Oakland: University of California Press, 2017.
Kushner, Barak. *Men to Devils, Devils to Men: Japanese War Crimes and Chinese Justice*. Cambridge, MA: Harvard University Press, 2015.
——— *The Geography of Injustice: East Asia's Battle between Memory and History*. Ithaca, NY: Cornell University Press, 2024.
Lao, She 老舍. *Chaguan* 茶館 [*Teahouse*]. Beijing: Beijing gongye meishu chubanshe, 2018.
——— *Luotuo xiangzi* 駱駝祥子 [*Rickshaw boy*]. Beijing: Renmin wenxue chubanshe, 2019.
Larry, Diana. *The Chinese People at War: Human Suffering and Social Transformation, 1937–1945*. New York: Cambridge University Press, 2010.
Lautz, Terry. *John Birch: A Life*. New York: Oxford University Press, 2016.
——— *Americans in China: Encounters with the People's Republic*. New York: Oxford University Press, 2022.

Lee, Leo Ou-Fan. *Shanghai Modern: The Flowering of a New Urban Culture in China, 1930–1945*. Cambridge, MA: Harvard University Press, 1999.

Lee, Na Young. "The Construction of Military Prostitution in South Korea during the U.S. Military Rule, 1945–1948." *Feminist Studies* 33, no. 3 (2007): 453–481.

Lefebvre, Henri. *Critique of Everyday Life*, vols. 1–3, trans. John Moore. London: Verso, 2008.

Leffler, Melvyn. *A Preponderance of Power: National Security, the Truman Administration, and the Cold War*. Stanford, CA: Stanford University Press, 1992.

Leng, Xin 冷欣. *Cong canjia kangzhan dao mudu Rijun touxiang* 從參加抗戰到目睹日軍投降 [*From joining the war of resistance to witnessing the Japanese surrender*]. Taipei: Zhuanji wenxue chubanshe, 1967.

Leong, Karen J. *The China Mystique: Pearl S. Buck, Anna May Wong, Mayling Soong, and the Transformation of American Orientalism*. Berkeley: University of California Press, 2005.

Li, Jet 李連杰, dir. *Zhonghua yingxiong* 中華英雄 [*Born to defend*]. Hong Kong: Sil-Metropole Organisation, 1986.

Li, Siyi 李思逸. *Tielu xiandai xing: Wanqing zhi minguo de shikong tiyan yu wenhua xiangxiang* 鐵路現代性：晚清至民國的時空體驗與文化想像 [*Railway modernity in China: The temporal-spatial experience and the cultural imagination of trains, 1840–1937*]. Taipei: China Times, 2020.

Li, Yaoyu 李耀宇. *Yige Zhongguo geming qinlizhe de siren jilu* 一個中國革命親歷者的私人記錄 [*A private record by a participant of the Chinese Revolution*]. Beijing: Dangdai Zhongguo chubanshe, 2009.

Li, Yaoyu 李耀宇 and Li Dongping 李東平. "Wo suo zhidao de Yan'an Meijun guanchazu" 我所知道的延安美軍觀察組 [The US Army Observation Group to Yan'an that I know of]. *Nanfang zhoumo* 南方周末 1045 (February 19, 2004).

Liao, Yuyang 廖宇陽. *Wanqinglou shici wenshi heji* 晚晴樓詩詞文史合集 [*A collection of poetry, literature and history of the Wanqinglou*]. Nanchang, Jiangxi: Jiangxi renmin chubanshe, 2015.

Lin, Hsiao-ting. "Taiwan's Secret Ally." *Hoover Digest* 2 (2012): 192–203.

Liu, Danian 劉大年. *Meidi qinHua shi* 美帝侵華史 [*The history of American imperialist aggression in China*]. Shanghai: Jiaoyu chubanshe, 1950.

Liu, Haiming. *From Canton Restaurant to Panda Express: A History of Chinese Food in the United States*. New Brunswick, NJ: Rutgers University Press, 2015.

Liu, Michael Shiyung. "Eating Well for Survival: Chinese Nutrition Experiments during World War II." In *Moral Foods: The Construction of Nutrition and Health in Modern Asia*, edited by Angela Ki Che Leung, Melissa L. Caldwell, Robert Ji-Song Ku, and Christine R. Yano. Honolulu: University of Hawaii Press, 2020, 89–108.

Liu, Ping 劉萍. "Zhanhou Meijun zaiHua chuzhi zhanfan wenti chutan" 戰後美軍在華處置戰犯問題初探 [Preliminary study on postwar American military's handling of war criminals in China]. *Minguo dang an* 民國檔案 3 (2016): 128–138.

Liu, Tong 劉統. "Guomin zhengfu shenpan Riben zhanfan gaishu (1945–1949)" 國民政府審判日本戰犯概述 (1945–1949) [Overview of the Nationalist Government's trial of Japanese war criminals (1945–1949)]. *Minguo dang an* 民國檔案 1 (2014): 72–84.
Lott, Eric J. *Love and Theft: Blackface Minstrelsy and the American Working Class*. New York: Oxford University Press, 1993.
Lu, Xun 魯迅, *Sanxianji* 三閒集 [*Triple leisure*]. Beijing: The People's Literature Publishing House, 1958.
Lüdtke, Alf. "Introduction: What Is the History of Everyday Life and Who Are Its Practitioners?" In *The History of Everyday Life: Reconstructing Historical Experiences and Ways of Life*, edited by Alf Lüdtke. Princeton, NJ: Princeton University Press, 1995, 3–40.
Lutz, Catherine, ed. *The Bases of Empire: The Global Struggle against U.S. Military Posts*. New York: New York University Press, 2009.
Maier, Charles S. *Among Empires: American Ascendancy and Its Predecessors*: Cambridge, MA: Harvard University Press, 2007.
Manela, Erez. *The Wilsonian Moment: Self-Determination and the International Origins of Anticolonial Nationalism*. New York: Oxford University Press, 2007.
Mann, Jim. *Beijing Jeep: A Case Study of Western Business in China*. Boulder, CO: Westview Press, 1997.
Mao, Zedong. *Selected Works of Mao Tse-tung*, vol. IV. Beijing: Foreign Languages Press, 1961.
Marchetti, Gina. *Romance and the "Yellow Peril": Race, Sex, and Discursive Strategies in Hollywood Fiction*. Berkeley: University of California Press, 1993.
Marolda, Edward John. "The U.S. Navy and the Chinese Civil War, 1945–1952." PhD diss., George Washington University, 1990.
Marsden, Magnus, Diana Ibañez-Tirado, and David Henig, eds. "Everyday Diplomacy: Insights from Ethnography." Special Issue, *Cambridge Journal of Anthropology* 34, no. 2 (2016).
McLuhan, Marshall, and W. Terrence Gordon. *Understanding Media: The Extensions of Man*. Corte Madera, CA: Gingko Press, 2003.
Meiguobing gunchuqu 美國兵, 滾出去 [*American soldiers, get out*]. Aiguo yundong chubanshe, 1947.
Millwood, Pete. *Improbable Diplomats: How Ping-Pong Players, Musicians, and Scientists Remade US-China Relations*. Cambridge: Cambridge University Press, 2023.
Minami, Kazushi. *How Americans and Chinese Transformed US-China Relations during the Cold War*. Ithaca, NY: Cornell University Press, 2024.
Ministry of Foreign Affairs, *Treaties between the Republic of China and Foreign States (1927–1957)*. New York: AMS Press, 1974.
Minjian yingxiang 民間影像, ed. *Wo de 1945: Kangzhan shengli huiyilu* 我的1945: 抗戰勝利回憶錄 [*My 1945: Memoirs of victory against Japan*]. Shanghai: Tongji daxue chubanshe, 2017.
"Minzhu shi pannixilin, ke zhiliao Zhongguo zhengzhi: Zhang Lan da jizhe wen" 民主是盤尼西林, 可治療中國政治: 張瀾答記者問 [Democracy is penicillin, and can cure Chinese politics: Zhang Lan answered reporters' questions]. In

Pu Xixiu jizhe shengya xunzong 浦熙修記者生涯尋蹤 [*Sketches of Pu Xixiu's journalist career*], edited by Yuan Donglin 袁冬林 and Yuan Shijie 袁士杰. Shanghai: Wenhui chubanshe, 2000, 380–382.

Mitter, Rana. "State-Building after Disaster: Jiang Tingfu and the Reconstruction of Post–World War II China, 1943–1949." *Comparative Studies in Society and History* 61, no. 1 (2019): 176–206.

———. *China's Good War: How World War II Is Shaping a New Nationalism.* Cambridge, MA: Harvard University Press, 2020.

Mitter, Rana, and Aaron William Moore, eds. "China in World War II, 1937–1945: Experience, Memory, and Legacy." Special issue, *Modern Asian Studies* 45, no. 2 (March 2011): 379–490.

Modern Girl around the World Research Group, eds. *The Modern Girl around the World: Consumption, Modernity and Globalization*. Durham, NC: Duke University Press, 2008.

Moe, Albert F. "'Gung Ho.'" *American Speech* 42, no. 1 (1967): 19–30.

Moon, Katharine H. S. *Sex among Allies: Military Prostitution in U.S.–Korea Relations*. New York: Columbia University Press, 1997.

Moon, Seungsook. "Regulating Desire, Managing the Empire: U.S. Military Prostitution in South Korea, 1945–1970." In *Over There: Living with the U.S. Military Empire from World War Two to the Present*, edited by Maria Höhn and Seungsook Moon. Durham, NC: Duke University Press, 2010, 39–77.

Morton, Louis. "Army and Marines on the China Station: A Study in Military and Political Rivalry." *Pacific Historical Review* 29, no. 1 (1960): 51–73.

Mote, Frederick W. *China and the Vocation of History in the Twentieth Century: A Personal Memoir*. Princeton, NJ: East Asian Library Journal in association with Princeton University Press, 2010.

Neubauer, Jack. *The Adoption Plan: China and the Remaking of Global Humanitarianism*. New York: Columbia University Press, 2025.

Ngai, Mae. *The Chinese Question: The Gold Rushes and Global Politics*. New York: W. W. Norton & Company, 2021.

Niu, Jun 牛軍. *Cong Heerli dao Maxieer: Meiguo tiaochu guogong maodun shimo* 從赫爾利到馬歇爾: 美國調處國共矛盾始末 [*From Hurley to Marshall: A history of the American mediation between the Nationalists and the Communists*]. Beijing: Dongfang chubanshe, 2009.

Oyen, Meredith. *The Diplomacy of Migration: Transnational Lives and the Making of U.S.-Chinese Relations in the Cold War*. Ithaca, NY: Cornell University Press, 2015.

Pang, Laikwan. "The Collective Subjectivity of Chinese Intellectuals and Their Café Culture in Republican Shanghai." *Inter-Asia Cultural Studies* 7, no. 1 (2006): 24–42.

Pang, Xianzhi 逄先知, ed. *Mao Zedong nianpu: 1893–1949*, xiajuan 毛澤東年譜: 一八九三——一九四九, 下卷 [*Chronological biography of Mao Zedong, 1893–1949*, vol. 3]. Beijing: Zhongyangwenxian chubanshe, 2002.

Parkyn, Michael. "Operation BELEAGUER: The Marine III Amphibious Corps in North China, 1945–49." *Marine Corps Gazette* 85, no. 7 (2001): 32–37.

Pascoe, Peggy. *What Comes Naturally: Miscegenation Law and the Making of Race in America*. New York: Oxford University Press, 2009.

Pauley, Edwin W. *Report on Japanese Assets in Manchuria to the President of the United States*. Washington, DC: United States Government Printing Office, 1946.

Payne, Robert. *China Awake*. New York: Dodd, Mead and Company, 1947.

Peck, Graham. *Two Kinds of Time*. Seattle: University of Washington Press, 2008.

Peffer, George Anthony. "Forbidden Families: Emigration Experiences of Chinese Women under the Page Law, 1875–1882." *Journal of American Ethnic History* 6, no. 1 (1986): 28–46.

Pepper, Suzanne. *Civil War in China: The Political Struggle, 1945–1949*. Lanham, MD: Rowman and Littlefield, 1999.

Piccigallo, Philip R. *The Japanese on Trial: Allied War Crimes Operations in the East, 1945–1951*. Austin: University of Texas Press, 2021.

Polenberg, Richard. "The Good War? A Reappraisal of How World War II Affected American Society." *Virginia Magazine of History and Biography* 100, no. 3 (1992): 295–322.

Pomfret, John. *The Beautiful Country and the Middle Kingdom: America and China, 1776 to the Present*. New York: Henry Holt and Company, 2016.

Poon, Shuk-wah 潘淑華. "Huniu yu shaniu: Wanqing ji Minguo shiqi Zhongguo niurou jingji yinqi de zhengyi" 護牛與殺牛: 晚清及民國時期中國牛肉經濟引起的爭議 [To kill or not to kill: Controversies over the beef economy and oxen protection in late Qing and Republican China]. *Shijie lishi pinglun* 世界歷史評論 3 (2021): 177–203.

Pozzi, Laura. "*The Revolution of a Little Hero: The Sanmao Comic Strips and the Politics of Childhood in China, 1935–1962*." PhD diss., European University Institute, 2014.

Pulos, Arthur J. *The American Design Adventure, 1940–1975*. Cambridge, MA: MIT Press, 1988.

Reist, Katherine K. "The American Military Advisory Missions to China, 1945–1949." *Journal of Military History* 77, no. 4 (2013): 1379–1398.

Remick, Elizabeth J. *Regulating Prostitution in China: Gender and Local Statebuilding, 1900–1937*. Stanford, CA: Stanford University Press, 2014.

Rieger, Bernhard. *The People's Car: A Global History of the Volkswagen Beetle*. Cambridge, MA: Harvard University Press, 2013.

Roberts, Mary Louise. *What Soldiers Do: Sex and the American GI in World War II France*. Chicago, IL: University of Chicago Press, 2013.

Rong, Qun 榮群, ed. *Meijun zaiHua de baoxing* 美軍在華的暴行 [Brutalities committed by US troops in China]. Shenyang: Dongbei renmin chubanshe, 1951.

Rotter, Andrew J. *Empires of the Senses: Bodily Encounters in Imperial India and the Philippines*. New York: Oxford University Press, 2019.

Ruskola, Teemu. *Legal Orientalism: China, the United States, and Modern Law*. Cambridge, MA: Harvard University Press, 2013.

Schivelbusch, Wolfgang. *The Railway Journey: The Industrialization of Time and Space in the Nineteenth Century*. Oakland: University of California Press, 2014.

Seelinger, Matthew J. "From the Jeep to the Humvee: U.S. Army Light Combat Vehicles, World War II to Present." *On Point* 11, no. 3 (December 2005): 8–13.

Shaffer, Robert. "A Rape in Beijing, December 1946: GIs, Nationalist Protests, and U.S. Foreign Policy." *Pacific Historical Review* 69, no.1 (2000): 31–64.

Shang, Haiming 尚海明. "Shanzhong, xiongsi yu sharen changming: Zhongguoren sixing guannian de wenhua chanshi" 善終、凶死與殺人償命: 中國人死刑觀念的文化闡釋 [Good death, violent death and a life for a life: A cultural interpretation of Chinese views on the death penalty]. *Faxue yanjiu* 法學研究 4 (2016): 61–78.

Shanghaishi zhengfu tongjichu 上海市政府統計處, ed. *Shanghaishi tongji zongbaogao* 上海市統計總報告 [Shanghai municipal general statistical report]. Shanghai: Longchang Printing House, 1946.

Shanghaishi gongwu tongji baogao 上海市公務統計報告 [Shanghai municipal public affairs statistical report] 2, no. 3, 1947.

Shanghaishi gongwu tongji baogao 上海市公務統計報告 [Shanghai municipal public affairs statistical report] 3, no. 8, 1948.

Shaw, Henry I. *The United States Marines in North China, 1945–1949*. Washington, DC: US Marine Corps, 1968.

Shen Yunlong 沈雲龍, ed. *Zhongguo zhanqu Zhongguo lujun zongsilingbu chuli Riben touxiang wenjian huibian* 中國戰區中國陸軍總司令部處理日本投降文件匯編 [Compilation of Japanese surrender documents handled by the Chinese Army General Headquarters in the China Theater]. Taipei: Wenhai chubanshe, 1945.

Simbulan, Roland G. "People's Movement Responses to Evolving U.S. Military Activities in the Philippines." In *The Bases of Empire: The Global Struggle against U.S. Military Posts*, edited by Catherine Lutz. New York: New York University Press, 2009, 145–180.

Sledge, E. B. *China Marine: An Infantryman's Life after World War II*. Oxford: Oxford University Press, 2002.

Smith, Mark M. *Sensing the Past: Seeing, Hearing, Smelling, Tasting, and Touching in History*. Berkeley: University of California Press, 2007.

Sollors, Werner. *The Temptation of Despair: Tales of the 1940s*. Cambridge, MA: Belknap Press, 2014.

Spector, Ronald H. "After Hiroshima: Allied Military Occupations and the Fate of Japan's Empire, 1945–1947." *Journal of Military History* 69, no. 4 (2005): 1121–1136.

In the Ruins of Empire: The Japanese Surrender and the Battle for Postwar Asia. New York: Random House, 2008.

Steege, Paul. *Black Market, Cold War: Everyday Life in Berlin, 1946–1949*. New York: Cambridge University Press, 2007.

Steege, Paul, Andrew Stuart Bergerson, Maureen Healy, and Pamela E. Swett. "The History of Everyday Life: A Second Chapter." *Journal of Modern History* 80, no. 2 (2008): 358–378.

Stephens, Harold. *Take China: The Last of the China Marines*. Bangkok: Wolfenden, 2002.

Strand, David. *Rickshaw Beijing: City People and Politics in the 1920s*. Berkeley: University of California Press, 1989.
"Symposium: Rethinking the Lost Chance in China." *Diplomatic History* 21, no. 1 (1997): 71–115.
Tao, Xingzhi 陶行知. *Xingzhi shigeji* 行知詩歌集 [*Collection of Tao Xingzhi's poems*]. Shanghai: Dafu chuban gongsi, 1947.
Teng, Emma Jinhua. *Eurasian: Mixed Identities in the United States, China, and Hong Kong, 1842–1943*. Berkeley: University of California Press, 2013.
Thomas, Nicholas. *Entangled Objects: Exchange, Material Culture, and Colonialism in the Pacific*. Cambridge, MA: Harvard University Press, 1991.
Tucker, Nancy Bernkopf. *Patterns in the Dust: Chinese-American Relations and the Recognition Controversy, 1949–1950*. New York: Columbia University Press, 1983.
United Nations Relief and Rehabilitation Administration. *UNRRA in China, 1945–1947*. Washington, DC: UNRRA, 1948.
United States Army Forces. *Here's How: A Handbook for American Troops in China*. Washington, DC: China-Burma-India, 1944.
United States Army Service Forces. *A Pocket Guide to China*. Washington, DC: US War and Navy Departments, 1942.
United States Department of State. *Foreign Relations of the United States: Diplomatic Papers, 1943, China*. Washington, DC: United States Government Printing Office, 1957.
The China White Paper, August 1949. Stanford, CA: Stanford University Press, 1967.
Foreign Relations of the United States: Diplomatic Papers, 1945, The Far East, China, Volume VII. Washington, DC: United States Government Printing Office, 1969.
Foreign Relations of the United States, 1946, The Far East: China, Volume IX. Washington, DC: United States Government Printing Office, 1972.
Foreign Relations of the United States, 1948, The Far East: China, Volume VIII. Washington, DC: United States Government Printing Office, 1973.
United States Joint Chiefs of Staff. *Joint Publication 3–0*. Washington, DC: U.S. Government Printing Office, 1995.
United States Marine Corps. *A Marine's Guide to North China*. San Francisco, CA: First Marine Division, 1945.
United States Navy Naval History and Heritage Command. "Casualties: U.S. Navy and Marine Corps Personnel Killed and Wounded in Wars, Conflicts, Terrorist Acts, and Other Hostile Incidents." www.history.navy.mil/content/history/nhhc/research/library/online-reading-room/title-list-alphabetically/c/casualties1.html.
Van de Ven, Hans. *China at War: Triumph and Tragedy in the Emergence of the New China 1937–1952*. Cambridge, MA: Harvard University Press, 2018.
Vine, David. *Base Nation: How U.S. Military Bases Abroad Harm America and the World*. New York: Henry Holt and Company, 2015.
Wagner-Pacifici, Robin. *The Art of Surrender: Decomposing Sovereignty at Conflict's End*. Chicago, IL: University of Chicago Press, 2005.

Waldron, Arthur. "China's New Remembering of World War II: The Case of Zhang Zizhong." *Modern Asian Studies* 30, no. 4 (October 1996): 945–978.

Wan, Kuiyi 萬揆一. "Minguo shiqi Kunming xiangyan shihua" 民國時期昆明香煙史話 [Accounts of cigarette history in Republican Kunming]. In *Kunmingshi Panlongqu wenshi ziliao xuanji di 8 ji* 昆明市盤龍區文史資料選輯第8輯 [Historical literature of Panlong District, Kunming, vol. 8], edited by Zhongguo renmin zhengzhi xieshang huiyi, Yunnansheng Kunmingshi Panlongqu weiyuanhui, wenshiziliao weiyuanhui 中國人民政治協商會議雲南省昆明市盤龍區委員會文史資料委員會, 1993, 83–109.

Wang, Chaoguang 汪朝光. "Haolaiwu de chenfu: Minguo nianjian Meiguo dianying zaiHua jingyu yanjiu" 好萊塢的沉浮: 民國年間美國電影在華境遇研究 [Rise and fall of Hollywood films in China]. *Meiguo yanjiu* 美國研究 2 (1998): 113–139.

Wang, Dong. "The Discourse of Unequal Treaties in Modern China." *Pacific Affairs* 76, no. 3 (2003): 399–425.

Wang, Gaopeng 王高朋. "Qingmeisu zai jindai Zhongguo de chuanbo yu jieshou" 青黴素在近代中國的傳播與接受 [The dissemination and acceptance of penicillin in modern China]. Master's thesis, Hebei University, 2018.

Wang, Guanhua. *In Search of Justice: The 1905–1906 Chinese Anti-American Boycott*. Cambridge, MA: Harvard University Press, 2001.

Wang, Jianlang 王建朗. "Zhongguo feichu bupingdeng tiaoyue de lishi kaocha" 中國廢除不平等條約的歷史考察 [A Historical investigation into China's abolition of unequal treaties]. *Lishi yanjiu* 歷史研究 5 (1997): 4–18.

Wang, Jianzhu 王建柱. "Tiananmen guangchang de shiwuci yuebing" 天安門廣場的十五次閱兵 [Fifteen military parades in Tiananmen Square]. *Hongyan Chunqiu* 紅岩春秋 10 (2017): 8–13.

Wang, Qi 王淇. "Yijiu sisan nian 'ZhongMei pingdeng xinyue' qianding de lishibeijing jiqi yiyi pingxi" 一九四三年《中美平等新約》簽訂的歷史背景及其意義評析 [The historical background and analysis of the 1943 Treaty between the United States and China for the Relinquishment of Extraterritorial Rights in China]. *Zhonggong dangshi yanjiu* 中共黨史研究 4 (1989): 9–15.

Wasserstrom, Jeffrey N. *Student Protests in Twentieth-Century China: The View from Shanghai*. Stanford, CA: Stanford University Press, 1991.

Watt, Lori. *When Empire Comes Home: Repatriation and Reintegration in Postwar Japan*. Cambridge, MA: Harvard University Press, 2009.

West, Philip. *Yenching University and Sino-Western Relations*. Cambridge, MA: Harvard University Press, 1976.

Westad, Odd Arne. *Decisive Encounters: The Chinese Civil War, 1946–1950*. Stanford, CA: Stanford University Press, 2003.

White, Theodore H., and Annalee Jacoby, *Thunder Out of China*. New York: William Sloane Associates, Inc., 1946.

Wilkinson, Mark. "American Military Misconduct in Shanghai and the Chinese Civil War: The Case of Zang Dayaozi." *Journal of American-East Asian Relations* 17, no. 2 (2010): 146–173.

Wilson, Paul E. *China Marine*. North Charleston, SC: BookSurge, 2008.

Wong, Sin Kiong. *China's Anti-American Boycott Movement in 1905: A Study in Urban Protest*. New York: Peter Lang, 2002.

Wu, Hong 武宏. "Yexi Meijun danyaoku" 夜襲美軍彈藥庫 [Night raid on US ammunition dump]. In *Ninghe wenshi ziliao di 2 ji* 寧河文史資料第2輯 [*Historical literature of Ninghe*, vol. 2], edited by Zhengxie Tianjinshi Ninghexian weiyuanhui, wenshi ziliao weiyuanhui 政協天津市寧河縣委員會文史資料委員會, 1991, 137–138.

Wu, Jingping 吳景平. "Kangzhan shiqi ZhongMei zujie guanxi shuping" 抗戰時期中美租借關係述評 [A review of Sino-American lend-lease relations during the Sino-Japanese War]. *Lishi yanjiu* 歷史研究 4 (1995): 48–62.

Wu, Lin-Chun 吳翎君. "1946 nian ZhongMei Shangyue de lishi yiyi" 1946年中美商約的歷史意義 [The historical significance of the 1946 Sino-American Treaty]. *Guoli zhengzhi daxue lishi xuebao* 國立政治大學歷史學報 21 (May 2004): 41–66.

Wu, Wenshi 武文士. "Hankou 'Jingming dalou shijian' zhenxiang" 漢口"景明大樓事件"真相 [Truth of the "Jingming building affair" in Hankou]. *Wenshi chunqiu* 文史春秋 4 (1994): 43–46.

Xinhua shishi congkanshe 新華時事叢刊社, ed. *Meijun zhuHua shiqi de xuezhai* 美軍駐華時期的血債 [*The blood debts incurred by US troops stationed in China*]. Beijing: Renmin chubanshe, 1950.

Xu, Dingding 徐丁丁. "Penicillin (Qingmeisu) Zhongyiming de bianqian" (青霉素)中譯名的變遷 [The evolution of penicillin's Chinese translations]. *Zhongguo kejishi zazhi* 中國科技史雜志 36, no. 3 (2015): 325–335.

Xu, Guoqi. *Chinese and Americans: A Shared History*. Cambridge, MA: Harvard University Press, 2014.

Xu, Jiajun 徐家俊. "Tilanqiao jianyu: Zhongguo jingnei diyige shenpan Riben zhanfan de changsuo" 提籃橋監獄: 中國境內第一個審判日本戰犯的場所 [Tilanqiao jail: China's first venue for the trials of Japanese war criminals]. *KangRi zhanzheng yanjiu* 抗日戰爭研究 4 (1998): 215–222.

Xue, Liyong 薛理勇. *JiuShanghai zujie shihua* 舊上海租界史話 [*Accounts of old Shanghai's foreign concessions*]. Shanghai: Shanghai shehui kexueyuan chubanshe, 2004.

Yan, Changhong 嚴昌洪. "Jindai renli chefu qunti yishi tanxi" 近代人力車夫群體意識探析 [Analysis of the group consciousness of modern rickshaw pullers]. *Huazhong shifan daxue xuebao* 華中師範大學學報 6 (2007): 63–71.

Yang, Bingheng 楊秉亨. "Yexi Meijun danyaoku de qianqianhouhou" 夜襲美軍彈藥庫的前前後後 [The complete story of the night raid on the US ammunition dump]. In *Ninghe wenshi ziliao di 3 ji* 寧河文史資料第3輯 [*Historical literature of Ninghe*, vol. 3], edited by Zhengxie Tianjinshi Ninghexian weiyuanhui, wenshi ziliao weiyuanhui 政協天津市寧河縣委員會文史資料委員會, 1995, 87–93.

Yang, Fan. *Disorienting Politics: Chimerican Media and Transpacific Entanglements*. Ann Arbor: University of Michigan Press, 2024.

Yang, Kuisong 楊奎松. "1946 nian Anping shijian zhenxiang yu Zhonggong duiMei jiaoshe" 1946年安平事件真相與中共對美交涉 [The truth about the 1946 Anping incident and CCP-US negotiations]. *Shixue yuekan* 史學月刊 4 (2011): 60–74.

"Zhongjian didai" de geming: Guoji dabeijing xia kan Zhonggong chenggong zhi dao "中間地帶"的革命: 國際大背景下看中共成功之道 [*Revolution in the "middle area": The CCP's road toward success in the international context*]. Guilin: Guangxi shifan daxue chubanshe, 2012.

Yang, Shangkun 楊尚昆. *Yang Shangkun huiyilu* 楊尚昆回憶錄 [*Memoir of Yang Shangkun*]. Beijing: Zhongyang wenxian chubanshe, 2001.

Yang, Yuqing 楊雨青. *Meiyuan weihe wuxiao? Zhanshi Zhongguo jingjiweiji yu ZhongMei yingdui zhi ce* 美援為何無效? 戰時中國經濟危機與中美應對之策 [*Why is American aid ineffective? Wartime Chinese economic crisis and Sino-American responses*]. Beijing: Renmin chubanshe, 2011.

Yang, Zhiguo. "United States Marines in Qingdao: Military–Civilian Interaction, Nationalism, and China's Civil War, 1945–1949." PhD diss., University of Maryland, 1998.

Yao, Liang. "Nationalism on Their Own Terms: The National Products Movement and the Coca-Cola Protest in Shanghai, 1945–1949." *Modern Asian Studies* 51, no. 5 (2017): 1439–1468.

Yeh, Wen-hsin. *Shanghai Splendor: Economic Sentiments and the Making of Modern China, 1843–1949*. Berkeley: University of California Press, 2007.

Yen, Hsiao-Pei. "Body Politics, Modernity and National Salvation: The Modern Girl and the New Life Movement." *Asian Studies Review* 29, no. 2 (2005): 165–186.

Yen, Rhoda J. "Racial Stereotyping of Asians and Asian Americans and Its Effect on Criminal Justice: A Reflection on the Wayne Lo Case." *Asian Law Journal* 7, no. 1 (2000): 1–28.

Yeo, Andrew. *Activists, Alliances, and Anti-U.S. Base Protests*. New York: Cambridge University Press, 2011.

Young, Arthur N. *China and the Helping Hand, 1937–1945*. Cambridge, MA: Harvard University Press, 1963.

Yu, Dafu 郁達夫. *Yu Dafu sanwen* 郁達夫散文 [*Essays by Yu Dafu*], edited by Yi Qi 亦祺. Hangzhou: Zhejiang wenyi chubanshe, 1999.

Yu, Huamin 于化民. "Dui Ri shouxiang quan zhengduan beijing xia de Zhonggong yu Mei guanxi" 對日受降權爭端背景下的中共與美關係 [CCP-American relations amid disputes over the right to accept Japan's surrender]. *Shixue yuekan* 史學月刊 12 (2011): 64–78.

Yue, Nan 岳南. *Nandu beigui 3: Libie* 南渡北歸 3: 離別 [*Southward migration, northward return 3: Parting*]. Changsha: Hunan wenyi chubanshe, 2015.

Yuval-Davis, Nira. *Gender and Nation*. London: Sage, 1997.

Zanasi, Margherita. "Frugal Modernity: Livelihood and Consumption in Republican China." *Journal of Asian Studies* 74, no. 2 (2015): 391–409.

Zeiger, Susan. *Entangling Alliances: Foreign War Brides and American Soldiers in the Twentieth Century*. New York: New York University Press, 2010.

Zhang, Hong. *America Perceived: The Making of Chinese Images of the United States, 1945–1953*. Westport, CT: Greenwood Press, 2002.

Zhang, Leping 張樂平. *Sanmao jiefang ji* 三毛解放記 [*Sanmao's liberation*]. Shanghai: Shaonian ertong chubanshe, 2020.

Zhang, Longlin 張龍林. "Kangzhan houqi zhuHua Meijun zhuanshu guanxiaquan yanjiu" 抗戰後期駐華美軍專屬管轄權研究 [Research on the exclusive jurisdiction of US forces in China during the late war period]. *Xibei daxue xuebao* 西北大學學報 42, no. 1 (2012): 80–86.

Zhang, Weizhen and Tao Peng. "The Qingdao Pattern and U.S.-Chinese Crisis Management: The KMT, the CCP, and the U.S. Marines in Qingdao during the Chinese Civil War (1945–1949)." *Journal of Cold War Studies* 25, no. 2 (2023): 150–178.

Zhang, Xianwen 張憲文, and Zhang Yufa 張玉法, eds. *Zhonghua minguo zhuantishi* 中華民國專題史 [*Special history of the Republic of China*, vol. 16]. Nanjing: Nanjing University Press, 2015.

Zhang, Yun. "The Emerging Modern Woman: Representations of the 'Girl Student' in Early Twentieth Century Urban China." *Harvard Asia Quarterly* 16, no. 3 (2014): 50–59.

Zhang, Zhenkun 張振鵾. "Zaishuo 'ershiyi tiao' bushi tiaoyue: Da Zheng Zemin xiansheng" 再說"二十一條"不是條約: 答鄭則民先生 [Again on "Twenty-One Demands" are not a treaty]. *Jindaishi yanjiu* 近代史研究 1 (2000): 238–252.

Zhao, Xiaojian. *Remaking Chinese America: Immigration, Family, and Community, 1940–1965*. New Brunswick, NJ: Rutgers University Press, 2002.

Zheng, Yanqiu. "A Specter of Extraterritoriality: The Legal Status of U.S. Troops in China, 1943–1947." *Journal of American–East Asian Relations* 22, no. 1 (2015): 17–44.

Zheng, Zemin 鄭則民. "Guanyu bupingdeng tiaoyue de ruogan wenti: Yu Zhang Zhenkun xiansheng shangque" 關于不平等條約的若干問題: 與張振鵾先生商榷 [Some questions on the unequal treaties: A discussion with Mr. Zhang Zhenkun]. *Jindaishi yanjiu* 近代史研究 1 (2000): 215–237.

Zhonggong Beijing shiwei dangshi yanjiushi 中共北京市委黨史研究室, eds. *Kangyi Meijun zhuHua baoxing yundong ziliao huibian* 抗議美軍駐華暴行運動資料彙編 [*Collected materials on the Anti-American Brutality movement*]. Beijing: Beijing daxue chubanshe, 1989.

Zhonggong Qingdaoshiwei, dangshiziliao zhengweihui bangongshi 中共青島市委黨史資料徵委會辦公室, ed. *Qingdao dangshi ziliao di 4 ji* 青島黨史資料第四輯 [*Historical materials of the CCP in Qingdao*, vol. 4]. Qingdao: Qingdaoshi chubanshe, 1989.

Zhonggong zhongyang dangshi yanjiushi 中共中央黨史研究室. *Zhongguo gongchandang lishi (diyijuan)* 中國共產黨歷史(第一卷) [*History of the Chinese Communist Party*, vol. 1]. Beijing: Zhonggong dangshi chubanshe, 2010.

Zhongguo zhanqu Zhongguo lujun zongsilingbu shouxiang baogaoshu 中國戰區中國陸軍總司令部受降報告書 [*Report on the acceptance of the Japanese surrender*]. Zhongguo lujun zongsilingbu 中國陸軍司令總部, 1946.

Zhuang, Lang 莊浪, drawings by Ding Hao 丁浩, *Meijun zai Zhongguo de baoxing* 美軍在中國的暴行 [*Brutalities of American troops in China*]. Shanghai: Dadong shuju, 1951.

Zou, Zhenhuan 鄒振環. "Xican yinru yu jindai Shanghai chengshi wenhua kongjian de kaituo" 西餐引入與近代上海城市文化空間的開拓 [Introduction of Western food and the expansion of Shanghai's urban cultural space]. *Shi lin* 史林 4 (2007): 137–149.

Zumwalt, Elmo R. *On Watch: A Memoir*. New York: The New York Times, 1976.

Zuo, Chengying 左承穎, and Yang Yuqing 楊雨青. "Hequ hecong: Anping shijian hou guogongMei sanfang dui zhuHua Meijun de yinying" 何去何從: 安平事件后國共美三方對駐華美軍的因應 [What next: Communist, Nationalist, and American responses to US forces in China post-Anping Incident]. *Junshi lishi yanjiu* 軍事歷史研究 34, no. 1 (2020): 76–86.

Zuo, Shuangwen 左雙文. "1946 nian Shen Chong shijian: Nanjing zhengfu de duice" 1946年沈崇事件: 南京政府的對策 [The 1946 Shen Chong Incident: Nanjing government's policies]. *Jindaishi yanjiu* 近代史研究 1 (2005): 65–103.

Zuo, Shuangwen 左雙文, and Liu Shan 劉杉. "Lengzhan chuqi Sulian de 'zhanlipin' zhengce ji Sujun zai zhanlingqu de junji wenti" 冷戰初期蘇聯的"戰利品"政策及蘇軍在佔領區的軍紀問題 [Soviet "spoils of war" policy and military discipline problems in occupied areas during the early Cold War]. In *Lengzhan shiqi de Meiguo yu dongya shehui* 冷戰時期的美國與東亞社會 [*The United States and East Asian societies during the Cold War*], edited by Du Chunmei 杜春媚. Taipei: Showwe, 2023, 213–233.

Index

8th Route Army, 23, 38

Abarra, Petro, 120, 121
Amerasia, 145
American goods. *See also* theft of American goods
  Chinese consumption of, 155–169
  Chinese rejection of, 192–195
  versus national goods, 169–176
American military vehicles
  causing traffic accidents, 102–106
  street politics, 106–112
American soldiers
  dissatisfaction with mission in China, 45–47
  extraterritorial rights in China, 7–10
  GI/Jeep duality, 102–105
  lifestyle, 59, 61–68, 81, 91–92, 117
  misconduct, 4, 18, 116, 143–144, 166
  multiple roles and identities, 16–18, 91–93
  privileges, 67–68, 162, 207
  and rickshaw men, 112–118
  withdrawal from China, 24–25
American Volunteer Group, 124. *See also* "Flying Tigers"
III Amphibian Corps (IIIAC), 3, 27–30
Anping Incident, 39–41, 47
anti-American boycott 1905, 175–176
anti-American sentiments, 95, 203
  contemporary narrative of, 197–204
  gendered nationalism, 145
  popular sentiments, 13, 192–197
  and reckless GI driving, 106
  and rickshaw puller cases, 121
Anti-Brutality movement, 12, 149, 151. *See also* anti-American sentiments
Arnett, Warren Jefferson, 76
Astor Hotel in Tianjin, 27, 62
asymmetric warfare, 206–207

Bai Chongxi, 190
Ballard, J. G., 157
bargaining and economic transactions, 86, 117
"Beijing Jeep", 123, 210
Bernstein, Richard, 206
biracial babies, 130
Birch, John, 48
black market, 168
  American participation in, 182–183
  Chinese government control on, 189–190
black troops, 6, 150
black truck drivers, 98
Born to Defend, 203
Bousquin, Sylvio L., 109, 162
Boxer Uprising, 12, 59, 61
Buck, Pearl S., 142
Bucklew, Phil, 68

Cabot, John M., 192
canned food, 155, 156, 158, 164, 174, 175
Cao Guiming (Ts'ao Hui-ming), 184, 191
Carlson, Evans Fordyce, 85
Carter, Jimmy, 196–197
Cathay Hotel, 62
CBI (China-Burma-India) Theater, 82, 85, 97, 98, 140
ceasefire negotiations and agreement, 47
Chen Baocang (Chen Pao-tsang), 33
Chen Cheng, 129, 170
Chen Xiangmei, 139
Chennault, Claire Lee, 51, 139
Chiang Kai-shek
  condemning anti-American sentiment, 11
  on GI misconduct, 9, 55, 56, 147, 192
  as head of Nationalist Governmemt, 2, 7, 24, 34, 41, 43, 53, 97, 149, 151
  on Japanese surrender, 22–23
  on jurisdiction and sovereignty, 55–57, 67, 190–192

287

288   Index

Chiang Kai-shek (cont.)
  promotion of modern Chinese life, 75, 131, 170
Chiang Kai-shek, Madame, 11, 142
Child, Julia, 82
Child, Paul, 21, 82
"Chimerica", 211
China Expeditionary Army of Japan, 56
The China Weekly Review, 105, 159
China's Committee to Deal with War Crimes, 54
"Chinaman's chance", 88, 109
Chinese Communist Party (CCP)
  anti-American boycott, 156, 175–176
  anti-American propaganda, 11–14, 44–45, 48, 106, 123, 153, 175, 192, 198–202
  and the civil war, 2, 11, 23, 24, 45, 148
  confrontations with American military, 37–48
  guerrilla tactics, 38–45
  narrative of moral superiority and self-reliance, 195
  victory of, 94
Chinese Exclusion Act, 141, 175
Chinese Industrial Cooperatives Movements, 85
Chinese National Relief and Rehabilitation Administration, 39, 81
Chinese women
  attraction to American men, 137–138
  dichotomous portrayal of, 151–153
  GIs' views on, 139–144
  marriages between GIs and, 128
  as victims of GIs' sexual violence, 144–151
Chongqing Negotiations, 94, 95, 168
chopsticks diplomacy, 78
Coca-Cola, 161–164
coffee, 158–161
colonialist mentality, 150
Communist victory of, 11
compensation
  politics of, 110
  for rickshaw pullers, 121
  for shooting victims, 184–185
  system, 109–111
Concordia, 66
Congressional Investigation Committee on Demobilization, 47
Cooke, Charles M., Jr., 63, 77, 180, 187
coolies, Chinese, 115, 116
cultural diplomacy, 66, 76
Cultural Revolution, 123, 153, 203

Curley, Walter J. P., 34, 182

DDT, 75, 164–166
Deng Chumin, 176
Deng Xiaoping, 196
ding hao, 85
distrust
  of the Chinese legal system, 52
  against Chinese witnesses, 120
Dixie Mission, 99, 168
Dong Shijin, 132
Doolittle trial, 54
Dorn, Frank, 82
Double Tenth Agreement, 94
Dream of the Red Chamber, 136
Du Jianshi (Tu Chien-shih), 190

economic desperation
  and compensation politics, 110–111
  and survival theft, 178–180
  and war refugee women, 126–127
Ehrhardt Bureau case, 51, 56
Eight-Nation Alliance, 12, 61
Eisenhower, Dwight, 96
Enloe, Cynthia, 15, 140, 152
Evans, William K., 56
everyday/quotidian encounters
  contact zone, 14–16
  micro-macro dynamics, 18
  micropolitics, 16
  sociocultural impacts of, 86–87, 91–92, 109–110, 118, 121–122, 131, 144, 170–172, 181–182, 191–192, 203, 208–209
Executive Yuan, 9, 113, 147, 190, 191
extraterritoriality, 7–10. *See also* US military justice. *See also* violence
  and governmental impotence, 111
  and legal impunity, 56–57, 145–147

Fairbank, John King, 155
Fairbank, Wilma, 181
feast and hotel taxes, 67, 68
February Ninth incident, 176
"Flying Tigers", 11, 139, 163, 205
food
  cultures of beef, 80
  as cultural symbol and soft power, 161–164
  drinking rituals, 80
  as relief and survival, 157–158
  as symbol of national power and identity, 169–171
food diplomacy, 78

Index

Forrestal, James, 25
Frey, Richard, 169
Fu Manchu, 45

gan bei, 80, 92
Gao Ruofan, 184, 185
German residents in China, trial of, 52
Gillem, Alvan Cullom, 55, 56, 145
GIs. *See* American soldiers
Glist, Lou, 126, 142
The Good Earth, 142
Graham, Burton E., 183
Griffith, Samuel B., 63
gung ho, 85
Guo Gen, 126
Guo Moruo, 176

halt-or-shoot policy, 176–188
Hankou trial, 50, 51
Hao Wenqing (Ho Wen-ching), 178
Harding, Frank R., 184
Hersey, John, 112, 115
Hinke, Frederick W., 67
Hong Shen, 132, 151
Hoover, Herbert, 64
Howard, Samuel L., 41, 61, 181, 190
Hu Shi, 154
Huang Renlin (Huang Jen-lin), 80–81
Huang Shang, 170
Hurley, Patrick J., 94

immigrants, Chinese, 88, 141, 211
informal diplomacy, 2, 147, 197, 208
interpretation and misinterpretation, 84–89, 181. *See also* linguistic barriers/control
interpreters, ban on, 69
Isaacs, Harold R., 91

Jacoby, Annalee, 41, 42
Japanese surrender ceremonies, 29
  show of force during, 27–37
  sword surrender act, 30, 33, 36
Japanese war crimes trials, 48–51
Jeep. *See also* American military vehicles
  as cultural symbol and experience, 94, 102
  diplomacy, 112–118
  domestication of, 123
  street politics of, 106–112
"Jeep babies", 130
Jeep girls, 101. *See also* Chinese women
  agency of, 135–139
  cartoons, 104
  class divide among, 125–128
  college students as, 131, 137–138
  name of, 102, 126
  silencing and symbolism of, 130–131, 151, 153
  social stigma and debates on, 128–134, 135
Jet Li, 203
Jewish refugees in China, 76, 83
Jiang Ermao, 115
Jiang Qing, 153
judicial sovereignty, 57

Kitts, W. A., 120
Klim, 157
Korean War, 123, 153, 198, 201
Kung Hsiang-hsi, 81
Kunming, 21, 129, 183, 210

Lao She, 117, 153
Laoshan Iltis Mineral Water Co. Ltd., 162
"leech gang", 189
legal discrimination. *See also* extraterritoriality
  against Chinese witnesses, 120
  and systemic injustice, 8–10, 88–89, 119–122, 145–147
legal Orientalism, 52
lend-lease, 155, 167
Li Gongpu, 40
Li Xianliang (Lee Sien-liang), 190
Li Yannian, 34
linguistic barriers/control, 83–86, 88–89, 181
Lockwood, William W., 91
loss of China, 1, 18, 197
Lü Wenzhen, 35
Lu Xi, 135–136
Luo Jialun, 134

Ma Yinchu, 173
MacArthur, Douglas, 34, 53, 103
Maddocks, Ray T., 53
Manchuria, 3, 24, 34, 130, 147
The Manchurian Candidate, 45
Mao Zedong, 11, 42, 94, 95, 123, 148, 168, 193, 195
Marine Air Force, 31, 37
Marine legation guard, 61
A Marine's Guide to North China, 143
marriage(s)
  between GIs and Chinese women, 128
  "marriages of convenience", 142
  patterns and legal barriers for GIs, 138–141
Marshall, George C., 1, 2, 41, 45, 46, 48, 53, 96, 100, 161, 208
Masataka Kaburagi, 50

May Fourth Movement, 134, 193
McCartney, Arthur Jack, 89
Miles, Milton E., 28
Military Advisory Group in China (MAGIC), 25
Military Assistance Advisory Group, 207
Military Operations Other than War (MOOTW), 24, 206
Military Police (MP), 68, 105, 112, 143, 183, 203
Ministry of Economic Affairs, 67
Ministry of Foreign Affairs, 54, 55, 103, 190
Ministry of National Defense, 53, 54
Modern Women, 134
Moon, Lottie, 196
Mote, Frederick W., 38

Nagano Eiji, 33
Nanjing Massacre, 51
Narum, Leslie F., 183
national dignity
　and ban on interpreters, 69
　and GIs' contempt for the Chinese people, 89, 111
　and masculinity, 152
　and Nationalist Government, 170
　and rejection of American goods, 195
　and student resistance, 185–186
National Products Movement, 175
Nationalist army, 23, 35, 46, 48, 76, 97, 189, 261
Nationalist Government. *See also* Chiang Kai-shek
　on American-led war crimes trials, 4–5, 8, 52–57
　asymmetric relations, 191
　ban on rickshaws, 113, 114, 118
　dilemma of dealing with the American military, 5–10, 147–148
　on extraterritoriality, 7–9, 111
　legitimacy crisis, 2–3, 9, 11, 49, 57, 198
　and national dignity, 170
　political exploitation of incidents, 11
　toward prostitution, 126, 148
　on theft of American military goods, 180, 189–190
　treatment of the Japanese, 22–23, 48–57
New Culture Movement, 134
New Life Movement, 75, 113, 131
Nixon, Richard, 78
The North China Marine, 141

O'Connor, Jeremiah J., 52

Okamura Yasuji, 33, 56
old China hands, 61, 69, 205
Olive, William, 122
Operation BELEAGUER, 3, 206
The Opium War, 7, 88
"Opposing the US Support of Japan" movement, 12, 193
Ott, Eugen, 53

Page Act of 1875, 141
Patton, George S., 96
Paulucci, Jeno, 210
Payne, Robert, 126
Peck, DeWitt, 38, 39, 40, 61, 140
Peck, Graham, 5, 48
pedestrians, 93, 102–103, 108, 110, 118, 184
Peffer, Nathaniel, 145
Peking rape incident, 4, 12, 124, 144–149. *See also* Shen Chong
Peking siege, 59
Penicillin, 17, 143, 156, 167–169, 174, 193
people-to-people diplomacy, 197
Perry, Matthew C., 34
Pfeiffer, Omar T., 63, 176, 179, 180, 188
pidgin language, 83–84, 86, 87, 92, 181
Pierson, William Gaither, 145
ping-pong diplomacy, 197
A Pocket Guide to China, 143
Port Arthur (Lüshun), 3, 64
Post Exchange (PX) stores, 161
Pritchard, Warren, 145

Qingdao
　as naval base, 7, 24, 64, 176, 182
　prohibiting the use of rickshaws, 118
　rickshaw puller case in, 120
　surrender ceremony, 31–35
Qingdao International Club, 66
Qu Jinpei, 190

Rabb, William R., 46
racism, 67–68, 88, 98, 114, 139
　Chinese biases, 141–142
　Chinese critiques of, 149–150
　and Chinese rickshaw pullers, 114–116
　and Chinese women, 138–139, 141–142
　and colonial mentality, 66, 144, 182
　and Orientalist discourse, 68–71, 116–118
　racialized smells, 72–75, 90–91
　systemic tolerance and racial prejudice, 87–89, 116, 137, 140, 141, 150–151
Red Cross club, 66
Rickshaw Boy, 117

Index

rickshaw men (pullers), 112
  bargaining by, 83, 117
  civilization narratives, clash by, 117–118
  collective actions by, 121–122
  as guides, 113–116
  as Oriental symbol, 69, 90, 92, 95, 112–118, 119
  as victims of GI's violence, 90, 112–122, 203
Rockey, Keller E., 29, 30, 41, 46, 61
Roderick, Edward, 119
Roosevelt, Franklin D., 80, 96
Rosset, Barney, 209, 210
Russian refugees in China, 83

Sanmao, 199, 201–203
Sassoon, Victor, 62
Shanghai stocking industry, 174
Shen bao, 168, 171
Shen Chong, 1, 88, 145, 147, 153. *See also* Peking rape incident
Shen Lusha, 136
Shepherd, Lemuel C., 27, 33, 34, 36, 37, 66, 183
Simms, John B., 25, 27, 42, 59, 86, 179
Sino-American Treaty for the Relinquishment of Extraterritorial Rights in China and the Regulation of Related Matters, 7
Sino-Soviet split, 123
Sino-Soviet Treaty of Friendship and Alliance, 3
Sino-US reciprocity
  entangled relations in, 92–93
  uneven reciprocity, 5–10
Sledge, E. B., 27, 42, 59
Smith, Arthur H., 88
smuggling of American goods, 173, 174, 182–183. *See also* theft of American goods
Smyth, Robert L., 53
South China Morning Post, 139
Soviet Union, 3, 6, 7, 21, 23, 31
Stars and Stripes, 142
Stars and Stripes rickshaw derby, 115
Stilwell, Joseph W., 82, 97
Strong, Anna Louise, 48
Stuart, John Leighton, 10, 145
student protests, 2, 11, 13, 67, 147, 185–186, 192, 203, 204
Su Mingcheng case, 120, 122, 186
Sugamo Prison, 50
Sun Lianzhong, 35
Sun Yugui (Sun Yu-kuei), 178, 188
Suzhou Hutong, 126

Taierzhuang, Battle of, 35
Taiwanese prisoners of war, trial of, 49, 54. *See also* Japanese war crimes trials
Tang Yongxian, 191
Tao Xingzhi, 167
Teahouse, 153
theft of American goods. *See also* black market
  American biases toward, 188–192
  by American personnel, 183
  Chinese measures against, 189–192
  shooting suspects, 176–178. *See also* "halt or shoot" policy
  survival theft, 178–180
Tianjin
  GIs' impression of, 59
  incidents in, 38, 39, 61, 74, 84, 86, 103, 110, 130, 140, 165, 178, 179, 182, 189
  recreational and sports facilities in, 66–67
  surrender ceremony in, 33–36
Tilanqiao Prison, 50, 52
Tojo Hideki, 167
Tokyo Trial, 50, 52
traffic accidents
  American military vehicles causing, 102–106
  and vehicular politics, 106–112
  as visible form of American misconduct, 102–106
Treaty of Friendship, Commerce, and Navigation, 9, 175
Truman, Harry S., 2, 24
Tsao, Charles, 105

US Legation in Beijing, 61
US Military Commission, 48–49
US military involvement
  adjudication of war criminals, 48–57
  hypermasculine culture, 89–90, 140–144
  occupation of North China, 3–5
  show of force, 27–37. *See also* Japanese surrender ceremonies
  untenable position, 24–26
US military justice, 182. *See also* extraterritoriality
  Chinese complaints of, 192
  double standards, 183–184
  institutional bias and hypocrisy, 120, 145–148
  systemic injustice, 8–10, 119–122, 145–151
  trials, 48–60, 119–122, 145–151

Index

US property, guarding, 176–188
"US Troops Quit China Week" campaign, 11
Uchida Ginnosuke, 30, 221
United Nations Relief and Rehabilitation Administration (UNRRA), 25, 81, 155, 157, 163, 169
United States Army Observation Group. *See* Dixie Mission
USS *Missouri*, 34

Vandegrift, A. A., 43
vendors, 1, 70, 83, 87, 92, 156, 160, 176, 184, 187
violence. *See also* extraterritoriality
 against Chinese civilians, 176
 and the halt-or-shoot policy, 176–188
 against Jeep girls, 131–132
 against rickshaw men, 112
 sexual, 106, 139, 144, 146–147, 148, 185, 192, 207
 and systemic racism, 90, 118
Vogal, F. H., 190

Wagons-Lits Hotel, 62
Wallace, Henry, 167
War Brides Act of 1945, 138, 139, 141
War Fiancées Act of 1946, 138
Watson's Mineral Water Company, 162, 163, 174
Wedemeyer, Albert C., 24, 47, 48, 62, 68, 116, 140, 147
Wen Yiduo, 40
Wenhui bao, 121
West Wind, 134, 135, 151, 155

White Russians, 83, 126
white superiority, 114, 117. *See also* racism
White, Theodore H., 41, 42, 88
Williams, Thomas E., 44, 78
Willys-Overland Corporation, 97
Wong, Anna, 208
Wong, Anna May, 141
Worton, William A., 27, 28, 29, 30, 36, 37, 61, 140, 143
Wu Hong (Woo Hung), 41, 76
Wu Liusuo (Wu Liu-so), 178

XABU, 66
Xi Jinping, 197
Xinhe (Hsin Ho) Ammunition Dump, 41, 46
Xinhua ribao, 121
Xinmin Evening News, 154

Yang Shangkun, 168
Yang, L. C., 52
Yanks, 141

Zang Yaocheng (Zang Dayaozi) case, 113, 118–120, 199, 203
Zhang Dongsun, 144
Zhang Lan, 168
Zhang Leping, 199
Zhang Zhizhong, 94, 95
Zhao Xueyao, 110
Zhou Enlai, 37, 47
Zhu De, 23
Zhu Ziqing, 193, 194
Zumwalt, Elmo R., Jr., 28–29, 82, 140

For EU product safety concerns, contact us at Calle de José Abascal, 56–1°, 28003 Madrid, Spain or eugpsr@cambridge.org.